The Journey of Dagny Taggart

The Journey of Dagny Taggart

A COMMENTARY ON
AYN RAND'S *ATLAS SHRUGGED*
VOLUME 2

Frederick H. Cookinham

Pereset Press
New York, New York

2025

A Pereset Press Book

First hardcover printing in 2025

Pereset Press
355 South End Avenue, Suite 10M
New York, New York 10280
info@peresetpress.com
www.peresetpress.com

Copyright © 2025 by Frederick H. Cookinham

All rights reserved. No part of this publication may be reproduced, distributed, or transmitted in any form or by any means, including photocopying, recording, or other electronic or mechanical methods, without the prior written permission of the publisher, except in the case of brief quotations embodied in critical reviews and certain other noncommercial uses permitted by copyright law.

Library of Congress Control Number: 2025904759
ISBN: 978-1-7373088-4-3

Names: Cookinham, Frederick H., author.
Title: The Journey of Dagny Taggart : a commentary on Ayn Rand's Atlas Shrugged , volume 2 / Frederick H. Cookinham.
Description: New York, NY: Pereset Press, 2025.
Identifiers: LCCN: 2025904759 | ISBN: 978-1-7373088-4-3
Subjects: LCSH Rand, Ayn. Atlas shrugged--Criticism and interpretation.| BISAC LITERARY CRITICISM / American / General
Classification: LCC PS3535.A547 C66 2025 | DDC 813.52--dc23

To the young reader who is curious enough
to tackle very long books

and

Always to Belen,
best of wives and best of women

When it shall be found that much is omitted, let it not be forgotten that much likewise is performed.

Samuel Johnson (from the Preface to his English Dictionary)

A dwarf has an excellent way of making himself taller than a giant: it is by perching himself on the giant's shoulders. That the giant should allow it – there is the wonder. And that he should praise the dwarf for his height – there is the folly. Ah, the simplicity of mankind!

Victor Hugo, *The Man Who Laughs*

Table of Contents

How to Use This Commentary xv

Foreword xvii

Preface xxi

Acknowledgments xxix

Introduction xxxi

   Rand's Writing Career xxxi

   Rand's Critics xxxiii

   It's About Dagny xxxv

Abbreviations xxxix

Main Positive Characters xli

Main Negative Characters xliii

Timeline xlv

PART III A Is A (Dagny and Galt) 1

   Part Overview 2

1. Atlantis 3

   Chapter Overview 3

   Scene 1: Dagny meets Galt, Wyatt, Mulligan, and Akston. She sleeps before dinner 3

   Scene 2: Dinner at Mulligan's. The mind on strike. Dagny sleeps in the "anteroom." 26

2. The Utopia of Greed 39

   Chapter Overview 39

Scene 1: Ragnar appears. Dagny offers to be Galt's housekeeper. 40

Scene 2: Francisco arrives. Galt will not let him contact Hank 46

Scene 3: Dagny is relieved to learn that Galt spends his evenings lecturing 52

Scene 4: Halley plays for Dagny. Kay Ludlow. Motherhood. Akston on superhuman creatures 61

Scene 5: Dagny, Galt and Francisco at the mine. Hank's plane appears 72

Scene 6: Galt, Akston, Mulligan and Francisco ask Dagny whether she plans to stay or go. 77

Scene 7: Galt flies Dagny out of the valley 83

3. Anti-Greed 85

    Chapter Overview 85

    Scene 1: Stadler and Ferris at Project X 85

    Scene 2: Dagny returns to New York. Meigs and Eddie, Dagny and Jim. Lillian blackmails Dagny into speaking on Scudder's radio show. 94

    Scene 3: Dagny on the radio, and with Hank in her apartment. 102

4. Anti-Life 109

    Chapter Overview 109

Scene 1: Jim comes home and wants to celebrate his deal to nationalize d'Anconia Copper. 109

Scene 2: Cherryl and Dagny. 117

Scene 3: Lillian visits Jim. They have sex. 120

Scene 4: Cherryl catches Jim and Lillian in flagrante delicto, confronts Jim, and kills herself. 123

5. Their Brothers' Keepers 129
Chapter Overview 129

Scene 1: The breakdown of Taggart Transcontinental. Francisco blows up d'Anconia Copper. Hank and Dagny see Francisco's farewell message. 130

Scene 2: Hank and Philip. Hank in divorce court. Wet Nurse asks for a real job, warns Hank that something is up. 138

Scene 3: The Minnesota wheat harvest. 141

Scene 4: Dagny called away from looters discussing the latest disasters. Has sex with Galt for the first time. 144

6. The Concerto of Deliverance 159
Chapter Overview 159

7. "This is John Galt Speaking" 179
Chapter Overview 179

Scene 1: Dagny hears Galt's speech with Mr. Thompson and the nation's leadership...................179

Scene 2: Galt's Speech...183

8. The Egoist 227
    Chapter Overview 227

    Scene 1: Dagny with the leadership in the studio after the speech...228

    Scene 2: Dagny and Eddie after the speech..............232

    Scene 3: Thompson hears public reaction to the speech, asks Dagny for advice...........................234

    Scene 4: Dagny goes to Galt's apartment..................237

    Scene 5: Thompson's first visit with Galt...................243

    Scene 6: Thompson confers with Dagny. Francisco sends Dagny a note. Thompson, Ferris, and Stadler visit Galt. Eddie leaves for California......................247

    Scene 7: Galt forced to ballroom for broadcast........255

9. The Generator...263
    Chapter Overview 263

    Scene 1: Stadler to Project X. Meigs blows it up. ...263

    Scene 2: Ferris, Jim, and Mouch get Galt to the torture chamber. Dagny hears of the collapse of the Taggart bridge, meets Francisco, and gives the oath. 266

Contents

    Scene 3: The torture scene. 271

10. In the Name of the Best Within Us 277

    Chapter Overview 277

    Scene 1: Assault on Project F. 277

    Scene 2: Eddie is stranded on the Comet 288

    Scene 3: Dagny and Galt in the Gulch. Strikers plan for the future. 293

Appendix A Rand Qua Writer 297

    The Journey of Dagny Taggart 297

    The Atlas Theme 298

    Some Lovely Passages 299

    Rand's Sense of Humor 300

    Parodies of Christianity 301

    Rand's Words Refute Critical Attacks 302

Appendix B A List of the Strikers 305

Appendix C My Fifteen Favorite Stickers 307

Appendix D My Dreamcast for *Atlas Shrugged* 309

Bibliography 311

About the Author 319

Advance Echoes 321

Recurring Themes Index 325

Index to Volume 2 333

How to Use This Commentary

To get the most benefit from this Commentary, you should be aware of several features. Most importantly, it is keyed to the hardcover edition of *Atlas Shrugged*, published by Random House in 1957. The Commentary proceeds sequentially from the beginning to the end of *Atlas Shrugged*, and on the left-hand side of each page in this volume, you will see an entry for the page in *Atlas Shrugged* that is under discussion. Any references to page numbers in *Atlas Shrugged* always reference the page numbers in the novel's printed edition and always take the form "AS #." Any English-language edition of *Atlas* will likely have the same pagination. I can't say the same for any foreign translations.

If you have never read the novel or only read it long ago, it would be best to familiarize yourself with it before engaging with the Commentary. The more studious among you will probably want to place a copy of *Atlas Shrugged* alongside the Commentary, following along from one to the other. Others who are less devoted might be satisfied keeping a copy within arms' reach and checking it out only when the Commentary touches on something you want to know more about. For those less industrious, the Commentary contains many features that will help you follow and enjoy the flow of *Atlas Shrugged*.

Rand divided the novel into three parts: *Non-Contradiction, Either-Or,* and *A is A*. These are the Aristotelian principles of logic. To help reflect the flow of the story, secondary titles have been added to the part names: *Dagny and Francisco, Dagny and Hank,* and *Dagny and Galt*. These three alternative titles guide the reader through Dagny's intellectual and emotional journey.

Each chapter has an overview of what takes place within. Each chapter of the novel has places where a break in the narrative shifts your attention elsewhere. This is a common literary practice. On those occasions, a Scene description indicates what follows.

When commenting on the specific language in *Atlas*, a brief excerpt usually appears in italics at the beginning of a paragraph.

The Commentary frequently refers to the *Recurring Themes Index*. This fantastic resource will be an essential reference tool for anyone wishing to explore or write about *Atlas Shrugged*. The commentary includes an "Advance Echoes" listing, a collection of places where Rand appears to have used a phrase or idea that she paired with a similar usage earlier in the novel.

The Commentary also includes a summary of Rand's literary career, a timeline of events in the novel, a list of the good guys, a list of the bad guys, a list of the strikers, and an appendix containing several quotes from *Atlas Shrugged* that highlight her literary skills in several categories. As you read through *Journey*, these should help you follow the action and know who and what to look for.

In addition to the *Recurring Themes Index*, each volume includes a general topic index. The index in Volume 1 covers only Volume 1; the index in Volume 2 covers only Volume 2. All page numbers in the general indexes, the *Recurring Themes Index*, and the Advanced Echoes listing refer to page numbers in *Atlas Shrugged*. You can use the *Atlas Shrugged* page numbers as a reverse index that will locate the Commentary page number by finding the *Atlas Shrugged* page number. Since *Atlas Shrugged* page numbers appear sequentially, you should easily find them.

Foreword

As a long-time fan of Ayn Rand's writings, I take great pleasure in publishing *The Journey of Dagny Taggart: A Commentary on Atlas Shrugged*, Frederick Cookinham's massive two-volume study of all things *Atlas*. I am especially delighted that he focuses a significant amount of attention on Rand's skills as a writer in general and a novelist in particular, traits often overlooked by many of even Rand's most dedicated fans, who concentrate more on the polemics and philosophy in *Atlas* than on her literary talents. (I love the polemics too, but unlike many of Rand's fans, I never tried to memorize Francisco's speech on money or Galt's address to the nation.) After all, Rand is, first and foremost, a novelist and deserves evaluation as such. Cookinham does a terrific job of bringing her abilities to the fore.

The title of the Commentary reflects the attention to literary detail. While Galt and Francisco gather most of the fan love, from a scholarly standpoint, they belong in the background, populating the environment through which the novel flows. Dagny, by contrast, holds down the foreground. Her intellectual and emotional journey from opponent to the strike to hard-core rebel moves the story forward and glues the various parts together, as does her romances with the three leading male characters, Francisco, Hank, and Galt.

I have known Fred and his dedication to Randian studies for more years than I care to count. Yet, happily, I still learned many new things from his Commentary on Rand and *Atlas*. At the same time, Fred's observations capture a spirit that returned me to my earliest intellectual explorations, a journey into nostalgia.

I first encountered *Atlas* over the Christmas holiday during my first year at Brooklyn College. I found it on my father's nightstand, and it hooked me for many of the reasons Fred describes in his Preface. I read non-stop for two days until I finished it. It came at a time when I had seriously started examining political and economic ideas. I was excited when I finished. It helped me justify what I believed.

Although I grew up Jewish in a predominantly Jewish area of Brooklyn that voted overwhelmingly for ultra-liberal Democrats, I somehow developed a contrarian persona. I was born during World War II and went to grade school during the Korean War. School air raid drills routinely had us march into the hallways to be seated with our heads between our knees.

I knew I was militantly anti-Communist and anti-socialist from a young age. Still, I envied some of my left-wing high school classmates who seemed to have a more profound knowledge than I of current events and politics, throwing around names I barely knew and cabinet posts I didn't know about. I lacked a similar understanding of the anti-communist intellectual environment. My first intellectual turning point came unexpectedly from an article by a left-wing TV columnist for the New York Post, who also had a weekly political column.

Back then, the NY Post, founded by Alexander Hamilton, was so left-wing that people joked that Moscow didn't have to write editorials for them because the Post did such a better job.

Her column that particular day attacked anti-socialists as irrational because governments ran public schools and subways and libraries; they were socialist institutions, and who could be against them?

Ka-Ching! She was right. I no longer believed in public schools, libraries, or government-run subways. By my senior year in High School, I started aggressively reading free market-oriented books.

When I attended Brooklyn College, it had a reputation as a quality educational institution with reasonably high academic standards. It was known, mostly, however, for educating future teachers. It was, not surprisingly, an overwhelming liberal-left faculty and student body. (One of my economics professors never heard of Milton Friedman or Ludwig von Mises.)

Luckily, shortly after finishing *Atlas*, I discovered the campus had a "Students of Objectivism" club. (Rand had told her fans they should

Foreword

call themselves *students* of Objectivism and not Objectivists so that people could distinguish between how she defined her philosophy and how her fans might have mischaracterized her philosophy.)

Over the next four years, the club sponsored an annual speech by Rand at the school's theater hall. Despite the overwhelmingly liberal environment, Rand filled the 2000-seat auditorium year after year. One of the club members' great highlights from this annual event was the private luncheon with Rand and Branden after her talk, where the members freely conversed with and asked questions of our two esteemed guests.

On other occasions, we brought Branden and others from Rand's inner circle to speak on campus, again with lunch afterward. When Branden came, Rand joined us. We also brought von Mises and other economists and journalists to lecture. One of our other traditions was an annual exhibit in the school library of books about Free Enterprise and Objectivism. Yes, Liberals believed in free speech back then.

Club members frequently lunched together in the school cafeteria and exchanged much of the type of speculation you see in Fred's Commentary. Who did Rand base so and so on? What part of New York did she describe? What influenced her writing? And, of course, gossip about the movement and cultural breakthroughs. (Was there really an elevator in the PanAm building with a plaque identifying it as the John Galt Express?) We were ready to save the world—news at 10:00.

Great times, Fred! Thanks for the journey back and the journey forward.

Gary Greenberg
Publisher
Pereset Press
2024

Preface

I wrote this book between September 6, 2019, and December 18, 2021, with further tinkering in 2022 and beyond. I combed every line of *Atlas Shrugged* for the little touches and details I fear many readers don't notice.

Rand packed a lot of meaning into short sentences, short paragraphs, and scenes that a skimmer will probably miss. Her book is long not because she could not be concise but because there were so many scenes and characters and layers of meaning to be concise about. Rand's theme, after all, is "The role of the mind in man's existence." That covers a lot of territory and offers up a lot of dramatic possibilities.

I sometimes mention the same point many times because that point serves a purpose. If I repeatedly show Dagny falling in love step by step with Hank in Part I, it is because that is how you build characterization and plot. Dagny falling in love with Hank is a long, gradual process. In a huge canvas like Atlas Shrugged, the reader might forget a point before he sees it mentioned again five hundred pages later. If you use this commentary as a reference work, you won't notice the repetitions. If you read it cover to cover, bless you.

The "soap opera" scenes and characters like Jim Taggart yield fewer notes for this commentary than the scenes where the heroes interact. The heroes being people to whom ideas matter, they are more articulate. They have something to say to each other. Dagny does not talk as much to Jim as to Hank, for example, because Jim is not listening. Rand loves her heroes and embellishes them with more description, more metaphors, more layers of meaning, more emotion, and more conflict.

In large part, this commentary is just for fun. It is fun to hear an author claim that she can explain the purpose of every word in a giant tome and then do so.[1] It is fun to figure out from clues in the text where in Iowa Project X must be located, and to find on Google Maps the Yardley, Pennsylvania steel mill, and to imagine it to be the real Rearden Steel.

It is fun to read about the real J. Robert Oppenheimer, and see how Rand turned him into the fictional Robert Stadler. It is fun to imagine what Rand and Oppenheimer talked about, when they met, and what they said about each other afterward to others.

It is fun to find other works of fiction that can be compared with *Atlas Shrugged* in some (limited) way, like James Clavell's novel *Shogun* or Noel Coward's play *Fumed Oak*. It is fun to find out so much about an historical figure like Ayn Rand that you start to get inside her head and think along with her.

∞∞∞

I was thirteen years old when I first read *Atlas Shrugged*. One goal of this commentary is for this long-in-age adult to speak to the modern twenty-first century teen who has read Atlas for the first time and point out the interesting, thought-provoking, and inspiring points I don't want such a reader to miss or misinterpret. Or, to turn that around, this is the book I wish I had read alongside *Atlas* at thirteen.

When I call a favorite line of mine a "sticker," I mean it is a line that has stuck with me over the years. The line sometimes comes to mind unbidden. If I tell some personal anecdotes in my commentary, there is a reason. Many young readers of *Atlas Shrugged* will see much of their own story in mine. (Hey! Cookinham had the same reaction I did!) But if they see in my stories a very different reaction to *Atlas Shrugged* from theirs, that's fascinating too. (Oh! Well, that's a completely different way to interpret this scene!)

---

[1] One of Rand's friends challenged her by picking a paragraph at random in *Atlas Shrugged* and asking her to explain every choice of words in that paragraph. You will find her analysis of that paragraph on page 135 of Nathaniel Branden's *Who Is Ayn Rand?*

Preface *xxiii*

Spoiler Alert!

This commentary is one big spoiler. It is designed for the reader who has already read the novel, or has seen the three movies (Atlas Shrugged Part I, Part II, and Part III) and who now wants to study the novel more intensely. If you haven't yet read Atlas Shrugged or at least seen the movie, you might be deprived of the pleasure of first discovery by reading this book.

∞∞∞

The front and back covers of *Atlas Shrugged* along with the inside teaser induce the casual browser to buy the book and read it. The sheer size of the book makes you notice it on the rack; the width of the spine allows you to read the title while it sits on the shelf. Such a large and impressive volume suggests that this is an important book, like the Bible, *Gone with The Wind,* or *War and Peace.*

I found *Atlas Shrugged* on my older brother's bookcase. Inside, one of his high school classmates had written her name. She, or someone before her, must have seen the book on a book rack and bought it, probably for the above reasons, and others. It was the gold paperback, the one with the cover showing a male figure, his hair blowing in the wind, spreading his arms and hands, and looking up in anguish, as if asking Zeus, "Why are you doing this to me?" Or as they say now in 2024, "WTF!" Behind him, a dark background suggests the glowing ruins after a fire. This painting establishes the somber mood of the story perfectly. The title's lettering on the cover jiggle up and down, suggesting a shrug. Clever. But they also suggest an earthquake, or the vibration of a violent explosion. All this supports the mood of *Atlas Shrugged* as a sort of "disaster" novel.

There is no teaser on the front, only the title and the picture, and the words, "The widely discussed new novel by the author of The Fountainhead." If you get that far and turn the book over, you read on the back cover, "The astounding story of a man who said he would stop the motor of the world – and did." That's the grabber.

Then follow two short paragraphs, written by Rand herself and consisting of full sentences with subordinate clauses. People used to write that way in ads back in the old days. The key words include "challenging," "daring view of life," and "brilliant story-telling power." More grabbers.

This is about story telling. In spite of what professors told their classes, that Rand was merely using fiction as a recruiting tool for her cult, buyers pulled this book off the shelf or the rack. They wanted to read a story and they got one.

Besides the teenaged science fiction fans, there is another group of AS buyers and readers: housewives. Publishers have told us for years that women read novels more than men do. Many women read themselves to sleep with a novel, usually one involving romance. They too get what they wanted.

Inside the cover we find more teasers. The big headline is "What Moves the World?" Here, Rand lists some of the characters enshrouded in mysteries, such as "why a composer gave up his career on the night of his triumph."

She saves the best for last, "why a beautiful woman who runs a transcontinental railroad fell in love with the man she had sworn to kill." The grabber here is not just the drama of a woman swearing to kill a man (picture Bette Davis at the beginning of the movie *The Letter*), but the idea of a woman, and a beautiful one, running a railroad. That alone is worth the price of admission, which was just 95 cents for this Signet paperback back then. (My keyboard doesn't even have the cents sign anymore.) This was 1963 and the book was already in its thirteenth printing.

Before 1968, Atlas was dedicated to both Frank O'Connor and Nathaniel Branden. That changed. Why it changed is a long story told in books by the Brandens and Anne Heller.

Chapter titles entice further. The ones that struck this reader were "Atlantis," "The Generator," and "In the Name of the Best Within Us." Atlantis is a perennial attention-getter for any young science fiction reader. Any reference to a generator, or any machine, ditto. And the last chapter title has the ring of a last chapter title. It sounds like a grand summation. Someone has reached a decision, and not an easy one, and must justify it to others with a resounding moral principle.

After seeing the covers, the teasers, and the chapter titles, this thirteen-year-old reader was puzzled. It kind of looked like science fiction, but not exactly. Another mystery, and another reason for a voracious young reader to dive in. Why Rand?

When a young reader, such as I was many years ago, encounters heroes who show that they value honesty and other virtues, he feels a sense of relief. I'm not crazy, the world is crazy. The young reader learns that ideas matter. Branden told Rand that she had in effect brought him up, long distance, through *The Fountainhead*. ("Long distance" was a telephone term from before the era of cell phones.) Many of Rand's moral ideas reinforced virtues already taught to us not only by our parents, but through Captain Kirk, the Lone Ranger, James Bond, and other fictional heroes.

Besides the virtues defined by John Galt in his Speech (AR 1018 to 1021), the virtue, or value, which jumped out at this thirteen-year-old from the pages of Atlas was normalcy. You get from the novel the impression of Rand coming down from Mount Sinai with the Commandments of God and announcing a fundamental change in man's whole way of life. But what is the nature, the content, of this big new revelation by Rand?

It was simply "Be Normal!" Go about your personal business, pursue happiness, don't bother others doing the same thing. No gods or supernatural beliefs, no talk of sacrificing self to others or others to self or anybody to anybody. No talk of enemies. No class enemy rah-rah, or race enemy, just a world full of individuals cheering each other on to greater personal fulfilment and happiness. Aristotelean self-actualization. Your self-interest does not consist of the ruin of others. There is no necessary conflict between the rights of one and the rights of another, and ditto the interests of one and the interests of another, at least not at the fundamental level. All mankind will prosper together as soon as we stop killing each other out of primitive tribal fear. This is Rand's message of hope, as seen by one thirteen-year-old reader, who then went on to read about Gandhi. Galt's argument about the "Sanction of the Victim" follows the same principle as Gandhi's doctrine of "Non-cooperation with Evil."

What might interest the 21st century reader?

My methodology was one of brute force. I read each page, from AS 1 to AS 1168, and wrote down anything that might be of interest to the first-time Atlas reader in his teens. In 2024 and beyond, that must of necessity mean a reader born in the 21st century. Our teen does not know what mailing addresses or telephone numbers looked like in Rand's day, before ZIP codes and area codes. Our teen will be puzzled by all the bowing and formality that this native of 1905 St. Petersburg, Russia was used to. Our teen does not know what a "phone booth" is. So, what I was looking for on every page of Atlas was 20th century references the young reader needs explained.

- Internal references I can spare the readers having to look up themself
- Themes Rand touched on before in *The Fountainhead* or elsewhere
- Lines that had a profound impact on me in my youth and why
- Points readers miss because they read too fast
- Possible sources upon which characters were based, or the origin of a character's name, or a real incident that influenced a scene. For example, did movie star Carole Lombard's death in a plane crash give Rand the idea for Dagny crashing in Galt's Gulch? Maybe the answer to questions like that lie buried somewhere in the Ayn Rand Archive.
- Rand anecdotes culled from a lifetime of Rand study that will provide young readers with clues to Rand's artistic choices in the novel, or answer such questions as What sort of person was Ayn? How did she come to write this book?

Other books about Rand you might enjoy

Following her death in 1982, Rand's intellectual heir, Leonard Peikoff, a philosophy professor, founded the Ayn Rand Institute and it remains very active today. It has also spawned a rival, the Atlas Society. Both organizations publish articles promoting Rand's work and philosophy.

A number of books about Rand, pro and con, continue to be published forty years after her death. *Atlas Shrugged* continues to sell

150,000 copies every year. If there is ever an Ayn Rand Museum (ARI has a small one), a big part of it will be the ever-growing library of books *about* Rand, on top of the books *by* Rand. For those who want more information on Rand, I would recommend the following works, just for starters.

- *Ayn Rand: The Russian Radical*, by Chris Sciabarra. Once the Soviet Union fell, Chris took advantage of the chance to send researchers looking for things like Rand's records at the University of Leningrad, whom she studied under, and what she learned in philosophy. Dr. Sciabarra also edited the Journal of Ayn Rand Studies, until recently.
- *Ayn Rand and the World She Made*, by Anne C. Heller. When I met Anne, she said she was considering whether to undertake a biography of Ayn. But she said she did not know much about her yet. I said that was a good thing.

Barbara Branden's strength as a biographer was also her weakness. She was close to Ayn for eighteen years. What she gained in access, she likewise lost in objectivity.

Anne, by coming at the project from ignorance, brought a fresh pair of eyes to the subject, as proofreaders say. She had no axes of her own to grind, no prejudices or preconceptions. Anne died in October 2022, after publishing her Rand biography in 2009 and later, a biography of Hannah Arendt.

- *Judgment day: My Years with Ayn Rand*, by Nathaniel Branden. I recommend this one with reservations. See above about access versus objectivity. Read this for the style and drama, then read other, later, more objective biographical writing for accuracy. And read between Nathaniel's lines. Both he and Barbara try to be fair and show the bad with the good about Rand and about themselves. But they do not always succeed.
- *100 Voices: An Oral History of Ayn Rand*, by Scott McConnell. Let people who knew Rand speak for themselves and make up your own mind. But be aware that McConnell used, in at least one case that I know of, only a fraction of what an interviewee told him. You will wonder why McConnell included some Rand quotes that

the Rand Bashers have gleefully seized on from this book because they cast her in a bad light.

I also recommend any of the talks and articles I have seen by Shoshana Milgram Knapp. She teaches literature at Virginia Tech. Just seeing a real literature professor take Rand seriously as a fiction writer is all by itself a rare pleasure. Literature is my focus too, in this book: *Atlas*, contrary to what you have heard, is a novel. It is not a manifesto or a treatise on politics or economics. Naturally, economists see an economics textbook in *Atlas*, and political types see a political statement. But it is a novel, with characters, plot, theme, narrative passages, descriptive passages, dialog, and all the things a novel is supposed to have.

Acknowledgments

I have to thank Gary Greenberg, my editor at Pereset Press, for his many valuable suggestions for improving on my original manuscript.

I was also greatly encouraged by the seventy-eight people who asked to see the earliest version of this book.

Anne C. Heller. Thank you for sharing some of the journey. Anne took all of my Ayn Rand tours while writing her biography, *Ayn Rand and the World She Made*. We had fun for six years sharing information about the subject before she published her book in 2009. She died during my final editing.

Introduction

Ayn Rand was born Alisa (Alice) Rosenbaum in Saint Petersburg, Russia on February 2, 1905. She came to the United States in 1926 intending to make her living as a Hollywood "scenarist" (screenwriter) and writing any other kind of fiction.

Rand's Writing Career

Rand worked in Hollywood as a script doctor and wrote screenplays for Warner Brothers and Hal Wallis. She wrote four plays, two of which were performed during her lifetime. The Night of January 16th had a successful run on Broadway; The Unconquered much less so. In the summer of 1937, during a break from researching The Fountainhead, she wrote the novelette Anthem.

In 1936, she published her first novel, *We the Living*. But it was her second novel in 1943, *The Fountainhead*, that made her famous.

In late 1943, Rand's friend Isabel "Pat" Paterson told Ayn that she should write a non-fiction book expanding on the political and economic implications of The Fountainhead. Pat insisted that it was Ayn's duty to give her novel ideas to the world.

Rand replied that she had no such duty and added, "What if I went on strike? What if all the creative minds went on strike?" Frank said that would make a good plot for a novel.

To make a long story short, Rand wrote such a novel and called it Atlas Shrugged. Her first notes for the novel appeared on January 1, 1945, and she started full-time work on it in April 1946. April through August of that year saw Rand in the planning and research phase. She started the actual writing on September 2, 1946, which is why she uses September 2 throughout the book as a guide to the passage of time.

The action takes place over a three-and-a-half-year period. She worked on *Atlas* from 1945 to 1957.

Her style was to portray heroes who were not skilled at swordsmanship, archery, or swinging on ropes through Sherwood Forest; they were heroes of the mind. They had ideas, and cared enough about them to express those ideas with well-chosen words. That is why *Atlas Shrugged* has some long speeches. They explain a character's reasons for taking certain actions. And characters making decisions is what Ayn Rand meant by "plot."

Many readers have complained about these long speeches. Some skip Galt's Speech in its entirety. But as I point out in the commentary, certain lines in the Speech relate directly to the story and the characters, relations you will miss if you pass over it.

Her first notes for Galt's Speech, considered a distillation of her philosophy, date to July 29, 1953. It took her till October 13, 1955–more than two years–to write the whole speech. After that, finishing the novel was fun for Ayn, writing action and tying up the loose ends.

She finished in November 1956. Because of the success of *The Fountainhead*, she did not have to look for a publisher. Publishers looked for her. She chose Bennett Cerf's company, Random House. Then came the editing, the copy editing, and the proofreading.

Random House published the novel on October 10, 1957. The book debuted at number 13 on the Times best seller list, and peaked on December 8 at number 3. It made the list for 22 consecutive weeks. Despite savage reviews and ridicule, it survives in print sixty-five years later. By 2019 it had sold nine million copies.

Cerf had much to say about Rand in his memoirs, as did her editor, Hiram Haydn. Both men were admiring, irritated, fascinated, and puzzled by this unexpected phenomenon of a novelist. They eagerly waited for her next novel.

When a quote of hers was read into the Congressional Record in the early Sixties, Cerf congratulated her, saying, "Now that you have made the Congressional Record, there is only one mountain left for you to climb. I refer, of course, to *Playboy* magazine." She reached that peak too, in the March 1964 issue.

Rand wrote no more fiction after *Atlas Shrugged*. So many young readers asked so many questions about the philosophical implications of Atlas that Rand's young protégé, psychologist Nathaniel Branden, suggested to her that they could market a series of lectures fleshing out what she had suggested in the novel. Branden opened the Nathaniel Branden Institute in 1958 as a profit-seeking venture. It succeeded beyond his wildest dreams. It closed in 1968 after a personal dispute between Rand and Branden.

Rand died in 1982. Yet socialists and so-called progressives never seem to tire of making anti-Rand rants and spewing invective whenever her name arises. Nevertheless, millions remain curious about her views and her life.

In 1991, the Book of the Month Club and the Library of Congress conducted a survey. They asked about two thousand Book of the Month Club members which book had influenced them the most in their lives. 778 responded. 166 of those cited the Bible. Seventeen cited *Atlas Shrugged*. All the other responses trailed down from there, including *Lord of the Rings* and *To Kill a Mockingbird*.

The editor of India Abroad magazine told this reader that "In India, everyone knows Ayn Rand's books."

The US Postal Service has issued an Ayn Rand stamp. There is a sculpture of Rand at the entrance to a museum near Nashville, Tennessee and a bust on the campus of Universidad Francisco Marroquín in Guatemala City. A quote from *The Fountainhead* appears on a monument in Disney World. Rand has even appeared in computer games. For explorers, there are five Ayn Rand walking tours offered since 1998 in New York.

Rand's Critics

If the intellectual establishment feels the need to attack Rand year after year, there must be a reason. They accuse her of causing the "Great Recession" of 2008. They accuse her of fascism. They call her the "gateway drug" that leads young dupes to Trumpism.

People on the street all over the world, if they have any intellectual pretensions, have heard of Rand. But they are often very fuzzy about her life and the contents of her novels. Those over fifty will often tell you that they read either The Fountainhead or Atlas Shrugged in their teens or twenties, and today, they likely remember not what the books actually said, but the jokes told them about Rand by their professors. But if they are young, and have read Atlas once, then they may want to study it in greater detail, and this will be the book they should turn to.

Barbara Branden observed, and my own experience confirms this, that for all the accusations of cultism from Rand's critics, people who read her as teens seldom join the Moonies or the Hare Krishnas or Scientology or some other real cult. The mentality is just not the same. Readers who are all gung-ho for Rand at fifteen, and then find reasons to criticize her, join the establishment, not the cults. Even Hillary Clinton admitted going through an Ayn Rand phase in her teens. The typical Ayn Rand reader follows a lifelong interest in science and scientific philosophy, not religion.

One often-repeated complaint against Ayn Rand, and especially against Atlas Shrugged, is that Rand's characters are one-dimensional. Her characterizations are paper-thin. They mean that Rand telegraphs too soon and too clearly who constitutes the hero and who functions as the villain. But Rand has a reason for this telegraphing.

In her Romantic style, it is important to establish quickly who is who, to get the conflict started right away. Without conflict between hero and villain, there is no drama and no plot. On that foundation of conflict, you can then add layers of detail and nuance to the characterizations, as long as those details don't get in the way of the plot. If readers would slow down their reading, they would notice those layers. In this commentary, I point them out.

In addition to the heroes and villains, there are also swing characters, such as Gail Wynand in *The Fountainhead* and Robert Stadler in *Atlas Shrugged*. Rand keeps us in suspense for a long time as to whether these characters will end up good guys or bad guys.

Some complain that Rand's heroes have no inner conflicts. Yet, the entire plot of Atlas Shrugged revolves around the heroes' inner conflicts over whether or not to go on strike. Rand shows how that conflict over the strike intertwines with other conflicts in the characters' lives, like Hank's marriage to Lillian, and Dagny falling in love with the man she had sworn to kill. Hank Rearden goes through a long, slow, agonizing development, showing us a heroic inner struggle with certain mistakes he made in his thinking earlier in life. Nearly every page shows Dagny's inner struggle in great detail, right up to the moment she does go on strike (on AS 1138).

Rand divided the novel into three parts, naming them after Aristotle's three laws of logic: Non-contradiction, Either-Or, and A is A. These titles don't directly reflect the content within each part and some critics have pointed to this as a fault: the part titles have nothing to do with the parts. While the part titles serve as an homage to Aristotle's teachings, the critics overlook the fact that the laws of logic provide a major thread throughout the novel, as the role of the mind and the awareness of intellectual surroundings guides various characters on their intellectual journeys.

Rand's Atlas portrays what many see as an unabashed defense of laissez faire capitalism. That economic system, they charge, with great contempt and anger, denies government benefits to the poor. Rand was not an economist or a political theorist and still less a political leader or candidate for office. She was not even a philosopher, in that she had no doctorate in the subject, or even a master's degree. She was a fiction writer. She dabbled in philosophy, but writing fiction was her profession. It's just that she believed that ideas matter, and so her heroes try to apply philosophical ideas to everyday life, without actually getting degrees in the subject. This makes her works, especially *Atlas Shrugged*, appear to be propaganda for her philosophy. That just means that your professor never heard of such a thing as a novel of ideas that wasn't just propaganda. The teenaged reader will, if he wishes, have no trouble finding works on economics for or against capitalism. But his interest will have been stimulated by this novel of ideas, and that is what a novel of ideas is supposed to do.

It's About Dagny

Rand's three major works, *We the Living*, *The Fountainhead*, and *Atlas Shrugged*, followed her lifelong interest in philosophy, from politics down to the underlying ethics, and then down to the underlying epistemology and metaphysics (today called ontology). Her themes went from What happens when you lose your political freedom to What happens when you lose your personal and professional dreams and ambitions, to What happens when you lose your grip on reality itself?

In *We the Living*, the conflict is simple: man versus the totalitarian state.

The Fountainhead gives us four characters – Dominique Francon, Peter Keating, Ellsworth Toohey, and Gail Wynand – whose lives revolve around the assumption that there are no men of integrity. Then they all meet one. Howard Roark. Rand sets this dreaded apparition down in their midst as a cat among the birds, and they all panic and scatter, each in his own characteristic way.

Atlas Shrugged unfolds along a higher plane and on a larger scale. This is not about the problems of a dozen or so acquaintances in the Petrograd of 1924 or the New York of the 1930s. This is not about New York City or about the United States. It is about all of mankind and his whole world and the ages. It is not about a turning point in the life of one character, but a turning point in the life of the whole human race. But you can't write a story about an entire species or all of a planet. You have to focus on the life of a few characters, while making clear that their individual lives and problems are being painted against the backdrop of world-changing events that those individual characters are typical of.

One of my chief goals in this book is to show that, contrary to what you have heard, John Galt is not the main character in this story, and his Speech is not the climax of this story. Dagny is the protagonist. We see the story more through her eyes than anyone else's. The story is about her discovery of the motor, her discovery of the strike, her discovery of John Galt, and her decision to join the strike.

The "headline" of *Atlas*, or the "plot-theme" as Rand called it, is this: Will Dagny join the strike? Everything else is subplot. In integrating Dagny's search for the destroyer, the inventor of the motor, and her "man at the end of track" with the spectacle of industrial civilization collapsing for want of that man, Rand is likening Dagny to the pilot of a plane that is going down. She is in a tailspin. The propeller is not turning. The altimeter hand is going counterclockwise toward zero. Industrial civilization is collapsing.

Yet Dagny does not bail out. Why? Because she still believes that she can pull up the plane's nose and land safely. She believes that the nation and the world will come to their senses and change the government's disastrous policies, and the underlying philosophical premises that made those policies possible, and inevitable. She believes that she and Hank and a few others can lead by example, and then say, like Roark, "The defense rests."

Will Dagny succeed? Will she crash? Will she bail out? That is, will the world change its ideas? Will Dagny go down with New York City and die in the ruins? Will she join Galt in the Gulch? In fact, Dagny does pilot a crashing plane, at the end of Part II. Let that scene serve as a microcosm of the whole novel. And there on the ground to meet and rescue Dagny – and the world – is John Galt.

There are many, many characters and subplots. That is what makes second-time readers, and third and fourth and tenth. There is also the mystery angle. Rand was a big fan of Agatha Christie, Raymond Chandler, her friend Mickey Spillane, and other mystery writers. Mysteries are fun to read.

That too keeps readers coming back for more. But in the end, the story revolves about Dagny's journey of discovery, as to her inner self and the nature of the world collapsing around her.

Abbreviations

AH	Anne C. Heller or her book Ayn Rand and the World She Made
AR	Ayn Rand
ARI	Ayn Rand Institute
ARL	The Ayn Rand Letter
AS	*Atlas Shrugged*
Atlas	*Atlas Shrugged*
BB	Barbara Branden, or her book *The Passion of Ayn Rand*
JAR	*Journals of Ayn Rand*
JARS	*Journal of Ayn Rand Studies*
LAR	*Letters of Ayn Rand*
NB	Nathaniel Branden, or his memoir, *Judgment Day*
TEAR	*The Early Ayn Rand*
TF	*The Fountainhead*
WTL	*We the Living*

Main Positive Characters

Dagny Taggart	Operating Vice-President of Taggart Transcontinental Railroad.
Eddie Willers	Special Assistant to Dagny.
Henry Rearden	Owner of Rearden Steel and inventor of Rearden Metal alloy.
Francisco d'Anconia	Heir to d'Anconia Copper of Buenos Aires. Dagny's first lover.
John Galt	Physicist at Twentieth Century Motor Company and inventor of a motor that draws static electricity from the air and converts it to current. Organizer of the strike.
Dr. Hugh Akston	Taught philosophy to Galt, Ragnar and Francisco. Striker.
Ellis Wyatt	Oil field owner. Developed a new technique for getting oil out of depleted wells. Striker.
Kenneth Danagger	Coal mine owner. Striker.
Ragnar Danneskjöld	Close friend of Galt and Francisco who helped them start strike. Studied philosophy, then turned pirate.
Cherryl Brooks Taggart	Shop girl whom James Taggart married. Became disillusioned with James.
Owen Kellogg	Engineer, assistant manger of Taggart Terminal. A striker.
Judge Narragansett	A judge of the Superior Court of Illinois. Striker.
Midas Mulligan	A Chicago banker. Striker. Owns Galt's Gulch.
Tony the Wet Nurse	A government official sent to regulate Rearden Steel. Turns against the government's strong-arm tactics and dies trying to save Rearden Steel.
Gwen Ives	Rearden's secretary. Joins him in strike.

Main Negative Characters

James Taggart	President of Taggart Transcontinental Railroad. Dagny's older brother. Good at trading favors with government and business figures.
Wesley Mouch	Rearden's Washington lobbyist. Betrays Rearden in deal for position in government planning board. Becomes economic dictator.
Mr. Thompson	Head of the State. Becomes more ruthless as economic picture turns desperate.
Cuffy Meigs	On government's Unification Board. Runs Taggart Transcontinental for government. Dreams of conquering Canada and Mexico. Seizes Project X and accidentally destroys Iowa.
Orren Boyle	CEO of Associated Steel – Rearden's larger, older, more politically connected competitor. Trades favors with Jim Taggart.
Lillian Rearden	Hank's wife. Intellectual hostess. Brings famous intellectuals to her parties. Makes Hank miserable.
Philip Rearden	Hank's younger brother. Demands money and a job from Hank.
Paul Larkin	Manufactures mining equipment. Buys Rearden's ore mines.
Dr. Robert Stadler	Director of the State Science Institute. Former physics professor to Galt, Francisco and Ragnar.
Dr. Floyd Ferris	Works for State Science Institute. Uses Stadler's prestige to acquire government power.
Kip Chalmers	Climbs the bureaucracy in Washington, then runs for Legislature from California. Dies in Taggart Tunnel disaster.
Tinky Holloway	A top government bureaucrat, but AR never names his exact title.
Chick Morrison	The Government's "Morale Conditioner": a sort of propaganda minister.
Eugene Lawson	Headed a bank in Wisconsin, later a Washington bureaucrat.

Fred Kinnan	Head of Amalgamated Labor, the biggest labor union in the country. Much more realistic and honest than Taggart and Boyle and the Washington leadership, but just as ruthless.
Claude Slagenhop	Head of the "Friends of Global Progress," of which Philip Rearden is a member.
Bertram Scudder	Has a magazine of fashionable opinion and a radio show.

Timeline

Year	Date	Page[†]	Event
1	September 2	4	Dagny trying to build Rio Norte Line
2	January 29	174	Rio Norte becomes John Galt Line
2	September 2	382	John Galt Line finished; Dagny and Hank have started their affair and have found the motor; Dagny interviews Quentin Daniels
3	September 2	428	Jim has married Cherryl; Dagny has tried to find the motor's inventor; Hank has been tried.
4	May 1	550	Government issues Directive 10-289
4	June 28	802	Dagny is about to leave the valley
4	August 5	864	Jim brags to Cherryl about double-crossing Francisco
4	August 5	866	Chile will nationalize d'Anconia Copper on September 2
4	August 6	905	Cherryl kills herself
4	September 2	921	Francisco's farewell
4	September 14	39	Minnesota harvest
4	November 22[‡]	1005	Mr. Thompson is supposed to speak, but Galt speaks instead

[†] Page numbers refer to the page in *Atlas Shrugged*.
[‡] The last scene takes place in the winter of Years 4 and 5. So the story unfolds over about three and a half years.

xlv

PART III
A Is A
(Dagny and Galt)

Part Overview

AS 699

Compare these next two chapters, in their visual impression of light and beauty and filled as they are with beautiful, rational characters, to two movie scenes: In *The Wizard of Oz* we see Kansas in black and white, then suddenly we see Oz in color. In *Blade Runner* we see a Los Angeles that is crowded and dirty, and where it always seems to be a rainy night, and fear stalks all the characters. Then suddenly the hero and heroine are in an aircraft flying over a California landscape that is natural, colorful and flooded with sunlight. The contrast is breathtaking—like the sudden appearance of the word "I" at the beginning of the last two chapters of *Anthem*.

1. Atlantis

Chapter Overview

Dagny comes to. Galt takes her home. She meets the strikers. Galt explains the strike to her at a dinner at Mulligan's house. She sees the powerhouse and the strikers' oath. Dagny sleeps in the guest room.

AS 701

Scene 1: Dagny meets Galt, Wyatt, Mulligan, and Akston. She sleeps before dinner.

like a blessing pronounced upon the universe. Compare this to the line back on AS 108: "a feeling greater than happiness, the feeling of one's blessing upon the whole of the earth . . .." And what was the cause of that feeling? The after-glow from her first sex with Francisco.

AR is already hinting at the heaven/earth theme she will develop later, on AS 721, with Ellis Wyatt. And these whole two chapters in Galt's Gulch play with that theme. This is Atlantis, Elysium, and Valhalla.

BB, on the last page of her AR bio, notes that Kensico Cemetery is in the village of Valhalla, New York.

The village Board chose that name because Kensico and other big cemeteries were already established there, giving the new village its base industry. BB pictured AR arriving in Valhalla, greeted not only by Frank and other departed spirits, but also her fictional heroes.

The rest of this page is devoted to Dagny's first visual impression of Galt. The first-time reader must be thinking: This must be John Galt! Who else could it be?

no mark of pain or fear or guilt. In the chapter by that name, Eddie ascribes that quality to the face of the worker in the cafeteria (AS 652). It is not that Galt has never experienced pain or fear or guilt, but that these experiences have not coarsened him to the point of taking his bitterness out on others, as early adversity did to Toohey.

the angular planes of his cheeks. AR worked in Hollywood in the era when "classic Hollywood good looks" became a part of world culture. Frank O'Connor and Gary Cooper were two examples.

arrogance . . . scorn . . . yet the face had none of these qualities. Galt does *not* look arrogant. He looks like he has reached the state that the arrogant man wants you to *think* he has reached. Did you catch that fine distinction?

a ruthless innocence. Who but AR could put those two words together? And yet it makes perfect sense. A child has a ruthless innocence. His trusting look challenges you to be the being he expects you to be. He demands the best within you.

as if his eyes imparted a superlative value to himself and to the world. "It is my eyes which see, and the sight of my eyes grants beauty to the earth" (*Anthem*). It takes two to tango: it takes both a seer and a seen to create meaning in the seeing.

to the world for being a place so eagerly worth seeing. In her interview with Tom Snyder, AR called this world a very wonderful one. That is another theme AR should have expanded on. Maybe if she had left more sketches, or expanded from sketching into painting, readers would know this about her. AR is not using the word "eagerly" quite correctly here. "Worth seeing" is not eager. *You* are eager to see the world.

chestnut-brown hair. Neither Galt nor Dagny is a blond (There is a final E on "blonde" for the females, no E for the males in medieval French, but in English today, both spellings are correct). And Galt's eyes are green, not blue.

Reading Atlas for the first time at thirteen, this reader was struck by the fact that AR is describing a sexy, handsome, hot guy. But he is an inventor! You mean you can be a nerd, a scientist, a bookworm, a pocket protector-wearer—and still get the girls? Unheard of!

AS 702

this man was a total stranger. This reflects AR's belief, and NB's, that you can tell everything about a stranger with a close look at his face. Naturally, a fiction writer would want to think that.

John Galt. Where did AR get that name? She was good at finding character names that had just the right sound. She wanted you to read her books aloud, not just silently. "John Galt" is American in style: short and to the point, not long and flowery and overloaded with European titles of nobility or Soviet *nomenklatura*. Some claim to see the German word *"Geld"*: "money," in "Galt." Actually, it is a Scots name, meaning "pig" in the Border Dialects. And one of Rand's confirmed themes in this novel is "Man as god." One syllable, starting with a hard G. God.

Another German word (and remember, AR could read German) is *"Held,"* meaning "hero." There was a cartoonist named John Held (1889-1958) of whom AR would certainly have heard. He drew illustrations for *The New Yorker, Harper's Bazaar,* and *Vanity Fair* magazines. He is remembered as the visual immortalizer of the Jazz Age. If you have seen illustrations of flappers, they are his. AR might have played around with his name until Held had become Galt. In her research on scientists and inventors, for Galt's characterization as an inventor, AR might have encountered John Dalton (1766-1844), who discovered that an element's atoms have a characteristic size and weight, and that chemical bonds are electrical. Rand knew a lawyer named John C. Gall. He was one of her conservative intellectual friends of the forties who proved so ineffectual at spreading any moral arguments for capitalism. She should have written a book about them and called it "For the New Ineffectual."

But if we are looking for words that have the right sound, as possible inspirations for the name "John Galt," how's this? "Galt" rhymes with "exalt."

All this is speculation, until and unless someone turns up a written statement from AR saying where she got the name of her hero.

Why are you frightened? This reader must admit he was shaking when he met AR, and NB.

What is this valley? AR might have seen the 1930s serial *Buck Rogers,* where the aircraft of the Hidden City fly into a giant door that opens up in the side of a mountain. *Lost Horizon* is set in a utopian community hidden in the Himalayas.

AS 703

The Taggart Terminal. Galt knows that this is the end Dagny has been seeking, and that he is the man she imagines standing at the end of the tracks. Thanks to Eddie and his big mouth, Galt knows Dagny very well indeed.

For just a few moments. This was Dagny's reaction to the brakeman whistling Halley's Fifth Concerto, back on AS 13.

AS 704

an image refracted. This is one of the places where the reader becomes aware of the science fiction aspect of the novel, although Galt's motor and Rearden Metal are previous examples. But science fiction purists will insist that the science has to be central to the plot to make a story officially science fiction. Galt's and Rearden's inventions are important, but they are not central to the plot. Dagny's uncovering of the strike and her struggle to put off joining it—that is the plot.

except a courage such as yours. So that is what caused the crash. Not accident, and not foolhardiness on Dagny's part, flying so low, and not some shooting down of her plane on Galt's part, but courage.

Some of the rays are the kind that kill magnetic motors. Readers would read, many years later, about the EMP, the Electro Magnetic Pulse that is generated in a hydrogen bomb blast. If a bomb explodes a hundred thousand feet in the air, it will kill the motor of every ground vehicle below. This was not widely known before the movie *The Day After* in 1983. AR did her homework.

masculine simplicity . . . feminine, overdetailed lace-work. Here is Ayn the poet. A fir tree is like a pyramid, and birch trees are like lace. Masculine and feminine. AR is making sure on these pages that we don't miss the sexual tension that is building up. And the line "like sculpture reduced to an essential form" shows what kind of sculptor Ayn would have been.

as if learning it from him. Another revelation for this reader, and one applied many times in the long years since 1967. You do not have to look away as if caught, if you and the person you are looking at have nothing to fear from honesty, and from each other.

AS 705

She heard the sound of the waterfall. In this paragraph, Dagny hears two sounds that become one in her mind for a moment, the falling water and the music, until she and Galt pass the waterfall and draw closer to the music. It is Richard Halley playing his Fifth Concerto (the brakeman, AS 13).

Has that ever happened to you? Perhaps as you are just falling asleep or just waking up. Falling water that seems to be music, or music that seems to be words? AR must have been able to introspect well enough to record and remember, and use, some altered states of consciousness.

She didn't think much of drugs—looks like she didn't need any. And, of course, what else does "Fallingwater" mean to AR? "Fallingwater" was a famous country home designed by Frank Lloyd Wright in 1936. He built it over a waterfall.

It was not a town. AR must have thought of the Boy on the Bicycle: "He saw a town. Only it was not a town." (TF 535)

AS 706

The gold dollar sign is three feet tall. Much has been made of the floral dollar sign at AR's calling hours and burial.

anniversary present. So there is a Mrs. Mulligan? There is no other mention of her.

they emerged suddenly from behind a rocky corner. This happens in the Gary Cooper movie *For Whom the Bell Tolls*. Out comes Ayn's notepad: this is an interesting way for a character to enter a scene, because it happens so suddenly. This is just speculation.

AS 707

Do you suppose I was killed in that crash? AR will come back to the theme of heaven and earth later.

scab. This is a word that strikers use for workers who fail to join or support a strike.

understudy. a word that would come naturally to someone with AR's recent experience in the theater. Frank, a former actor himself, might have suggested it, too.

Galt was watching her face intently. Remember how Galt reacted when Eddie told him about Hank and Dagny on AS 653?

AS 708

intently and that she saw an instant's change in his. Remember that Galt has found out only two or three days ago from Eddie about Dagny and Hank.

golden ray hit her eyes, sweeping over her forehead. We will see Akston brush a comma of hair off Galt's forehead on AS 736, Francisco give Hank the same gesture on AS 998, and on 999 we will see the red glow of the mills sweep over Hank's forehead, "as if in salute and farewell."

as another connection fell into place. What fun AR must have had, writing this chapter, revealing all the secrets.

Don't let him go! See AS 655, 1163, 1165, 1166, and ARL Volume I, Number 4.

AS 709

as one would say to a dead friend, in a dream, the words one regrets having missed the chance to say in life. Did Ayn have such dreams about her family? About Leo—Lyolya—her boyfriend back in Leningrad?

memory of a telephone ringing. This happened on AS 334.

One must always see for oneself. This is one of the things a thirteen-year-old needs to hear from a hero in a book.

a sheet of glass for most of the front wall. How appropriate such a wall would be, Roark is thinking, for a client who seems pure consciousness, his faculty of sight being his best-loved tool (AS 701). Imagine Roark meeting Galt! And designing his house!

He carried her across the threshold. A hint of wedding bells to come, as is a line on AS 791 where Akston calls Dagny by her first name, and on AS 799, in the paragraph beginning "His wife."

a frontiersman's cabin . . . super-modern skill. A sticker! You can have it both ways. The future does not have to be unrelieved white in every direction, as in *Things to Come, 2001: A Space Odyssey,* or *THX*

1138. And Santiago Calatrava's "Oculus" at the new World Trade Center. You can go back to nature AND be futuristic!

AS 710

mercilessly perceptive eyes. AR returns to her eye theme, again, as on AS 701.

That's the contradiction you had to resolve. Let us put this line into the "Check your Premises" collection: pages 199, 331, 489, and 618.

I never had any wish to be talked about. Galt neither welcomes nor fears fame. It was an accident. When he makes his speech, he will use that fame. But he does not let it use him.

AS 711

an engine checked by an expert mechanic. Here is another of the metaphors of mechanics and electricity that AR either got from Isabel Paterson or was already inclined to before. She was initially going to call TF *The Mainspring*, for example. Mechanical, and therefore masculine. But here is how metaphors can get you into trouble: A nurse, very well read, especially in science fiction, and a poet herself, did not like this metaphor. "When I take care of patients," she said, "they do not feel like a machine. They feel like a person I care about." But of course, that is not what AR meant here.

AS 712

sparkling in the sun on the polished table top. Light, light, light!

When did you sleep or eat last? Hendricks is the doctor, but Galt is Dagny's nurse.

On their way to Stony Creek, Connecticut, for their 1936 vacation, Ayn and Frank passed Hendricks Point, on the Saugatuck River in Westport. But, as always, it is just as likely that Ayn got the name out of the Manhattan or Los Angeles phone book.

In any way you wish. Boy, has he ever got her number! He's practically making out the guest list for their wedding. But then he has had twelve years to fall in love with her.

She let a moment pass. NB uses this formula on his record "Discovering the Unknown Self." See AS 714 below.

toasting bread, frying eggs and bacon. See Dr. Akston cooking on AS 327. This is a moment that this reader longed to see on the screen. It did not make it into the *Atlas Shrugged Part III* movie script. It shows Galt and Dagny in one of those "humanizing" moments. Such moments of mundane activity throw the high relief of the mountaintop moments into even higher relief, by contrast.

That, among other things. Understatement! Great line. Especially because in it we see whole scenes, in our minds, that AR did not need to include in the book. We see Dr. Akston, the proud mentor, with Galt, Ragnar, and Francisco, talking about Plato over a plate of hamburgers and potato salad.

AS 713

It's built? It's working? It's functioning? Dagny is talking about a machine that draws power from the air. Only AR could make Dagny sound as excited about that as most readers and writers of 1957 would sound on being told that Jesus Christ is in the next room and wants to meet you. What do Jack Kerouac's characters get excited about in his novel *On the Road*? Meeting people they can sponge off for alcohol and drugs? Why do the professors want us to see that novel as "serious literature" and not this one?

AS 714

as if deliberately letting her see. This is NB's formula again, as on AS 712, and on AS 371 and 401. I will give you a moment to hear yourself, and to let you know that I hear you.

Couldn't he give it to you as a courtesy? Dagny would not have said "give," she would have said "lent." AR cheated a bit, putting in the word "give," because Galt's reply is about the forbidding of the word "give."

we have no laws in this valley. This line is crucial, especially for those who insist that AS is not a novel, but a manifesto, and that AR wants you and me and everyone in the world to live literally and exactly like the people in the valley live. She does not.

This valley is Midas Mulligan's land, and these people—AR thought in terms of no more than a thousand, and they appear to this reader to be many fewer than that—are here by invitation for one month a year.

This is a community that springs into being every June 1 and disappears every June 30, like *Brigadoon*, a Lerner and Lowe musical

Atlantis

that premiered on Broadway in 1947, as AR was writing AS. This is not a Utopian society, despite the next chapter title. It is a bunch of friends, vacationing and going to a marvelous party.

So go ahead and feel free to use the word "give." Just don't demand human sacrifices in its name.

AS 715

This whole page was one of the greatest stickers for this reader. The moment that Quentin Daniels describes, when Galt came to him and said that he was the one who invented the motor, and then asked Daniels to come away with him: it recalls the movie *Death Takes a Holiday*, and a Twilight Zone take-off on that movie, starring Robert Redford. Or the 1985 Ron Howard movie *Cocoon*. Someone comes to take you away from the unsatisfying life you are living. Surely a universal human fantasy. Beam me up, Scotty!

In the 1966 Hitchcock movie *Torn Curtain*, there is a scene between two physicists at a blackboard. Coincidence? Or did someone read the scene Daniels recounts to Dagny here?

AS 716

The sun had trickled down the peaks. It looks like AR took the trouble to observe a sunset in Ouray and write down a description of it in her notepad. But how many readers stop and smell the descriptive passages in this book? And look how beautifully AR's description of the valley and the peaks becomes a narrative passage of Dagny's thoughts and feelings. "Joyous, proud comfort": Dagny has found everything she wanted within the granite walls of this valley. Mainly Galt. (Actually, the rocks around Ouray are red and clearly layered, and so are sandstone, not granite.)

a sense of the finite. Leonard Peikoff, in a talk called "Why Ancient Greece is my Favorite Civilization," explained that the ancient Greeks had no religious faith at all. They had no use for the mystical, the unexplainable, the infinite. They liked to know, to quantify.

Mulligan's house ... granite walls ... terraces. Was AR thinking of Taliesin, Frank Lloyd Wright's estate in Wisconsin? Wright and his wife invited the O'Connors for the weekend in 1947, as Ayn and Frank drove from LA to NYC and back.

herds of sheep. Shouldn't that be flocks?

herds of cattle. That's better.

AS 717

Sanders Aircraft. In 1948, Liberty Films produced the Frank Capra film *State of the Union*, in which Spencer Tracy plays Grant Matthews, an aircraft manufacturer. Matthews proudly says, "I started with a monkey wrench and built the Matthews aircraft."

Perhaps AR had Tracy in mind for Dwight Sanders. Angela Lansbury's character lauds Matthews' managerial brilliance. "He's never even been threatened with a strike!" Like Rearden, Matthews is another fictional businessman hero who, far from grinding down the laboring masses, takes care of the workers who take care of him.

crashed with forty passengers each. What are you talking about, Ayn? Don't we all know that air crashes are caused by greedy capitalists who lobby government to gut needed safety regulations? This is the challenge for libertarians: to persuade a skeptical public on regulatory issues like that. Movie star Carole Lombard died in a plane crash as AR was finishing work on TF.

In gold, Miss Taggart. One open-minded reader read AS and asked this reader "Why is gold significant?" That was her first question. This was an educated woman. She really did not know why gold should be important. Her teachers and professors had seen to that.

AS 718

Your laws forbid it. FDR did that, but not for all gold. Only bullion.

He pressed the starter and drove on. Notice that AR does not show us Sanders saying "Be seeing you" or such to Dagny. It must have happened, but AR leaves it out. It is not necessary to the scene.

motionless water. AR must have thought of the first page of TF here. "The water looked immobile, the rock, flowing."

the blue of the sky and the green of the mountains. Blue-green! Ayn's favorite color. This must be a big part of why Ayn called her native world a wonderful one: lots of color in nature, as well as in the built world. And you thought she had no use for nature. See her *Tomorrow Show* interview with Tom Snyder.

Good day, Miss Taggart. These cameos of Galt's strikers are like the scene in the movie *Fahrenheit 451* where Montag meets the members of a secret community of readers of forbidden books. Each one calls himself by the name of the book he has memorized. (Ray Bradbury published the novel in 1953, so it is possible that AR read it or heard about it while writing AS.)

What was it that you betrayed me for. Dagny is happy to see these men, but the pull of her old life is still strong. She is still angry at McNamara for checking out just when she needed him.

I'm the utilities man. Perhaps AR was thinking of Wendell Willkie, the Republican presidential candidate she worked for in 1940. He was a utilities man too, running an electric power company in Indiana. Ayn saw him as betraying her, and all those who had worked hard on his campaign or voted for him, by his ineffective campaign and indifference to ideas. That same complaint could be leveled at every Republican from Hoover to Trump.

AS 719

he taught that you can't consume more than you have produced. That would be Henry Hazlitt (1894-1993). His wife Frances worked with AR at Paramount Pictures, where AR was a reader. The Hazlitts introduced AR to Ludwig von Mises and other conservative intellectuals (yes, there were a few back then). Hazlitt wrote *Economics in One Lesson.* The one lesson is this: You can't consume what you have not produced.

the inhabitants of slums were not the men who made this country. AR had not yet met Robert Hessen, who became her secretary, and who was then studying American History at Columbia University.

He was in Murray Rothbard's circle, so he did not meet AR till after AS was published and Rothbard wrote Rand a fan letter. The farther back you go in American history, the more the Great Man theory of history becomes the norm, so many older historians would subscribe to it. The Great Man Theory versus the Masses Theory of history deserves a longer discussion than this paragraph.

he taught that men are capable of thinking. This describes NB and also NB's psychology advisor at NYU, Dr. John Tietz. NB liked him because he began his course by saying "Ladies and gentlemen, I shall conduct this class on the assumption that you are all conscious." NB recalls "I had burst out laughing in appreciation, and he and I had grinned at each other" (*Judgment Day*, page 170). The joke was that the Behaviorists were just then coming into vogue, and for them consciousness was either non-existent or irrelevant.

the guiltlessness of his face. Compare this paragraph to Dagny's negotiation with Hank on AS 83. These are two people who can be brutally frank and honest with each other because they respect each other, and themselves.

Ahead of them. The writer with large eyes appears. This is AR's Hitchcock-like cameo in her own novel. Alfred Hitchcock, one of AR's and everyone else's favorite movie directors, played a small part himself in every movie he made when he was just starting to work, just because he was short of money and could not afford extras. Then he made it a tradition to put himself in every one of his movies.

Michelangelo put himself into his mural *The Last Judgment*, as an empty skin that Christ is throwing into hell, perhaps to suggest that Michelangelo's flesh was going to hell because of his sins of the flesh. He was gay.

hopelessness, serenely accepted. Ayn portrays herself here as hopelessly dreaming of Galt. How did Frank feel about that? Doesn't it suggest that in Frank Ayn was settling for a man somewhat short of her ideal man? Did she have higher hopes for Nathan? (His friends called Nathaniel Branden "Nathan.") Or is the fishwife not meant to be seen that literally as Ayn?

AS 720

a stab of jealousy. More sexual tension.

fishwife. That is how Ayn wants us to see her, apparently. "Carping like a fishwife" is an ancient expression. In the musical "1776," Franklin says to Adams "Stop sounding like a Boston fishwife!"

laminated rock. This is AR's way of saying sedimentary rock, which is, in fact, what makes up the cliffs around Ouray. But in this case, it is apparently shale—with oil in it.

Buena Esperanza. Good Hope. Ellis Wyatt had discovered it already, back on AS 249. He must have explored a pass that extended onto Mulligan's property.

What am I paying you for? For heaven's sake, Wyatt, he turned away from his task for only a moment. Those of us who lack confidence in our ability to do our jobs wince at this paragraph. But it sounds like Wyatt is more joking than serious. Also, Wyatt's wording suggests an American attitude: you should be working diligently because that is what I am paying you for.

The Old World attitude would be: You should be working diligently because you are afraid of me. Baron Steuben found that he could not expect mindless, machine-like obedience from American soldiers as he had expected of German soldiers. In this brave new world, you have to give the soldiers a *reason* for following each order. Hence, AR saying that Aristotle should be considered America's *real* Founding Father.

best fishwife, best grease-monkey, best pupil. Best, best, best. How does the roughneck on the rock wall feel about that? If there are all these "bests," then there must be others who are second best, even here in the Gulch. Well, maybe they live in hope for greater accomplishments later. See the truck driver, thirteen lines below.

AS 721

aristocrats. Would it ever even occur to you, in 2024 and beyond, to use the word "aristocrat" at all?

AR was born in 1905 in a European capital, remember. "Aristos" means "the best," and "crat" means "ruler." Aristocracy means "rule by the best" (best at fighting, that is, winning battles for his king). But AR's point, in AS and in her whole career, is never about anyone ruling anyone, so it would be better, especially today, to just avoid using that term at all. AR, as always, though, is giving the word her own new and deeper meaning.

There is no such thing as a lousy job. When readers remember from Atlas nothing but the high-powered main characters, they sometimes think that AR had contempt for anyone in a position lower than CEO. But she did not. "All work is creative work if done by a creative mind," she said. Because even a janitorial job involves problem solving, which is what makes us human.

He looked like a truck driver. Google a picture of Oscar Hammerstein II. He looked like a truck driver.

eager for acknowledgment. This is what NB called "psychological visibility."

the eagerness of an artist at the opening of his show in a gallery. In the late stages of writing and editing AS, AR would have been to a few gallery openings. Frank was a student at the Art Students' League, their friends Joan Mitchell Blumenthal and Mary Ann Rukavina Sures were studying art. When did AR meet José Manuel Capuletti? She wrote about him for the December 1966 *The Objectivist*, so she had probably not yet discovered him in the AS period.

while you were on earth. Here AR creates an alternative to the traditional division of reality into heaven above, hell below, and earth in between. In her view, this earth is not a vale of tears. Earth is the Good Place, when people make it so, and the Bad Place when people make it so. Earth is better than heaven, because while you are still on earth, action is still possible for you. The thing AR feared above all others was a situation where she could not act. Once a loved one dies, no further action is possible on your part to help or save your loved one. Therein lay AR's fear of death. Is this going to be a sticker for you?

displaying the greasy stains as a treasure. The dignity of creative, productive work.

Mine. . . . what that word means . . . what it feels like. This takes practice, because we were none of us brought up to see things this way. Back on AS 715, Quentin Daniels says "I want to make money. I want to make millions." He and Wyatt are talking about the money that comes to the creative thinker who figures out *how* to get oil out of shale or electricity out of the air. The act of problem solving is the point of pride. Under socialism, the inventor will get a shiny medal that reads "Hero of Socialist Labor" and a hearty handshake from Bernie and AOC, and the thanks of a grateful nation. Cue Sammy Davis Junior singing "For once I can say this is mine, you can't take it" and "Yes, I can," and the line from the show "Shenandoah": "This land is Anderson land! By the strength of my hand and the sweat of my brow . . . ." That's what it feels like. You have to look hard for examples of AR's themes in pop songs and shows, but, every once in a while, you will find one.

AS 722

I'm manufacturing time . . . as pricelessly mine as if I moved my grave two further hours away. What a great way of looking at creative, productive work! Did Ayn think this up? Did she get it from Isabel Paterson or Henry Hazlitt? It recalls what Arthur C. Clarke wrote in *2001: A Space Odyssey*: In creating language, man had won his first great victory over time and death. Now, a man's knowledge and wisdom need not die with him. And it recalls what this reader's grandfather said on reaching eighty: I am trying to arrange my life so that everything I do is because I *want* to and not because I *have* to." Those two hours have been freed from the "have to" column and put into the "want to" column.

work for use, not for profit. This was one of the many socialist slogans of the twentieth century. You will see AR refer to it in the Author's Foreword of *Anthem*: "The slogan 'production for use and not for profit' is now accepted by most men as a commonplace . . . ." Actually, in a free society, people produce things for use and not for profit all the time. It is called "hobbies." But they do it because they choose to do it, not at the point of the state's gun.

Only those who produce, not those who consume, can ever be anybody's market. This is a corollary to Hazlitt's Lesson.

He chuckled. This paragraph does a better job than Francisco's Money Speech at describing man's struggle to survive. Big sticker!

Wyatt shows Dagny a plant trying to grow out from under a rock: Contrast AR's use of weeds as symbols of decay on AS 31, 446, 560, 572, 609 and 659, and especially on AS 519, where Dagny impulsively uproots a weed at the entrance to Roger Marsh's electrical parts factory in Colorado. Here, the plant is, for Wyatt and for Dagny, a fellow living thing trying to survive, so AR's symbolism suggests the exact opposite of the hated and feared weeds.

NB, in *The Psychology of Self-esteem*, has a charming passage where he describes sitting in his living room looking at his dog Muttnik and a philodendron plant. He asked himself what it is about the plant that makes him feel different from how he feels toward all the other objects in the room. It is the fact that the plant is alive, just as he and Muttnik are alive.

He felt a fellow-feeling for the plant because it faced, as he and every living thing does, the daily alternative of life and death. This is also why AR spoke of "ethics for weeds": if your ethical system is based on life and death, then for every plant and animal, and every pusillanimous creature that slinks through slimy seas, all that which makes life possible is the good, and all that which destroys it is the evil.

On the struggle to survive, compare also Countee Cullen's poem "The Shroud of Color," on the theme of finding the courage to live when you are tempted, like Shakespeare's Hamlet, to end it all with a bare bodkin. Compare also with the "Boy on the Bicycle" vignette at the beginning of Part IV of TF, on the theme of finding the courage to plunge into life when you graduate school.

And again, we do not hear Wyatt saying goodbye. As in a movie, AR just fades to black after each of these short scenes.

AS 723

potato plants and cabbages. This image might have come either from fields AR saw around the ranch in Chatsworth, or from the car or train crossing the country, or an image Frank supplied. Less likely, but possible, would be something she saw from the train crossing the USSR, or heading from Leningrad to Berlin and Paris. Russia, the Baltics, Poland and Germany certainly have enough fields of potatoes and cabbages. Frank liked working on the ranch; AR was ever the city girl. But she sees and remembers the *colors* of the fields. It's a beautiful world!

Roger Marsh. The weeds appear again, and AR goes back to their usual meaning: decay.

lustrous tile front. Marsh's factory sounds like it has an Art Deco façade.

The road was descending to the bottom of the valley. The Gulch is apparently much bigger than Ouray's valley. In fact, AR said it was (LAR 509). Maybe AR was getting some of these images from mountains and valleys she saw with her family on vacation in Switzerland in 1913. Ironically, the Alps were also Nietzsche's inspiration for Zarathustra's mountaintop. At the beginning of *Also Sprach Zarathustra*, the prophet comes out of his cave and sees an alpine sunrise. Richard Strauss captures that sunrise in the opening bars of his tone poem, as you hear at the beginning and end of the movie *2001: A Space Odyssey.*

making shoes. AR is using, as an example of the humblest trade, the very *pedestrian* trade of cobbling.

ruined competitor. Sticker!

AS 724

The ruined competitor is doing alright, it seems.

She wondered. This is another of AR's acid trip passages. The thought of Hank Rearden makes Dagny think of this foundry as the kind of place where Hank had started. Then that makes her think of youth in general, and that reminds her of a quote about youth, and that, in turn, reminds her of the tramp in a diner who had said that John Galt had found the fountain of youth (AS 178). Before her eyes, as she goes through these associations, she sees the fog of the foundry "drawing time into an odd circle."

The quote about youth is what this reader chose, in 1972, as his high school yearbook quote: "To hold an unchanging youth is to reach, at the end, the vision with which one started." AR does not say where this quote comes from, and a quick google search gives no answer other than AR. It was BB who brought the quote to my attention, by using it as the epigraph for her biographical essay "Who Is Ayn Rand?"

In this paragraph, Dagny remembers that line as a quotation, but this is the first time it appears in AS. Did an earlier appearance get left on the cutting room floor?

and while a dim thought went floating. AR sets up the quote in a very odd and mysterious way. Not her usual clarity. "like the streamer of an unfollowed sentence": What does 'streamer" mean? Webster and Google cannot help us here. It sounds like "streamer" might mean an ellipsis at the end of a sentence, but Google and Wikipedia show no such meaning. After all, a series of dots leading across a page in a table of contents is called "leaders," so maybe at the end of a sentence . . .. But no, there is a word for those dots: an *aposiopesis*. There's your new word for the day.

AS 725

the tortured hour of waiting. See AS 440.

a promising child. AR knew as well as anyone what it means to be a promising child.

I've always been short on time in my life, never on what to use it for. That is why this reader could never understand co-workers who say "It was busy today, but that's good. It makes the day go faster."

That's the only sort of men I like to hire. Major sticker!

Have you come to think that one man's ability is a threat to another? No, and AR's corollaries are that one man's rights are no threat to another, and no man's interests are a threat to another. These are the big challenges to a skeptical world from anyone wishing to promote AR's ideas.

AS 726

Another fade to black.

Oh, yes. Yes, Galt knows what it is like to have to wait.

musical comedy. AR hated Gilbert and Sullivan, so what does she like about the thought of musical comedy here? Bright colors. Dagny's mother wanted her to notice the lights, the colors, the flowers, the music of her first ball. "Red cubes, green circles, gold triangles." And how creative! The cubes are bins of tomatoes, the green circles are barrels of lettuce, the gold triangles are pyramids of oranges. Frank was not the only one in the family with a visual sense. Sight was Ayn's best-loved tool.

an attractive young woman . . . her posture light as a showgirl's. AR often pairs the images of industry with the ultimate end in view: luxury, enjoyment of life, bright sunshine and colors, and youth. Whom did she have in mind for this young woman?

Atlantis

AS 727

On the edge of the road. In this paragraph, AR introduces us to the movie star Kay Ludlow, who, just like Kay Gonda in *Ideal*, was inspired for AR by Greta Garbo. And here at last is a character who really did disappear. Garbo stopped making movies at the age of thirty-six and became almost a recluse until she died at eighty-five. She did not seem to be going on strike against anything, but no one to this day seems to know just why she did stop working.

glorifying the commonplace. See Kurt Vonnegut's 1961 short story "Harrison Bergeron."

Mulligan's bank is made of rough granite. Picture the Seamens Bank at 74 Wall Street at Pearl Street. Banks usually want their architects to design a building that looks like it has stood since the earth cooled, and is all one solid block of impregnable rock.

but the dates stamped upon them were of the past two years. Here again we enter the Twilight Zone: What years were those? AR does not say. AS exists in a timeless dimension. It is a myth.

objective values. This means that a dollar today is worth whatever the government says it is worth—supposedly and subjectively. And that's why other nations, after Nixon's cutting of the last ties between the dollar and gold or silver, no longer wanted to hold dollars. A currency that seeks its own market value in the give and take of a world market is objective.

AS 728

the Taggart Bridge. an advance echo of a disaster yet to come.

a rare wedge of sunlight. AR may have pictured the forest scenes in Fritz Lang's 1924 silent movie *Die Nibelungen: Siegfried.* AR admired Lang as her favorite director.

AS 729

the smooth, shining, untouched serenity of glass. Roark's best-loved tool.

Let's see who'll do greater honor. AS 101. Help me to remain. AS 114.

that was all she could read in his face. Notice that AR shows, over and over again, how Galt never misses anything—Dagny is an open book to him—but she can almost never read anything in his face.

She had caught the sound of suffering. Note well! John Galt suffers. But only down to a certain point. He knows about Dagny and Francisco, and about Dagny and Hank, from Eddie. But he has probably not had time, since the slapping scene on AS 640, to hear from Francisco about Francisco and Hank knowing about each other. Unless that was the reason Galt was nervously chain smoking when Eddie joined him on AS 652.

AS 730

a simple granite cube, the size of a toolshed. Maybe it *was* a toolshed—the toolshed of the gardeners of Bryant Park, in midtown Manhattan. It stands on the northeast corner of Sixth Avenue and West 40th Street, a spot now officially called "Nikola Tesla Corner."

Tesla, in the years before he died in 1943, used to hang around Bryant Park, feeding the pigeons. In 1899 the Tesla Company, Inc. was located at 8 West 40th Street. Tesla died in his suite at the New Yorker Hotel, at West 34th Street and Eighth Avenue.

FBI agents swooped in and ransacked the suite for drawings, plans or models of the death rays he had announced his invention of. They found nothing . . . so far as Tesla's biographer knows. AR might even have seen Tesla in the park. She might have spoken to him. She might have told him that she had written a play about an evil inventor in her play *Think Twice.*

Or not. But how about such a meeting as a premise for a play? In any case, Tesla would certainly have come up in AR's thinking about inventors, while she was planning her characterization of John Galt. His obituary would be fresh in her mind in 1945.

She might, at any rate, have had that toolshed in mind for Galt's powerhouse. It's just concrete, though, not granite.

He obeyed. In this paragraph we see another "as if": "a moment uniting her beginning to her goal."

Just as in Dagny's sex scene and her Morning After scene with Rearden (AS 250), AR is showing us both thoughts that are going through Dagny's mind and thoughts that *would* go through her mind and come out as words if she had the time to tell us the meaning of everything that happens to her.

She stood looking up at the structure. In this paragraph, AR lays those layers of meaning pretty thick. Cerf and Haydn's blue pencil fingers must have been itching. But the reader, especially the high school and college-age reader, is getting memorable visual images here that will stick long after he has gotten over any impatience at AR's verbal overkill.

spiral-shaped convictions. Sticker! Great image.

oxygen tube. Maybe AR is thinking of Frank's brother Nick at the VA hospital in Tupper Lake, New York. He had been gassed in World War I.

not to look down to, but up to. This comes from Dagny's meeting with Stadler on AS 358.

She thought of this structure. This paragraph is AR's answer to the Greens. The whole trend, and the whole point, of civilization, is to learn to do more with less. Clean, green electric power is made possible, in this story, by an inventor who is looking for ways to prevent waste.

Burning coal converts one millionth of the fuel into energy. The other 999,999 parts are waste, and become pollution. Fissionable uranium is a thousand times more efficient, but that just means that one *thousandth* of the fuel is converted to energy and the other 999 parts are waste—and a particularly dangerous kind of waste. If Galt's motor drew static from the atmosphere and turned it into current, then efficiency would be his main goal, but two side benefits would be clean air and preventing lightning. Galt, like Franklin, *"eripuit coelo fulmen et sceptrunque tyrannis"*: "He tore lightning from the heavens and the scepter from tyrants."

to lift one's head from one's task and glance at the sunlight. and see Dominique looking down at you in the quarry. AR must have pictured Gary Cooper when she wrote this line.

a month's journey through the whole, open width of the world. AR's "wonderful world" again. Nature hater?

on a ticket paid for by one day of one's labor. AR, the hater of the poor? It is new technology that has liberated the working man far more than all the government policies.

This is where we see AR fulfilling Henry Adams's prophecy in "The Virgin and the Dynamo." Electricity is not just a physical force. It is also a moral force.

AS 731

Have you noticed that, once we got into the "Atlantis" chapter, there has been a lot more to comment about, in this commentary?

there is no meaning in motors . . . but in man's enjoyment of his life. Your professor will try to dismiss "capitalism" as just the "Protestant Work Ethic." I have heard this line personally. But the object of working is not just to work. It is getting needed work done so that leisure time can commence. No one would agree more readily than Dr. Franklin, who was always on the lookout for ways to get more work done with less effort. There is a charming juvenile play called "The Laziest Man in The World," in which Franklin tells a grandchild that he invented things only because he was lazy. Why work if you can invent a machine that does the work for you? Nikola Tesla's boss, George Westinghouse, was once, as a boy, set to work by his father sawing broom handles. His father came home to see George playing, and was ready to give him a licking, until his son showed him how he had rigged the saw to do the work in a fraction of the time it used to take. The rest of George's day was his—as if he had pushed his grave two hours further away. And that sort of story, AR teaches, is not just a practical parable, but a moral parable. It is something for every human being to pursue as a moral goal.

the meaning of life. There it is. Achieving one's happiness is the meaning of life.

cut in the granite. Probably cut by that sculptor on AS 724.

an ancient temple—and she knew what rite was the proper form of worship to be offered on an altar of that kind. A sticker—and a puzzler. What rite is AR referring to?

Human sacrifice comes to mind, in connection with ancient temples, especially Aztec. Maybe AR knew about the prostitutes of Hindu temples, but throughout her career AR shows no sign of knowledge of non-western religions. She writes of non-western societies only with contempt. But if she mentions ancient rites, doesn't your mind automatically go to sex and death? AR would be more likely to think of Stravinsky's ballet *The Rite of Spring*, in which the sacrificial maiden dances herself to death to ensure good crops or something. But what kind of rite is Dagny thinking of? From the context of the paragraph, it is clearly sex. After all, she has been thinking impure thoughts about Galt since the moment she opened her eyes. She does not seem to have yet brought that into conscious awareness, but the reader sure has.

his eyelids drawing narrow. Dagny is aware that Galt is having even more trouble concentrating than she is, and this pleases her no end.

AS 732

Then you'll have to learn which one of us is wrong. This reflects Francisco's admonition to "check your premises." See Recurring Themes index.

the machinery inside would collapse into rubble. See AS 1096.

the secret of the motor. The secret of the motor has to be a secret from Dagny throughout the novel, because of the novel's theme: the role of the mind in man's existence. Dagny encountering the motor and trying to unlock its secret (literally, here) focuses our attention on the nature of knowledge. Nature will not give up her secrets without a struggle.

then smiled oddly, quietly at some thought of his own. What thought could that be? About Hank? Eddie? Francisco? Or just the secret he is about to entrust to her, on the honor system: the secret of how to open the door? The key words are right there in front of her, cut in stone.

AS 733

At last a page with no comments! Why? Because it ends the scene.

AR has no more surprises to spring on us; she has only to wrap up the scene's narrative and put an exhausted Dagny to sleep.

It is a little hard to believe that Dagny survived an airplane crash, and was unconscious for only a few minutes. If she lived at all, she should have been out for a day, and in a hospital emergency room for as long. It would have helped if Dr. Hendricks had said, "Your plane hit some tree tops, and that helped slow your plane's momentum. Otherwise you would be dead." Dagny might have added that she was nearly out of fuel, which fact prevented the plane exploding on impact.

Scene 2: Dinner at Mulligan's. The mind on strike. Dagny sleeps in the "anteroom."

AS 734

More sexual tension.

AS 735

Judge Narragansett has a face like a marble statue of Justice: blindfolded. AR must have thought of Enjolras, her favorite character in *Les Miserables*, the revolutionary who dies fighting on the barricades. Hugo describes him as the "marble lover of liberty."

We do not tell—we show. Dr. Akston throws down a moral challenge to us all.

Akston. Did AR get this name from Lord Acton, who said that "power corrupts, and absolute power corrupts absolutely"? Or maybe AR is suggesting the word "action," as in: "Actions speak louder than words." "Akston" starts with A, like Aristotle. And Aquinas. And "A is A." And "Hugh Akston" sounds like "Human Action," the tome published by Ludwig von Mises in 1948.

the great men you would like to meet. This reader has a long list. Not only because I want to meet them, but because I want to listen to the conversations they would all have with each other. What would Ayn have to say to Aristotle and Aquinas, for starters? And Hugo and Dostoyevsky.

AS 736

Well done. This line from Ken Danagger brings Dagny to tears, and almost this reader too. Since reading this line at thirteen, I have made it a point to tell everyone "Well done!" whenever they have accomplished anything. Like Akston, I don't want them to have to wait to hear it only in heaven. Sticker!

Mulligan and Akston serve dinner together. They grow tobacco together. Could it be . . . aposiopesis?

small silver trays, to be placed on the arms of the chairs. Google the video tour of Taliesin, Frank Lloyd Wright's estate in Spring

Green, Wisconsin. See the living room, with small tables built into the banquettes.

the wealth of selection, not accumulation. This is AR's answer to *Citizen Kane*, and endless parables from the altruist world written to drive home the moral that the rich are all crazed hoarders. That is one of their excuses for taxing you.

It seems to have been true of William Randolph Hearst, Orson Welles's model for Kane, but it is not true for Gail Wynand, in TF, who was also inspired by Hearst.

Wynand collects sculpture, but only sculpture that is meaningful to him. Likewise, see the Bennett Cerf story on AS 156 above. Sticker!

AS 737

moving sentence by sentence to a goal. Just as Galt intends, Dagny is being led to the point of decision. This is one of the places that show this book's thesis, that Dagny coming to decide to go on strike is the main plot of the novel, and when she finally does, that is the main climax.

More aposiopeses. AR is using her Eddie one-sided dialog technique on Dagny.

this concerto said everything I had been struggling to say and reach. This, apparently, was AR's own view of AS: she never wrote fiction again, because she had written her final word on the ideal man. See NB's article in *Reason* magazine, "Thank You, Ayn Rand, and Goodbye." And NB said the same thing himself, to me, at the "Atlas 50" seminar in Washington in 2007, sponsored by the Atlas Society. I asked him whether he had any new projects in the fire, and he said, "No. I've said everything in psychology I had to say."

beyond these mountains. AR must have been thinking of Thomas Mann's novel *The Magic Mountain*, which she mentions unfavorably in *The Romantic Manifesto*. Mann does what your professors say AR does: the novel is nothing but speeches, she says. I have not read it, so I will not assert, since I cannot show.

not a word of my method will be heard outside. This reader has a problem with a doctor who fails to use a method that could save lives. But if the good doctor happens to be traveling outside the Gulch, and someone in his presence looks like he may be having a stroke, perhaps he would use his technique in view of the sudden emergency. There is a premise for a play. But it sounds as though his method could not be used to cure, but only *prevent* a stroke.

justice is the act of acknowledging that which exists. His Honor is anticipating a point in Galt's Speech.

non-objective law. This came up on AS 436, 477 and 596, while gold as an objective value came up on AS 578 and 727. "Non-objective law" is the same as saying no law at all. "Martial Law" also means no law at all because it means the replacement of civil law with the whim of the commanding officer.

Check your premises. One funny line in Dora Jane Hamblin's article "The Cult of Angry Ayn Rand," in *LIFE* magazine, April 7, 1967, was this: "The primly belligerent way they all say, 'Check your premises' always inspires a vision of a burly night watchman with one of those long flashlights, checking the premises."

AS 738

All work is an act of philosophy. Important point. Dr. Akston means that all work is problem-solving, and therefore epistemology, and all work is an act of choosing to do what all human beings must do to stay alive, and is therefore an act of morality.

I am writing a book on this subject. Here the first-time reader might ask why AR didn't just write that treatise herself. The answer is that she was not a philosopher. She had no Masters or Doctorate. She did not teach. She did not write for the academic journals (except once). She was a fiction writer who put a lot of philosophy into her fiction, but it was still fiction.

slowly up her cheek to her temple. Integrated into Galt's exposition is Dagny's emotional reaction. She is almost terrified by Galt's words.

Through all the ages. Here begins a paragraph that takes up almost three pages: Galt on the mind on strike.

AS 739

build the jails into which they threw him. AR might have been thinking of Lenin's famous line: "The capitalists will compete to sell us the rope we hang them with."

See also Roark's speech: "He was probably burned at the stake he had taught his brothers to light." (TF 724)

reckless generosity. Here and in the Speech, Galt lists generosity among the virtues of egoism. Rearden supported his brother Philip for a long time because he could not believe that what Philip was doing was evil, and that he himself was evil to support Philip in his evil. The whole theme and plot of AS is the legal principle of complicity: being an accessory to the crime—co-operating with evil. But note well. AR does endorse generosity as a virtue.

the mystics and the kings. Here begins the theme that AR expanded on in *For the New Intellectual*: the Attila and the Witch Doctor.

No one has ever believed in the irrational. Ever notice that line before? When people seem to believe in the irrational, they are either evading reality or trying to put something dishonest over on someone. In either case there is a pay-off.

If people try evade reality, their pay-off is making the bogeyman disappear by closing their eyes. If they try to put something over on someone, they want the other person to fight the bogeyman for them. But however muddled this thinking, they believe in that moment, that the irrational will work, and will therefore be rational. In this sense, then, no one ever does anything irrational.

This is the new ideal. Galt means From Each According to His Ability . . . . AR may have also been punning on the slogan "the New Deal." "New Ideal" has been the name of an Ayn Rand Institute online publication since 2018.

the common man. AR does not mean that in Aaron Copeland's sense of the untitled peasant coming to the American colonies and declaring independence in order to free himself from the despotism and corruption of the titled nobility. (Cue Aaron Copeland's orchestral piece "Fanfare for the Common Man.") She means here a man of no accomplishment or distinction.

AS 740

We will work under directives and controls, issued by those who are incapable of working. Do not take this literally. Napoleon had a tremendous appetite for work. He had plenty of ability, and yet he was a tyrant and a monster. It is not that the tyrant lacks the ability or the willingness to work. It is that he does not understand the difference between construction and destruction, and neither do the voters he tricks into voting for him.

the sanction of the victims. See AS 454, 470, and 477. It is the title of Chapter IV of Part II. It was also the title of AR's last speech, to the National Committee for Monetary Reform, in New Orleans in 1981.

But that code was intended to be broken. Exactly Dr. Ferris's point, on AS 436.

AS 741

It is evil to enjoy one's existence in this world? Those of us who suffer from chronic depression and low self-esteem find it difficult to believe that we even *have a right* to take proper care of ourselves and enjoy life. Remember the laziness of Ben Franklin (AS 731).

the zero—the mark of death. Maybe, in the subconscious flow of words as she wrote this, AR saw the word "zero" she had just written, and was reminded of "The Mark of Zorro."

This must have been the speech that made Bennett Cerf argue to AR that she had already said before in the book much of what Galt says in the Big Speech.

People would not employ a plumber who'd attempt to prove his . . . Dr. Akston makes the same point made by Deborah Lipstadt, author of *Denying the Holocaust*. She refused, as a historian specializing in the Holocaust, to debate those who claimed the Holocaust had never happened. If you were an expert on the French Revolution, she says, would you waste your time debating someone who claimed that the French Revolution never happened?

permits no co-operation. No Caesars. See Francisco on AS 636.

AS 742

I am complying. This is typical of AR's technique. See the reference to Edward Albee on AS 620. Mulligan, the banker, says that Akston, the philosopher, had quit on the principle of sound banking, while he had quit on the principle of love. Another favorite technique, like the first page of TF: "The water looked immobile, the stone flowing." Paradoxes that turn out, on closer examination, to make perfect sense.

the Hunsacker case. AS 313.

I was born on a farm. I knew the meaning of money . . . facts, proof, and profit. AR was thinking of the scene she had objected to in the movie *The Best Years of Our Lives*. Fredric March's character scolds his boss at a bank for not letting him make a loan to a young farmer with no collateral.

faith, hope and charity . . . facts, proof and profit. Another AR alternative to the slogans of Christianity and other religions.

AS 743

objective rule of conduct. Richard Halley tells his story.

Of all these men and their stories, Halley speaks for AR, since they are both in the arts. She wrote fiction for the public and he writes music. What Halley says about the fickle public liking his music only after hearing about him suffering, rather than judging his music on its own merits, is similar to what AR wrote about murderer William Hickman, and swindler Ivar Kreuger: The editorialists were more indignant about these men being successful than indignant about their crimes. They wrote about Hickman being defiant on the witness stand, as if that were worse than his murdering a little girl. They hated Kreuger for being rich more than for being a swindler. Halley finds the public wanting to hear about him suffering rather than wanting to hear his music. This is AR's outrage at the inhabitants of "The Little Street" (JAR).

an abyss to be filled by the bodies. In school in Russia, AR would have heard about the Mongols of Chinggiz Khan (Genghis Khan) filling in moats with bodies.

self-esteem. also mentioned on AS 490. NB recalls AR and himself bouncing ideas off each other, she from the point of view of a moralist and he as a psychology student.

the goal of my music. AR would give a Ford Hall Forum talk on "The Goal of My Writing."

AS 744

waiting for me in the light of a lamppost. A good visual. It has been used before—Galt may have to share the lamppost with Lili Marlene—but it is a good visual.

or my choice of patients. The Rand Basher will jump on that line, out of this whole paragraph. He will say that this is code for not treating Black patients. Making that kind of claim is easy enough for any Rand Basher worth his salt.

and do the cooking besides. This is AR's humorous characterization of Ellis Wyatt. He, like Francisco, gives some occasional leavening to the heavy, angry speeches of Galt and the others.

the men I was fighting were impotent. Here is AR's new understanding of evil as the irrational, and therefore the impotent.

AS 745

if there are degrees of damnation. It is unusual for AR to express doubt. She says "if" here. She has not made up her mind on whether there are, in her moral theory, degrees of damnation. This comes up on AS 303 and 1023 as well.

the longest-range murderer on earth. AR will return to the theme of the misuse of science on AS 1126, when Dr. Stadler goes to see Project X.

original sin. This probably comes from Frank. Brought up in a Catholic family, Frank remembers that even as a child he resented the idea that every baby is born in sin. "In Adam's fall/ We sinned all," as the colonial primer says. He found it outrageous that he was expected to believe that a baby is born already damned, before he has a chance to do anything, moral or immoral.

It was their father's property. But their father was dead! And so was the company, Galt could see, once the heirs took over. But it is a great image: the motor hiding in plain sight, like the oath on the powerhouse, plain for anyone to read.

AS 746

We've all gone through it. Sympathy—from the implacable Galt. A humanizing touch. And on the previous page, Galt's unamused chuckle and faraway look was another.

when you walked out of the Twentieth Century. A double meaning!

flame-spotter. AR probably heard this term in California or traveling through the west, but there is a fire watch tower preserved as a historical relic in Marcus Garvey Park in the middle of Harlem.

Flame-spotters used it in the 1800s. She might have seen one in the Adirondacks, too.

walking delegate of this strike. A "walking delegate" is a union organizer who visits workplaces to get the workers to join his union.

Galt is a scientist who is also a gifted orator—a rare combination. In a more rational world, he might have had his own science show on TV, like Carl Sagan or Bill Nye "the Science Guy."

My two best friends. You know one of them. AR chose not to mention Ragnar's name just now, perhaps because Dagny might ask questions that would get this discussion off point.

AS 747

The valley is not listed on any map. How could that be if Mulligan bought the land from ranchers?

camouflaged beyond anyone's power to discover. 1957 was about the last year that the concealing of a valley in Colorado would be conceivable. Ironically, six days before Atlas was published (October 10, 1957) Sputnik was launched (October 4). The Space Age began. By now, in 2024, Google Maps allows me to look down on almost any spot on earth. Even Area 51! You can zoom down to the 100-foot magnification there. You can almost spot the aliens waving to you.

I stocked this place to be self-supporting. This makes Mulligan sound like what they are calling a "Survivalist" today.

man is a social being. One Marxist professor, in his Sociology class, brought in a couple of his British comrades to preach to us. One of them said "Man is a social animal"—as if that was all she needed to say to justify socialism. She seemed unaware of the difference between co-operation and coercion, between voluntary organizations and the State. But what exactly does "social" mean then?

AS 748

Judge Narragansett is to act as our arbiter. Aha! So this is an agreement the strikers have made for their month-long vacation. AR was the plaintiff in a contract dispute with the producer of *Night of Jan. 16th*. The parties agreed to abide by the decision of the American Arbitration Association. Thus, AR herself once participated in what anarchist theorists like Murray Rothbard and Morris and Linda Tannehill were writing about: non-governmental justice (AH 90, BB 123). Or at least this would be partial anarchy since the government stood behind the agreement between the contending parties and the arbitration organizations.

The world is crashing faster than we expected. This is the evolution through which AR's own thinking went in the early stages of writing Atlas. Originally, she planned on Dagny learning of the strike in its third generation. The unexpected acceleration of the collapse does not seem to be because of anything the strikers do, as much as the looters just doing what they always do. Directive 10-289 was the looters' doing, and undoing.

whatever rationality is still left in them. This is one of many lines in the novel that suggest that the strikers see everyone outside of the valley as looters: stupid, crazy and evil. That is just what a thirteen-year-old wants to hear. The grownups are all dumb. But there are just as many indications that AR sees the average person as a sane, rational, honest human being who is a *victim* of the looters.

when they have no pretense of authority left. When, for example, a pure con man accidentally occupies the White House, and people learn to ignore his lies and double-talk.

When they collapse and the road is clear. Galt will proclaim the road clear on the last page of the novel. But it will not happen by itself. As civilization collapses under Directive 10-289 and the like, everyone will join looter gangs and kill each other. Just seeing the world collapse will not give people the ideas they need to survive. So Galt *has* to give his speech, and many more afterwards. All the strikers will have to become advisors to the world. Some of them may even have to run for office.

the end of track. This is Dagny's image of the *man* at the end of track, but AR does not mention that man here, as she did on AS 220, 611, 634, 635, 641, and 703, because that would be too obvious. Dagny is still not admitting to herself that the man she dreamed of is standing right here before her. She knows, but she does not yet *know* she knows.

AS 749

everything I had ever wanted. Dagny the very feminine woman struggling with Dagny the Operating Vice-President.

you still think that it does not have to be one or the other. Either-or. No Caesars. In a revolution, you cannot sit on the fence forever. You have to come down on one side or the other.

the abnormal white brightness of the soil. Soil? Does AR mean the moonlight reflecting off the rock of the cliffs? Odd. No, wait! She is talking about the soil of the moon! Look at the photos taken on Luna by the Apollo astronauts, just twelve years after AS was published. You think you are looking at black and white photos, taken by one astronaut, till you see the lander or the other astronaut, and you see a speck of color, and you realize that black and white is the natural colorless color of Luna's soil.

like the print of a photograph on a cloud. Where does she get these images? Tell me Ayn wasn't a poet at heart!

It looked like a city sinking under water. The Atlantis theme again, as on AS 438, 633, and 637.

She knew what he saw in her face. What was that? On the previous page, read the paragraph beginning "He saw her looking at him."

AS 750

She saw a faint movement of his lips. Note well! Galt is suffering! Galt is human, contrary to what you have heard. Galt is a human character in a work of fiction, not just a mouthpiece for propaganda. Galt is breathing hard, and Dagny is looking at him so closely that she can see it. What Galt saw in Dagny's face was eagerness—an eager acceptance of this valley and all that it means. He sees that she is his—almost.

The sexual tension on this page crackles. This is some of the writing that Dora Jane Hamblin (*LIFE* magazine) and your professors do not tell you about when they make fun of AR's prose.

More "as if's."

neither of them would move his face. In pre-PC times, people referred to both parties as "he" and "his" even though one was a woman. Now, in the name of gender equality, teachers and moralists instruct us to use "they" and "their" for single persons of indeterminate sex, the individual becoming a plural. So, "We" has replaced "I" Welcome to *Anthem*. Actually, persons of indeterminate sex should be called "it." People don't like being called "it." They don't like to be de-sexed by pronouns. But they don't mind being collectivized by pronouns.

their hair mingled like the rays of two bodies in space that had achieved their meeting. Had AR been looking through a telescope? Perhaps what she is doing, in these astronomical images, is to steal the heavens from religion. See her ecstatic article "Apollo 11." Religion no longer has a monopoly on the sky.

you wanted to shoot me on sight. This may be an advance echo of Dagny shooting the guard on AS 1148. When the moment comes, and it is war, and it is Galt's life or the guard's, Dagny shoots and kills the guard—a man who wants only to dodge responsibility, but who has a gun, and who can warn the other guards, and who holds Galt's life in his hands. And Dagny's.

AS 751

The inscriptions on the wall: In the Atlas movie, Part III, you see these. One of them is "Andrea Millen Rich." She was this reader's boss, circa 1980, at Laissez Faire Books, the libertarian bookstore in Greenwich Village. She bought the store from its founders, John Muller and Sharon Presley.

One fan of that bookstore was Greenwich Village resident and Cold War history figure Alger Hiss. He spoke at Cortland State College, and I met him. I said "I'm a big fan of Ayn Rand, and I have been trying to remember whether she ever mentioned you in print. I don't think so."

"No, I don't think she did. She is kind of the darling of the anarchist set, isn't she?"

"Yes, but it's an unrequited love."

"There is a bookstore in my neighborhood run by two lovely young people that sells her books."

"Oh, that's Laissez Faire Books. John Muller and Sharon Presley run it."

Alger Hiss. Laissez Faire Books. Who would have thought it?

Everyone has to enter the valley through my house. "No one can come to the Father except through me"? (John 14: 6) This is another of AR's parodies of Christianity. But Galt's meaning could not be any more different from that of Jesus. Galt is merely letting initiates sleep in his guest room so he can be there to counsel them if they are having trouble adjusting. Jesus means that you need salvation, and I am the only one who can give it to you. This is the old snake oil come-on.

This is also another clue that Galt intended Dagny to come to this house as his bride. He *has* carried her over the threshold, after all.

2. The Utopia of Greed

Chapter Overview

Ragnar arrives. Dagny offers to work as Galt's housekeeper. Galt will not let Dagny inform Hank that she is alive. Francisco arrives, and explains to Dagny his strange behavior these twelve years. Dagny asks Galt where he goes in the evening, afraid he has a girlfriend. When he is out, Dagny waits for him so impatiently that she realizes she is already in love with him. Galt tells Dagny that Francisco had warned him, at the beginning of the strike, that Dagny would be the last, toughest holdout.

Dagny hears Halley's story, and Kay Ludlow's, and others.' At dinner at Akston's house, Dagny hears about the professor's three students, and about Stadler's betrayal. She grasps that Akston already sees her as Galt's wife. At the copper mine, Dagny and Galt frankly discuss the romantic triangle between themselves and Francisco. Galt will not let Dagny stay with Francisco the last week of their vacation.

Dagny sees Hank's plane. He has not given up searching for her wreck. She knows that she too cannot give up the world—even though she can no longer return to Hank, having met Galt.

Dagny meets with Galt and the others, to decide whether she will remain in the valley or go back to the world. When she decides to return, only then does Galt say that he too is returning to New York, and Dagny knows why.

Dagny has a drink with Galt and Francisco, and Francisco shows that he now realizes that he is out of Dagny's life, and Galt is in.

Galt and Dagny tensely settle that he is going back to New York to be ready to bring her to the valley, and the strike, when she is ready, because he wants her . . . there. Their love for each other is clear to both. He flies her out of the valley.

Scene 1: Ragnar appears. Dagny offers to be Galt's housekeeper.

Page 752

In one of her essays, AR wrote that she does not spend her time inventing utopias. Why, then, does she use the word "Utopia" in this chapter title?

Perhaps because years later and in another context, she said she did not spend her time inventing utopias. And because she was writing in that essay about planning an actual utopian community, as opposed to what she did in AS, where she simply described a fictional one-month-a-year utopia among friends.

Another cheery morning, smile and all, as on AS 443, 458, 530, 566, 576, 583, 612, and 705. More poetry. More love of nature. A benevolent universe.

the cane I left in the car. She forgot the cane, and so did he. They both had other things on their minds.

some sudden memory of his own. What could that be? Maybe he is remembering bonding with Dr. Akston over breakfast. Or maybe Akston told him that Dagny had once offered him a job cooking. Maybe he remembered that he is expecting Ragnar for breakfast.

Won't it be fun if Dagny hears a stranger introduce himself as Ragnar Danneskjöld? Or maybe Galt has imagined waking up with Dagny. This is what NB meant when he pointed out to Ayn that she never takes us inside Galt's mind. Only up to the door, but never inside, like the powerhouse on AS 731.

AS 753

It was strange to feel. AR cut out a few words at this point, showing how Dagny appreciates little things, like the sound of water coming out of the faucet. Again, AR puts it poetically: "the crystal singing of a jet of tap water." This is another sign that Dagny is falling in love.

as if she owned its owner. Already she is Mrs. Galt in her mind.

dancing. Robert Berole recalls teaching Ayn ballroom dancing. (See BB 326.)

direct, imperious manner of an aristocrat or a roughneck. Layers of meaning! An aristocrat is used to giving orders because he was born privileged. A roughneck is used to speaking with others frankly, because he does not care how aristocratic you were born. An American roughneck, that is.

prehistorical mirage. This shows Dagny's current estimation of the strike—an estimation that she already knows may be proven wrong eventually. She has the greatest respect for the people of the valley, but she is not yet convinced that a strike is necessary. Therefore, in her estimation, the need for a strike, or perhaps the effectiveness of a strike, is a mirage.

AS 754

AR makes no mention of Ragnar's voice. Surely, he must have at least a bit of a Norwegian accent. But Dagny has no idea who this stranger is, and if he asks, "Got any *lutefisk* for breakfast?" that would give the secret away too soon. AR is building up to another big reveal.

the only woman left in the outer world. Surely Ragnar must mean that Dagny is the only woman left on the list of major industrial players they hope to recruit for the strike. But there may be other, incidental, women, like the fishwife, who are not famous yet, or whose loss will not cripple the nation's economy further as Dagny's will.

courage and prodigality. Note well! Prodigality is an Objectivist moral virtue. It means being super productive. So productive that, like Rearden, you can support your worthless brother and never notice the burden. In *Anthem*, Equality 7-2521, after he renames himself Prometheus, carves the word EGO on the front of his house. "*Ego*" is Latin for the pronoun "I." Not "me" (which in Latin is also *me*), but I. Contrary to what you have heard, Egoism is not about getting—it is not about me—it is about the I: what you *do—you* as the subject of the sentence, not the object.

Ragnar's point here is that Dagny has so much confidence in her own ability to solve the railroad's problems, through an outpouring of willing hard work and genius, that she still thinks that the country's, and the world's, economy can be saved.

their handshake came an instant too late. Sticker!

AS 755

It's what they're doing to you. Wow! Dagny must have noticed, or heard from Hank, what Ragnar had told him, back on AS 576: that he had never attacked a military or commercial ship. He had attacked only the loot ships. She probably had not heard that from the papers, if the government had been suppressing all stories about Ragnar, although rumors may have flown, so she probably heard it from Hank. Ragnar is quite right to tell Dagny that she will not long remain a scab, if that is how she sees him.

you won't remain a scab for long. Another "heart attack" for Dagny. AR must have gone back and forth over the pages of her manuscript thousands of times, inserting advance echoes or cross references like this one, to make sure there would be clues and steps toward the climax sprinkled all over the novel, always just enough of a clue, not too much or too early.

Below, on AS 922, Hank tells Dagny, for the first time, that he has met Ragnar, and Dagny replies "He told me."

Let me help you. AR makes Galt walk right into a predictable retort from Dagny. This may be an example of the complaint that NB heard, that AR sometimes makes her characters do things that contradict their previously established characterizations. NB says that there is *some* truth to this criticism. Galt has not yet been subjected to any retorts by Dagny up till now, but she was injured and in shock and bewildered by Galt's Gulch, and by Galt. Now she is feeling better and getting her bearings. And Galt wants to help her because he has gotten in the habit of helping her now, because of her injuries, and because he is in love with her. Or, perhaps, evidence of AR's depth of characterization undermines the Rand-Basher claims that her characterizations are paper-thin or cartoonish. Or it may be evidence that Dagny does not yet understand, as Galt does, the difference between help and self-sacrifice.

like a woman in a ballroom. Remember Dagny's first ball, on AS 102?

like an actress on a stage. Kay Ludlow will come out of the wings in four pages.

but all of those ahead. Sticker! Galt's storied past is all in front of him.

Never mind the centuries. Galt is concerned about Ragnar's safety and that of his men. He does not want to hear, right now, about his own glory. He is not a narcissist.

Lost any men? This three-word line reminds us of the reality of Ragnar's unique strategy for fighting the looters. He must have lost men before this. Galt shows his compassion here. Those men of Ragnar's crew are also members of *his* crew: they have taken the oath and will soon start building their homes in the valley (AS 1158).

AS 756

He's a man who saved my life. Rearden saved Ragnar's life back on AS 583.

So you weren't in any danger. Galt shows his concern about his friend, and this line shows how well he listens.

a tinge of violence. Eddie and his big mouth! (AS 653) A humanizing touch for Galt. He is jealous of Rearden, over Dagny, but later, on AS 959, we will see the other reason Galt is jealous of Rearden.

She studied Galt's face intently. As usual, we see the scene from Dagny's point of view. We do not know that this stranger is Ragnar Danneskjöld until Dagny learns it. We do not know why Galt reacts with anger at Hank's name. We see inside Dagny's mind. She thinks that Galt would have no way of knowing about her affair with Hank. AR never takes us inside Galt's mind. NB asked her why. He says that her reply was "It almost seems like an invasion of privacy. One of my themes in the book is 'Man as god.' And you don't go inside the mind of a god." We do not, of course, know for sure that this is exactly what AR said to NB. But if the Albert Ruddy theory is correct, and Atlas should be seen as mainly a love story, then AR's main focus would be on how Galt looks through the eyes of the woman who is falling in love with him. He is her man.

AS 757

as if challenging him. AR is almost taking us inside Galt's mind, but not quite. A teaser.

I've defied the law of gravitation . . . You've always done that. Why does Galt say that Ragnar has always defied the law of gravitation? In any case, this is another allusion to science.

mid-Atlantic. Apparently, Ragnar has a plane on his ship, or flew a float plane to his ship and then on to Colorado.

On my first reading, at thirteen, I pricked up my ears at this and thought, "Has Ragnar found Atlantis? The literal one?" That was the science fiction fan's take.

None of them approve. AR provides only a glimpse of the case for Ragnar taking up piracy. The idea seems unbelievable, though. How could Ragnar somehow evade the navies of the world, for example, and *why*, for another.

violence is not practical. AR turns the hard-to-believe dramatic premise into a moral point.

force ruled by a mind. Ragnar says the same thing in his meeting with Hank (AS 581) and after the rescue scene (AS 1157).

I had the moral right to choose. Another indication that this is war and revolution. The gloves are off.

Directive 10-289 is the main reason for this. But Ragnar had turned pirate long before the Directive.

He is draining the soul of the world, I am draining its body. This is AR's familiar theme of the mind-body dichotomy. See AS 564 and 636.

the naked essence. AR means naked in the sense of plain for all to see, as on AS 739.

AS 758

The first paragraph on this page has three ellipses, an aposiopesis, indicating that Dagny is thinking about Ragnar and sizing him up, as he gives her a financial report which AR does not show us.

When you hear readers complain about AR putting too much in the book, think of all the things she did *not* put in. The paragraph takes us inside Dagny's head, to show yet another step on her road to striking.

His physical perfection was only a simple illustration. Fascinating! AR is using a simple illustration, and then she self-references: she refers to a fact of the story being, for Dagny, a simple illustration. In

The Utopia of Greed

a way, this is like her fishwife cameo. She is almost coming out of the story to tell us about a literary symbol in the story.

Taggart Transcontinental has taken its share of the looting. Note well! AR names big corporations as among the looters. Your professors told you that AR was for the rich and against the poor, for Big Business and against The People. Wrong.

AS 759

"Kay Ludlow". NB, in his taped lecture "Love and Sex in the Philosophy of Ayn Rand," says that when he read the manuscript and saw that Ragnar came from his plane to Galt's house for their traditional breakfast, he said to Ayn, "You cannot do this! He hasn't seen his wife for eleven months, and he arrives and says 'I'm alive. I'll see you after I have breakfast with John and Francisco.'"

AR responded, 'You're right. I'll have him arrive in the middle of the night.'"

Look back at AS 755. When did Ragnar arrive? "Late last night." Ragnar and Kay don't even get a conjugal visit around Christmas? BB adds that when she was reading in the manuscript about how attractive Ragnar and Kay both are, she suggested to Ayn that she make a couple of Ragnar and Kay. Ayn agreed. Kay, unlike Greta Garbo, does not want to be alone.

we are free to fight it. Kay can stand the eleven months because she is confident in her husband's ability to foresee and forestall any danger. Ragnar told Hank about friends in some astonishing places. Perhaps in the navies hunting for him.

AS 760

I'm going to hold you simply because I want you here. Galt could not make himself any plainer.

fully intends to fight, but hopes to lose. Dagny also makes her meaning plain. Does Galt pick up on what is in her face? We cannot know, since AR does not take us into Galt's thoughts.

of a kind I am not entitled to collect. How gracefully Galt alludes to the elephant in the room!

What started on the previous page as Dagny's proud refusal to take Ragnar's gold now leads dramatically up to Dagny proposing that she work for Galt as his housekeeper. Dramatic structure! But your professors say that AR couldn't write her way out of a paper bag.

he laughed as if he were hit beyond his defenses. In a battle, what hits beyond your defenses? Artillery fire, or aerial bombs. Is this a metaphor AR got from Nick, or some other veteran of World War I? That war consisted of artillery duels more than other wars did. Why Galt is laughing here will be explained on AS 960 below.

as if this were his victory—and hers. His victory over Hank Rearden. He has Dagny where he wants her—almost. And if it is his victory over Rearden, it must be hers too, because Galt knows that he, and not Rearden, is the man at the end of track.

AS 761

as if amusement could be transmuted into some shining glory. Galt is very, very happy. It shows. Human after all.

I shall be the first man in this valley to hire a servant. The idea of servants leaves a bad taste in this reader's mouth. Times have changed since 1957. If Galt is the first in the Gulch to hire a servant, what happened to Wyatt's faithful Indian companion? Did Wyatt leave him behind? Did he leave Wyatt's employ as a servant (AS 248)?

Scene 2: Francisco arrives. Galt will not let him contact Hank

trying to explain . . . ow she had come to beat him to his destination. This example shows what an author puts in and leaves out. We understand that Dagny here recounts to Kellogg what happened to her, but since we already know all that, we don't have to hear Dagny tell the story again. That is the difference between fiction and real life.

AS 762

Did the Comet reach San Francisco? Dagny's first thought is professional, her second personal.

tossed it contemptuously. Always, in Dagny's characterization, we see the anger at being handicapped. Dagny wants action! Purpose!

AS 763

barring the sky in the east. and a few lines later, "eastern": East, for Dagny, means Hank, back in Philadelphia.

The Utopia of Greed 47

as if the sight of her were all he wished to allow into his consciousness. Again, AR skates pretty close to going into Galt's mind, but not quite, because she frames this sentence in Dagny's point of view. Dagny can see how much Galt enjoys the sight of her.

in deliberate denial. In denial of what? His look, and how much she enjoys his look.

the left elbow worn through. With this reader it is always the right elbow that wears out, but I am right handed. Is Galt a southpaw? Frank? Ayn herself? (AR was right handed, unless the photo on page 83 of Britting has been reversed.)

the treason she had wanted to escape. She feels guilty for thinking about Hank now that she is falling in love with Galt. She also feels guilty about wanting to give up the railroad and Hank in favor of Galt and the strike.

AR said that her heroes could never feel fundamental guilt. But she meant the Catholic doctrine of Original Sin or some similar *unchosen* guilt. Dagny certainly feels guilty at the moment, but she knows that she will make a choice and stand by it in the end.

if no secret of yours were given away? This was the subject of another criticism from NB. Everyone who knows Dagny, but especially Hank, thinks she is dead. Can't Galt make an exception just once, and let Hank know that Dagny is alive? After all, Galt expects both Dagny and Hank to join the strike pretty soon. Would it harm the strike and its purposes any if Hank received a note saying, "Dagny is safe"?

It is inhuman to make Hank suffer needlessly. NB says that AR explained that Galt's characterization needed some hardball to make him more realistic. He still smarts over his discovery that Hank has the woman who should have been his, as well as the fame and fortune that should have been his. So, for now, Galt almost hates Hank. This is all part of the theme of how much the strikers have paid for the strike.

AS 764

And when Galt does offer to make an exception, Dagny turns him down. Why? And doesn't Kellogg tell Galt and the others about the world thinking that Dagny is dead? Doesn't Galt realize that both

Hank and Francisco would be searching for Dagny's plane? Well, he is about to find out, when Francisco arrives.

fumbling effort at an unfamiliar task. There is irony, maybe even comedy, in this image of Dagny, the woman who makes the trains run on time, who rescued Colorado, trying to teach herself how to patch a shirt. She does it because she is in love with the owner of that shirt, and because she has been hired and paid for the purpose. She is too damn proud to let Galt see how untutored she is in domestic chores.

Dominique had something of the same experience, in TF: "We'll take a house here—like one of these—and I'll keep it for you—don't laugh, I can—I'll cook, I'll wash your clothes, I'll scrub the floor. And you'll give up architecture" (TF 492). Dominique was trying to get Roark to "go on strike."

The voice was Francisco's. AR never fails to give Francisco great entrances. Even when she does not say he stands like he wears a cape waving in the wind, she does.

That's something I want to see for myself! Another of Francisco's abrupt changes of mood. See Recurring Themes Index.

she noticed dimly that it was Galt who closed it, leaving them alone. What was Galt thinking? He knows about Dagny and Francisco, and Dagny and Hank.

AS 765

Were you afraid when he made me say it? Hank, that is, whereupon he slapped Francisco. AS 638.

you who were the final argument that made me leave you. Irony. And why did seeing Dagny persuade him to leave her and d'Anconia Copper? Because of "what awaited you in the future." The strike, and its walking delegates, began their campaign for Dagny at that moment. Francisco saw that he had to save her from a crazy world.

You were everything that he was seeking. And now he has her, and you have lost her, Francisco.

AS 766

I saw the government regulations passed to cripple me. This sounds more like New Deal America than Francisco's native Argentina,

The Utopia of Greed 49

where the biggest and oldest company would be in bed with the oldest families and the most corrupt politicians. These fulminations of AR's must be taken as attacks on a principle, not as attacks on a family like the d'Anconias. It is not the rich individuals who suffer, it is the principle of free competition and responsibility that suffers, and therefore the young, poor entrepreneur who suffers. The company the entrepreneur *might* have founded remains unfounded, its inventions and innovations unrealized. The "loafing failures" would be the playboy heirs that Francisco pretends to be one of.

magnificent machinery. Here AR gives us a rapid-fire visual montage of the industrial world and what it means to her. There have started to be some paintings of this sort painted by artists inspired by AR. See Quent Cordair, Objectivist art dealer.

unshaved humanitarian. BB said AR distrusted men with beards. She believed they tried to hide some great moral or psychological fault (BB 208.) Or he is just too lazy to shave.

basement beer joint. That might be Hitler, haranguing his followers in Munich's *Bürgerbräukeller* (City Brew Cellar).

virtue must be penalized for being virtue. AR's definition of envy: hatred of the good for being the good.

He had quit the Twentieth Century. A *double entendre*! He certainly did quit the Twentieth Century . . . if this *is* the Twentieth Century, in the story.

and when we would see the lights of New York go out. And we will, on AS 1158. But on the next page, 1159, AR reminds us of this passage way, way back on AS 766, in case we had forgotten it.

AS 767

with your eyes still held straight ahead. Francisco's variation on the theme of the Man at the End of Track.

the towers of a city. AR must have been thinking of the Stephen Vincent Benét story "The Place of the Gods" in the *Saturday Evening Post* in 1937, the story that inspired her to write *Anthem*.

fat, soggy, mindless cripple. Most people might not accept this long adjective-heavy conversation in real-life. Does this make AR a bad writer? No.

In art, the rules are different. AR creates images. The lights of New York going out. It is her poetry.

not to any child who had your kind of look when he faced the future. This too is being captured on canvas today.

See, for example, the Quent Cordair art catalog. See also "child's look" in the Recurrent Themes Index under "Smile of morning."

and I knew that if I were to lose you, it was still you that I would be winning with every year of the battle. Note well! Even if I lose Dagny, I am fighting for the principle that makes Dagny Dagny.

the wreckage of your plane! After all the poetry, AR yanks us back to the reality of *why* Francisco is so ecstatic: Dagny is alive!

Francisco, I've hurt you in so many different ways. Compassion! She has hurt him with the agony of fearing her death, she has hurt him by her years of hatred, and she has hurt him by being Hank's mistress. These are not her fault, of course, but these things did hurt him, and she feels his pain. "Com" meaning "with," and "passion" meaning "pain."

it's a man who might never hear it from me. A great dramatic twist! Dagny now realizes and accepts the fact that she has fallen in love with Galt. Galt has replaced Hank in her affections. Francisco does not know that yet.

But you do. With this paragraph, Francisco rises to the level of a mahatma—a Great Soul—who rises above pain and envy.

AS 768

every desire is driven by the same motor. AR's "motor" theme and metaphor, on the Recurring Themes list.

Will you forgive me? Not sure why she feels the need to ask for Francisco's forgiveness, after what he has just said. As mentioned 11 lines above, the ways Dagny has hurt Francisco were not her fault.

AS 769

I see. Galt still does not want to tell Hank that Dagny is alive.

Do you wish to give any outsider any relief from the consequences of remaining outside? This is Galt's moral argument for not telling Hank about Dagny. It does not wash. How can Galt wish to punish Hank for remaining outside, when Hank does not know there is any *inside*?

The Utopia of Greed

What does it accomplish, torturing Hank further? Is that going to get Hank out on strike any quicker? And yet Francisco agrees with Galt.

AR uses the word "pity." From her, this reader understood pity to mean compassion without respect. Compassion *with* respect is "sympathy." People become enraged if they think you are offering them pity, because you are implying that you don't respect them.

unrhythmical abruptness of the involuntary. So, he, too, feels discomfort and conflict in the moment.

He respects Rearden, but he also experiences years of accumulated resentment toward him due to his success and, now, over Dagny. But in this moment, he feels bad about taking Dagny away from his friend Francisco. That is the "beating" he says Francisco is taking.

you're the one who's taken the hardest beating. We have now seen demonstrations of the deep love that Galt and Francisco and Ragnar have for each other.

Even in the depths of his own anguish over Hank's possession of Dagny, and Hank's lifestyle, which Galt is denied because of the strike, Galt still cares about how much Francisco has suffered by giving up Dagny and so much else, like his having to play the humiliating charade of a worthless playboy.

Galt as track worker, Francisco as playboy, Ragnar as pirate—all three have spent twelve years having to play humiliating and unnatural roles. They have been deprived of their own real selves. Galt must be thinking that while he has hope for winning Dagny in the future, Francisco has the memory of having possessed Dagny in the past and then having to give her up.

He certainly does not pity Francisco, because he has too much respect for him.

looking, not at him, but at her. Galt wants Dagny to know that he does not pity or have sympathy for Hank, his rival for her affection. He is merciless in his refusal to relieve Hank of the consequences of remaining outside. Galt's leitmotif is ruthless justice.

This is the quality that AR so admired in NB when he passed harsh moral judgments on his NBI students.

Years later, though, NB said "You do not make people moral by condemning them. It does not work when the Church does it, it does not work when our parents do it, and it does not work when Ayn Rand does it."

Scene 3: Dagny is relieved to learn that Galt spends his evenings lecturing

AS 770

no time could be wasted on the comfort of its start. Compare this to Hank's start in an iron mine, Roark working his way through architecture school, and Wynand sleeping on his office couch and driving himself to build up the *Banner*.

And of course, AR herself, who wrote in her diary, "You are only a writing engine. . . . Stop admiring yourself—you are nothing yet." (Paxton, 79.)

a fresh wooden scaffolding erected to shelter the birth of a skyscraper. Neat metaphor! AR would have seen the plywood barriers around the excavations and erections of Rockefeller Center in the late 1930s. That was the only major construction project to keep construction workers busy in New York City during the Great Depression.

superlative aristocrat. Here again, AR the Russian, growing up in a European capital and living through a revolution against inherited power, reminds us that modern, purposeful individual achievement creates the reality of which kings and horses and coaches and palaces and gaudy uniforms and ceremony are merely a pretense.

they won't be able to afford even its heating bill. Sticker! How succinct an illustration of the difference between achievement and pretense.

Charles M. Schwab, of Bethlehem Steel (1862-1939), built a huge mansion on Riverside Drive between 73rd and 74th Streets. He left it to New York City. They could not afford its heating bill, and Mayor LaGuardia did not want to use it as the official Mayor's residence, so they tore it down.

Photos of the mansion now decorate the lobby of the apartment building now occupying that site. See Hessen, Robert, in the Bibliography. Hessen was Rand's secretary and a historian.

The Utopia of Greed 53

AS 771

to conquer the world. AR has made plain by now that "conquering the world" means pretty much the opposite for Francisco from what it meant for Napoleon and Hitler. And Putin.

born, not of chance and blind tribal warfare. Many historians have made similar points.

The US was invented and based on philosophical principles. It did not just grow. You can call that "American Exceptionalism" if you like.

redeemed the world. Well, the US did not do that all by itself. Britain and France were also in the spearhead of the Enlightenment.

AR puts two aposiopeses in this paragraph, so it looks like a monolog, but it is really a dialog. As with Eddie and Galt, we can infer Dagny's questions from Frisco's answers.

return to reason. Is this where Paul Lepanto got his title? He wrote a 1971 book on Objectivism called *Return to Reason*.

mine by right. Francisco describes an entire world of political stability, free enterprise, and free trade.

This corresponds to how Wendell Willkie, in his book *One World*, defined his goal of "political independence and economic dependence for the nations of the world."

AS 772

A remarkable page! It is all about Dagny trying to reconcile her past love for Francisco with her new relationship with him, and her emerging love for Galt with her inability to give up the railroad and the world. Her present feeling for Francisco confirms everything he just said on AS 764 to 767.

She and Francisco feel their old childhood excitement, looking at plans for a smelter and talking about their plans for a future filled with productive, creative work. Not just *getting* money but *making* money: creating new real wealth. Even without a romantic, sexual relationship, they still enjoy each other's company and shared values. Dagny is introspecting—seeing down through the layers of her own thinking, and the implication of everything she is experiencing. AR is setting up another remarkable scene beginning on AS 791.

scraps in a junk yard. see AS 95.

some vision of the unattainable shining ahead. See the four paintings by Thomas Cole, "The Voyage of Life."

The second of the series is called "Youth." It shows a youth pointing to a vision of the unattainable shining ahead. The quartet of paintings is in the National Gallery in Washington.

she would have no right to look at him if she were to renounce her railroad. This is what holds Dagny back from joining the strike.

on some future street. Imagine how it would feel if you awoke in an alternate future where you and your mate had never met, but you know it and he does not, and he passes you on the street and does not recognize you. Imagine the anguish and the tragedy. Yup. AS is a love story, all right.

AS 773

he did not choose to feel. If you want to emulate Galt, do not take this paragraph to mean that you can and should repress unwanted emotions. NB spent a career explaining why. Rather, see this paragraph as evidence that Galt is, at the moment, as conflicted as Dagny is. Galt is struggling not to resent his friend for having had Dagny as a lover. But he has had years to do that.

A harder task is to deal with his resentment of Rearden. Or maybe Dagny is mistaken in her interpretation of Galt's mien. It is not that he is choosing not to feel about Francisco and Dagny, it is that he is tortured by the thought of Dagny and Hank.

Throughout the novel, you can see the tremendous amount of information the characters get from looking at each other's faces. AR laid great store by what you can see in a face.

the sordid shape of self-sacrifice. This is what we will see dramatized beginning on AS 791. Dagny not only wants him, she wants him to want her—want her too much to give her up even for his best friend (and she still does not know that he knows about Hank).

All the talk since AS 769 about Galt's tender feelings toward Francisco are intended to raise the reader's doubt and tension on this point. Is Galt going to "nobly" sacrifice Dagny to Francisco in the name of friendship? Contrast this love triangle with Dickens's *A Tale of Two Cities*: Would it really be a "far, far better thing I do" for Galt to give up Dagny

The Utopia of Greed 55

for Francisco, as Sidney Carton gives up his life for a friend? Maybe a little of Hemingway's *The Sun Also Rises*: Jake and his girlfriend Brett and her fiancé Mike. And the end of *Casablanca*. All these comparisons must have run through AR's mind as she wrote this.

as if pleasure, not pain, broke her resistance. AR puts a lot of "as if's" in these pages. Another of AR's clever reversals. The pleasure of watching Galt eat the food she had prepared gave her the right to get nosy about where he was spending his evenings. She is acting more and more like a wife.

that did not seem to be directed at his words. That did not seem—to Galt! Aha! Again, she almost goes inside Galt's mind. Just the merest peek.

two authors. So, there are two authors in the valley—the fishwife and—who? Maybe AR pictures Victor Hugo or Fyodor Dostoevsky going on strike. Or Isabel Paterson?

AS 774

Dagny and Galt spar. She wants to find out where she can find him outside of the valley. Galt sees through her.

the will to laziness. AR could not have written those words without thinking of Nietzsche's book *The Will to Power*. Nietzsche had a sister, Elisabeth Förster-Nietzsche, who was a proto-Nazi, and after her brother died, she brought together some unpublished pieces of his that he had written as he was going crazy from syphilis. These pieces make Friedrich appear closer to Elisabeth's positions than he really was. Creative editing. But when her friend Adolf came to power, he closed the Nietzsche archive in Weimar, so that scholars could not find out what he had really written.

In any case, his most popular work was, and remains, *Also Sprach Zarathustra*, which he wrote long before he went crazy. It is the book that AR read at fifteen. It was the first, but not the last, book she read in philosophy.

Also, what exactly did Nietzsche mean by "power"? Scholars differ on this. Nietzsche lacked AR's deep concern about the clarity of his writing. He was more concerned with his poetic style than with clarity. AR apparently did not mind putting a phrase in AS that would remind many readers of *The Will to Power*.

the will to a secret violence. In reading the next page, you don't have to be Fellini to figure out what kind of violence Dagny is thinking about.

AS 775

Here we have a page and a half that shows Dagny wrestling with herself. Introspection. She is honest with herself. She keeps asking herself "what do you want?" Her resistance to the real answer peels away, layer by layer.

the castrated performance. Wow! The idea of a woman de-sexed—castrated, so to speak. Drudgery in a kitchen is a thankless duty. Atlas was published in 1957—thirteen years before Germaine Greer's *The Female Eunuch.* Greer makes the same complaint, about women being de-sexed by kitchen drudgery, but she blames it on "consumerism" and living in the suburbs.

AR stretches out the paragraphs on this page with dots, both inside and between sentences. This supports the picture of Dagny pacing, lighting cigarettes, watching the hours drag by . . ..

the weary distaste of a substitute purpose. Dagny can never be satisfied without a real purpose to follow.

When nothing seems worth the effort, it's a screen to hide a wish that's worth too much. Here's a rivieting insight that could serve as a defense against chronic depression.

At the bottom of the page, AR drops the bomb. The whole page has been leading up to the words "the one superfluous, protective word in that sentence." I want him *back.*

AS 776

There is so much characterization on this page, so much sexual tension, so much psychology, that it is astonishing to hear NB say, in his *Reason* Magazine interview in 1971, and again in his talk on the "Benefits and Hazards of the Philosophy of Ayn Rand," that AR told him herself that she did not really understand human psychology.

By 1971, she may have convinced herself that humans are just crazy and unfathomable, but earlier in her career, as a fiction writer, as a creator of the psychologies of characters, she understood human psychology just fine.

When did you see me for the first time? Compare this to her question to Francisco on AS 97: "What do you like about me?"

This is Dagny's femininity. All of Rand's heroines are very feminine. The male teen will be astonished and intrigued by the idea of a woman running a railroad. Later, he will notice how well Dagny combines that with being feminine.

AS 777

transparent blouse. This is the third or fourth time AR has mentioned it. Every time AR puts in that term, it makes us wonder how much Galt can see through that blouse.

hand-printed in violent colors. Colors on a printed skirt? Violent? Here, AR's fondness for the adjective "violent" may have gone over the top. "Bright, vibrant colors," yes, but "violent"? Whom are they violating? Well, it gets the job done. It gets the point across.

high-heeled pump. Dagny is wearing high heels at home, to do housework? Was she walking down the track with Owen Kellogg in high heels?

her body had become an instrument for the direct perception of his. Three paragraphs down, you will see what AR is leading up to.

he who had never started or lost a battle against himself. Dagny does not know Galt well enough yet to decide that. AR must mean this only in regard to the brief time Dagny has known Galt. He will tell her about one battle against himself on AS 958. And what does it mean to say he had never *started* a battle against himself?

Then she felt a sudden, blinding shock. Dagny, looking at Galt's posture, his body, has had a bodily reaction of sexual desire, let us say.

At the top of AS 780, Dagny has a thought about Galt that she experiences as "flowing as a dark warmth through her body." Compare the line in the Barbra Streisand movie *Yentl*: "Flowing through my body is a river of surprise" (Alan and Marilyn Bergman, lyrics.) Perhaps Dagny is having two reactions—one of which Galt might spot through that transparent blouse.

One of NB's favorite passages in WTL was on page 69. It is the second meeting of Kira and Leo. "He rose in one swift, supple movement and she sat looking up with admiration, as if hoping to see him repeat it." (Already in WTL we see that familiar "as if" formula.) NB, reading this as a teenager, wished that someday a woman would feel that way about him and vice versa. Telling this story in the 1980s, NB reported that both hopes had since been realized.

AS 778

We don't intend to reclaim him. This ties up a loose end.

Although we will see a lot of Stadler in the pages ahead, his arc is already closed. He sold his soul, and he will not enter the city of Galt.

endurance, courage and consecration to your work. As with Ragnar, on AS 754, speaking of Dagny's "courage and prodigality," Galt identifies the crucial problem of the novel: When will Dagny see the light and join the strike? Not as long as she keeps solving the problems of her railroad.

By chance. It was late at night. Galt hesitates for the length of an ellipsis, being careful not to give away the secret of where he works. But he has to tell her the story of what he saw when he first laid eyes on her.

Compare Galt's first sighting of Dagny with Hank's, on AS 562.

you would stand there naked. "Naked" is not a metaphor this time. Galt names exactly what is on his mind.

the tunic of a Grecian goddess. Another reference to ancient Greece. Leonard Peikoff gave a lecture on board a cruise ship in the Greek islands, called "Why Ancient Greece Is My Favorite Civilization." The answer is: the Greek worship of man and his understandable world, rather than of gods and the supernatural.

imperious profile of an American woman. It is hard for us to see that, who have seen so many movies with European goddesses like Garbo, Dietrich, and Bergman. Does just being an American woman give you an imperious profile?

AS 779

curtained apartment. Galt had not been haunted before this by the image of a glamorous woman in a glamorous apartment, but now he was seeing Dagny in both a glamorous setting and in the setting that makes glamor possible. Her railroad, and her work in the railroad, and productive, creative work in general—Dagny had inspired him with the need to see both together: the reward and that which makes the reward possible. Note that Galt says he had not been haunted by glamor before. He is an inventor. A nerd. He was motivated by motors in his youth. He is not at all like Trump, who thinks of nothing but impressing others, whether he respects their judgment or not, with his gaudy, flashy status symbols.

wealth, grace, extravagance and the enjoyment of life. "Grace" is what Rhett Butler longs for at the end of *Gone with the Wind*. The gracious, courtly Old South, as opposed to the crass, money-making New South.

But Galt must mean something different here. This needs to be the theme of a new novel or movie. Is there some other kind of extravagance, one with grace but without the crass showiness of Trumpism?

The answer appears in Galt's fourth term, the enjoyment of life. On the same day that Rand died, John Belushi also died—of a drug overdose. He had wealth and fame. He could impress others, but not himself. He lacked self-esteem and a sense of purpose. "Money will take you wherever you wish, but it will not replace you as the driver" (AS 411).

its proper gods. Greece again. Picture a sculpture of Dagny!

Oh, why didn't you speak to me, then or later? This sounds more like what Dagny thinks, not what she would say out loud, but apparently the barriers on both sides start to drop down rapidly.

if he had come to claim her, then or later. Again, AR sets up AS 958.

she would shoot the destroyer on sight. This is not about the Second Amendment or the NRA. This is Hollywood talking. This is Bette Davis, shooting a man in the opening scene of *The Letter*. This is AR at the Biltmore Theater on West 47th Street, in 1940, persuading her producer to fire a bad actor in the production of her play *The Unconquered*, and then seeing the actor's rich wife come storming in demanding to know why they had fired her husband. This lady was so over the top, Ayn recalled, that "if it were on the stage, I'd be sure she'd pull a gun." (BB 151.)

AS 780

reduce him to the helplessness of pleasure. Sticker. As a thirteen-year-old reader, I found this description a crystal clear explanation of some portion of the mysteries of sex.

Every man that your railroad needed. Galt sounds like he is going through all the torture that Dagny is going through, and this taunt is his way of pushing it away.

I have pulled every girder from under Taggart Transcontinental. AR must have thought of Roark blowing up Cortlandt Homes, and the story of Samson in the Bible.

It was her voice, more than her words, that made him stop. Careful! You are taking us inside Galt's mind. Just a peek.

He waited, to regain his breath. Ditto. Galt starts to anger and become stressed, wound up in his rant to Dagny. Galt has emotions. He is a human character, not just an excuse for speeches. He is a fictional character, and Atlas is a novel, not a manifesto as you have been told.

It's your acceptance of this place that I want. See the Bennett Cerf bracelet story on AS 156 above. The deeper meaning, the personal meaning, is all that matters, not the shallow appearance or price.

AS 781

the judge who seemed to observe her. Back on AS 775, Dagny heard a "stern voice" and it was "as severe as a judge."

This is the voice of introspection, of self-criticism, of conscience, of what NB and Carl Gustav Jung called the "higher self." The Disney Pinocchio's Jiminy Cricket.

Why is it his body you want, and no other? Major sticker! This and many other lines in AR and NB taught this teenager that there is no such thing as purely physical sex. Francisco's sex speech explained this more fully, but not completely.

the sound of a step and the click of a cigarette lighter. This reader has always wondered about this line, not being a smoker.

Dagny hears those two sounds (thin walls) and concludes that Galt is awake but will not come. Galt lighting a cigarette indicates that he is still up, but his lights are off (she saw no light from his window on the tree trunks outside). So, he is not sleeping, but neither is he working or reading Agatha Christie.

Perhaps he is doing the same thing that Dagny is doing: at the bottom of AS 780 a "moaning violence" was filling her mind that "seemed only a sensation of her muscles." AR and 1957 were not ready for today's sexual explicitness, so AR does not come right out and say it, but the reader might gather that necessity has made both of these star-crossed lovers take care of the immediate problem by other means.

In any case, here ends a scene of such sexual tension—sexual tension integrated with deeper meanings and with plot and theme, that we can only say, with Yale's revered Harold Bloom, "Rand couldn't write her way out of a paper bag."

Scene 4: Halley plays for Dagny. Kay Ludlow. Motherhood. Akston on superhuman creatures.

prodigal magnificence . . . flowing monument. There is that word "prodigal" again. Like a fountainhead. The spring. The source. Man—from whom all blessings flow.

a concept which equates the sense of life with the sense of beauty. That line still needs some chewing. Here, AR presents her "sense of life" concept. When she introduced her play *Night of January 16th*, she described it as "a sense of life play."

as if spit by the infected throat of a loud-speaker coughing its malicious hatred of existence. Whew! A mouthful, but AR has a reason for these long descriptions: They make the reader have to slow down and read the whole passage.

People tend to read too fast. When you slow down and read more carefully, and you encounter this unpleasant visual of a coughing, strep-infected loud-speaker, it will remain with you for a long time. I have seen a loud-speaker cough in an old cartoon from the 40s. She was complaining about the cough-like sound of modern music back on AS 66.

hatred of existence. Here again is the theme of the mind warped by fear, that does not want to live by achievement, or even by parasitism. It does not want to live at all. It craves only avoidance of anxiety, and so achieves nothing but anxiety.

AS 782

Emotions be damned! AR must be echoing William H. Vanderbilt's line "The public be damned!" which she has Dagny mention on AS 230. In this paragraph AR talks about her art, speaking for anyone who presents anything to the public for contemplation.

Not the fact that you felt, but that you felt what I wished you to feel. Major sticker! When AR's play *Night of Jan. 16th* became a Broadway hit in 1935, she commented, "I wanted raves that raved about the right things." (AH 77).

Even if an author gets raves, if the raves praise the wrong things, then no communication has taken place. The success is random and accidental; the author is not assured of any future success.

I do not care for blindness in any form, I have too much to show—or for deafness, I have too much to say. Sticker! Ernest Thompson, who received an Oscar for his screen adaption of *On Golden Pond*, said, "I have something to say and a burning need to say it."

An artist is the hardest and most exacting of all traders. Sticker!

with the moonlight draining its color. The Moody Blues portrayed the same vison on their album *Days of Future Past*, singing, "Cold hearted orb that rules the night/ Removes the colors from our sight/ Red is gray and yellow white/ But we decide which is right/ And which is an illusion."

who happens to be tone deaf. a tiny humorous aside. AR's own humor tended to take that form.

Mort Liddy and Balph Eubank. At Lillian's party, AS 133, and Jim's wedding, AS 404.

AS 783

all work is an act of creating. Back on AS 721, Ellis Wyatt said there is no such thing as a lousy job.

Likewise, Martin Luther King urged young people "If you can't be the sun, be a star/ It's not by your size that you stand or you fall/ Be the best at whatever you are."

which means. Jerome Tuccille, in *It Usually Begins With Ayn Rand*, reported a conversation among the old Objectivist "Collective" in which they were finishing each others' sentences. See Recurring Themes under "Which Means."

how to build an electric motor For more parallel references, see the entries in the Recurring Themes index under "Motor Theme."

That sacred fire. For more parallel references, see the entries in the Recurring Themes under "Ring of Sacred Fires."

the discoverers of new germs or new continents. After breaking with AR in 1968, NB and BB moved to Los Angeles and with Ed Nash formed a mail order book service called Academic Associates. (See Tuccille in the Bibliography.) One book offered was *Microbe Hunters*, by Paul de Kruif, about the discoverers of new germs. Objectivists like to remember and honor inventors and innovators.

Aposiopesis! Dagny interjected something that AR chooses not to share with us.

the earth does turn. AR refers to the famous (but disputed) story of Galileo recanting at the Church's insistence his claim that the Earth rotates, then walking out of the church muttering, "But still it turns!"

an alloy of steel and copper. Presumably, AR and Halley refer to Rearden Metal, but previously someone had called the Metal an alloy of copper and aluminum. Maybe the Metal contains all three elements and more besides. Or maybe AR did this deliberately, not wanting some nerdy thirteen-year-old reader to think she really invented such an alloy. Some readers do anyway.

You can read long discussions online of how Galt's motor might be built. It's just a story, kids.

he will not bear false witness. AR plays on the Ninth Commandment.

a severity no army-drilling sadist could impose. Sticker. Perhaps AR was thinking of the Foreign Legion commandant in *Beau Geste*. Or Captain Bligh in *Mutiny on the Bounty.*

we are, in fact, the only people capable of feeling. AR means that the person who is honest with himself and others spends his time pursuing values and feeling happy when he succeeds, while the chronic evader of reality can never feel anything but anxiety. If you are really far gone in repression of your unpleasant feelings, you find out that if you deny the unpleasant feelings, you lose the ability to feel the good feelings, too.

Then, as NB said in *The Disowned Self*, life offers you only two possibilities: bad days, when you feel screaming pain, and good days, when you feel nothing. But too many young readers come away from AS thinking that "feeling" is a dirty word, and that repression is a virtue.

Halley gets pretty wound up in this speech, but he is telling the story of his life to his most appreciative fan, and he is letting out a lifetime of anger. Feelings!

they are first to be exterminated. Not exterminated usually: bought off. See the movie *Mephisto*, about a German actor who becomes a protégé of one of the Nazi leaders, and then finds out that there are strings attached to his patron's patronage.

AS 784

the streets of the valley. On AS 726 AR said, "the valley's single street." Growing fast.

purposeful selectiveness of art. Another of AR's clever reversals, the artist as businessman and businessman as artist.

clapboard concert hall. Perhaps AR thought of the humble theater in Stony Creek, Connecticut, now called the Puppet Theater, where Frank acted in a summer stock production of *Night of January 16th* in 1936, while Ayn was rowing out onto Long Island Sound, thinking up plot ideas for TF.

picked from the hand-me-downs of the centuries. In these paragraphs about Kay's play, we see Ayn commenting on her own profession, fiction writing, more directly than anywhere else in the book.

beauty of spirit matched her own physical perfection. Some Rand Bashers have made fun of the author for making her heroes beautiful and her villains ugly. AR's friend, actress and mystery writer Kay Nolte Smith, said that AR telegraphed too early and too clearly who was going to be a hero and who a villain by how they looked and moved. But there is a method to the madness. The reader never has any trouble remembering who is who in a Rand novel. Even just from the dialog, you always know who is speaking. That is simple, old-fashioned characterization. It works. It helps to tell the story clearly. But sometimes, as with the Galt's Gulch truck driver whom Dagny thought was a philologist because he looked like a truck driver, the author will, for dramatic contrast and impact and irony, give a deformed body to a character with a beautiful soul. That leads to characters like Quasimodo in Victor Hugo's *Notre Dame de Paris*, or John Merrick in *The Elephant Man*.

always to be beaten at the end by the little girl next door. Watch movies from Ayn's era and look for the Hollywood cliché that Kay complains of. One example would be *Beyond the Forest*, a 1949 Warner Bros. release starring Bette Davis (it is in this film that she says, "What a dump!"). Bette, as usual, plays a fiery, dynamic character, but she is evil and dies in the end. She is having an affair with a man with a bland, uninteresting wife. Some reviewers see this movie as a take-off on *Madame Bovary*, Flaubert's novel about a woman who sacrifices her husband and their security for love and meets a horrible end. This is why it is such a stunning relief to see a woman rebelling against convention and getting away with it, as in AS, or in Ibsen's *A Doll's House*.

the sense of having studied some aspect of a sewer there had been no reason to see. Sorry to report, Ayn, but it has only gotten worse since 1982. You would think by now they would have run out of sewers.

AS 785

two fearless beings, aged seven and four. Another myth about AR is that she must have hated children because there are none in her fiction. She doesn't have many, but here are two, and she has one in WTL.

Patrick O'Connor, of New American Library, was AR's last editor. See *100 Voices*. He said that AR was not a bad writer of adult fiction, but a good writer of juvenile fiction.

AR wrote AS during the years when the marketers were pigeonholing us all into strictly separated markets, especially in radio. Teenagers were expected to listen to "Top 40" radio stations and only "Top 40."

But AR learned her craft before all this strict segregation. If you asked her which market she wrote for, she would have said human, period. In this, she, as usual, bucked a popular trend. Also, in reading AR's sparse mentions of children, remember that when she was born, 1905, parents strictly and sternly taught even the youngest children that they were expected to act like miniature adults. That is how AR saw herself, rushing ahead to adulthood as fast as she could, and in this she was, perhaps, just internalizing what she was being taught by her parents and governess. Her native precociousness just reinforced this teaching. Movies and TV shows that cry out in anguish about "let the kid enjoy being a child for a while" are a more recent phenomenon.

Also, AR had a need to feel in control. That is why she told Isabel Paterson that she was now spoiled for riding in a passenger car after riding in the cab, and even being allowed to drive the train (AH 212). She wanted to be the engineer, and not a helpless, passive passenger. Childhood, therefore, did not suit her.

to convince him that reason is impotent. One high school film strip in 1977, about philosophers, called Immanuel Kant "the father of modern philosophy."

condensing into a soft blue vapor far below. One thing this reader noticed only now, after fifty-five years studying this book, is how lovingly AR describes the beauty of nature and a small town. You get so used to her big-city bias that you would think she would take one look at this Rocky Mountain valley and say, "What a dump!"

AS 786

There are three ellipses in this paragraph that indicate that Dagny is asking Akston questions that the reader does not need to see, because we can infer Dagny's questions from Akston's answers.

superhuman creatures. This is crucial! This is for the "Rand is a Nietzschean" crowd.

they're normal men. This supports this reader's impression of the novel on completing my first reading. Rand seems to be announcing a new dispensation for mankind, with all the drama of Cecil B.

DeMille coming down the mountain with the Ten Commandments, but what exactly is this new philosophy? Are we all to wear funny hats and pray toward the Empire State Building five times a day? No! Rand's message to the world is simply Be Normal! Just go about your peaceable business, pursue creative, productive work, use your mind, and enjoy life. No weirdness, no drama. Ayn Rand is the apostle of normalcy.

conditioners be damned! Here is our familiar theme of Vanderbilt's line "The public be damned!" again. But this time the object of Rand's jeremiad is the new school of psychology that was rising to challenge Freud in the 1950s: Behaviorism. Instead of throwing out free will and reason in favor of Marx's economic determinism or Freud's determinism of the Id, or Calvin's determinism of pre-destination, we are throwing them out in favor of "conditioning": everything determines your behavior—except you! Thus does B. F. Skinner, the latest star-chologist in the 1960s, take us "beyond freedom and dignity."

some forsaken crossroads in Ohio. That would be Lorain, Ohio, hometown of Frank O'Connor. Frank's father was a steel worker.

left home at the age of twelve. Twelve? A little hard to believe. How did he evade the truancy laws? Howard Roark also came from Ohio, and worked his way east. Maybe Galt and Roark were seatmates on the same train to Cleveland and Patrick Henry University. Galt got off there, but Roark continued east to New York and worked in the building trades.

Minerva, the goddess of wisdom. Another Greek allusion. For similar references, see the Recurring Themes Index under "Atlas." The Greek Athena became the Roman Minerva.

It is typical of AR to have Akston think of Galt as being without a past or a family. AR saw herself that way. She was reluctant—and some of her cheerleaders are too—to let herself be thought of as coming from anywhere or anyone. This is where Chris Sciabarra, in *Ayn Rand the Russian Radical*, caught some resistance when he wrote about her philosophy courses at Leningrad U. Didn't she just figure out all of philosophy by herself?

Oddly enough, Minerva had been Frank O'Connor's mother's name, but she "crossed the Tiber" and converted to Catholicism when she married Frank's father. She changed her pagan name to Mary Agnes, a nice Irish Catholic name.

They were sitting at the back of the classroom. Galt sits at the back of the room at the Twentieth Century meeting. There was an Objectivist meeting at NYU many years ago. One man, older than college age, sat in the back of the room while ten or twelve students sat down front. He looked like he was imitating Galt.

which Plato hadn't had the sense to ask of himself. Sticker! Isn't it great when you play "Stump the Professor" and get away with it? That is the kind of teen who read Atlas.

AS 787

physics and philosophy. Sticker! This line made this reader aware, all through high school and college, of the importance of balance—in this case, balancing the abstract and the tangible, the inductive and the deductive, the Plato and the Aristotle (in the Raphael painting *The School of Athens*).

these children knew it too. We are talking about college men. AR refers to Galt as a "boy of 26" on AS 1138. That sets the threshold of adulthood a little high. Ladislas Farago, in *Patton: Ordeal and Triumph*, described the private slapped by Patton "as a boy in his midtwenties (page 316)." Perhaps the 2000 generation is more sensitive to offending youth by calling them boys and girls.

Feminist sensibilities have slopped over to the male side. We no longer dare insult a young woman by calling her a girl, and we have learned to extend the same consideration to young men, especially if they are Black.

John worked in a railroad roundhouse. Doesn't Dagny twig to the possibility that Galt works at the Taggart Terminal (which he mentioned as he carried her down from her plane wreck, and again on AS 777).

Don't sit on the ground! Richard Cornuelle, author of *Healing America*, knew AR in the early 1950s. He recalled, to the *Big Apple Libertarian*, a party on a roof where Ayn nervously watched Frank standing near the parapet. She warned him more than once not to stand so close to the edge of the roof. She was afraid Frank would fall off! "The parapet was five feet high," recalls Cornuelle. "I don't think Frank could have vaulted it if he had wanted to." It looks like AR's source for Dr. Akston's solicitude was herself. She did claim to be a good at introspection.

helpless self-mockery. Akston does not mock himself to tear himself down in his own eyes or in Dagny's. He does so because he sees in Dagny's astonished look the irony of his concern about Ragnar catching cold when Ragnar spends eleven months of the year fighting the navies of the world, which, by the way, means that he has to kill military men, even though he says he never attacks naval vessels because defense is a legitimate function of government.

"Ragnar's First Battle" might be the title of a play or movie showing Ragnar wrestling with the implications of his chosen profession—and pursuing it despite the disapproval of Galt and Akston. After all, he might catch a cold on the high seas.

Akston's gesture is another of those "humanizing" touches that Rand is not supposed to have in her works.

a tall bluff over Lake Erie. Did Ayn and Frank visit someone on a bluff over the Pacific in Los Angeles? At Stony Creek, Connecticut? At Lorain, Ohio?

granite mountainside. In this paragraph, Akston mentions that they had been looking over the lake instead of this granite mountainside, and both images have been stickers for this reader.

AS 788

I always felt as if it were early morning. See the "Smile of morning" in the Recurring Themes Index. Remember Ronald Reagan's campaign slogan in 1984? "Morning in America."

They never spoke of what they wished they might do in the future. This is what BB reports Frank saying about Ayn in her early years in America (BB 87). Truman Capote used to do the same thing.

It was everyone and no one. This is the point of the tunnel disaster.

simpering social worker incapable of earning a penny. Another swipe at social workers. See the Recurring Themes Index.

bureaucrat scared of his own shadow. AR describes what the 1776 revolutionaries called a "placeman," a man who gets a lucrative government job and spends the rest of his career trying to keep it. Keep your ass well covered.

pushed by the hand of every would-be decent man. This is a codicil to the Atlas Principle: If it is the men with virtue who hold up the world, it is the same men who hold up the evil world. This is why Jim Taggart is not the villain of Atlas—Dagny is. It is she who must realize her mistake and stop supporting the looters.

unenslaved thought. Look at the uproar over John T. Allison's funding of college Business School courses on Business Ethics. He required, as a condition of his grant, that these courses include Francisco's Money Speech among all the other readings the professor might require. The socialist professors spewed forth angry articles claiming that the evil capitalist was forcing Rand down the throats of students. They would define "unenslaved" thought as "tax-supported socialist thought." Any money with the attached string of Francisco's speech they would see as "enslaving" thought.

the long white rays of airports. That tall bluff must be about 500 feet tall for Akston to be able to see the runways of an airport in the distance. Maybe AR saw LAX from the Hollywood Sign or Griffith Observatory.

moved this world. I put "moving the world" with "holding up the world" in the "Atlas" entry of the Recurring Themes Index. These are related metaphors.

the greatness of which they were the last descendants, they would win. If they are the *last* descendants of greatness, then that means they will not win. If they win, then there will be further descendants of greatness. Akston should have said the "latest" descendants.

misguided attempt. For AR, religion acted as a primitive attempt at philosophy. Our ancestors were short on facts, but long on imagination. They peopled the earth and sky with gods and demons.

AS 789

like a railroad car imbedded in the sky. Notice how AR uses railroad similes when Dagny is present, just as she spoke of the "alloy" of Rearden's emotions on AS 30.

The Utopia of Greed

Don't frown, John. Galt has emotions! We have seen him emoting before, and we will again.

Well, so did I. You can tell that this is not a speech. It is a conversation, and you can see Dagny asking a question in another seven ellipses in this paragraph. Akston was talking about his own relationship with his three students on AS 788, and now he is telling the contrasting story about their relationship with Stadler. No one objects to Akston sharing all this private information with Dagny, an almost total stranger. Not Galt, not Francisco, not Ragnar and not Kay. Is Dagny the only one present who does not yet see that she and Galt are *Basherts?* (Yiddish: "predestined soulmates").

survivors from some vanishing age. AR's familiar "fall of Rome" image. AR was a short-term pessimist but a long-term optimist.

ivory-tower philosopher. Was it ever true that philosophers were up in an ivory tower, aloof from the workings of the world? Not in the 1940s and 50s, according to Ellen Schrecker—see the Bibliography.

AS 790

I could gather, from your question. Can you see inside Ayn's mind in this line? She is thinking about how she is making the reader infer Dagny's questions from Akston's answers, just like Eddie and Galt, and that gave her the idea for Akston's next line. Dagny met Stadler on AS 185 to 192.

realm of malevolence. AR's Benevolent/Malevolent Universe theory.

Unspeakable. Good word. Full of syllables.

might is right. Lincoln, in the Great Hall of Cooper Union College in New York in 1860, said "Let us have faith that right makes might." He should have said "There is an understandable, natural, logical *reason* that right makes might."

Ferris, Mouch, and Pritchett: This is the pay-off for all AR's hard work writing, and our hard work reading, about these characters earlier in the novel, and for Rand giving them such fitting names. Ferret, mouse and preach-at.

AS 791

Every man builds his world in his own image. This is a much more important aphorism than the AR quote that has been making the rounds of the Internet lately, the one about "who is going to stop me?" It is another example of the Nietzsche quote in AR's Introduction to TF. She has given a new and deeper meaning to an old religious formula. The Bible says that God created man in his own image. Some hip, modern Christians say, "Man created God in his own image."

the necessity of choice. Some say, "the tyranny of choice." The human who sees choice as tyranny does not want to live. He goes in the Recurring Themes Index under "Life is not their Purpose."

uncorrupted by any concession to the will of others. This is the Howard Roark Principle—independence—the rejection of the strategy of kissing ass.

whoever brings into reality a matchstick. AR is thinking of Ralph Waldo Emerson: "The man who builds a better mousetrap, or preaches a better sermon . . . ." But AR had no respect for Emerson: see *Philosophy: Who Needs It?*

made in the image of his thought. See up eleven lines.

he . . . is a man . . . virtue. Vir is the Latin word for man. To have virtue means to be a man. To be a *mensch.*

none of the others had caught. That's hard to believe.

Those eyes of Galt's that miss nothing and that challenge Dagny to name even the unnamed—if Galt is Akston's son, then Dagny is his daughter . . . in-law.

Scene 5: Dagny, Galt and Francisco at the mine. Hank's plane appears

a small cut on the face of a mountain. You can see those cuts on the slopes all around you as you drive from Farmington, New Mexico to Durango, Silverton and Ouray, Colorado. Below the mouth of a mine, you will see tailings spilling in a delta down the mountainside.

AS 792

This . . . was the story of human wealth. Dagny is again seeing the deeper meaning in the sight of Francisco's mine.

the machinery did most of the work. President Kennedy asked, "When a machine does the work of ten men, where do those ten men go?"

Good point.

But these men are happy to have jobs operating machines to do what they would otherwise have to do by hand.

an unlivable moment. see AS 640.

some purpose of its own. When Dagny looks at land, she asks herself if laying track would make it easier to get from A to B.

When novelists build up a character's persona, they should, from time to time, remind the reader that the characters also have jobs. They don't constantly live amidst life's *Sturm und Drang*. They don't always spend their time in exciting airplane chases. They don't always frolic through passionate love triangles.

only a few dots of single trees were left. Ayn was there! Frank would have been walking beside her as she wrote these descriptive lines in her notepad, as they stopped for lunch in the town of Ouray, at something like Hugh Akston's diner.

naked rock. This time (see the "Naked" entry in Recurring Themes) "naked" means that there is nothing, such as grass or moss, hiding the cruel rocks—rocks that nearly killed Dagny when she crashed, and rocks that challenge Francisco's mining machinery and the track Dagny wants to lay

In this context, "naked" means not that we stand unprotected in the face of danger, but that the danger to us lies unconcealed. It is the danger that is naked, instead of the victim.

AS 793

the intensity with which the two men were watching her face. They are wondering whether Dagny has decided to stay in the valley.

steel trestle . . . across that gorge. We are reliving the building of the John Galt Line!

AS 794

You'll have to hear about it. Sticker! Galt is characterized as an avenging angel reminding us not to be cowards, not to ever wish to evade reality. Tough love.

You'll hear about the collapse of the Taggart Bridge. This foreshadows that very collapse on AS 1138.

Nobody stays here. This will be echoed on AS 797.

AS 795

the three of them into the hopeless waste of self-sacrifice. This is where AR pulls perhaps the most important switcheroo in all her fiction. You have seen love triangles before. In *Casablanca*, Rick gives up Ilse to Victor. Perhaps this is what AR was thinking of here. "You're part of his work; the thing that keeps him going," Rick says. "I'm no good at being noble, but it doesn't take much to see that the problems of three little people don't amount to a hill of beans in this crazy world." As much as Rick loves and wants Ilse, he knows that Victor's importance to the war effort dictates his giving up Ilse. *C'est la Guerre.* But AR is going to show why the altruist world's idea of "noble" actions is bad for all concerned. And notice how AR set this up back on AS 773.

I knew how much he had given up for the strike. Look back at AS 769: "Pity, John?"

this was not the answer to the one question she feared. What question is that?

Francisco's approaching figure. Awfully convenient that Francisco was called away just at that moment.

AS 796

a dark excitement. Remember Dagny's first ball? " . . . acknowledged by all as high adventure" (AS 103). Dagny is playing the *femme fatale* for just a moment, but for very high stakes.

Then—no. Peter O'Toole says, in *Becket*, "That's tiresome of you—I fancy her myself. And where *that* subject is concerned, friendship goes by the board." That movie was produced by AR's old boss Hal Wallis.

it would have destroyed the valley in her eyes. Not just destroyed Galt in her eyes, but the valley too. The two are one.

AS 797

an unchanging sunlight. This is a variation on the "smile of morning" theme. Recurring Themes.

Francisco took the sudden brightness. Francisco keeps missing things in these valley chapters, but that has been established earlier in the book, as on AS 491: "Francisco missed the significance of the

The Utopia of Greed

first two words . . . ." He does not read Dagny as well as Galt does, but that is because he does not know that they are in love.

Part of the intensity of her relief. Read this paragraph over a few times, in light of Ayn's affair with NB. She was, as always, living out her fiction in her real life. She would not fake reality in any manner whatever. If she believed she loved NB, and he loved her, then neither could settle for second best.

AS 798

cry in despair that life is frustration. The Benevolent v. Malevolent Universe debate.

Sure, there are many vicissitudes we cannot control, like Covid, but just as many of our prisons are of our own making. Read AR's article on a woman president in light of this paragraph (in Peikoff's *The Voice of Reason*).

one another's weakness, deceit and stupidity. Recently, Rand Bashers have called her a "sociopath," the fashionably collectivist replacement for "psychopath."

A psychopath sees every other human as an enemy, and looks to see how much he can get away with when hurting others. In this paragraph, we see on the contrary that Rand, in a sense, comes across as the only one who is *not* a psychopath in an altruist world. For Rand, no necessary conflict exists between the rights and interests you and I share. Everyone else, except, I hope, you, dear reader, scoffs at this position of hers as naïve and unrealistic.

die never having been born. Wow.

glittering roofs of the valley . . . as clear and firm as sun and rocks. This time, the rocks are *not* naked in threatening hardness and injurious sharpness, but reassuring in their solidity and sureness. And the sun again—Ayn should have been a sun worshipper. Well, she grew up in cloudy St. Petersburg. What a contrast with sunny southern California!

there is no conflict of interests among men. This is crucial! This is one of AR's most important insights. There is no necessary conflict of interests, or of rights—at the fundamental level, and not if men do not expect the unearned.

that the unearned cannot be had. This, in economics, is Henry Hazlitt's "One Lesson": You cannot spend what you have not earned.

the destruction of a value which is, *will not bring value to that which isn't.* When someone from India approached Richard Attenborough about making a movie about Gandhi, he kept the idea in the back of his mind for some years before deciding. Upon learning that Gandhi had said, "I have never understood how some people think they can gain honor from the dishonor of others," he committed to the project. In the same vein, a popular internet meme holds, "Blowing out someone else's candle does not make yours shine more brightly."

AS 799

summer day … a carefree youth … sunlight. More sun and youth worship.

His wife—she thought. Now Dagny has said the word. Now we know what will happen after the end of the novel, when the road is cleared. Just like Roark and Dominique, the Galts will become a married couple. Or more like the Danneskjölds. A married couple with a colorful past, but with a future devoted to doing all the *normal* things that circumstances have prevented them from doing these past twelve years. A return to normal life in a normal, sane world.

not an army model. Hammond fears an invasion of the valley by the forces of Wesley Mouch. Another very tiny, subtle suggestion of the approach of the USA to fascism.

AS 800

safer than an underground vault. Irony.

the number that belonged to Hank Rearden. Have we established that Hank flies and owns a plane, and that Dagny would remember his license number? Barely. On AS 648, Dagny suggests to Hank that he fly his own plane to meet her in Colorado. But nothing about her flying with him and learning his license number.

AS 801

Dagny is pulled back to the world by the sight of Hank still not giving up on her. A minute ago, she was over the moon about Galt refusing to share her with Francisco, but now she sees Hank. She has no intention of going back to Hank as a lover, any more than she intends to return to Francisco, but she now realizes that Hank is

The Utopia of Greed

still going through the torture of looking for her dead body. Still, Nathaniel Branden's question remains: what would be so terrible if Dagny sent a message to Hank saying, "I am alive"?

On the night of January 16th (ironically), 1942, movie star Carole Lombard and others died when their plane crashed into Mount Potosi, 32 miles southwest of Las Vegas. They had refueled at Las Vegas, and the navigation beacons around the airport had been turned off so they could not be used by invading Japanese planes.

This was such a famous tragedy that AR, a member of the "movie colony" of Hollywood, must have had it in mind for Dagny's crash.

Lombard's husband, Clark Gable, flew from Los Angeles to Las Vegas to claim his wife's body. He did not have to personally search, as Hank is doing here, and as Francisco did earlier and on foot. The Red Cross and others had found the wreckage of the plane and recovered the bodies. A year later, Gable was reading TF on a train. He wired MGM saying that he wanted to play Roark in any possible Fountainhead movie.

a mirage of primordial savagery. What a neat metaphor. The ray screen projects an image of primordial, tangled, and broken rocks. Additionally, the ideas of the outer world also suggest a mirage of primordial savagery.

Scene 6: Galt, Akston, Mulligan and Francisco ask Dagny whether she plans to stay or go.

AS 802

your heart and your mind. Plenty has been written on this theme—beginning with Thomas Jefferson's famous letter to his girlfriend Maria Conway about the conflict between his head and his heart.

You have no duty to anyone but yourself. This is a big old springboard for discussion too. If others get you to accept an unchosen duty toward them, isn't that slavery? All of these bits of advice to Dagny are good lessons in decision making.

AS 803

the burden of his abdication of choice. From this paragraph, you might want to look back to the Jeff Allen sequence beginning on AS 656, and forward to Dagny shooting the guard, on AS 1147.

no action could be lower or more futile than for one person to throw upon another the burden of his abdication of choice. Not a sticker on the first reading or the fourth, but the fifth time was the charm. "Lower or more *futile*." Notice that AR, as usual, locates the moral *with* the practical, and the immoral *with* the impractical. The two are not conflicted in AR's system, as they are in the altruist system.

map of a railroad. This foreshadows Dagny's decision to go on strike, on AS 1137.

there's only ten or twelve men. Shouldn't it be "there ARE only ten or twelve men"? Is AR deliberately giving Mulligan a less than perfect command of singulars and plurals, because he is a rags-to-riches businessman, without a lot of education?

AS 804

you're not returning to New York this time. This whole page sets up the societal collapse we will see played out from this point to the last page of the book. This is why Whittaker Chambers, in *National Review* magazine, could try to get away with the claim that AS was written out of hate. Rand's rejoinder might be: No, it is written out of drama. You have to put your hero in danger, and more and worse danger, right up to the climax. See the comparison to Albert Speer's book on AS 589 above. Society is cracking up. AR is doing to us what Galt did to Dagny on AS 794: "You will have to hear about every train wreck...."

open violence. The violence will come mostly from Directive 10-289, which makes workers into medieval serfs, legally tied to their jobs.

They're suspecting something. This is a necessary development. How could the disappearance of key men in the economy *not* arouse suspicion? AR might have heard from Oppenheimer himself how he had called all the top physicists in the US and asked them to go to a secret location to work on a secret war project. He could go so far as to say it was in New Mexico. The men he called had started to notice their colleagues disappearing from campus. See the documentary *The Day After Trinity.* Nineteen minutes into the film, you will hear physicist Stan Ulam remembering how this happened after Pearl Harbor. He was teaching at the University of Wisconsin,

Madison. Hans Bethe asked him whether he would like a secret government job in New Mexico. He went to the library to read a guide book to New Mexico and found that that book had been borrowed by all the physicists who had then disappeared. A real-life Maguffin!

AS 805

lags a few steps behind his vision. Who gave AR the idea for this look? Frank? Nick? Pat?

Pick out passages like this from the book and you will have a whole treatise on the human face and what it reveals.

the only thing I want from the world. This is an advance echo of a line on AS 1156.

looters or neutrals or scabs. So, Galt admits the existence of neutrals.

I'm now free to risk it. Galt has not felt free to risk his life up to now, because of "our work," taking more key men out on strike. So as Galt said on AS 748, "We did not know whether we would live to see the liberation of the world." So, Galt saw himself as *El Libertador*.

suddenly glimpsed a question. Francisco *still* has not twigged? But Akston has.

a world falling apart. See the paperback cover art showing Dagny, eyes down, and the world cracking in pieces.

just think of their railroads. Mulligan is skating close to tipping Dagny off on just where Galt works.

AS 806

When the rails are cut. Shut up, Mulligan! You're giving Galt's secret identity away to Lois Lane! Nevertheless, this line pre-explains just why the collapse of New York will be caused by the bridge being destroyed on AS 1137. The lights of New York go out on AS 1158.

in the midst of the growing stillness. Nice literary touch—too nice to sound natural coming from Mulligan in this kind of dialog, even though he did say he wanted Galt to picture the coming collapse.

No, it won't! Ah, now we see what AR has been building up to these past three pages.

by default of the courage of your convictions. This line of Akston's makes a point similar to the climactic line of the movie *A Man for All*

Seasons, which Objectivist philosopher Doug Rasmussen cites as the youthful influence that led him to philosophy.

Sir Thomas More, pressured by government officials, refused to approve King Henry VIII's divorce and marriage. One of the others cajoles him, "Come on, Thomas, won't you go along just this once, for fellowship?"

"And when we die," More replied, "and you go to heaven for doing your conscience, and I go to hell for *not* doing mine, will you join me then, for fellowship?" This riposte, worthy of John Galt, devastates *because* it applies philosophy to a real-life crisis, and integrates philosophy with the plot and theme of its story.

AS 807

If you want to know the reason. This is Zinovy Rosenbaum speaking, refusing to leave Russia, hoping that people will come to their senses and throw the Communists out.

Do they? This is the big question: Do they really want to live, or do they merely want to avoid the necessity of choice? See the Recurring Themes Index.

Without this insight, the strike would not be necessary. If only people *wanted* to live—*wanted* to be selfish—*wanted* to discover their true, long-range self-interest.

there need never be any conflict among your desires. We all live in prisons of our own making. We all have mistaken premises that need checking. This is AR's message of hope.

You are right. This is the climactic line from Victor Hugo's novel *Ninety-Three*.

AR told BB that she heard, as a child, from her bedroom, someone reading this aloud. She was supposed to be asleep, so she could not ask, the next morning, what it was she had heard. Years later, she discovered the book, and it contributed to her desire to become a writer. The hero has been about to escape from his enemies, but has gone back into a burning castle to rescue two children who would have burned to death. As the enemy arrests him, the lines are: "*Je t'arrête.*" "*Je t'approuve.*": "I arrest you." "You are right."—as Ayn translates the line.

AS 808

Your plane has been repaired. Ah, her plane. A loose end. Did Ayn remember to take care of that detail? Did Hiram Haydn remind her?

The last is the hardest. Dagny means the last night in Galt's house. That's why she asked him to take her out of the valley tomorrow and not day after tomorrow. One night of torture instead of two to bear.

The only man never to be redeemed is the man without passion. Not "the man without a purpose," as on AS 99, and in AR's interview *with Playboy*? Are passion and purpose the same thing? No, but they are related. To have purpose is to have passion. An irrational passion for an irrational purpose would be something different, an obsession rooted in fear.

AS 809

I'm not sure whether I'll be back in New York. He will—to post his farewell message on the calendar. See AS 925. It will be dangerous for Dagny to see Francisco because he will be wanted for the destruction of d'Anconia Copper.

True, Dagny. You're not. Why is Dagny not entitled to see Francisco anymore? It must be that once she leaves the valley, she is once again the enemy.

But of course. Francisco finally figured it out. Now he says that he saw it coming twelve years before.

AS 810

Take it. Do you see what AR is doing here? This is the Last Supper. Jesus says "Take, eat, this is my body." Then he takes the cup and says, "Drink from it, all of you." Francisco has given Sebastián d'Anconia's silver goblets to Galt and Dagny, and takes a wine glass for himself. He has bowed out. This is perhaps the most dramatic scene in the book. AR does not show us anything in the scene after they drink, even though this is not the end of a chapter or even a scene. Fade to black. Jump cut. In the next paragraph Dagny and Galt are walking home. Anything in the scene after they drink would be anti-climactic. AR is writing for the screen.

AS 811

No matter what future evidence you observe. In this dialog, you can see AR uniting philosophy and drama perfectly. This is how human beings should talk to each other and to anything that can pass the Turing Test. This is dialog as it might be and ought to be.

as if she had absorbed his kind of frankness. Dagny did that before, on AS 704, as Galt is carrying her down from her crash site.

at the straight lines of his eyebrows. Yes, Galt certainly does have a lot of *Frank*-ness about him. Ayn made that clear to BB. Frank had straight eyebrows—until Ayn sketched him with arched eyebrows in order to make him appear imperious. He wasn't. See Britting, in the Bibliography. Ayn's sketch of Frank is in Britting's book.

poured-metal planes of his skin. See Art Deco-style portraits, with their chiseled Hollywood good looks. See Nicholas Gaetano's Ayn Rand postage stamp.

AS 812

the unattainable shape of Atlantis. AS 633. This was the paragraph AR analyzed in NB and BB's *Who Is Ayn Rand?*, page 135.

Aloud, she said. This is another intense, extraordinary paragraph. AR is interspersing Dagny's spoken words to Galt with her unspoken words. When she says, "the valley," she mainly means Galt.

shape in the image of my highest values. See AS 791: this is another version of "Every man builds . . . ."

the day when I am able to deliver to you the whole of the world. This is the most plausible argument Dagny has made for not joining the strike. She does not expect to stay in the valley—she expects to raise the whole world up to the standards of the valley.

to be worthy of you on the day I would have met you. This is 12-year-old Alisa, with a bandit's gun in her back, thinking "If I die, I will try to think of Enjolras at the end, and try to be worthy of him." (BB 30)

some circuit not yet to be broken. This is Isabel Paterson's "circuit of energy" metaphor. See *The God of the Machine*.

AS 813

you must enter it naked and alone. This time, "naked" carries three meanings at once. First, naked in the sense of visible to others

The Utopia of Greed

and unashamed. Second, in the sense of unprotected but unafraid, and third, in the sense of unencumbered.

As Lincoln said, "We must disenthrall ourselves . . . ."

"Thrall" is another word for "slave." We must dis-*enslave* ourselves from the false beliefs of the past. *"with no rags from the falsehoods of centuries."*

Go out to continue your struggle. Go on carrying unchosen burdens. AR may be thinking of another line from Hugo's *Ninety-Three*: "Go on! Make yourselves dwarfs!" (Lantenac to Cimourdain, at the climax).

it's real, it's possible—it's yours. This line is echoed in the Speech, on AS 1069.

but his eyes breaking the circuit. AR means the circuit mentioned on the previous page—the imagining, in Dagny's mind, of Galt saying: I heard the words you did not say, and you know I heard them.

as if she were sitting at his feet. Sitting at someone's feet is a powerful image for Ayn. A friend of Ayn's showed visitors a snapshot of Ayn sitting at Frank's feet, smiling, and resting her arm on his knees. Niece Mimi Sutton remembers Ayn sitting at the feet of Isabel Paterson—something Ayn did not do with anyone else except Frank.

in this manner. Notice that AR used this same expression at the top of AS 812. You can see her finding another use for this phrase just a page later, and you can imagine her hesitating for just a moment. Is it going to attract attention and look silly for the reader to see the same phrase on two successive pages? Apparently, she decided to take that chance. Hiram Haydn writes that one writing rule of AR's that he found silly was to never use two rhyming words in the same paragraph. I just used the word "silly" twice in the same short paragraph. Did you find it distracting? Maybe I should change one of those "sillies" to "ludicrous." I don't want you to think that "silly" is the only word I know for this kind of situation.

Scene 7: Galt flies Dagny out of the valley

AS 814

if she were not so far away. A beautiful way of describing how far away from everything but Galt Dagny feels right now.

motor . . . engine. AR uses both words in this short paragraph, perhaps to avoid the awkward sound of using the same word twice so close together. Read the paragraph aloud as is, then with two "engines" and a third time with two "motors," and hear the difference. We have discussed the fact that an airplane is powered by an engine and not a motor, because an engine converts mass to energy and a motor converts energy in one form to energy in another.

memory of the sound of words. Shouldn't that be "sound of *his* words"? Did AR leave a word out?

In any case, *we* should listen to the sound of words in this book. It is poetry, and poetry is meant to be read aloud and heard. Slow down, and take the time to read aloud AR's words, especially these passages that describe either scenery or thoughts and feelings. AS is an epic poem, like Homer's *Iliad* and *Odyssey*, or like Stephen Vincent Benét's *John Brown's Body*. Did that and Benét's *The Place of the Gods*, which inspired *Anthem*, also inspire AR to treat AS as her own epic poem?

Then there was nothing but the stillness. Compare this line with "Then there was nothing but the ocean and the sky and the figure of Howard Roark."—the last line of TF.

Did AR ever take a ride in a small plane during her writing, just to see what it felt like? Later she professed to be afraid to fly (because she did not trust the psycho-epistemology of the young hippies she was afraid the airlines might hire these days as pilots), but in 1950? Remember always that the readers of 1957 were not yet blasé, as we are in 2024. Flying a plane, and especially flying your own plane, was more impressive, more special, than it seems today. People used to dress up to fly.

AS 815

You will not find me. But she does! On AS 954. Or did Galt somehow arrange for that to happen?

On AS 694, Galt's plane looks to Dagny like a cross. On AS 799, Hank's plane looks to Dagny like a cross. Now, Galt's plane looks like a cross again. Well, maybe it's nothing, but maybe it is meant as a suggestion. But see AS 1140.

3. Anti-Greed

Chapter Overview

Thompson, Mouch and Ferris preside at the unveiling of Project X. Stadler reluctantly reads the speech Ferris has written for him.

Dagny reaches New York. She calls Hank to tell him she is alive. Cuffy Meigs, the government's Director of Unification, under the Railroad Unification Plan, is running Taggart. Jim tells Dagny she is expected to appear on a radio show. Lillian comes to Dagny's office to tell her that if she does not appear, Lillian will tell the world of her affair with Hank. Dagny takes the mic and tells the world herself about the affair. Then she sees Hank, who points out that on the radio, Dagny spoke of the affair in the past tense. Hank has guessed that Dagny has met her final romantic choice. Dagny confirms this. Hank is still not willing to give up Rearden Steel, but now he knows that there is someplace for him to go if he does. "If" is rapidly becoming "when" for both of them.

Scene 1: Stadler and Ferris at Project X

AS 816

some insect buzzing to reach his wet temple. A little touch, to make you feel the heat of the summer sun in a field, and also the heat of Stadler's discomfort.

pulp-magazine. Pulp is the cheapest grade of paper. The earliest science fiction magazines, in the 1920s, were called "pulps," along with detective fiction and other cheap magazines.

AS 817

resin sparkling in the sun. Again, you can feel the heat.

grandstands. The first test of the atomic bomb, in New Mexico on July 16, 1945, was not public. Hundreds of scientists and technicians, and soldiers, watched, but no one else. A cover story was released saying that an ammunition dump had blown up, accounting for any sight or sound of an explosion anyone had detected from miles across the desert at 5:30 in the morning. But Ayn and Frank were present in grandstands at Cape Canaveral, Florida for the launch of NASA's Apollo 11, the first moon landing mission, on July 16, 1969. Keep your eyes and ears open next July 16.

what looked like a group of aging rowdies . . . the press. H. L. Mencken would love that line.

AS 818

a large dome, grotesquely too heavy for the rest. This sounds like a radar dome of the DEW Line: Distant Early Warning. These were being built across arctic Alaska, Canada, and Greenland at the time AR was writing, to warn of approaching Soviet bombers.

Ferris's office in Washington. So, Ferris has an office in Washington now, while Stadler, Director of the State Science Institute, is still up in New Hampshire at the Institute. AR is showing us how Ferris, like Hitler's secretary Martin Bormann, is gradually becoming his boss's boss.

the demands for his loyalty. The word "loyalty" was ominous indeed in the late 1940s, and for J. Robert Oppenheimer in the 1950s. There is even a play about his loyalty hearing, called *In the Matter of J. Robert Oppenheimer*, Kipphardt.

like the folding gear of a mechanism. Landing gear? Maybe she did take a flight in a small plane, or at least visited an airport.

he thought it, not by means of words, but by means of . . . an emotion. This is what NB was talking about when he said that Ellsworth Toohey, in TF, knows that Roark is the enemy, but he does not know it in the terms that Roark uses in his speech. Toohey does not have that deep an abstract understanding of what Roark is all about. He knows it rather in terms of the fear that a man like Roark invokes in him.

What Stadler knows is that he must not look too deeply into his own favorite mantra: "What can you do when you have to deal with

Anti-Greed

people?" (AS 188). That is an exact quote from J. Robert Oppenheimer. That is what he said to AR when she interviewed him for background for a movie about the Manhattan Project. She saw that line as the key to Oppie's "Faustian bargain," as Freeman Dyson called it.

AS 819

the mark of uncertainty. But elsewhere, AR has commented on uncertainty being what the professors want us to see as the mark of intellect. T. E. Lawrence (of Arabia) refers in his book *The Seven Pillars of Wisdom* to "doubt—our modern crown of thorns."

sweeping his arm at him, in the manner of a tourist guide. AR's first job was that of a tour guide (tourist guide is an older term) at the Peter and Paul Fortress, St. Petersburg.

AS 820

wilted linen suit. Read these paragraphs about Mr. Thompson before reading Galt's meeting with him, and you will get a clearer picture of this character, and of his inspiration, President Harry Truman. In this case, as in the "What can you do" line above, you can see that AR expects the reader to have a very good memory, or else expects him to re-read the book very soon after reading it the first time, to catch these repetitions of lines or images from their first mention, sometimes hundreds of pages back.

AS 821

movie theater ushers. Some of the biggest movie theaters of 1957 may still have had ushers. They were a phenomenon of the 1920s, when the movie industry was fighting back against competition from radio by building huge, gaudy movie palaces with uniformed ushers. One of the biggest such extravaganzas was the Roxy, on 50th Street between 6th and 7th Avenues. 5,920 seats. It stood from 1927 to 1960. Cole Porter wrote:

You're romance, you're the steppe of Russia,

You're the pants on a Roxy usher . . . .

magnified by the microphone inventor's ingenuity. David Edward Hughes, of England, and Thomas Edison independently invented the carbon microphone, the first practical one, but Edison got the patent in 1877 after a long legal dispute, and made further improvements.

AR, as always, is urging us to remember that everything we use had to be invented by some determined soul, somewhere, sometime.

social loyalty. Ferris is combining the socialists' favorite word, "social," with a word heard much in the US while AR was writing AS: "loyalty."

such staggering scope. Was it at this point that AR interrupted her writing of the novel to put on her ad writer's hat and dash off the teaser on the inside of the dust cover?: "Tremendous in scope, breathtaking in its suspense . . . ." She wrote those words for Random House.

naked ribs of the roof. Naked implies decay since the ribs of a roof are not supposed to be visible. A carpenter would call them "rafters," but AR uses the term "ribs" and makes them naked, to paint a word picture of a decaying body, with the skin rotting and revealing the ribs. She is setting up the horror of what will happen when the operator pulls the lever. And that in turn sets us up for the greater horror of what is to come on AS 1132.

a tractor with its treads in the air. Oops! A tank or a bulldozer has treads, but a tractor does not. Some recent, heavy and high-tech models do, but not likely in 1957. Rancher Frank should have caught that one! The picture of a vehicle with its treads or its wheels in the air suggests a dead animal with its legs in the air, and AR is almost subliminally setting us up, because that is exactly what we are going to see in three pages.

sun-scorched weeds. Here is another reference for the "weeds" list. Here, we can either feel sorry for the weeds, dry and sun-scorched as they are, or feel sorry for the farmer who had to abandon his cornfield *to* the weeds. The weed can be, symbolically, both a villain and a victim.

AS 822

one must be darn careful. . . . We shall see, on AS 1132, how careful you have to be with the Xylophone.

Dr. Stadler found pleasure in watching the kid. Compare AR's rapturous description of this kid with the *kids* in the valley, on AS 784. AR does more than just mention children, she paints a deeper meaning of childhood for us: "the joy of discovering its own existence." Also compare Stadler's pleasure here to his pleasure at a patch of sunlight on a distant hillside at the Institute on AS 340 and AS 349.

Taggart Bridge, Des Moines, Fort Dodge, Iowa, Austin, Minnesota, Woodman, Wisconsin, Rock Island, Illinois. All real places, except the bridge. Woodman is near Platteville, in the southwest corner of Wisconsin. AR names these places clockwise, assuming that the Taggart Bridge is on the Mississippi about between Muscatine and Burlington, Iowa. Project X would be a little south of Waterloo, Iowa. The places she names are all at about a one hundred—mile radius of Waterloo. Ferris mentioning the Taggart Bridge is another set-up for us, planting a seed in our memories that will sprout on AS 1137.

AS 823

AR mentions Rearden Metal, as she had the Taggart Bridge, as another of the hundreds of tie-ins she needs, to keep this whole huge story together. But it is interesting that Ferris, of all people, calls it Rearden Metal when he should be calling it by its new government name, Miracle Metal. This is an early example of what Rearden's lawyer will mention on AS 934: the looters want something from Rearden.

the pawn of a silent machine. Elsewhere, AR will explain that it is ideas, not conspiracies, that determine the course of men and nations. If all the evils of the world depicted in this novel were the work of a conspiracy, then we need only discover the ringleader and arrest him. But the whole world, from Mr. Thompson and the big shots down to the lowest Taggart track worker, follows the clichés and assumptions of altruism and statism: the *ideas*.

Dr. Blodgett. In the newly-released second volume of AR's letters, Letter number 092, August 28, 1943, is from AR to a fan named Helen Blodgett. Having read TF, Ms. Blodgett probably would have read AS when it was published fourteen years later. How did she feel about an unattractive character bearing her name? She must have figured that her last name had gone into AR's file of useful future character names. Near Cortland, NY is a crossroads called Blodgett Mills, so AR could have gotten the name from a map. But it is even more likely that she just went through the Los Angeles or Manhattan phonebook looking for names with the right sound for heroes, villains, and other types of characters. She describes Dr. Blodgett as "youngish, fattish, and effeminate." Did AR recall, as she used that name, that a fan by that name had written a glowing fan letter for TF just a few years before?

no entities, only actions. AR is not kidding. R. Buckminster Fuller had many good ideas, but his book title *I Seem to Be a Verb* was not one of them. AR is, as always, showing the relevance of philosophy to everyday life. Ferris is speaking to an elite crowd, so he is not using old saws, but the latest prospective clichés—the clichés of the future—of hip philosophy, with Dr. Pritchett himself, the author of some of those enormities, in the audience. Ferris is flattering Pritchett, a useful political ally in academia, and also showing off his own intellectual hipness to the elite crowd in the grandstands.

Mr. Thompson looked blankly bewildered. Shtick! Shtick in *Atlas Shrugged*!

AS 824

The farmhouse tore into strips of clapboard. You have seen this. I have seen this on TV countless times—a film of the early atomic bomb tests in Nevada. Houses blown apart, and mannequins melting and burning. Google "atomic bomb test house." We realize that Project X is AR's take on the atomic bomb. She may have also been thinking of the hints that Nicola Tesla dropped, toward the end of his life in 1943, that he was working on some kind of death ray. When he died, the FBI swooped down on his suite at the New Yorker Hotel (Eighth Avenue and 34th Street, later the HQ of the Moonies), to search for any weapons designs that might be useful in the war effort, or that might be stolen by Axis spies, or back-engineered, or independently invented by the Axis.

Anne Heller found an article in the *New York Times* of September 22, 1940, called "Death Ray for Planes." Scientists, like Nicola Tesla, and science fiction writers, were giving the public, from the 1920s on, the idea of death-dealing rays of energy.

he realized that he was looking for the kid. A nice, slightly redeeming touch for Stadler. The whole scene is seen through Stadler's eyes. It invites comparison with Oppenheimer's famous words on seeing the Trinity atomic test. He recalled two lines from the *Bhagavad Gita*: "If the brilliance of a thousand suns were to burst at once upon the sky, that would be like the splendor of the Mighty One," and "Now I am become Death, the shatterer of worlds."

floorwalker. Are people still familiar with this term? It was first used in 1876. "A person employed in a retail store to oversee the salespeople and help customers."

she was sick at her stomach. This reader grew up hearing the expression "sick *to* her stomach." This looks like another of AR's old-fashioned expressions.

AS 825

handouts from this country. Here we see more sharply what Ragnar was talking about: the Marshall Plan after World War II. But Stadler is calling Ferris's bluff: he does not buy Ferris's national defense argument for Project X. What national enemies do we have to fear anyway? Ferris then drops the other shoe: "Internal enemies can be as great a danger as external ones." This is the "social loyalty" consideration Ferris mentioned on AS 821. In 1950, the McCarran Internal Security Act was passed. It provided for prison camps for anyone, during a war or other emergency declared by the president, considered dangerous—by that same president, or his Attorney General. Some of these camps were left over from the internment of the Nisei during World War II, including some friends of Ayn and Frank's. President Truman vetoed the bill, not because it was too draconian, but because it was not draconian enough: detainees could still get out through *habeus corpus*. (Lincoln had suspended *habeus corpus* during the Civil War.) It was passed over Truman's veto. One camp was at Allenwood, Pennsylvania, and has since been used as a minimum-security federal prison. Some criticized it as a "country club" for prisoners, such as the Watergate conspirators, who were white, rich, and had friends in the federal government.

No private businessman or greedy industrialist would have financed Project X. Sure they would, and did, especially as AS was being written in the Cold War era. Not for commercial sale, but for government contracts.

AS 826

An announcer, with a voice like a machine gun spitting smiles. Great line.

sparkling snake-head of the microphone. Another.

the signaling arm of Wesley Mouch. Here, as on the last several pages, you see that Mouch (another Bormann) is the conductor and Thompson the lead soloist, but not in charge.

AS 827

Mr. Mouch's function. This is another twist on the Nietzsche quote: "It is not my function to be a fly swatter." Also on TF 353, and ARL 382.

off-color story. An old expression meaning slightly pornographic.

face-saving. This is an Asian expression that caught on in the west long ago: if you lose honor, you "lose face."

Dr. Stadler's answer disturbed him. This whole scene is about political power relationships: Mouch's power over the Head of the State, Mr. Thompson, and Dr. Ferris's power over Dr. Stadler.

Lack of faith is the only thing we got to fear. This is a twist on President Franklin D. Roosevelt's famous line "The only thing we have to fear is fear itself." This was in FDR's first inaugural speech. This speaker is described as "beefy," and AR gives him a misused "got," so she is suggesting the thuggish, blue-collar types you see coming to power under the Nazis, Communists, and suchlike promoters of the proletariat, with the tweedy professor types tagging along, to show how hip and proletarian they are. For a bizarre account of this last social phenomenon, see Tom Wolfe's *Radical Chic and Mau-Mauing the Flack Catchers*.

AS 828

Scientists have never been popular with the masses. See the "Doctors' Riot" in New York City, 1788. See also the movie "Son of Frankenstein," with its familiar scene of the peasants, with pitchforks and torches, storming Dr. Frankenstein's castle. Finally, there is Trump and his anti-vaccination and generally faith-versus-science mob.

The professorial elite likes to call the people they profess to love "the masses," as if they measure their dependents by the pound and not by the individual, and call anyone who disagrees with them the running dogs of the elite.

a tall, willowy woman. This is an image that goes back to WTL, where Kira attends a speech by visiting British female comrades who have come to gush over the noble Soviet experiment. (They are visiting Swedes on WTL 156, and Brits on 182.) "Willowy" means "gracefully tall and slender."

Eleanor Roosevelt was tall, but was she graceful? AR might have been thinking of her.

order must be maintained by any means available. This line sounds like a premonitory echo of Malcolm X's famous slogan "by any means necessary." Mr. X was becoming known and feared by White Americans around the time AS was published in 1957. Both lines reflect the ever-popular old saw "The ends justify the means."

A fat, jellied woman, with an inadequate brassiere under a dark, perspiration-stained dress. This poor lady will appear only once in this novel, and only in this one sentence, so AR has to load all her adjectives into one burst. AR was no stranger to women's club meetings. See BB 196: Ruth Beebe Hill's "wishful thinking" story. See, or rather hear, Anna Russell's comedy routine on women's club meetings.

AS 829

An uncontrolled radio station? Many readers, including this one, recalled much from AS about the loss of free enterprise in the fictional USA of the novel, but not so much about the loss of civil liberties. So note that Mouch and the various factions, around Jim Taggart, around Kip Chalmers, and around Ferris, are eroding freedom of speech, too. After all, if government controls, or owns outright, all media, then as Ferris says, "how would he make himself heard?" A dissident, that is.

AS 830

It looked like a walk to mount either a pedestal or a guillotine. AR must have thought of Hugo's *Ninety-three* or Dickens's *A Tale of Two Cities*. The line recalls someone's description of Kira in WTL as looking like either a saint or a prostitute, and a very similar line in the musical *Evita*: "A fantasy of the bedroom, or a saint." AR is not the only writer to use startling comparisons like that.

AR always says *the* Patrick Henry University. Was this an old-fashioned wording, or a Russian one?

corrupt ... favor ... pull. This describes the bad guys in *Atlas* in a nutshell. But your professors have told you that AR makes poor people the enemy.

AS 831

hazel green eyes. These eyes, on top of the announcer listing the chairmanship of the physics department of Patrick Henry University among Stadler's accomplishments, reminds Stadler of Galt. The memory of the face without pain, fear, or guilt arouses exactly those emotions in Stadler.

your press card and your work permit. This is Directive 10-289 at work again. This is why Dagny, reading the Directive for the first time, said "I will not work as a slave or as a slave driver."

AR must have been thinking back to Petrograd, where Communist government ration cards were distributed in schools and workplaces. Therefore, if you were unemployed and not a student, you could starve (AH 37).

Just because the story of Project X was inspired by the atomic bomb, do not expect to find AR marching next to Bertrand Russell in peace marches.

Do not take this as a literal, topical diatribe against The Bomb. She lived in the Cold War Era as a refugee from the Soviet Union, and she and her contemporaries had to, like it or not, evaluate The Bomb as one more possible desperate measure for survival in an age of desperate measures for survival. This scene is an unpleasant one, and this commenter is glad to see the back of it.

Scene 2: Dagny returns to New York. Meigs and Eddie, Dagny and Jim. Lillian blackmails Dagny into speaking on Scudder's radio show.

Dagny has been living for a month in heaven, and is now back in hell. AR must have thought of the pessimism of Russians, and the optimism of Americans, as she writes about Dagny wanting to shake people by the shoulders and say, "Snap out of it!"

where the airport bus had left her. That, in AR's time, would be the Airline Terminal Building, on the southwest corner of Park Avenue and East 42nd Street. It stood there from 1940 to 1980. It was a little Art Deco gem, designed by architect John B. Peterkin. The Dean, in TF, mentions a Professor Peterkin, and this must be where AR got that name. It was demolished for the Philip Morris Building. The Art Deco stylized eagles on top of it now grace the entry of the Philip Morris world HQ in Richmond, Virginia. Over the door of the building was a map of the world, curving concavely around the entryway, just like the world map in Wynand's office in the TF movie, and this viewer would be surprised if that was a coincidence. Philip Morris is now Altria Corporation.

AS 832

incomprehensible language. AR certainly had this experience on trains, in Germany, France, Ukraine, and, with her still-limited English, traveling from New York to Chicago to Los Angeles in 1926.

She watched the prairies. Since AR flew only twice in her life, both long after she wrote these words, she must have asked others what flying is like, and she could glean what impressions she could from movies. There is such a scene in *The Best Years of Our Lives*, the very 1946 movie that she did not get a chance to analyze for HUAC. Returning veterans, in one scene, are looking down on the Midwest from a low-flying plane.

AS 833

a child, not yet able to read. Did the precocious Alisa remember doing this herself, or did she see her younger sisters Natasha and Nora do it? Or did Zinovy tell her, "You know, Alisa, before you learned to read, do you know what you used to do?"

Los Gatos, Colorado. John Steinbeck lived in Los Gatos, California early in life. Also, AR was a cat person. *Los Gatos* means The Cats.

AS 834

resents any effort as an imposition. And a few lines down, it looks like this woman failed to get Miss Ives's message to Hank when he came back to the hotel. All over the book are passages like this, about incompetent underlings. But there is also Miss Ives. There is Eddie, and there are many others. And there are so many *overlings* too—both good and evil. Intended or not by AR, these passages work on the adolescent reader. Don't we all identify with the heroes, and assure ourselves that we would always be Miss Ives, and not the desk woman at the Eldorado Hotel? And does that not inspire us to make sure that we *are* Miss Ives when we put down our Ayn Rand books and get our first jobs?

My plane crashed . . . in the Rockies. In *The Unsuspected*, a 1947 murder mystery starring Claude Rains, a woman arrives in New York by air from Brazil after being reported lost in a sinking on the Atlantic. AR may have gotten the idea of Dagny's cover story from that movie. And the story was first serialized in the *Saturday Evening Post,* which is where AR first read her favorite novel, *Calumet "K,"* by Merwin and Webster. The climax of this movie is a radio speech by Rains. Not as long as Galt's.

AS 835

She telephoned her secretary. Having found dramatic uses for Gwen Ives, AR keeps Dagny's secretary down to pure function. No name, no development.

AS 836

Cuffy Meigs. Another Ivy League nickname, like Kip Chalmers and Tinky Holloway, but Meigs does not fit the "Tennis, Anyone?" image. He is a thug, pure and simple.

AS 837

Punchboard. The only place this reader has seen punchboards was Fairbanks, Alaska in 1990. You buy a cardboard block the size of a mobile phone and stick a pen point into holes in the board. The pen point pushes a coil of paper out. A number is printed on the paper. If you get the winning number, you win a prize. It is usually used for fundraising.

AS 838

Eddie, on this page, acts as explainer, as he did after Dagny's Woodstock interlude, and as he did in the cafeteria with Galt. He gives Dagny, and us, a picture of Taggart Transcontinental under the sway of Meigs.

Her map . . . the picture of Nat Taggart were on the wall. This is another subliminal advance echo of what is to come on AS 1137.

AS 839

People in Washington and . . . and others. What others?

cracking his knuckles . . . the shrillness, the aura of panic were new. Note well! AR is introducing new aspects of Jim's character. Development. This is what a good writer must do to hold the reader's interest. But the change must have a reason.

In this case, the reason is that Jim is progressively cracking up, "going to pieces" as Dagny sees. Earlier, what we saw in Jim's conversation, when he wasn't hysterical, was the speech of private schools and Ivy League universities, as you would expect in an heir and future corporation president.

AS 840

He wore a jacket which was not, but looked like, a military uniform. AR has already shown us that she respects the military: Ragnar does not attack military ships. The military is a legitimate function of government. But here, a military-like jacket on so sinister a character as Meigs takes on a sinister hue too. It looks like Meigs is affecting a military look in order to intimidate people, and to steal, you might say, the respect usually due a man in uniform.

pooling their resources. This is what Mussolini called "corporatism." The companies in every industry are forced to pool their revenue, and accept prices and policies dictated by the Fascist government. The Fascists also wanted "autarky": economic self-sufficiency for their empire. FDR's advisor Rexford Tugwell was an open admirer of Mussolini's economics.

AS 841

on the basis of its need. The old "From each according to his ability . . . " theory that Jeff Allen described, from the Twentieth Century Motor Company (AS 660).

So you've got nothing to worry about. AR shows the difference between Dagny and the typical businessman in real life. He would be content to ride on a government plan that ruined his competitors. But Dagny sees farther than a few days into the future.

AS 842

the strongest plants around him. AR begins the paragraph with a plant analogy, but then switches to an animal analogy: Jim is now a mountain lion, pouncing on a carcass. This reader is not sure why AR used a plant analogy, or whether it might have been better to use the same analogy throughout the paragraph, unless that would have been distractingly cute.

Dan Conway. It is a good idea, in a novel this long and complex, to remind us of Dan Conway and other characters and incidents from way, way earlier in the story, and tie them to the theme of this scene. See AS 77.

a cracking bone between the pouncer and the abyss. Strange image. Did AR see such a scene in a movie? Strange but vivid.

she saw that they knew it. Here again, AR is getting at her theme that these people do not really want to live. They just want to evade. Their motivation is fear, not the willing embracing of life with its uncertainties. Nothing ventured, nothing gained, says the man who wants to live, to try, even in the face of the possibility of failure. Nothing admitted into consciousness, nothing risked, believes Jim Taggart.

AS 843

We couldn't permit a railroad like Taggart Transcontinental to crash! In the economic downturn of 2008, the government bailed out certain big banks that were judged "too big to fail." But that policy is as old as banking itself, or as individuals with friends in high places.

In the long run, we'll all be dead. This is the famous tag line of economist John Maynard Keynes, but he meant by it the opposite of what most people think he meant.

This reader believed for years that Keynes meant that the future does not matter, because in the long run we are all dead. But he was really using that line to pooh-pooh the kind of economist who disregards the crises of the present by painting a rosy picture of how good times will be after the current crisis is over.

(Keynes then wrote of how good times will be once the current crises, like World War II, were over. In the not-too-distant future, he wrote, most or all humans will have almost all leisure time and little or no work time.) This is Cuffy Meigs's favorite expression. He says it again on AS 947.

So be careful, writer, that your most quotable quote expresses your own thoughts and not your opponents' that you are lampooning.

the little girl. Meigs is giving offense, AR says. Betty Friedan would agree. In fact, AR and her circle very publicly approved of Friedan's book *The Feminine Mystique.* See *The Objectivist Newsletter,* July 1963.

AS 844

They don't believe the newspapers. This reflects the growing fear of the Russian people as the Communists took over—fear that resulted in young Alisa burning her diary, lest the secret police search the apartment and read what she had written.

It also brings to mind the pols and pundits of 2020 accusing each other of "fake news."

all those big industrialists who've vanished into thin air. Another necessary tie, or reminder. The strike is getting noticed, and adding to public panic.

no decent man will work for those people. AR surely had her own father in mind here. Zinovy Rosenbaum refused to work for the Communist government of Russia. The alternative was to starve.

unrest. There was a report online, on Friday, October 30, 2020, four days till the presidential election, that Walmart has removed guns and ammo from display in their stores, in case of "unrest."

an industrialist of the old school. "Old school" is an old expression that is currently enjoying a new vogue.

reactionary. a Marxist term. After any move toward liberation by The People, the Establishment will react with violent suppression. Anyone, like AR, then, who is not on the socialist program is dismissed by your professors as a "reactionary."

AS 845

She had listened. The words of Hank's that AR quotes in this paragraph were back on AS 378.

If they put you on a torture rack. Another advance echo, anticipating Galt being tortured, though on a "leather mattress," on AS 1140.

the Morale Conditioner. This reflects the fact that as AR was writing *Atlas* in the 1950s, the "conditioned reflex" theory of psychologist B. F. Skinner was rising to challenge the Freudian system. "Conditioning" was the word of the day. AR was hearing from NB about the latest trends in psychology.

But I promised it!" "I didn't." This characterizes all the dialogs between Dagny and Jim. Jim is always hysterical, caught in his own machinations, wheedling and evasive. Dagny's answers are always short and to the point, and cut through Jim's evasions. These dialogs are among the biggest stickers for a young reader who is seeing in Dagny the kind of straight shooter he wants to be.

AS 846

He was shaking. This is a good paragraph to look back to, to help explain Jim's psychology when he finally cracks up altogether on AS 1145 and 1146. Some readers may be just sick and tired of reading about Jim and are not paying attention anymore. They are going through Character Fatigue. So maybe there is such a thing as *over-characterization*. This paragraph also shows AS as epic poetry: AR is taking her time in showing Dagny's inner thoughts about what she sees in Jim's mental state. Any novel has to be paced. It can't just be climax all the time.

awed by the enormity of the sight. Here you can take "enormity" in both senses: enormous and catastrophic.

Well, Eddie. Another sight of Dagny's warm side, both in what she says and the way she says it. No wonder Eddie not only respects her, but loves her. Notice that it is the greedy capitalist who is concerned about preventing train wrecks.

AS 847

at an angle considered smart. "Smart," in the sense of up-to-the-minute in fashion, neat and well-planned, "put-together," elegant and dignified, but with just a touch of youthful insouciance, was an expression current in the 1920s when AR was learning English. The magazine *The Smart Set: A Magazine of Cleverness*, ran from 1900 to 1930. H. L. Mencken and George Jean Nathan co-edited it from 1914 to 1924. The magazine introduced many future great writers to the

Anti-Greed   101

American audience, including a Rand favorite, O. Henry. Mencken would later write Rand a fan letter about WTL. Mencken and Nathan left TSS in 1924 and founded *The American Mercury*.

Harold Ross founded *The New Yorker* after TSS ended, modeling the new magazine on the old. A writer for *The New Yorker* once asked AR for an interview. Rand said sure, as soon as the magazine retracts the insults it has paid me in the past.

Dagny inclined her head gravely. AR's usual Old World formality. AR rarely made concessions to the changing customs of 1957 and beyond. She was still bowing to the audience in 1976 at the Ford Hall Forum in Boston.

Then proceed to support it. Here, as elsewhere, Dagny is always the polite and formal one, and the straight talker, while others speak in innuendoes.

AS 848

Compare this whole page and Dagny's reaction to Lillian's blackmail with Hank's reaction to Ferris's blackmail, on AS 557. Hank still has a lot of guilt to work through, and he is working through it. Dagny is beyond all that.

in all of their propaganda. Perhaps this is why Ferris called it "Rearden Metal" instead of the approved "Miracle Metal" on AS 823. The looters have changed their minds and have given up the "Miracle Metal" name for the original "Rearden Metal" because Rearden is becoming more popular than they are. They want to appropriate his fame with the name of his metal, and appear to get on his side, as well as make it appear that he is on their side.

AS 849

Odd: AR does not put a comma in "Oh yes," but on the previous page, she put one in "Well, yes" and "Oh, of course."

the line of the fault in the stone. AR is thinking back to Roark's quarry scene. Everyone else snickers about director King Vidor focusing on Gary Cooper driving that phallic drill ever deeper into the stone, but AR, as usual, looks for a deeper meaning than the Freudian one.

sharp planes, the firmness of the mouth. AR is picturing Greta Garbo again. And Katherine Hepburn.

Dagny noticed. AR is shifting Points of View: first she describes Lillian's reading of Dagny's face, and now the reverse. Writing teachers will tell you to restrict a scene to a single POV, but here it works. Writing teachers will sometimes admit that a clever writer can break at least some of the rules some of the time and get away with it.

It was I. Compare this to Toohey telling Roark "It is I who've done it." It is in the Fountainhead movie, but not in the book, in the scene on TF 408.

dollars which you're able to make and I'm not. A line no one would say in real life. Everyone would say "those dollars you get from exploiting the workers."

I am doing it without gain. Another "non-material tiara" for Lillian. See AS 308, 386, 398 and 399.

AS 850

as if too much of her was seen and as if she were not seen at all. Roark also makes people feel that he sees too much and does not see them at all. See TF 7: the Dean Scene.

Scene 3: Dagny on the radio, and with Hank in her apartment.

the great social program of our leaders. More signs of government propaganda replacing a free press.

AS 851

Scudder calls Dagny's "the extreme, conservative viewpoint": Then as now, "conservative" means not fashionably statist.

the glass of a protective wall. Another advance echo, since on the previous page AR had described Dagny and Scudder as being in a glass cage. And it shows AR's associative mind at work: she thought of this simile because she had just been thinking of the "glass cage" description. AR had been on the radio at least once, back in the 1930s (AH 96). Was there a glass partition in that studio?

This was not the way I wanted you to learn it. Dagny does not know that Eddie had told Galt about her and Hank. The microphone is made of Rearden Metal: great touch, since it sharpens the pain of

Dagny having to end her relationship with the man who invented it. Also, it makes more real to us the fact that Rearden Metal has come to widespread use and importance. There is a reason why the looters wanted to seize and take credit for it.

and it was suddenly easy. AR, and Dagny, feared the unknown, but not the fightable. That explains why AR feared to fly. The passenger has to sit back passively and hope the pilot knows what he's doing.

AS 852

let your estimate be your own concern. You can't blackmail a victim who has no shame. This is true of Dagny, whose standards are her own.

AS 853

On these pages, 851-853, we hear Dagny making a speech. Short, but well delivered.

empty dreams. This is the Johnnie Dawes Principle, from *Ideal*, again. Life is of no account, but who has made it so? Not those who cannot dream, but those who can *only* dream.

those who make steel, and railroads, and happiness. Who but AR would put those together?

your only knowledge is in your hatred. This is the point about evil that NB made on his first "Seminar" record when a questioner asked how Toohey could knowingly choose the evil over the good. NB explained that Toohey does not understand good and evil. He could not have given Roark's speech if he had wanted to, as many readers think. He does not have that kind of abstract understanding of Roark. He knows that Roark is the man he cannot intimidate or manipulate, so Roark is the man who has to go, but Toohey knows this only in terms of the fear that a man like Roark invokes in him. Toohey is not a brilliant person. He is a shrewd person, a cunning person, which is a different thing entirely. This came up before, on AS 818.

hate me then. If this be treason, make the most of it! AR loved to quote Patrick Henry's famous words of defiance.

AS 854

like the limbs of an animal lying in the road, intact but dead. Scary, but effective. Is this from a note AR made while driving cross country with Frank?

Nobody stays here. That was back on AS 794 and 797.

mere acknowledgment of the coins. When was the last time you gave a tip in coins?

AS 855

Almost this whole page is narration, not dialog. It reads almost like one of AR's early scripts for a silent film, with the acting in the faces more than in the words.

to sit at his feet. See AS 813.

he knew her pain and felt it. This is compassion: "with-pain." Or sympathy: "same pain." But not "empathy," which everyone incorrectly says these days.

insulting cruelty. See AS 254.

she had seemed as the stronger of the two. Why the "as" here? This line is a sticker for this reader. We have seen repeatedly how Dagny is farther along the path to enlightenment than Hank is. (See AS 368.)

Nevertheless, when it all becomes too much for Dagny, on this page, she needs Hank's strength. And he is about to catch up to her on that path, as you will see over the next five pages. In those passages in which Dagny does seem the stronger of the two, we see AR's feminism.

she whispered guiltily. AR said to Alvin Toffler of Playboy magazine that her heroes could never feel fundamental guilt. Here, Dagny feels guilt, but it is not fundamental guilt, and this is a good example of why the word "fundamental" is so important to AR. By "fundamental guilt" she means Original Sin. Dagny is just a little embarrassed because she has broken down in tears in front of Hank for the first time, that's all.

AS 856

the kind of hell I let you go through in the last month. Here, and elsewhere over the past few pages, Dagny sounds awfully regretful about not asking Galt to make an exception and let Hank know that she is alive.

to prove her strength. When AR appeared on the Phil Donahue Show the second time, just after Frank died, she said that she had agreed to appear partly to assess whether she could handle a TV interview so soon after his death.

AS 857

same pride and the same meaning. This paragraph could stand in for Hank's speech to Dagny on their first morning together (AS 254) and Dagny's reply, and for Francisco's whole Sex Speech (AS 489). Those and Hank's speech that begins here can be regarded as, among other things, AR's defense of Frank against the suffocating Catholicism of his childhood. Original Sin was the doctrine that turned him against his parents' religion.

I loved you from the first day I saw you. Gary Cooper says the same line (except for "moment" instead of "day") in the Fountainhead movie.

I want you to know how fully I know what I am saying. There, briefly, is the reason for all the long speeches in the book, but especially this one. This is why the speeches have to be there, to advance the plot.

AS 858

the highest of moral values, to be defended above one's life, because it's that which makes life possible. That is all you need as a base for a moral system. What makes life possible?

jabbering incompetents. Hank does not mean that it is immoral to be incompetent. There are plenty of skills that even Galt and Francisco do not possess. That's not the point. The evil lies in devoting your life to learning and practicing the skills of manipulation, as Jim Taggart and Peter Keating and Ellsworth Toohey do. They could have instead learned honest skills.

I did not know that the force unleashed against me was my own. We have met the enemy and he is us.

wealth is only a means to an end. This is the point, and it is all over this book, that showed many teenaged readers that the altruist image of Citizen Kane mindlessly accumulating money and junk is not what wealth is all about.

a brother who plotted for my destruction. AS 467. But we will really see it on AS 932 and 966: Philip is the punk.

Bennett Cerf wanted to cut Galt's Speech because AR "already said it." The reason she left this speech in is because it is *Rearden* saying it.

AS 859

people think that a liar. This could be a chapter, nice and concise, in an ethics textbook, about why you should not lie. But you have been told that John Allison is an evil capitalist buying academia by endowing chairs for a course in business ethics that includes Francisco's Money Speech among other readings.

the world's slave from then on. This is the lesson learned by another great swing character in AR's fiction: Gail Wynand. But your professors told you that there are no swing characters in AR's fiction. There are no conflicted characters.

AS 860

This page requires a lot of chewing and digesting, like the line "a white lie is the blackest of all." You could write an essay just on that premise.

a public stoning. Perhaps AR is thinking of the Gospel story of Jesus saving Mary Magdalene from a mob. AR was fond of the image of the violent mob attacking the innocent. Jesus shames the mob by saying "Let him who is without sin cast the first stone."

the greater the loss behind me, the greater the pride I may take in the price I have paid for that love. This sounds like AR had read Lincoln's famous "Letter to Mrs. Bixby," who had lost five sons in the war. ". . . the solemn pride that must be yours to have laid so costly a sacrifice upon the altar of freedom." This is how characters used to talk in 19th century novels and letters.

AS 861

No other reason could have made you leave me. Could this be the answer to NB's criticism of AR having Dagny *not* ask Galt for an exception, so she could send a message to Hank saying that she is alive? Or would NB say, Still, what purpose is served for anyone by letting Hank go on thinking Dagny was dead?

Dagny did not know that Galt knew, thanks to big-mouth Eddie, that Dagny was having an affair with Hank. So, Dagny was thinking that if she asked Galt for an exception, Galt would twig to the fact that Dagny and Hank were lovers, and he would believe he had lost his chance with Dagny.

Hank's speech on the previous page, and the further points he makes here, was necessary for the purpose of explaining why Hank, like Francisco, can be big enough to let go of Dagny now that they know that she has met her "final, irreplaceable choice."

These two pages are also the reason why Karl Hess ridiculed AR's heroes for explaining in excruciating detail why they love each other. AR would reply: This is how all human beings should act: consciously. They should always be able and willing to explain important issues, such as why I love you, and in what exact way I love you. And we should all be willing to listen to each other's explanations.

What you'll give him is not taken away from me. This is why it is ironic that the looters accuse the heroes of "greed." Perhaps this is the reason AR called the previous chapter "The Utopia of Greed" and this one "Anti-Greed": The anti-greed faction is building a death ray to control the population, and they excuse it by pleading that they are not motivated by greed and that makes it alright. And Lillian speaks of her "non-material tiaras" while she is practicing blackmail.

I've watched you struggle to discover it. Another sign of Hank being a swing character, struggling to achieve clarity, in this novel where, you have been told, the heroes never struggle. Hank could certainly never have delivered this speech back when he was murderously angry at Francisco for having been Dagny's lover in the past. He is growing in understanding, partly through hearing Francisco's Sex Speech.

AS 862 & 863

Perhaps these two pages could be the trailer for a new and better *Atlas Shrugged* movie.

AS 863

compassion. Hank has compassion for Dagny. Compare AS 769: Galt for Francisco.

4. Anti-Life

Chapter Overview

Jim exults over his advance knowledge that Argentina will be declared a People's State, and that Chile will nationalize d'Anconia Copper. He brags about this to Cheryl, who had become disillusioned with him when she learned that Dagny, not Jim, had kept the trains running. In a flashback, Cheryl traces the steps toward her disappointment.

   Dagny misses Galt terribly. Cheryl comes to apologize for insulting her at the wedding. Dagny sees how upset Cheryl is about Jim. She is concerned for Cheryl, but does not see how close Cheryl is to breaking.

   Cheryl goes home to find Jim in bed with Lillian. She commits suicide.

Scene 1: Jim comes home and wants to celebrate his deal to nationalize d'Anconia Copper.

AS 864

the beggar's mood matched his own. Jim does not care whether he lives or dies. Not as Dagny would. This is the Life-is-not-their-purpose Principle in action. Contrast Jim's beggar with Jeff Allen, Dagny's hobo, on AS 656.

he could not admit what it was he wanted to celebrate. We will learn what Jim wants to celebrate on AS 897.

AS 865

This is a good page to show to people who think that Rand's heroes are all businessmen and her businessmen are all heroes.

progressive. We are hearing this 1930s term more often these days than in the previous thirty years.

bar built like a cellar on the roof of a skyscraper. AR took us there once before, on AS 44.

Interneighborly. Google Fred Koch and Cyrus Eaton to learn about their efforts to do business in the Soviet Union during the 1920s and 30s.

southern hemisphere. AR seems to mean only the American part of the southern hemisphere, not Africa or Australia. This is AR's own Monroe Doctrine: she is concerned only with the western hemisphere.

The parties Jim goes to on these pages recall Eugene Burdick's book *The Ugly American*. This was famous and talked about, but not heeded, when it was published in 1958. It is a series of short stories that the authors say present fictional, but typical, situations involving Americans in a fictional, but typical, southeast Asian nation.

Jim Taggart makes deals with both business and political figures from Latin America. The theme here is corruption, as in the southeast Asia of *The Ugly American*. Some of Burdick's characters straddle the Communist and non-Communist worlds, surviving by being useful to both the old and the new regimes. In the terms of WTL Russia: NEP-men: the fixers in Lenin's New Economic Policy. Today they would be Putin's oligarch friends.

not as beautiful as she assumed. Ha!

AS 866

which most of those men had had no reason to seek. Does AR hint that these men are gay, or is it just Taggart sizing them up as gay?

The party had bored him. Albert Speer, in his memoir, describes the boredom of a weekend at Berchtesgaden: "We were all exhausted from doing nothing." Speer could be seen as a Stadler, since he had more brains than the rest of the Nazi leadership put together.

September 2. See AS 925. AR sets up another surprise from Francisco.

This page is devoted to Jim's crazy thinking processes. It helps to explain his final mental breakdown on AS 1144. Why does Jim feel like celebrating tonight? Because Chile is about to nationalize d'Anconia Copper mines and other properties, and Jim can sell his d'Anconia stock and avoid the catastrophe. Avoid, not avert. Taggart has dodged another bullet.

Anti-Life

unprovoked tips. This is a typical AR funny line, like "ungulfable bridge" (BB 165).

AS 867

This page is just more vivisection of Jim. We see more of the "Do they want to live?" theme: Jim's purpose is to avoid all purposes; all reality; not to live, but to escape responsibility. Where did AR get all these insights into a mind as warped as Jim's? There is a little Jim, as well as a little Dagny, in all of us. Don't you have moments when you don't know your destination, and don't want to? And don't you have other moments like Roark's "stops—points reached—and then the typing flows on again"? (TF 578)

AS 868

Ditto.

like a foghorn within him, blowing, not to sound a warning, but to summon the fog. Great line!

the severe simplicity of its lines serving as her only ornament. Compare this to Dagny's bare shoulder at Hank and Lillian's anniversary party, on AS 136. On this page, we see how Cherryl has matured quickly over a year of marriage to Jim, and has now had enough of him. And Jim is afraid of Cherryl now, because he can see that she is no longer afraid, or overawed, of him.

AS 869

The spark vanished. Don't miss this little touch. Cherryl lights up at the words "skill and timing," but loses interest when Jim adds "psychology." In his *Reason* magazine interview, NB says that AR once told him that she did not understand or like his field, psychology. It was the dark side of psychology she was thinking of. Cherryl knows that, in Jim's vocabulary, "psychology" means manipulation.

Wait till they hear about it. Jim's inner judge is, in part, Dagny, along with Hank and maybe Francisco. The people in his life who do not fear reality as he does.

control every industrial property south of the border. In Jim's description of his big deal, you see the economics of fascism, mercantilism, and what the socialists *call* capitalism. Every ism but free enterprise. AR's villains represent corruption and domination.

AS 870

That's what you've always admired, isn't it? Wealth? It depends. NOTA BENE! This is one of AR's lines that give the lie to the Bashers when they say that she cares for nothing but money. She cared for *production*. For *making* money, not just *getting* it.

I want to show you that I can do it. Contrast Jim's offer to Cherryl with Hank buying Dagny a famous ruby, on AS 367-8.

Hank wants to make the ideal real, for his own pleasure and Dagny's. Jim wants to impress and awe Cherryl with his political pull, even though he does not respect Cherryl's judgment. He is coming to fear her, though, because she is not as easily fooled as she was a year ago.

AS 871

from under his forehead. This is a mannerism of Jim's. He did it before, on AS 8. It is a Hollywood mannerism.

Can't you just see Boris Karloff or any other Hollywood villain looking up, snake-like, from under his forehead? Did AR get this from tall, skinny, balding J. Robert Oppenheimer?

as if in cynical breach of some hallowed restraint. What does AR mean here?

AS 872

Was there some big broadcast figure in the 1940s or 50s whom people were afraid of? Father Coughlin was in the 30s. He is one of the figures of that period you might look up for background on AS. If you do, notice how Coughlin decried socialism while wanting to nationalize industries. Rand mentioned Coughlin on LAR 44.

AS 873

His blow had upset his water glass. After Cherryl's line "It seems much longer," near the bottom of this page, we go into a flashback that does not end until AS 883, when we see a spreading water stain on the dinner table, and that brings us back to the present. This is another of AR's cinematic devices.

It's the date of our first wedding anniversary. Compare this line with Lillian doing the same thing to Hank on AS 35. But Cherryl is wistful where Lillian is sly.

Anti-Life

not to get scared, but to learn. We feel sympathy for Cherryl, not pity. Sympathy is compassion with respect, and pity is compassion without respect. We respect Cherryl because she knows that she has much to learn and she is trying as hard as she can to learn it.

AS 874

It was in the bewildered loneliness of the first weeks of her marriage to Jim. AR must have felt like Cherryl when she first arrived in the US, but from being a stranger in a strange land, not from marrying the wrong husband.

recapture her vision of him. Cherryl had a "man at the head of track" too! Too bad it was Jim.

AS 875

Coney Island. That entertainment mecca was starting downhill as AS was going to press in 1957.

distant headlight advancing upon her. AR will develop this simile over the next few pages. It is the inverse to Dagny eagerly waiting to meet her Man at the Head of Track. Cherryl feels a runaway train about to come down the track and hit her. The big red headlight on Frank's Atlas cover represents hope for Dagny, but fear for Cherryl. For Galt, it represents a stoplight. He promised to stop the motor of the world.

crumbling ruin of a gutted warehouse. Nice metaphor.

AS 876

"*she felt only that the headlight moving upon her had grown larger.*"
"*She had learned, in the slums of her childhood, that honest people were never touchy about the matter of being trusted.*" Two good lines in these two above quotes.

AR's fellow exile to the middle-brow ghetto, Harold Robbins, gives a similar line to George Peppard in the movie *The Carpetbaggers*: "I've learned that an honest man always asks for less than he really needs." There is no shame in writing middle-brow juvenile novels that teach young people valid lessons.

I'd like to believe that you love me for myself, not for my railroad. Jim's line and another on AS 886 came from AR's friend Isabel Paterson (BB 205.)

AS 877

Happy days are here again! The title of FDR's 1932 campaign theme song.

drug addict. When did AR ever have any experience with drug addicts? Maybe in Hollywood.

Will it knock them flat! An expression of AR's time. Compare AR's play title: *Knock Me Flat!* on TF 286.

hugging their children or their dreams. Another line that seems a bit too literary or poetic for Jim Taggart. Compare it to his line on AS 1000, where he uses a steel plant simile. "The news ran through the mills like one of those furnace breakouts." Wouldn't a railroad man say, "like a runaway train"? Is Jim Taggart the kind who would make a literary turn of phrase at all? Well, he did start in Taggart's Public Relations Department. Maybe wordsmithing, and not making trains run on time, was really his calling all along.

AS 878

They'll be brought down! They'll be—. This may be a foreshadowing of Jim's final breakdown on AS 1144. There, he is about to say that he wants Galt to die, even though he knows his own death would follow. Here, he looks like he is starting down that same crazy line of thought.

AS 879

the strain of their manner at the mention of their boss. We have seen, many times, Dagny being a good boss. Now we see Jim's opposite effect on his underlings.

The railroad workers were more specific. Notice, again, AR's respect for the working man. Just as Fred Kinnan, the union boss, is the most honest of the Washington bigshots, so the blue-collar Taggart workers are more honest with Cherryl, and with themselves, than the executives, who have to play along with the boss's lies and delusions.

AS 880

the severely literal simplicity of his words. In other words, Eddie gives straight answers. AR was herself a very literal person in how she answered questions. She then gives that quality to Eddie.

never encroaching on her emotions by any sign of concern for them. Here is a real-life example of how AR talks about a real problem. A woman called her grown daughter to give her the news that an old friend of the daughter's had killed himself. The mother cried and blubbered so much that the daughter felt that she could spare herself no grief over her friend's suicide, because she had to comfort her mother.

The daughter explained that this was an old trick of her mother's. She had done this before. The mother was, so to speak, stealing her daughter's emotions, stealing her grief and suffering. I am calling you, not to comfort you, but to manipulate you into comforting me.

Eddie respects Cherryl and her suffering, and shows it by not trying to steal Cherryl's suffering. Did AR know an emotion-thief personally?

AS 881

More development of the scene ensues. Perhaps this page could have been edited out without the reader missing the point of the scene. But on this page, Cherryl has gotten, gradually, to the point of asking Jim "Why did you marry me?"

This scene has to be this long, because of Cherryl's disbelief that the hero she had looked up to and married could be as rotten as she now sees him to be. She could not have reached this conclusion any faster. We see her illusions fall one by one. That takes time.

the rational being who was not present. This would be Cherryl's inner judge, and her Man at the End of the Track. And NB's and Carl Gustav Jung's "Higher Self."

AS 882

the brilliant fire of hero worship. If you *really* want to edit AS down, you might be left with only these words.

the gnawing drabness of pity. This is a typical Rand line. She finds unusual ways of putting things.

The one who was she . . . the passive stranger who had taken her place. This sounds like the dialog in Lord of the Rings: Return of the King, between Gollum and Smeagol. This is self-alienation. Cherryl is "of a divided mind" about Jim.

who said that they were adult. AR has always shared this young reader's dim view of the grownups.

She had to learn to understand the things that had destroyed her. AR wants us to see that when Cherryl throws herself over a parapet, she is only snuffing out the lingering heartbeat of a creature that has already suffered from brain death yet still remains alive enough to want to understand how she came to die.

AS 883

the headlight was closer and in the moment of knowledge she would be struck by the wheels. This is the headlight metaphor from AS 876.

a drying stain of water on the table. This ends the flashback that began on AS 873. That flashback was all in Cherryl's head, as she looks back over a year of trying to make sense of Jim.

In a movie, the camera would begin and end the flashback with a focus on the overturned glass. The camera would be an active teller of the story, not just a passive recorder of a stage play. This is what Alfred Hitchcock called "pure cinema, which I have always believed in." This may be one of the cinema techniques AR learned from Cecil B. DeMille.

To be loved for! This is the whole Isabel Paterson paragraph that we saw a preview of on AS 876.

AS 884

swaying dangerously between caution and some blindly heedless impulse. This is the mentality of the bully. In a sense, he *wants* to get caught and stopped. He provokes you, hoping to get a reaction out of you. He pushes you, hoping that you will push back. He wants to be told that he has gone too far.

Don't you ever feel—just feel? This reader has not heard this line, but I have heard someone say, in complete seriousness, "Can't you forget about logic for a minute and just *believe*?"

However, most people, most of the time, are too cagey to blurt out what they are really thinking.

gold-digger. This term was first used in 1911. It means a woman who cultivates marriage or mistress-hood with a man in order to get his money. The expression was popularized by movies in the 1930s: AR's time in Hollywood.

gold-digger of the spirit. Compare Toohey in TF: "I play the stock market of the spirit . . . and I sell short." TF 315, and in the Enright House party in the movie.

Anti-Life 117

Without . . . the necessity . . . of being. Cherryl hits a nerve here. The whole scene has been leading up to this moment. Here again is a premonition of Jim's final breakdown on AS 1144.

AS 885

But he had to stop, because the butler entered. This is the price you pay for being rich enough to afford servants: you have no privacy in your own home.

Scene 2: Cherryl and Dagny.

AS 886

All right, even this. NB describes a similar feeling, in his book *The Psychology of Romantic Love*, that he had after his second wife, Patrecia, died. Each day, he had a different reaction: denial, bargaining, agony, tenseness, obsessing about everything Patrecia had ever done that annoyed him.

At each stage, he felt, this is my day to experience denial. Bargaining. Agony. I have to go through every stage. Even this.

You knew it—she told herself severely. This is one of the many times in the book that we see the heroes being ruthlessly honest with themselves, and others. This is Dagny's Inner Judge.

There were no buildings near the height of her office. This was true in 1957, but not anymore, around the New York Central Building at 45th and Park.

wondering whether some invention of his own. This is one advance echo that has no later realization. Galt never reveals any such invention. It is only in Dagny's mind. Maybe this passage should go in the "naked" entry. Dagny wants Galt to see her.

AS 887

a flare of distress . . . or a lighthouse. Dagny wonders. Am I hoping to give in and join the strike, or am I still stubbornly offering my Pharos light to protect the world? This is concisely the crux of the novel.

Would you permit me to speak to you, Miss Taggart? It would be great to see two actresses perform this scene.

What a distance to travel in less than a year! Dagny is perceptive, kind and generous throughout the scene.

AS 888

a faint, tremulous crease of her mouth, as if, together, they had completed a single smile. Great line, and one I never noticed till now.

No, through our own choice. A big old sticker! I have savored this line for years.

What is important to each of us is only what each of us freely chooses for himself. Dagny is graciously choosing Cherryl for a sister. Why? Look down to the line "But that you value all the things I value . . . " Besides, poor Dagny grew up with no sisters, and only Jim for a brother. And a big brother at that. No wonder she grew up to be so self-sufficient. She must be eager to acquire a sister. See AH 93: Though she never met Frank's father, Dennis O'Connor, AR inscribed a WTL first edition to him, calling Dennis "my American father." AR must have yearned for a family to replace the one she had lost in Russia.

not because you suffer, but because you haven't deserved to suffer. Major sticker! This is a much more important quote from AR than the one currently making the internet rounds, about "who will stop me?" This is the difference between altruism and mutualism, between pity and respect, between charity and justice.

This line should be in neon lights. It should be a chapter title in books written to argue against altruism and for mutualism—the principle that one hand washes the other.

some bracing current were relaxing her features. Was there such a thing before 1957 as electric muscle-relaxing paddles?

AS 889

the only thing still left for me to do. I never noticed this line till my *fourth* reading of the book for this commentary! And Dagny missed it, too. This is Cherryl's suicide note.

Well, observe that you never hear that accusation in defense of innocence, but always in defense of guilt. Cherryl will see this on AS 906.

AS 890

You must never think that their existence is a reflection on ours. Yet elsewhere AR writes that "There is a degree of evil that contaminates even the observer." There's a theme to write on.

Anti-Life

but not by an explosion . . . the end of the world, not fire and brimstone, but goo. An extraordinary imagining of the end of the world.

The "explosion" probably comes from newsreels, and by now television pictures, of nuclear explosions. The "fire and brimstone" (sulphur) comes from the destruction of Sodom and Gomorrah in the Book of Genesis.

This top half of the page explains why Cherryl *must* commit suicide.

If Dagny could conceive of such despair, she would not have let Cherryl go home. She would knock her down and sit on her. But Dagny is not a trained suicide counselor. And there was no such thing in 1957.

AR may have been thinking of Robert Frost's line "Some say the world will end in fire. Some say in ice," from his 1920 poem "Fire and Ice," and T. S. Eliot's line from *The Hollow Men*: "This is the way the world ends/ Not with a bang but a whimper." (1925) Even before Oppenheimer started shattering worlds, people in AR's era gave a lot of nervous thought to the possibility of man destroying his own civilization, and even his own planet.

there have been centuries of philosophers. This is how people would speak if they not only read philosophy but applied it to everyday speech and action. This is how people would speak if they took ideas seriously.

Say it aloud, like the holiest of prayers. Here is one of AR's examples of investing "an old religious formula with a new and deeper meaning"—as she quotes Nietzsche in her 50th anniversary Introduction to TF.

And what is that holiest of prayers? "You know that what is, *is*." A is A. In Dagny's words of support to Cherryl, we may be hearing something of the words of support that AR gave to young friends, such as NB and BB, and the young Leonard Peikoff, and many others.

An animal knows who are its friends. That is why animals are so calming and therapeutic in nursing homes and mental hospitals.

No Jim Taggart, however crazy, can bullshit an animal, nor does he need to. The most fearful paranoiac can drop his defenses around a dog or cat.

it's great to break the spine of Hank Rearden. Shouldn't Dagny ask Cherryl what that was about? But Dagny knows to ignore Jim's hysterics.

How am I to deal with people? Ironic! That's Stadler's mantra, but with a difference. Stadler says "what can *you* do when you have to deal with people?" and Cherryl says, "what can *I* do?" Stadler is confident of his ability to beat others at their own game, and Cherryl is not.

AS 891

I wish I could wish to fight. Cherryl is too broken to survive her realization of Jim's and the world's nature. Her slum upbringing has made her too fearful to get through this crisis. She did get out of the slums, but this setback was too much for her.

AS 892

upon a few drops of fuel. This is one of AR's "man-as-machine" metaphors. *Cherryl, I don't want you to go home tonight.* See AS 890 above. Shouldn't there be a comma after the word "sway"?

She looked like a plant with a broken stem. Cherryl is a good weed. See "weeds" in the Recurring Themes index. It can be a metaphor for good or for evil.

Scene 3: Lillian visits Jim. They have sex.

Jim slumps down on a "davenport," a couch or sofa. This reader's grandmother called a sofa a "davenport" in the 1960s, but I have not heard the term lately. The farther we get in time from 1957, the more we will need a glossary to read Atlas.

Through the open door of his study. Jim has a study! Don't skip over this detail. It is one of those "humanizing" touches.

Just as AR's heroes need kitchens and bathrooms, to bring them down to earth, so Jim needs a study, to bring him *up* to earth. He can't be shown only drinking and screaming and getting hysterical. But this is a tiny, microscopic touch.

How many readers even notice it? AR should have shown Jim doing some actual, normal work, in his office. This is referred to, many times, but AR always sweeps these touches away in another burst of "I couldn't help it!"

AS 893

The sound of the doorbell startled him. This is an interesting little paragraph. AR has Jim startled by the doorbell, but she does not say

Anti-Life   121

that Jim sees any deeper perception of *why* it startles him. The deeper meaning is between Ayn and the reader.

The reference is perceptive, and it helps set up Lillian, her situation and her mood for this scene. And then this scene sets up Jim's infidelity, which sets up Cherryl's suicide, which contributes to Jim's crack-up.

I haven't run into Balph Eubank for months. Sounds like Lillian does not know as much as Jim does about who is in power and who is now out, in Washington.

AS 894

faces that look like butcher's assistants. AR pointed out that the idealists at the beginning of a revolution are later pushed aside by the Napoleons.

with the smile as license for insult. Ever been insulted by someone who dodges responsibility for the insult by smiling?

the deep shade of coagulated blood. This became fashionable at least as far back as the 1940s, and, like all nail polish colors, has gone in and out of fashion since then. It is called "burgundy." It is hard to maintain, for exactly the reason AR gives: it shows up too easily if it gets chipped.

AS 895

what made him start divorce proceedings. See AS 559: "The trip to Florida was not inexplicable to him any longer."

astonishing perceptiveness. Why would it be astonishing that an operator like Jim should be perceptive of peoples' weaknesses and how to exploit them?

AS 896

Real, stinking, hall-bedroom poverty! A hall bedroom was a 19th Century tenement bedroom that had no windows. It had only a door out to the hall. On TF 136, we read: "Dominique Francon went to live for two weeks in the hall bedroom of an East Side tenement."

worth nothing nowadays. This is AR's only hint in the novel that inflationary policies are destroying everyone's savings.

AS 897

everybody has something on everybody else. It is said that no president dared fire J. Edgar Hoover as Director of the FBI because he had dirt on everybody in Washington.

He was your friend, wasn't he? Cherryl said the same thing on AS 871.
this was the celebration he had wanted. See AS 864.

AS 898

He'd merely blame himself for not having moved out of the club's reach. This line became a sticker only on my fifth reading of the book. Never noticed it before. But it speaks volumes about the character of a man who takes responsibility for *everything* that happens to him. Even when he needn't. See AS 996. Hank does indeed get hit in the head with a club. Another of AR's subliminal advance echoes.

made sacred by his touch. AR's spirituality.

Caesar's wife. Gaius Julius Caesar's wife Pompeia hosted the Bona Dea festival at their house. Females only. A man named Clodius snuck in, dressed as a woman, to seduce Pompeia. He was tried for sacrilege.

Caesar did not testify against him and he was acquitted, but Caesar divorced Pompeia anyway, since "Caesar's wife must not even be under suspicion."

Do you remember what she was supposed to be? Pompeia, that is. Lillian is doing to Jim what Toohey does to Peter on TF 682: "Remember the Roman Emperor who said he wished humanity had a single neck so he could cut it?": That was Caligula.

Toohey, and Lillian, assume that their listeners learned these things in either World History or Latin class, or read *Quo Vadis?* by Henryk Sienkiewicz, as Ayn had. It was one of her favorite novels. We cannot assume that young people know anything anymore. Anything but computers.

AS 899

impotent hatred. AR has used the word "impotent" before, in reference to villains. This reference plants the suggestion of impotence in the reader's mind so as to reinforce the fact of Jim's literal impotence on the very next page. But what AR *really* means is that Jim is impotent of the kind of achievement Hank can boast, and so he can only lash out in hatred.

I'd like to hear him scream with pain, just once. Another premonition of AS 1144.

lay railroad tracks . . . erect bridges. AR is giving us hints, along with Jim now noticing Lillian's décolletage, that sex is rearing its ugly head. She may not have calculated putting in words like "lay" and "erect," but neither did she take them out once they appeared so close together. Perhaps she wanted to involve the reader personally in the scene, who may think, "I am seeing the not-so-subtle hint here, so maybe I am finding out something about myself. Maybe I am as smutty-minded as Jim. And Lillian."

I can't bring men down to their knees in admiration. Compare Guts Regan in *Night of Jan. 16th*: "to which one kneels." Another concept left over from religion.

AS 900

It was not an act in celebration of life. Hence the chapter title "Anti-life." This is not even sex, just envy: Jim and Lillian are both motivated only by envy of Hank. An acquaintance of Henry Ford II said, "Hank the Deuce is like a jackal: he pisses on any food he doesn't eat, just so no one else can eat it."

Scene 4: Cherryl catches Jim and Lillian in flagrante delicto, *confronts Jim, and kills herself.*

Like the Reardens, the Taggarts have separate bedrooms. This is something Old Money used to do.

a woman's hat with a feather. That and the two glasses Cherryl sees are two more Maguffins. Picture this scene as Hitchcock and his cameraman would shoot it.

Jim's voice had a tone of irritation, the woman's—of contempt. AR wasn't kidding, at the end of the previous subchapter, about the triumph of impotence. You can see here how creative polite writers used to have to be, to put sex between the lines. Today, anything goes.

AS 901

that mental chastity that recoils. Every other 20th century author wants to titillate us with evil. Only AR handles evil with tongs and gloves. Yuck. In the altruist world, evil is considered attractive. It isn't.

She had always thought of evil as purposeful. So did Alvin Toffler, until he interviewed AR for *Playboy* Magazine. Toffler asked her why she thought that the most depraved man is the man without a purpose. Don't murderers and dictators have a highly developed sense of purpose?

he could no longer say from whom. From the servants—the instinct of a man who has spent his entire life in mansions and penthouses full of ever-watchful domestics.

AS 902

would never be able to throw his deed of this night. Hank Rearden, that is. Jim compares himself habitually and unfavorably to Rearden. He envies Rearden.

AR defined envy as "hatred of the good for being the good." He would like to think that Lillian will tell Hank that Jim is better in bed than Hank is, but that did not work out. Another infuriating defeat for Jim, and his only consolation is the pleasure of torturing Cherryl. And "night," in AR's world as in Wagner's, is code for "sex," as in *Tristan und Isolde*, who yearn for night to hide their shame.

No, I wouldn't have. This is Hollywood's and the world's convention: every woman must be either a nun or a whore.

you had to love me. This is akin to Susan Alexander's climactic line in *Citizen Kane*: "Charlie Kane will do anything for you, but you have to love him."

AS 903

the headlight. See AS 876 and 883.

AS 904

It was too close to the unnamed. This is another foreshadowing of Jim's crackup on AS 1144.

not waiting to ring for the elevator. AR used this device once before: Francisco running to fix the furnace breakout on AS 456.

a littered sidewalk in a dark neighborhood. AR is once again thinking of her early uncompleted novel *The Little Street*. (JAR 20)

Why doesn't Cherryl flee right back to Dagny? She is in a suicidal mood because she sees no hope of finding anything but Jims. It is a world of Jims.

there was a thing with which one could not live. Mallory's beast, on TF 346.

Anti-Life

Why are you doing it to me? This is the question you can see on the lips of the figure on the front cover of the gold AS paperback. Prometheus, perhaps, or Atlas, looking up at Zeus and asking that question.

AS 905

social worker's from the personnel department of the five-and-ten. Did Woolworth's have social workers in their personnel department? Henry Ford had a whole department devoted to the betterment of his workers, although the unions saw these social workers as merely spies for Ford, coming into their homes.

veil of fog. This line recalls Dagny's apartment window view, that reminds her of the legend of Atlantis, on AS 633.

the reward of their achievement was martyrdom. Cherryl is going on strike against this martyrdom, just like Galt. But unlike Galt, she sees no way out but death. How different AS would be if AR had chosen a strike merely as a metaphor for death, and not as a revolution with hope for a better world! Cherryl is another Johnnie Dawes, from *Ideal*.

there was Dagny. But Cherryl is past hoping that even Dagny can save her. She figures that even Dagny is herself doomed. Cherryl is in a prison of her own making. She could go to Dagny, but she won't. In her mind, death is the only option.

the great skyscrapers in the distance. A bitter look back at the world of TF, a world that had been growing and not dying. But after the end of AS, man will begin again.

Who will write a Fountainhead for the time after Atlas—the next phase of growth and optimism for mankind?

AS 906

We have no concern for the pain of the innocent. These are the hucksters of religion, cashing in on guilt. Again, it shows the convention of guilt for any woman who is not a wife and mother. Rand herself could tell us the similarities and the differences between this "Young Women's Rest Club" and the Studio Club, an apartment building just for respectable single women, where Rand lived in Hollywood in 1926. This one sounds like what is today called a "Women's Shelter." But today the line is not "why aren't you married?" It is "What did your male chauvinist pig husband do to exploit you?" These two short paragraphs could serve as a springboard for a whole play, movie or novel. Remember that the line "We have no concern . . . " comes from Cherryl's terrified brain. It should not be taken as an official Rand position on all social workers, and certainly not today's social workers, who are professional health care workers and not Christian evangelists. This social worker is another Comrade Sonia (WTL), but in the religion racket, not the Communist Party.

She ran. These next two paragraphs are Rand's poetry. You can call her writing "wordy" if you wish—a lot of telling rather than showing—but here is the result. Rand gives us the word images of a poet. And then the bottom paragraph on this page begins "These were not words in her mind." AR is doing again what she did in Dagny and Hank's sex scene on AS 251, where AR writes "But what she felt, without words for it, was . . . ." Here, AR is showing us the words "which would have named, had she had the power to find them, what she knew only as a sudden fury . . . ."

Then the lights switched to red, dropping heavily lower. But the red lights on a traffic light are on top, not under the green ones.

AS 907

She could not deal with people any longer. See AS 890, above, for Stadler's favorite line, "What can you do when you have to deal with people?" Galt's alternative is on AS 1068: "You will live in a world of responsible beings, who will be as consistent and reliable as facts." Why? Because they have been taught from childhood that reality is their friend and not their enemy.

no voice that people would hear. AR must have thought of herself as Zola, writing his defense of Dreyfus. The writer can provide a public voice for the voiceless and reach millions.

even if this 'no' is all that's to be left of mine! This is similar to the point Richard makes to Geoffrey in the play and movie *The Lion in Winter*: The two sons think that their father the king will have them both executed for treason. Richard swears he won't grovel and beg forgiveness. He wants to go out with his head high. Geoffrey says "We've fallen. What matter the manner of the fall?" "When the fall is all there is, it matters."

Anti-Life 127

rotting water. Water does not rot. AR is shortening a phrase like "water full of rotting refuse" to just "rotting water." She is trying to be economical of words at the sentence level here. At the same time, she is laying on the adjectives, images, similes, and metaphors everywhere in the book. Why? Poetic imagery.

AS 908

till the parapet barred her way. A parapet at the end of a street would be tall enough to necessitate Cherryl climbing or vaulting over it. AR understandably does not take the time, at this climactic moment, to explain this, so we just have to fill in the wording for ourselves.

5. Their Brothers' Keepers

Chapter Overview

Jim tells Dagny that it is up to her to fix everything, as the nation's economy falls apart. This is yet another step toward her decision that she must go on strike. He also believes Taggart will have no trouble with copper after September 2, when Chile nationalizes d'Anconia Copper. But then the radio announces that d'Anconia assets all over the world have been blown up, and Francisco d'Anconia has disappeared.

Dagny and Hank see Francisco's farewell message. They plan for the Minnesota wheat harvest.

Hank hears clues that Washington is up to something. The Wet Nurse asks for a job, and Hank's brother Philip demands one. All these things are edging Hank closer to quitting. Hank begins to respect the Wet Nurse. The Minnesota wheat harvest goes to waste because of government corruption stopping transportation. Starvation spreads.

Dagny has to go to a conference of national leaders. She hears them evading the economic crisis, showing that they simply have no idea what to do about it, and instead start talking about invading Canada and Mexico. She gets a call from the Terminal: the signals are out. Trains cannot be moved in or out of the tunnels. She runs to the Terminal, calls together all the track workers, gives them instructions, and spots Galt among them. They rendezvous in the abandoned tunnels, make love, and talk. Again, Dagny says she might still defeat the looters by herself. He warns her not to try to find him. Don't let the looters' spies see them together.

130   *The Journey of Dagny Taggart*

Scene 1: The breakdown of Taggart Transcontinental. Francisco blows up d'Anconia Copper. Hank and Dagny see Francisco's farewell message.

AS 909

a slow, thin rain. One of AR's poetic descriptive paragraphs.

The men at the Division Headquarters. Like the tunnel disaster, this sequence shows how political breakdown causes moral breakdown: If you fear for your job, you learn to shift responsibility.

AS 910

telephone booth. Big enough for one person, in a store or restaurant or bar or office building lobby, or on the sidewalk, it contained a dial phone operated by inserting coins. It is a rapidly-disappearing bit of 20th century life from the era before cellphones and mobile phones. It looked like the Tardis of Dr. Who, except without the time travel capability.

her brother's office. Again, as on AS 892, we are shown a tiny, brief reminder that Jim has his normal, rational moments. In Romantic fiction, a character's only purpose is to propel the plot. This is not a character study, so we see no more of Jim's life than we need to see to advance the plot. But AR seems to assume a reader who is reading more slowly and attentively than many do.

An emergency file in her office. This was probably a management technique AR learned from A. H. Wright, the Vice President for Operations of the New York Central Railroad, whom she interviewed in 1947 at his office, while gathering material for Dagny's job.

ancestral map. The map is on Jim's office wall. But on AS 1137, the map will be in Dagny's office, not Jim's. Maybe they have one each.

AS 911

consumers' traffic. This is why Dagny was so dumbfounded on AS 837 when Eddie told her about cars ordered to Arizona to haul grapefruit. It's not that Dagny has something against grapefruit. It's that Taggart trains usually haul capital goods, not consumer goods. The shift toward consumer goods suggests a serious slowdown in the national economy.

Faulkton, Nebraska. Perhaps AR was recycling the name "Bjorn Faulkner" from *Night of Jan. 16*[th].

Their Brothers' Keepers

could not be allowed to collapse. "Too big to fail," as was said of Lehman Brothers and Goldman Sachs in the "Great Recession" of 2008. Some things never change. See the history of the British East India Company, and its role in provoking the American Revolution.

his brother's keeper. Hence the chapter title.

out of the common pool at the end of the year. See Mussolini's "Corporatist" system, and the pooling arrangement the Washington boys propose to Rearden on AS 980.

AS 912

It was some new trait in him. Jim seems more defensive and more dependent on Dagny since Cherryl's death. This is the *literal* meaning of "her brother's keeper."

Back on AS 839, Dagny noticed Jim cracking his knuckles as a sign of strain. Now the next step: he comes running to her instead of avoiding her.

AS 913

had long since gone. Compare with Galt's line about inventors being the first to go, on AS 1047.

that unknowable of mystic creeds that smites the observer for the sin of looking. AR might be thinking of the Medusa from Greek myth. Japanese parents used to instruct their kids never to look directly at the Emperor lest they be blinded. Perhaps she heard about that from her typist, June Kurusu.

horse farm in Kentucky. This is another sign that it is old-money fascists who have power in the US of the story, not Communists or socialists. Only old-money types own horse farms.

This whole page and the next are exposition on the subject of corruption. A whole book could be written on the real-life stories AR might have read in the papers as a basis for these snippets.

Voodoo. The authentic French spelling and pronunciation is *Voudou*. This is the religion in Haiti, a combination of African beliefs and Roman Catholicism. In 1957, the year of Atlas's publication, Haitians elected Francois "Papa Doc" Duvalier President. Through his expanding use of power he became President for Life. His death squad, the *Tonton Macoute*, murdered thousands, as he assumed totalitarian authority.

Having studied *voudou* in his earlier practice of medicine, he made use of it to cement his personality cult, further protected by his use of terror. In 1963 he claimed that he had placed a curse on President Kennedy, which caused the President's death. However, even before that, the term "voodoo" entered English to mean black magic used to cause harm.

the pull peddlers. AR used this title for an article in the September 1961 issue of *The Objectivist Newsletter* and in *Capitalism: The Unknown Ideal*.

AS 914

Imagine these two pages only slightly re-worded and inserted into a novel like *The Octopus*, by Frank Norris, a 1901 novel decrying "monopoly." You would not hear a peep of criticism from the lit-crit professors about AR being a bad writer or AS being too wordy or preachy ... as long as the message is anti-capitalist.

Humanitarians. See Isabel Paterson on humanitarian guillotines and Frederic Bastiat on philanthropic despotism.

shouting that man is his brother's keeper. That is this chapter's title.

when observing the awesome power of logic. Ann Druyan, in her introduction to her late husband Carl Sagan's TV series "Cosmos," spoke of the "awesome power of science." The point here is not that Druyan is drawing on AS for her wording, but that she does not have to. A is A.

the precise, mathematical execution of all the ideas men had held. Ideas matter.

AS 915

the champions of need and the lechers of pity. Comrade Sonia (in WTL) gets off on poverty. It made her feel needed. See Jim's lechery on AS 918, below.

What were they counting on? This reflects AR's Atlas theme.

tycoon. A Japanese word for a ruler. People apply old terms from the age of monarchy to businessmen. Hence "Robber Baron."

three generations. See Francisco's explanation of why he had to blow up d'Anconia Copper (that's about to happen on AS 918), on pages 617 and 765.

AS 916

This whole page is a rehearsal for Galt's chat with Mr. Thompson, such as Dagny's line "I'll merely take your orders." Especially the paragraph here starting "Give up."

AS 917

a hungry man is not free. a favorite line of all the socialist professors. This page is another discourse on the Atlas theme: Who is Jim counting on to make his life possible?

This whole page shows a great integration of philosophy and psychology—unfortunately, Jim's in both cases. Would you want to cut out the philosophy from this page when AR has shown so eloquently how Jim's philosophy and psychology are destroying the world?—even if Bennett Cerf was right in complaining to AR that Galt's speech should be cut because she has said everything in it several times before. This page advances the plot because it is another step toward driving Dagny out on strike. In these pages following her visit to Galt's Gulch we have seen her nod knowingly at each enormity of Jim's, and every disaster. She was indignant before, but now she sees each argument of the strikers confirmed. She is saying "Check. Check. Check. It's all coming true."

Dagny, I'm your brother. There's the chapter title again.

AS 918

My contentment is the measure of your virtue. You may live many years without hearing an altruist say things like this so eloquently and insightfully. This kind of high-flown language is, as Dagny knows, always said in the third person, by a professor in a book, not in the first person by a business executive who has no intellectual pretensions. Every once in a while, though, an altruist will, perhaps inadvertently, skate close to the edge of putting into words exactly what he really means.

effrontery to expound it in the first. Effrontery is AR's explanation for Jim's ethics lecture.

Actually, this is not so much out of character for Jim. He has had moments of such effrontery before, and the boarding school-and-Ivy League language to express it, as we saw on AS 877. He did start in the Public Relations Department of Taggart, so he is a word person at heart, not a logistics person like Dagny.

She wondered whether people. Here AR herself acknowledges that people do not usually say outright the things she has her villains say. This is because people are usually too cagey to come right out and say what altruism implies.

oddly lecherous anticipation. Hurting people is what Jim craves. His lechery is of suffering rather than sex.

The new head of the People's State of Chile, "who came to power on the moral slogan that man is his brother's keeper": This is the current chapter title again. For Señior Ramirez read *Presidente* Salvador Allende. (We met a Señor Martinez and a Señor Gonzales, both *Chilenos*, on AS 865, but this is a new one.) After three years of Allende's Marxist program, the inflation rate in Chile was 3,000 percent. His predecessor, Eduardo Frei, had begun the gradual nationalization of the Chilean properties of foreign copper mine owners Kennecott, Anaconda and Cerro de Pasco, through the buying of their stock. The junta that overthrew Allende never restored these properties, for all its supposedly "right wing" nature.

AS 919

the harbor, a few streets away. This is a bit of geographical poetic license on AR's part: Valparaiso, the port city, is 63 miles by air and 77 by car from Chile's capital, Santiago. Arthur C. Clarke moved Sri Lanka 600 miles south in his novel *The Fountains of Paradise*, so the island would be on the equator. This allows Clarke's hero to build, in Sri Lanka, a "Beanstalk": an elevator to orbit, which can be done only on the Equator.

the ore docks had been blown to bits. Like everyone else, AR says "dock" when she means "wharf."

the explosion had broken an electric transmitter. She very likely means "transformer."

Siam. The name of this nation was changed to Thailand in 1939, so this is another of AR's anachronisms.

Pottsville, Montana. This is not the foundry Francisco bought on AS 110. That was in Cleveland.

buried under tons of blasted rock. AR might have thought of the 1947 John Wayne movie *Tycoon* here.

had been handed their last pay checks, in cash. Checks or cash? Your professor's artificial "Ayn Rand" would have had her Francisco character blow up his properties with the workers still in them.

AS 920

not even a message of farewell. This sets us up for Francisco's message of farewell, on AS 925.

It was not a sentence, but the silent emotion of a prayer in her mind. As with Dagny's words when she and Hank began their beguine, AR is giving us the words Dagny would say if she had the time to explain her emotions.

like tiny commas squirming on the white field under the lens of a microscope. This is another of AR's similes that are so creative, so unusual, that they border on the psychedelic.

a worthy funeral pyre. This is AR's familiar Viking theme, but for Francisco this time, not Ragnar.

New York City, the only city on earth still able to understand it. This is AR's New York City snobbery. AR might as well be Fran Lebowitz.

the shadings of expressions appearing to sway and weave, as if cast by a distant flame. Look for words all over this page that use the images of fire and explosion to suggest the panic on people's faces and in their voices. That is imagery.

AS 921

victims who feel that they are avenged. This is totally unrealistic, at least in 2024. No one would feel avenged by Francisco's action. Everyone would have been in favor of nationalization of d'Anconia Copper, and every other evil corporation, for years.

a young boy still open to the enchantment of the unexpected. See the Boy on the Bicycle vignette on TF 535. Science fiction fans like to say that their genre gives them back their sense of wonder. This is AR's familiar "Youth" theme.

with their past still alive in their silent acknowledgment. This is how Dagny will relate to both Hank and Francisco after the novel is over, after the strike is over, and they are all rebuilding in a free world.

This will be what Dagny feels for her two former lovers after she has married Galt. This is a footnote to Francisco's speech to Dagny on AS 765 and Dagny's feeling of relief on AS 797.

the temple of Atlantis. We know what "temple" AR means, without needing explanation. AR calls Galt's power house a temple on AS 731.

sixty floors below. About the altitude of the Cloud Club, now long gone, at the top of the Chrysler Building, or the Rainbow Room at the top of the RCA Building at Rockefeller Center (closed from 2009 to 2014, and in 2020 during the Covid pandemic). The RCA Building was later called the GE Building, then the Comcast Building.

AS 922

two persons who dared to be certain of being right. This is leadership: Show that you are certain, and people will wonder what makes you certain. And then show that you know what you are doing, and people will follow you.

This line concludes AR's earlier fascination with the defiant rebel: William Hickman in real life, Danny Renahan in *The Little Street* (JAR 20), Bjorn Faulkner in *Night of Jan. 16th*, and Johnnie Dawes in *Ideal*. In those cases, AR, like many young, inexperienced writers, was overplotting. She was asking the reader to swallow too many flips, too many on-the-other-hands, too many qualifications on the idea of a "hero." Keep it simple.

Hank has not committed a murder. He has invented a new and better alloy. Hank and Dagny have had a sexual relationship, just like all those people who are now staring at them in a restaurant. It is much clearer in AS than in AR's earliest stories, that the hero is a hero. Not a criminal with some subtle heroism to his criminality, but an unambiguous good guy.

better ways to deal with nature. This is AR's concept of "purpose," which she had to explain to Alvin Toffler in her *Playboy* interview.

AS 923

That night, when they got Ken Danagger. This was on AS 449, the furnace breakout scene.

The effort by which. This begins the story of the Minnesota wheat harvest. AR must have been inspired by the efforts of Jim Hill, builder of the Great Northern Railway, to take care of the farmers who were his customers in the 1890s.

This issue was foreshadowed way back on AS 209, when a Mr. Ward, a harvester manufacturer, asked Rearden for five hundred tons of steel. See AS 924.

she knew what motive was still holding him to his job. In the army they say, "You may have had many different reasons for joining the army, but when you are in combat, you have only one reason to fight: to protect your buddies who are protecting you." Hank will not leave his post while his comrades-in-production are still trying to keep their companies and communities afloat.

Charity, hell! We're helping producers. This is not altruism, it is mutualism. One hand washes the other.

AS 924

the pull-peddlers. When economist Robert Reich went to Washington as President Clinton's Secretary of Labor, he gave a speech saying that the Clinton administration would undo everything done by the Reagan and Bush administrations, and that the lobbyists would hate it. At the back of the room, two of those lobbyists (AR's "pull-peddlers") looked at each other and smiled. "This guy doesn't know Washington," they said. If the Democrats undid everything they had just lobbied for, then their corporate clients would pay them to simply lobby for those favors all over again. Repeat business.

Ward Harvester Company. We met Mr. Ward back on AS 209, when he came to Rearden's office to ask for a shipment of steel.

no forgiveness is possible. Hank of the iron conscience is being too hard on himself, as usual. Why doesn't Dagny tell him so? When Hank slapped Francisco, on AS 638, Francisco said "Within the limits of your knowledge, you are right." No forgiveness is necessary for an action taken without full knowledge.

AS 925

said a woman with a schoolroom voice and a barroom mouth. Love it!

Brother, you asked for it! Ayn was searching for a farewell message from Francisco that would be relevant to the occasion and also in a style characteristic of Francisco. Frank suggested this. Ayn said

"Perfect!" and let her husband write the line into her manuscript in his own hand. Hank sees a double meaning: the message is addressed to him personally as well as to the world. No copper means no Rearden Metal—either for Hank and his customers or for the looters to loot. Asking for destruction is what Hank has been doing in this whole scene. Francisco is giving Hank the out he is looking for, and thus shows that he is still Hank's friend and comrade.

Rearden's laughter. This is the last of those heart attacks. See "Hank's heart attacks" in the Recurring Themes index.

Scene 2: Hank and Philip. Hank in divorce court. Wet Nurse asks for a real job, warns Hank that something is up.

AS 926

ocean liner . . . generators. Ocean liners are not propelled by generators, but by engines burning oil, but AR wants to get the word "generator" into the reader's head, to set us up for the torture scene on AS 1140.

a young man with a swift body and a brusque voice. Not all of the people who should be in Galt's Gulch have learned about it yet. This young man will no doubt be one of those building "modest communities on the frontier of mankind's rebirth" (AS 1067). Or maybe he will go rogue. His fate, like Eddie's, hangs in the balance.

Nobody can blame me! Are you getting sick and tired of hearing Jim say this and "I couldn't help it!"? AR means you to. She is manipulating your emotions. You may get tired of seeing AR writing those same lines over and over, but you will also get angry at Jim.

AS 927

Philip comes to the mill to spy and whine. Like Jim's whines, Philip's might seem repetitive. It's all he ever does. AR sticks him into this chapter to help lead up to the attack on the mill.

AS 928

More Philip. You have heard the slogan "Need, not greed." Here is Hank's answer.

AS 929

Can you do what they're doing? It is not rich versus poor. It is Hank and his capable, responsible employees against Philip, who thinks that his brother can just give him a job with no consequences. This was a sticker for this reader as a teenager.

entitled to a job which I must create for you? This is the *Atlas* theme.

AS 930

What do you expect to happen to me? Hank is catching on. Something may be likely to happen to him soon. Something is afoot.

AS 931

feeling for one's brother. There's the chapter title again. Dagny has Jim and Hank has Philip.

the act of treason is to let its vision drown in the swamp of the moment's torture. "Its vision" means the vision of joy. It is treason to let the suffering of the moment make you lose your desire for joy. See AS 214 and 374.

there is only pain and the absence of pain. In his lecture on "Discovering the Unknown Self," from his book *The Disowned Self*, NB wrote that some people experience only two kinds of days: bad days, on which they feel screaming pain, and good days, on which they feel nothing.

AS 932

the triumph over life, the zero! Like Jim Taggart, Philip does not desire joy or work to earn it. He aspires only to momentary relief from suffering, provided by Hank. Some teachers of fine writing frown upon exclamation marks.

It was like trying to summon emotion toward inanimate objects. AR had no interest in horses or horse racing (among many other things). Why would I bet money on "some animal's race" (AS 1053)? Like anyone else, AR could summon no emotion toward things she did not care about.

the anti-living. This is a form of a previous chapter title. It's not just people being bad at the game of living, it is people, in their fear and envy, destroying whatever *is* living.

AS 933

he saw resentment growing in their eyes. Compare this to the reaction to Roark of the people in the courtroom at his trial, on TF 723.

It was like blaming the victim of a holdup for corrupting the integrity of the thug. You have heard the slogan "blaming the victim."

AS 934

Are they planning something new against your mills? This, along with the appearance of Tony, the Wet Nurse, below, add two more steps in setting up the attack on the mill and the fate of Tony.

Not that I care. Hank is ready to be plucked.

if it's presumptuous, then just tell me to go to hell. Tony is just as obsequious to Hank as Cherryl was to Dagny. AR may be laying that on a bit thick, but it was 1957.

Okay, try it. Hank has an open mind, despite his former contempt for Tony.

If we don't use ugly words, then we won't have any ugliness. Hank remembers Tony using this formula back on AS 363.

But he saw the desperate earnestness of the boy's face and stopped, the smile vanishing. Hank, like Dagny, is not oblivious to the pain of others, and he is good at reading faces.

I don't know that I would be of much use to you. What a contrast with Philip's sulky demand for a job he is not trained for!

AS 935

looking off at the invisible vapor of rain over the flame of the furnaces. How can he see the rain if it is invisible?

deputy looter. Tony uses the word "looter" here, and Hank's lawyer did on the previous page. Is that term spreading?

Perhaps it is spreading from Hank himself, and Dagny, and maybe the strikers?

AS 936

they're getting ready to pull something here. This is another forewarning.

a tearing smile of pity. "tearing," as in paper, or "tearing," as in tearing up? Maybe both.

AR should have used "sympathy," not "pity." Hank is coming to respect Tony.

relativist, pragmatist, amoralist. AR will expand on these philosophical labels in her essays. People today use the term "amoral" all the time, always to mean "immoral." And they use "pragmatic" to mean either "practical," which is good, or "cynical," which is bad. Ideas matter to everyday life.

Scene 3: The Minnesota wheat harvest.

As Hank indicated in his last dialogue with Dagny, AR is portraying farmers, many of them poor, as heroes—heroes of creative, productive, work. But Brutus hath said that AR hates the poor.

men who had patched their trucks. This paragraph reads not only like an AR alternate version of Norris's *The Octopus*, but Steinbeck's *The Grapes of Wrath*.

advance echo. AR's use of this term here is the reason for the Advance Echoes index.

AS 937

seize all copper mines and operate them as a public utility. This was done in World War II to the coal mines, railroads and even to Montgomery Ward (see *Time's Time Capsule* book for 1944, under "Montgomery Ward" for the famous photo of soldiers carrying the head of the company out of his office.) Daniel Yergin, in his book *The Prize*, writes that railroads should be taken over and run as "public utilities." Sometimes, its hard to distinguish between doctrinaire socialists and establishment pragmatists.

Kip's Ma or Ma Chalmers. Might AR have had in mind Frances Perkins (1880-1965), FDR's Labor Secretary, and a radio show called *Ma Perkins* (1933-1960)? Frances had been a professor of sociology. "Ma" was not her nickname. Miriam "Ma" Ferguson (1875–1961) filled her impeached husband's term (1925–1927) and was elected (as her husband's puppet, as before) and served from 1933 to 1935. Former Texas Governor Ann Richards (1933–2006, Governor 1991–1995), now the subject of a one woman show *and* a rock opera, pointed out that she was not the first woman to serve as Governor of Texas.

The soybean is a much more sturdy. How times have changed on this particular issue! Today, much of Brazil is being called "Soylandia," and the Greens are against it—soy is replacing rainforest. But times have not changed a bit in the case of the content of Ma Chalmers's message. We hear this stuff every day. One economist on PBS recently said that if every nation consumed energy and resources at America's rate, the world was doomed. People around the office can be heard to say, "We are running out of trees!!!"

her voice always sounded as if it were falling in drops, not of water, but of mayonnaise. Great line!

AS 938

the greatest food for the greatest number. This is AR's play on the slogan of the Utilitarians: The Greatest Good for The Greatest Number. One devotee who was heard to use this cliche, at a Libertarian Party meeting, of all places, was former New York City Parks Commissioner Henry Stern. He said that that was his moral principle.

the peoples of the Orient. Today we are not supposed to use the word "Orient." It is just the Latin word for "East," but it has been declared tainted with European imperialism.

the People's Opera Company. AR must have been thinking of the New Deal's Federal Theater Project (1935-1939), part of the WPA: Works Progress Administration.

research into the nature of brother-love. There's the current chapter title again.

cameras, but no film. This was a common complaint in the Soviet Union. The stores were always out of some things but not others.

Air travel for private purposes had been forbidden. In the movie *The Shape of Things to Come*, 1936, socialist novelist H. G. Wells's hero sternly inform the owner of a private aircraft that "We don't approve of private aircraft."

the mind is a myth. So says Dr. Stadler. His co-optation is complete.

AS 939

This age of misery is God's punishment. One recent individual who had abandoned Orthodox Judaism recalled that she was taught as a child that the Holocaust was God's punishment on Jews who were not sufficiently observant.

thinking, logic and science. The god-peddlers are usually too cagey to come right out flat-footed and say this.

Cuffy Meigs, the man impervious to thought. AR might have gotten along without this subtitle to Meigs's name.

pistol . . . rabbit's foot . . . scorn . . . superstitious awe. This is the theme AR will expand on in the title essay of her book *For the New Intellectual*. In that essay, she summarizes Western history in terms of two archetypes she calls the Attila and the Witch Doctor: the man of action and guns, who scorns the intellectual but secretly fears him, and the intellectual, who scorns the man of guns but secretly fears him.

AS 940

Fear keeps everyone from dealing with a disaster, because they will be punished for admitting that the disaster exists. See Hitler and Stalin, especially Stalin's deliberate starving of the *kulak* farmers. When Stalin entered the theater, everyone stood and applauded for twenty minutes, they say, because no one wanted to be the first one to stop.

AS 941

More of the Minnesota harvest disaster. This is a narrative passage—for those who think the whole book is nothing but speeches.

AS 942

This and AS 943 tell the climax of the Minnesota disaster.

the Louisiana swamps. AR put Ivy Starnes in Louisiana, with looks and personality as droopy as her weeping willows. Now AR refers to the swamps of the state. Why pick on Louisiana? Between the bayous and Huey Long's dictatorial control of the state, AR and her readers both think of this state as swampy and filled with slavery, disease, and superstition. A literary metaphor. AR might have also thought of the climactic scene in the 1938 movie *Jezebel,* with Bette Davis riding off into the bayous to tend the sick Henry Fonda.

the newspapers kept silent. Civil liberties suffer when economic liberty suffers.

journal box. This is the box on the "truck" (wheel assembly) of a railroad car that contains the bearings and the lubricant that keeps the bearings and journals from overheating. The journal is the part of the axle that is in contact with the bearings.

It is probably called a "journal" because it moves, that is, journeys. This is a 19th century railroad coinage. Linguists haven't been able to come up with a good explanation for its origin.

AS 943

State Chief Executive of Minnesota. Just as AR makes Mr. Thompson the Head of the State, instead of President, so she changes this guy's title from Governor.

a progressive concern. The word "progressive", still used by the political establishment the way it was in 1957 and before that in Teddy Roosevelt's day, is code for socialist or semi-socialist.

Oriental austerity. AR referred elsewhere to the "austerity preachers behind the Iron Curtain." She angrily criticized Jimmy Carter for urging Americans to turn down the thermostats, wear sweaters, and drive less, as a way of coping with rising energy costs.

Then there was only the acrid stench. Compare the very last line of TF.

See AH 24: During World War I, AR saw or at least heard about Russian grain rotting at railroad stations for lack of transportation. So, when AR writes, in her Foreword to WTL, "I have seen the conditions of existence that I describe," she is referring not only to what she describes of Russia in WTL, but what she projects as the conditions in a USA that is starting down the road to serfdom.

Scene 4: Dagny called away from looters discussing the latest disasters. Has sex with Galt for the first time.

AS 944

the entrance to the terminal tunnels. That is at Park Avenue and 96th Street. The trains emerge out of the north side of Carnegie Hill and run on a viaduct over the Plain of Harlem.

like blood dammed by a clot inside a vein, unable to rush into the chambers of the heart. Frank's father, Dennis O'Connor, died in 1938, at seventy-four, of arteriosclerosis (AH 124). That is, his blood was dammed and could not rush into the chambers of his heart.

Ayn and Frank traveled from New York to Lorain, Ohio for the funeral. She must have gotten some impressions of a steel town on that trip. And she remembered years later having learned about what had killed Dennis. She got her similes and metaphors from all kinds of places.

make all their crucial decisions at parties. One reviewer of the 2011 *Atlas Shrugged Part I* movie wondered why so many of the scenes take place in bars. This paragraph explains why. This was even more the case in the 18th Century, when nearly all business took place in taverns.

the first step of their surrender. AR could have expanded a bit more upon this theme. It shows that there is still some method to Dagny's madness. She still has a strategy for overcoming the looters. But the reader may have, by now, waited impatiently for Dagny to see the light and go on strike.

she felt restlessly unable to accept that certainty. This is another of those inner conflicts that AR's heroes are not supposed to have, according to your professors.

AS 945

as if they hoped to gain. It is like Dagny's Coming Out party on AS 103: Do people think that the trappings of luxury will fool them into thinking they have something to celebrate? And compare Jim's wish to celebrate the nationalization of d'Anconia Copper on AS 864.

savages who devour the corpse of an adversary. AR, in a different forum, defined a "savage" as someone who had not yet learned the Law of Identity, and therefore thinks that a thing can act contrary to its nature. Devouring a corpse cannot, in fact, give you the man's strength and virtue. Building a model of a cargo plane cannot in fact make the cargo planes come back with food (the "Cargo Cult" described by anthropologists in the Pacific in World War II).

She wore a black dress. AR's heroines are all very feminine. This makes Dagny all the more admirable, sexually challenging, and modern when she is shown more than holding her own among the macho men of heavy industry. Here, she is pissed at Jim for telling her to look formal but humble at dinner, so she dresses in as gorgeous, but tasteful, a dress as she can find. The important point, though, is that this is the dress in which she will have her first sex with Galt, on AS 956 below. AR lavishes most of a long paragraph describing the dress.

like a transformer converting a flicker into fire. "Transformer" may not be the right word. A transformer raises the voltage of an electric current, but it is not supposed to start a fire. Maybe she does not literally mean an electric transformer. Mixed metaphor. An "accelerant" would transform a flicker into fire. In any case, this is another of AR's machine metaphors.

She regretted it now. Wow! Dagny regretted a decision made earlier in anger and spite. Your professors told you that AR is a bad writer because her heroes and heroines are impossibly flawless and one dimensional, and never change or grow.

Burlesque. From the Italian *burla*, meaning "joke." Originally it meant a skit that satirizes a well-known play. By AR's time it meant strip tease. The latter is said to have been invented at a bar now called Irving Plaza, on Irving Place, on the northwest corner of East 15th Street.

AS 946

the Mesabi Range. This is a mountain range in northern Minnesota. That's where the taconite comes from—iron ore. That mineral is named after New York's Taconic Mountains, where iron ore was mined in colonial times, but the Mesabi discovery put all previous iron mining regions in the US into eclipse. That's why native Minnesotan Hank Rearden gets his first job in the Mesabi iron mines. See the 2005 movie "North Country," starring Charlize Theron. A big goal that AR had for this novel was to pay tribute to American heavy industry and the men—and women—who built it.

AS 947

seceding from the union. Now we really start to see the United States coming apart. See the 1968 TV movie *Shadow on the Land*, *Seven Days in May* and others about the unthinkable: political instability in the US. That fear was another part of AR's world—the World Wars, the Cold War, dictatorships, putsches. And now we have seen January 6th, 2021.

India without any industrial development. According to the 1970 "population explosion" scare, everyone in India should have starved to death by 1980. A similar fate faced the US by 2000. Instead, India industrialized. On the subject of India and industrialization and its lack, see *Capitalism: The Unknown Ideal*, pages 84 and 113. There, AR discusses the economics books she read while researching the history of business and industry for AS.

It would be good for them. Have you heard people say, with a straight face, that another Great Depression would be good for people's characters?

In the long run, we'll all be dead. Thus spake British economist John Maynard Keynes, fashionable in the New Deal. Cuffy says it here and back on AS 843.

AS 948

Mexico and Canada. Note well! It is not AR's heroes who dream of conquest. It is not "supermen" conquering "subhumans." It is the Ship of State and its Big Business barnacles, like Jim Taggart.

This whole page shows AR's take on history: producers versus looters. This is another wordy page of AR preaching, but it is more than that. AR is showing us the inner workings of Dagny's mind. She is desperately trying to understand these powerful men. What she finds in their minds is frightening.

the industrialists had swept away. Here is a premise you could write books about.

In *Capitalism: The Unknown Ideal*, AR develops this theme of capitalism sweeping away the statism and endless tribal warfare of the past. AR's image of the indolent rajah and the starving peasant shows that she does not "hate the poor," as the Rand Bashers claim. Here you see her sympathy for the poor and her understanding of who made them poor.

they'll never produce so little but that the man with the club won't be able to seize it and leave them still less. A much better Rand quote than "who will stop me?" Delete the word "but."

feudal baron. Your professors want you to think that Jim Hill was a "robber baron." And who does Dagny find more rational than these powerful men who speak of conquest? The waiter.

AS 949

the stately lobby of the Wayne-Falkland. Batman comics always refer to "stately Wayne Manor." Did Ayn like the name "Wayne" because it contains "Ayn"? Or was she thinking of John Wayne, or Bruce Wayne, the secret identity of Batman? He would fit into her beloved "Zorro" formula for vigilante action fiction.

side mirror of a florist's window. Perhaps Ayn saw herself in such a mirror in the flower shop where Frank worked at one time. She might have written another note in her notepad, for future use!

she felt the enchantment of the full context. Full Context would later become the name of an Objectivist magazine. Who but AR would find enchantment in a "full context"? Most have never thought of it this way, but to a human being, it is enchanting to see, in your mind's eye, all the connections that lead down from the perception of the moment to the most basic premises. It makes you feel like a mechanic who has just gotten a broken machine to work perfectly.

a desolate voice kept asking her. This is Dagny's inner judge. Also, this reflection of Dagny's on the bitterness of an age where luxury has lost its meaning will be revisited by Galt on AS 959 below.

Yes! Say it honestly: what's in it for you? Even altruists must say that to themselves sometime. Dagny's reluctance to say that, even to herself, reflects her overwhelming sense of responsibility, not altruism.

the glowing entrance to the Taggart Terminal. If we recognize the Wayne-Falkland as the Waldorf-Astoria stand-in, Dagny might have found it more convenient to come out the east entrance of the hotel to catch a taxi. If she came out the Park Avenue entrance, she would be on the uptown side of Park Avenue. Besides, the ballroom elevators are at the Lexington Avenue end of the lobby, the east end. The taxi would go south on Lex from 49th Street and let Dagny off at the east entrance of the Terminal between 42nd and 43rd. It might have been just as quick to walk it.

AS 950

when the voice of her competitor came on the wire. Once again, as after the tunnel disaster, Dagny buys services from a competitor. That's the difference between a competitor and an enemy—as any "robber baron" would know.

Dagny's managerial genius is shown by the fact that she knows where to find competent men in an emergency—even among the ranks of her competitors. Perhaps A. H. Wright, Operating VP of the New York Central (AH 206, BB 219), told her of such an emergency.

the Hudson Line. This was one of the small lines either built or bought by Cornelius Vanderbilt to make up the New York Central Railroad. It runs along the east bank of the Hudson from New York to Albany—something that would not be allowed today, for environmental reasons.

Their Brothers' Keepers

AS 951

that hung in the darkness like a crown without a body. This sounds like AR means that the tower hung from the ceiling. Dagny climbs an iron stairway that goes up to the tower. There is no such suspended tower at Grand Central today.

There is a "tower," as the railroad men call it, as you walk from the concourse into the platform area. But this tower is just a small room with a bay window, so those inside can see at least a few hundred feet of the central platforms and the tracks between them. If you walk out to the very end of the central platforms, you will see another tower ahead of you in the darkness, and that seems like the one AR is describing here. It is not suspended from the ceiling, though.

The "iron stairway," which presumably is steel, not iron, goes from track level up to the tower. The NYCRR was incredibly happy, in 1947, to show all this to a novelist who was writing a novel about a railroad. Free publicity! Perhaps in those days AR saw a tower that looked more like the one here, but has since been dismantled, as the traffic controllers have come to rely more on electronics than line-of-sight visibility of these vast, dark tunnels under Park Avenue all the way from 42nd Street up to 96th Street. There, at 96th Street, in the daylight, you can still see a tower that looks like a tower.

though he had made no comment. Notice how observant Dagny is, and sensitive to the feelings of the people she is talking to.

dried channel. AR must have seen, out west, many rivers with "braided channels." Thirty or forty tracks, side by side under Park Avenue, but with little traffic, reminded her of those dry riverbeds of the southwest, with a trickle of water in only one channel at a time.

The wall of the relay room looks like the wall of a library, lined with books, and a protruding lever looks like a bookmark. That is AR thumbing her nose at the professor who scorns the practical men who make the trains run on time (which Mussolini promised to do and didn't, by the way).

no chance, no contradiction. Again, AR wants us to see the connection between abstract philosophy and everyday life.

AS 952

like the glass beads for which another breed of savages had once sold the Island of Manhattan. The lobby of Ely Jacques Kahn's Squibb Building at 5th Avenue at 58th Street displays on the lobby wall a mural of a powwow of Dutch and Indian figures with the number "24" in the center. This may the place, or one of the places, where AR got the idea for this line.

The figure of 24 dollars was estimated by someone in the 19th century as the value of the sale and probably has no relation to the buying power of 1626, let alone to the value *to the Indians* of what was offered to them by the Dutch West India Company. The deed of sale, or treaty, of Manhattan Island was later lost, so all we know is that the island was bought "for the value of 60 guilders." But 60 guilders worth of what? Four years later, the Company bought Staten Island for useful things like kettles, axes, hoes, and wampum. A good guess is that Manhattan was bought for similar trade goods.

When AR refers to 'glass beads," she should write "abalone shell beads," because that is what wampum was made of, although the Company may have traded any kind of bead that could be strung on strings of deer hide to make a belt of wampum. These belts were accepted by all the nations of North America as money, but they also were carefully preserved as records of treaties. The local chiefs would have shown them to the visiting chiefs of more distant nations as proof of the Lenape treaties with the Dutch.

Those peace and trade treaties would have given the Lenapes great leverage over more distant nations, since the Dutch had guns, making them a powerful ally. So, the Lenape probably valued the wampum and trade goods more than the privileges the Dutch got on the island through that deal. But since the treaty does not survive, we do not know exactly what those privileges were.

The treaty obviously did not mean that the Lenape on the island had to leave it, since many continued to live on the island for decades. So, the truth about the sale of Manhattan is far more complicated than either AR's description of "savages" or Comrade Professor's "White Imperialism" screed.

Their Brothers' Keepers   151

Yes, brother! Would a flawed hero be more realistic? There it is. AR says that Dagny "could not resist it." Dagny is venting her anger, fear, and impatience on the signal engineer. Her anger is directed at philosophy's influence on the everyday life and decisions of the non-philosophical, which is a good point that AR makes all over the novel. But it is misplaced here, since the signal engineer is hardly responsible for the epistemology taught in the modern classroom. AR knows this, so she apologizes for Dagny's fit of pique. It would be unrealistic, though, to *never* show Dagny losing patience, given the stress and strain she is under. Compare her snapping at Jim on AS 196.

AS 953

as its last memorial statues. An effective metaphor.

exhaustion of a labor that required no thought. AR urges us to take pride and pleasure in mental work, rather than valuing the privilege of lounging while peasants work for you, which is what our medieval ancestors valued. This is AR's modern American view of work. See Speer on AS 866.

the younger men who could now seek no chance to rise. Because of Directive 10-289.

but with the heavy indifference of convicts. Ayn and Frank saw a chain gang working on a road as they drove through Virginia. This sight inspired her quarry scene in TF.

she threw her cape back. Rational thought and effort are supposed to be rewarded with luxury. Only in the topsy-turvy world of altruism are there movies, like *It's a Wonderful Life*, where the hero is punished with duties and drudgery and denied the chance for the creative, productive, exciting life he had dreamed of.

AS 954

his weightless way of standing. In *The Romantic Manifesto*, AR explains that the theme of ballet is weightlessness, and that of Indian dance is bonelessness. (She was uninformed about the latter.) If ballet is a sort of pantomime of weightlessness, Galt has the knack even when he is standing still.

a hypnotic order given to herself. Hypnosis was often used as a dramatic device in movies in the 1950s, but its power to coerce was exaggerated. See the 1962 movie *The Manchurian Candidate*. George Axelrod wrote and produced it. See Bennett Cerf's memoir, *At Random*, for a funny story about Axelrod and AR.

a form of defiance against him. Dagny enjoys feeling overpowered by the mere sight of Galt, but she also enjoys fighting back and defying him. This is sexual challenge, going both ways between Dagny and Galt.

She felt as if. Read this extraordinary paragraph slowly. AR shows how the meaning, the implication, of entering the terminal tunnels sums up, for Dagny, the meaning of her life. She has always become excited with a sense of purpose and of her own future when entering the tunnels on a train. Now, in those same tunnels, there he is: the man she has always been looking for.

the sight of his face was like a speech in the form of a pressure at the base of her throat. Odd simile. AR means that seeing Galt's face suggests whole reams of meaning and consequences to Dagny, which she might put into words if she had the time.

AR gives us some of that speech on this page. AR's working in the word "speech" here is another one of those sneaky "advance echoes" of hers, since a speech is what we are shortly to hear from Galt. AR will mention this "speech" again on the next page.

AS 955

he had been the meaning and the promise. Galt is Dagny's "man at the end of track."

no, not by her wish, but by its total rightness. If AR had been a typical 19th century Romantic, Dagny would be living in a romantic fantasy where her wish would be fulfilled just by being her wish. But this is Ayn Rand, not a Spanish language Magical Realism writer, like Jorge Luis Borges, Mario Vargas Llosa, Isabel Allende, or Guillermo Del Toro. Dagny will get her wish just because she knows her own nature and Galt's, and she knows that he will act in the only way his nature allows. A is A.

The notorious wordiness of these two pages serves a dramatic purpose in that it gives us, the readers, plenty of time to imagine what will happen on the next page.

AS 956

the roots of the city. AR returns to Dagny's vision of the tunnels as the hollow roots of the tree-like skyscrapers of the city (AS 18), but now she adds Dagny's vision of herself and Galt as the nourishment brought through these roots.

the beat of the city. AR may have gotten this image from Stephen Vincent Benét writing of the beat of the city, "like a man's heart," in "The Place of the Gods."

as he had seen her for the first time. on AS 776.

the place that was its source. You find meaning in everything, if you pair up, in your mind, that which makes it possible with that which it makes possible.

When you are working hard, think of the luxury and security your hard work will make possible, and when you enjoy luxury, think of the hard work that you did to make the luxury possible. That way, Church and State will not be able to get you to submit to taxation and manipulation through guilt.

Then she was conscious of nothing. This paragraph brings together, integrates, even more than the Dagny-Hank sex scene, the physical pleasure and the meaning of that pleasure.

AS 957

radiant greed. Dagny.

driving greed. Galt.

Then she felt the mesh of burlap. This paragraph is, simply, "Liebestod" (from Wagner's opera *Tristan und Isolde*). Listen to the orchestra-only version, no vocals.

her teeth sinking into the flesh of his arm. See AS 253. Dagny is a biter, and so was Hank, AS 253, and Kira, WTL 121.

under the ground under your feet . . . your office at the top of the building. Compare this to AR's chapter title "The Top and the Bottom" in Part I, especially the point on AS 956 above about what-it-makes-possible. Think of Roark working in the quarry versus Dominique in her mansion, Eugene O'Neill's play *The Hairy Ape*, and other literary and cinematic images that contrast the vertical with the horizontal, or the high with the low.

In a transcript of a a discussion between François Truffaut and Alfred Hitchcock, Truffaut admires the contrast in *Psycho* between the Victorian verticality of Norman Bates's house with the Ranch Style horizontality of the Bates Motel.

AS 958

not with my eyes, but with the palms of my hands. Roark says something similar.

John, that night. AS 221, in the alley. Why does it seem so startling to hear Dagny call Galt "John"? Why does it seem natural to speak of Hank and Francisco, but to call Galt by his last name?

it was you, all my life. Albert Ruddy, producer of *The Godfather*, approached AR in 1972 about filming Atlas. He told her that he saw *Atlas* as a love story. AR replied, "That's all it ever was." This is the line where you see that Dagny has found her imagined "man at the end of track." Galt's recruiting of Dagny for his strike runs parallel to his falling in love with her, and she with him. It makes sense that he would be romantically attracted to the woman Francisco has warned him would be the toughest one to persuade to go on strike.

I knew it anyway. Odd that Dagny does not ask Galt *how* he knew it. These two pages are about the pain of the man whose face shows no pain, fear, or guilt.

AS 959

a manner of overbearing timidity. One of AR's insightful paradoxes, like the one on the first page of TF: "The water looked immobile, the stone, flowing." Today, "overbearing timidity" would be called "passive aggressive behavior."

I saw the world as he made it look. This is why AR called one chapter about Hank "The Man Who Belonged on Earth."

I saw that the world he suggested, did not exist. AR wants you to read the book out loud. That comma would give you pause. AR might instead have italicized the *he suggested.*

that it was right. In the same sense that Dagny finally consummated her love for Galt here in the terminal tunnels seemed right. Compare this line with what Francisco said to Dagny in the valley after he learned about her and Hank (AS 765), and to what Hank said to

Dagny after guessing from her radio speech that she had met the "man at the end of track" (AS 860).

If *Atlas* had been just about railroads, AR might have called it "End of Track" or "Clear Track Ahead."

Dagny, it's not that I don't suffer, it's that I know the unimportance of suffering. I had thought this line was in Francisco's speech to Dagny in the valley, but it is on the same point. All three, Francisco, Hank and Galt, have suffered the loss of Dagny. They all learned to stoically put up with it and move on.

AS 960

Do you see why I laughed as I did? He laughed on AS 760, at the thought that Dagny was to be his domestic servant while he was her lowest track laborer.

a smile of pure gaiety. Galt can smile with pure gaiety! Who knew?

Atlantis. Galt has not referred to the valley as Atlantis before.

error of your sight . . . optical illusion. This is a good simile.

darkest bottom of the underground. There is our "top and bottom" image again.

I love you more than my life. He means that literally. See AS 1091. But since it is only his life that makes his love for Dagny possible, how does this remark fit in with our what-makes-it-possible principle on AS 956 above?

my life might have to be the price. A dramatic point. So, this scene is not just another philosophical lecture by Galt. NB said, in his talk "*Love and Sex* in the Philosophy of Ayn Rand," "Five minutes after sex, Galt is back on his horse, talking like a philosopher again. I have reason to believe that Galt has a great many imitators around the country, and I'm here to tell you that it is driving wives and girl-friends crazy."

This line got a laugh, but reading this passage now, carefully, do you think NB is justified on this point?

Galt's long exposition about Hank is not a lecture. It tells Dagny something she needs to know about how he feels toward Hank. It is something they need to sort out before they can go any further in their relationship.

AS 961

I could not let this kind of moment pass us by. This must have been what Ayn and Nathaniel said to Frank and Barbara in talking them into reluctantly agreeing to the affair.

and if my life is the price, I'll give it. Here, Galt is skating close to Johnnie Dawes territory (in *Ideal*). He is willing to trade longevity for the ecstasy of one half-hour with Dagny. Willing to trade quantity of life for quality. Ian Fleming asked a fellow spy, during World War II, how he could make himself keep going back into enemy territory at the risk of his life. The spy replied "It's not how long you live that makes a life, old boy. It's what you pack into a life that counts."

My life—but not my mind. This line recalls the scene in *Gandhi* where Gandhi tells a crowd "They may beat me. They may break my bones. They may even kill me. Then, they will have my dead body. Not my obedience!"

Would you like me to repair that interlocking signal system? Galt may have something besides bravado up his sleeve: Here he is tempting Dagny, and forcing her to choose between him and the corrupt world. He is not just passively waiting for her to go on strike. He is pushing her.

I think that they're crumbling. Here is the conflict between Dagny and the man she loves, intensifying the sexual tension between them (because "a love story is all it ever was"): Dagny still thinks, even now, that the looters will disappear and she and Hank and a few others can pull another rabbit out of the hat, as they did with the John Galt Line. Like Ayn's father, she thinks that the "great, silent majority" (Nixon's phrase) is still sensible and will somehow get rid of the looters.

I can't let it go! Eddie will say "Don't let it go!" on AS 1165 and 1166.

what I've endured and wanted to spare you. If Dagny had not crashed in the valley, she would never have heard of Galt until his speech, and would not have met him until she was ready to take the strikers' oath. He would have knocked on her door, as he did with Ken Danagger.

Don't come to my home. That is exactly what she is going to do, after the speech. AR is again planting a suggestion in the reader's mind that will, perhaps subconsciously, set him up for AS 1086.

AS 962

chalk a dollar sign on the pedestal. Compare this to the passage in Charles Dickens's *A Tale of Two Cities* where a French revolutionary chalks or paints the warning "It is later than you know!" on the pedestal of a public clock.

temple of Nathaniel Taggart. Near the beginning of *Citizen Kane*, we see a sort of temple to the memory of Kane's banker. This is another example of modern man finding "new and deeper meanings" in "old religious formulas." See TF 50th Anniversary Edition Introduction.

its changeless light beating down on a deserted stretch of marble. Actually, the light in the Grand Central concourse *has* changed. In 1990, the City passed an ordinance requiring taxis and other vehicles in front of the Terminal, on East 42nd Street, to turn off their engines while standing. They are no longer allowed to idle. Within days, the air quality around, and inside, the terminal improved markedly. But that meant that the beams of sunlight coming through the windows do not appear any more, as they used to in old photos. Sunlight needs something in the air, like smoke, to reflect off, if a sunbeam is to be visible. The marble floor, of course, was a bit more deserted during the Plague Year 2020.

dust-smeared cape. Any terminal worker seeing her on the tracks or on the platform or in the concourse would have wondered about that.

Statue of Liberty . . . a red lantern that stopped the movement of the world. These are perfect images for this moment. This metaphor is appropriate to a railroad, and to Mulligan putting the Statue of Liberty on his gold coins in the valley. And Dagny is thinking this while sitting under the statue of Nat Taggart. But AR does not explain how Galt can disappear for half an hour with Dagny just when he knows the Tower Director is about to call his name and assign him duties.

6. The Concerto of Deliverance

Chapter Overview

The Unification Board slips new workers into Rearden's mills. The newspapers predict violence. Philip is spying on Hank and reporting to a lobbying group whose head reports to Tinky Holloway, of the Unification Board, a stooge of Orren Boyle, Rearden's competitor. Holloway invites Rearden to a conference in New York.

Philip, Lillian, and Rearden's mother all seem anxious that he go to that meeting. Hank knows this will be a trap, but he does not care anymore. Mouch, Taggart and the others propose a Steel Unification Plan. Rearden walks out and drives back to his mills. He sees them aflame. He sees a body beside the road. It is the Wet Nurse, who tells Hank that the government has staged an attack on the mills. Boyle and the others at the meeting are involved. They shot him to keep him from squealing to Rearden. He dies. Hank walks into his mills and is knocked out with a club. He comes to in his office and learns that a new foreman has taken charge of the defense of the mills. That foreman enters, and he is Francisco. Francisco gives Hank the "Strike Speech."

AS 963

AR sets up the coming *pogrom* against Rearden's steel mill. AR always refers to Hank's steel *mills*—plural—but she never mentions any plant but the one he works at outside Philadelphia. See the US Steel Fairless plant, on the Delaware River between Philadelphia and Trenton. That must have been about the location AR had in mind.

The Unification Board is able to manipulate both the Rearden Steel Workers Union (see AS 554 on Tom Colby, the head of this "company union") and the media, and prepares for both staging the attack and blaming it on Rearden. Compare the Reichstag fire, *Kristallnacht*, and the storming of the Capitol by Trump supporters on January 6, 2021.

Inequalities. What news story today does not end with a solemn finger-wagging about "inequality"?

AS 964

tuyères. We saw that French word for nozzle on AS 32. A tuyère is a water-cooled copper nozzle through which oxygen is forced into a blast furnace. It is one of many iron-working terms that slipped into English from French after 1500.

upsetting a ladle of molten metal within a yard of five bystanders. Maybe this was something she heard about at Inland Steel, in Chicago, or Kaiser Steel in Fontana, California.

wistful tenderness. Is this based on Ayn's feelings toward her family back in Saint Petersburg? She did not know for sure, but as she wrote this around 1950, Ayn figured that her family members were all dead. "What one feels for the dead is that no action is possible any longer": If so, this line provides a great insight into Ayn's personality, and it confirms what we know about her already: she was a creature of action. She was concerned about her family and so she had to act—she had to stay in touch with them and get them out of the Soviet Union. But Stalin stopped all communication in or out of the Soviet Union in the 1930s, and Ayn never saw her family again, except for her sister Nora. That story is told in BB and AH.

Have they? Hank is, in a way, already on strike at this point.

gold-haired pirate. see Ragnar back on AS 571. And Jim Taggart will mention the safe on AS 1000.

whose voice seemed to come sliding down the wire on its knees. Ha!

red tape. In the days when General Washington had secretaries, like Alexander Hamilton, to hand-copy letters, one copy would be sent by an aide on horseback to its intended recipient, and another copy was rolled up and tied with a piece of red tape (ribbon), and

The Concerto of Deliverance   161

filed in a trunk on the floor of the General's office. "Red tape" came to mean government or other paperwork. Red tape was used by other governments as well.

AS 965

This one did not seem to slide, but to bounce on the telephone wire. The first one apologized, the second one wheedles.

AS 966

That's what my punk told me. On AS 925, Philip snooped around. Now we know why.

"Punk" first meant a prostitute, then a small-time gangster, then a boy used by a male as a sex object, then an inexperienced boy. It also has meant wood that is so crumbly that it is useful only as kindling. By the time AR died, it was the name of a genre of pop music: Punk Rock.

The punk was Philip Rearden. Notice that AR does not give each side in this dialogue a separate paragraph. She wants us to read it quickly. It is not important enough dramatically for the usual paragraph drops. A punk paragraph.

set foot inside his mills. Around 2015 or so, everyone started saying "step foot," confusing two expressions: "step inside" and "set foot inside."

AS 967

On the morning of November 4. This is another poetic paragraph. It goes in the "smile of morning" entry in the Recurring Themes index. See the TF cover painting: Frank's impression of a sunrise that he and Ayn once saw in San Francisco.

It's got to be today. Even Hank's mother is in on the plot?

AS 968

a touch of tension in the air of the mills. More build-up for the coming attack.

of his guilt toward himself. He still feels guilty; the only difference now is that where he used to feel guilty of injustice toward his family, he now feels guilt for his ten years of injustice to himself.

blackmail-through-virtue. This is what AR meant by the Part II chapter title "White Blackmail."

on the city pavements. Today, calling the sidewalks the "pavements" is a British usage. Was that term used that way in 1957? And it is Hank's mother saying it—one of the older characters in the novel.

there had never been much love between Lillian and her. This reader does not remember that fact being established earlier, not that it is hard to believe about all three of these wretches (including Philip).

AS 969

AR develops the themes of Hank's family...

AS 970

...and carries them over to this page.

AS 971

Will it change the past? There is a difference between giving a sinner a second chance (if you think he might yet straighten up and fly right) and pretending that the past never happened. Which one does Hank's mother mean by "forgiveness"? Which meaning do you hear in most people's use of the word "forgiveness"?

A year ago, Rearden would have felt pity. The Atlas theme.

AS 972

errors of knowledge ... conscious evil. Every proponent of a moral system faces this problem. Errors of knowledge can be forgiven; knowingly doing evil can't. The Communist Party resolved this by trying members for deviationism. So did AR's inner circle (AH 266, BB 270).

So that's what you're afraid of. Another step toward Atlas's final shrug.

AS 973

the niche of the farthest window. Where he first met Francisco (AS 145.)

brother-cannibal love. Another of those notorious wordy explanatory paragraphs that some think can be done away with. But this reader sees them as AR's way of telling a story. She used them to set up the next dialog scene. If she had used dialog instead, the novel would probably be *three* thousand pages long.

We want to live! the Life-is-not-their-purpose Principle.

AS 974

And that's why you had to see me today. Hank has figured out his family's part in the plot, but he still does not see the *pogrom* coming.

The Concerto of Deliverance

the morning when she had learned the name of his mistress. on AS 525.

The sight of her face struck him like a last shred completing a circuit. AR's "man as machine" theme, and Isabel Paterson's "circuit" image. But you don't think of a shred as completing a circuit. Still, AR has a knack for making a mixed metaphor work somehow, like the article where she refers to a chicken hiding its head in the sand, and then adds in parentheses "(the ostrich is too big and dignified a bird for this metaphor)." This is in one of her essays.

Look at the bottom paragraph. AR's long explanation suggest similarities to ancient and medieval epic poems, like Homer's *Iliad* or the *Nibelungenlied*. AR practices old-fashioned narrative storytelling, but she writes plenty of dialog too. And when she writes dialog, you never have any trouble telling who is speaking at the moment.

AS 975

She had set out to break him. In TF, Dominique gets over this pattern of infantile behavior eventually. Toohey does not.

the vandal who smashed a statue. AR must have been thinking of Dominique here too. But in 2024, you might be reminded of the Taliban in Afghanistan blowing up Buddhist statues just because they were not Muslim.

the murderer who killed a child. AR must have been thinking of William Hickman (JAR 20-25) and Bruno Richard Hauptman, the Lindbergh baby kidnapper, "as if the murderer who killed a child were greater than the mother who had given it birth". What a nice line.

her desire to see him drunk, just once. There is no line earlier in the book where Lillian says anything to this effect. But it fits with everything we know about her.

her attempts to push him into infidelity. These are suggested obliquely on AS 144, 230, 385-6, 423, 524 and 525.

as if . . . his depravity would give her a right to hers. That's why a drunk always insists that others get drunk with him.

AS 976

the moral stature of one is at the mercy of the action of another. Oddly enough, you can find this principle dramatized in a TV show called *The Courtship of Eddie's Father*. Eddie has a chance to meet his idol, astronaut Gordon Cooper. A slimy corporate type wants Eddie's father to allow him to televise this meeting for filthy corporate gain. Eddie's father refuses.

The visitor tells Eddie's father that his company will make a large donation to charity, but only if he allows this televising. Eddie's father shakes his head and says, "You can't drop the problems of the world on me," or something like that.

He says that with a level look, and no sign of guilt or fear. The principle is that Eddie's father refuses to believe that he can be held morally responsible for an action of anyone else, such as this company. The episode, in the show's second season (1970–71), is called "Dear Mr. Cooper." We will see this principle at work again when Galt meets Mr. Thompson, on AS 1114. Reality is objective. Anyone, even a TV writer, can independently discover the same moral principle and use it in fiction.

the destruction of Lillian. This is the end of the last appearance in the novel of Lillian, Philip, and Hank's mother.

I would have forgiven the past. See AS 971 above on the subject of forgiveness. Hank would forgive their past behavior if they changed it. The future is more important than the past.

like two sunsets ending the day. Nice visual.

the greatest industrial achievement in the history of man. We are losing that image of New York City today. It may have been the star city of the world in the 20th century, as London was in the 19th, but there is too much competition right now. Dubai jumped out in front by 2020, but a hundred other cities all over the world are vying for the title of either the biggest, the typical, or the outstanding world city of the 21st century.

its only meaning was that which it meant to him. This echoes *Anthem*: "It is my eyes which see, and the sight of my eyes grants beauty to the earth." Also, see the Bennett Cerf bracelet story on AS 156.

AS 977

as if he were seeing it for the first time—or the last. "You only live twice. Once when you are born, and once when you look death in the face"—Ian Fleming.

The Concerto of Deliverance

The rest of this page is the familiar contrast of straight talk by one of AR's heroes and evasive baloney by the villains. Rearden does not mention it, but he is meeting here with Wesley Mouch, the very Washington lobbyist who had betrayed him back in Part I.

AS 978

what clout on my head. "Clout" means a blow, especially with the hand. Before that it meant a rag used as an archery target. The CPUSA used to have a slogan: "Vote Communist! The vote with *CLOUT!*" In that case, it meant power.

the general welfare. Much has been made, by the government welfare crowd, of the "general welfare clause" in the Constitution. But there is no such clause. "Promote the general welfare" is one of the promised benefits of the whole Constitution, promised by Gouverneur Morris, Secretary of the Constitutional Convention, in his Preamble.

He wrote that. He merely meant that constitutional government was better for the general welfare than total, irresponsible monarchy. In Hollywood, AR knew a writer named Gouverneur Morris, a descendant of the original.

AS 979

a vacant tennis court . . . answering his shots. See why AR described Tinky on AS 977 as a tennis player?

They are leading up to . . .

AS 980

The Steel Unification Plan! This is Mussolini's "Corporatism": You and your competitors will pool your profits. Tinky Holloway throws in the familiar slogans "dog-eat-dog" and "from each according to his ability, to each according to his need." FDR's economic advisor Rexford Tugwell was an open admirer of Mussolini and some parts of the New Deal went along these lines.

as if looking at a not too distant distance. Ha!

AS 981

Associated Steel owns 60 open-hearth furnaces. This paragraph has lots of numbers. Picture it with all these numbers written out. Would that help or hurt the expression of the whole idea of the paragraph?

Is Hank doing all this math in his head? He certainly knows some of these figures. If he needed a note pad to do the sums, why didn't AR say so? Was this deliberate, or an oversight? It wouldn't have interrupted the flow of the paragraph to say he did.

Perhaps Hank sat in a chair next to a table—this is Francisco's old luxury suite at the Wayne-Falkland hotel—with a notepad on it, with the letterhead of the Wayne-Falkland on every sheet. If you filmed this scene for a movie, you might show reactions on the faces of the men in the room as Hank does his figuring. You might have a quick close-up of his hand scribbling on the pad. It would look like the scene in the *Fountainhead* movie where Gary Cooper sketches while Raymond Massey waits.

AR's math is correct! 27,000 tons divided by 80 furnaces is 337.5 tons per furnace per day. Hank's 20 furnaces will mean he is paid for 6,750 tons per day.

Boyle's 60 furnaces, assuming they are all in use, mean he should be paid for 20,050 tons per day. I just did these sums on a pocket calculator, and of course those did not exist in 1957.

One of AR's teachers urged her to take up mathematics as a profession, since she was so good at it. Could she have done these calculations in her head? Does she imagine Hank doing so? It's impressive to see a writer also being a math whiz. Equal talents in words and numbers.

Nothing suggests a businessman, and an efficient one, like figuring tons of output on a pad. So, this scene is a perfect reinforcer of all that we already know about Hank. It helps his characterization. Perhaps Hank already did the calculations before the meeting, anticipating just this kind of pooling proposal.

And this is what any kind of "pooling" scheme comes down to. Inside every "we" there's a "you" and there's a "me."

preserving the country's natural resources—like factories. AR pointed out this tendency elsewhere to call people and their productions "natural resources" or "national resources."

Such a reference, perhaps from New Deal propaganda, must be somewhere in her Horror File.

AS 982

let Orren Boyle go broke. Free market economists and real businessmen urged the government to let Chrysler go broke. However, in 1979, Chrysler's president, Lee Iacocca, got the government to bail him out with a billion-dollar loan guarantee. See also the favors bestowed by the British government on the East India Company in the 1760s and 70s: one of the provocations of the American Revolution. Too big to fail. This came up before, on AS 911.

equalize the sacrifice. In the 1970s, this reader kept his own "Horror File" (see "Is Atlas Shrugging?" in *Capitalism: The Unknown Ideal*). I clipped a newspaper article in which George Meany, of the AFL-CIO, used those exact words.

That's why all this current talk about AR predicting 2008 or 2024 back in 1957 is bunk. She was not in the prediction business. She was not Jean Dixon. She was in the satire business, and satirized the kinds of government/corporate corruption one could find in 1957, 1757, or any previous year. There is nothing new in any of this.

AS 983

I can get away with it. The key to Trump.

that I am your friend. Francisco was tempted to call and save a ship loaded with copper for Hank's mill from being sunk by Ragnar, on AS 495.

without right to feel. Why?

AS 984

A year ago they would have shot him. Directive 10-289 meant full-tilt fascist economics and the beginning of a fascistic loss of all personal freedom. So maybe the persons in charge would have ordered him shot, or, more likely, they might have jailed him for desertion if he tried to disappear like Danagger.

However, as his trial proceeded, they began to realize that he would be more useful and less trouble if they corrupted him, because after Wyatt and Danagger disappeared, Rearden or Dagny might be the next to go.

In the movie *Becket*, the titular character advises King Henry, "A successful occupation does not crush. It corrupts. You must never drive your enemy to despair. It strengthens him. Kindness is better politics. It saps virility."

AS 985

you're conditioned that way. As AS was going to press, B. F. Skinner and his Behaviorist school of psychology began challenging Freud's popular Psych 101 cant. "Conditioning" became the word of the day.

tumbril. According to Webster, AR means "tumbler": a part of a lock that has to tumble into place before the lock will open. "Tumbril" means a farm tip-cart or the cart in which a victim is carted to the guillotine. You see that word a lot in Dickens's *A Tale of Two Cities.*

All those damned People's States. Someone said, around the time of World War II and AR's writing of this book, that anyone fleeing war, tyranny and corruption anywhere else in the world can always hope to get to the US. But if those evils come to the US, where can its own people hope to escape to?

mooch. See Wesley Mouch on AS 130 above.

you businessmen have been predicting disasters for years. AR also found a clipping for her Horror File to match this line, and quoted it in "Is Atlas Shrugging?" "Every time we went to the well, there was something there."

This is where your professor will show you a chart showing that one percent of the people own 99 percent of the nation's wealth and 99 percent own one percent, or some such ratio. He will tell you that the Laffer Curve has been discredited and that government can tax the rich up to 100 percent with negligible braking of the economy. The rich can be taxed enough for any amount of government spending.

What *Herr* Professor *Doktor* will not tell you is that government will not stop at taxing the richest one percent. They will tax the top two percent, three percent, your percent, every percent. This is where the debate has to be joined.

AS 986

the unsolved wounds of his life, the unbridled shapelessness. Three more mixed metaphors, but they work: you can see what she means.

a steel door dropping open at the touch of the final tumbril. This is the moment of Hank's going on strike.

The Concerto of Deliverance   169

All the clues he grasped throughout the novel have brought him closer to grasping that the unbelievable has happened, people really expected him and people like him to clean up their messes and make the unworkable work.

Notice that AR says that this was "only a sentence he had heard all his life." Sometimes there is a connection you never make, and then suddenly you make it, the hundredth time the lesson is repeated. And notice that AR uses steel metaphors for steelmaker Rearden.

This is an action paragraph. It may not look like James Bond throwing an electric cable and electrocuting Oddjob, but it is action: the action of Hank's *mind* solving a problem. The book's theme is: the role of the mind in man's existence. AR's action sequences naturally look like Miss Marple, Sherlock Holmes, or Perry Mason reaching a mental conclusion and solving a mystery.

Who is the guiltiest man in this room? See AS 417.

he, the rationalist. Notice the lower case "r" on "rationalist," meaning a rational person. But the upper case "Rationalist" means something different. It is the name of a school of philosophy.

AS 987

volumes of muddy philosophy. Ideas matter.

with no further activity of soul. See the novel *Hanta Yo*, by AR's friend Ruth Beebe Hill, set among the Dakota nation. Look in the glossary for the Dakota term *taku shkan shkan*: "something-in-motion; spiritual vitality." See AH 178.

But he felt as if he were speeding down a skyway suspended and coiling in empty space. He is! It's the Pulaski Skyway, between Jersey City and Newark, on the way from New York to Philadelphia.

AS 988

vanish into the haze equating earth with night. This is an odd use of "equate," but it works, sort of.

in the cool, white fire of crystal. This may even have been subconscious: was AR thinking of *Kristallnacht* as she wrote this?

blast furnaces standing like triumphal arches. Great use of visual parallels and symbols. Was AR thinking of *Triumph of the Will*? Or just Napoleon's *Arc de Triomph*?

arches ... colonnade ... imperial city ... garlands ... lances ... flags. See the painting series "The Course of Empire," by Thomas Cole, at the New-York Historical Society. The American republic is giving way to empire, like Rome.

a spot where no fire had reason to be. This is like *Star Trek's* Captain Kirk saying, "I know every sound this ship might make, and that's not one of them." This is the result of a lifetime of love and dedication to a steel mill, or a starship.

AS 989

forced the car to complete its half-circle. Ayn and Frank had a car accident in Virginia, driving from Los Angeles to New York in 1934 (AH 81, BB 119). Ayn recalled that "the car went out of control. We slid onto an embankment over a sharp drop...."

Frank may have used, or learned later that he should have used, the counter-intuitive trick of steering into the skid instead of against it. That embankment in Virginia becomes this fictional embankment in Pennsylvania (a guess).

Hank rescuing Tony from a roadside slag heap may have been inspired—a long shot here, but worth wondering about—by Jesus's parable of the Good Samaritan. The Samaritan rescues an injured man lying by the side of a road. A Samaritan means someone from Samaria. In the time of Jesus, Samaritans were practicing a deviationist form of Judaism that the rest of Israel considered heretical. It was as if Jesus told a 16th century Catholic audience that even a Lutheran could sometimes be a good person. Your professors will tell you that an Ayn Rand hero would never help those in need. Your professor never heard of mutualism, only altruism.

he had glimpsed an oblong shape. Was AR thinking of the climax of Victor Hugo's *Ninety-Three*? Lantenac is intent on leading a war, but when he sees two children about to burn in a burning castle, he rescues them at the risk of his own life and his cause. Rearden is intent on saving his mill, but when he sees a dying man, he, like Lantenac, has to make a hard decision. As important as his mill is, he cannot leave a man to die. AR explained that the theme of *Ninety-Three* is loyalty to values.

The Concerto of Deliverance

too wrong, too close a spot on the left side of the boy's chest. This is good wording. A sticker.

on orders from Washington . . . goons hired on the outside. AR would have heard from her father about anti-Jewish *pogroms* in the Pale, the region of Russia to which Jews were confined. She might also have been influenced by *Kristallnacht* in her depiction of the attack on Rearden Steel. On the night of November 9, 1938, under orders from Himmler and Goebbels, Nazis assaulted Jewish-owned shops throught Germany. Local and state police dressed in civilian clothes met back at their stations after dark and stormed out, smashing windows of Jewish shops.

Goebbels, Minister of Propaganda, publicized the incident as a spontaneous outpouring of anger by the German people against Jews. Goering, head of the Reichstag, rushed through legislation that vacated the insurance policies held by Jewish merchants, preventing owners from collecting from their insurance companies.

the intensity of a crusader's battle. "Crusade" means a procession of crosses, just like "parade," "arcade" and "cavalcade" mean a procession of shields, arches and horses. President George W. Bush learned the hard way that "crusade" is no longer a good word to use, if you are trying to sell a war in the Middle East after 9/11. It was alright for General Eisenhower to write a book about his role in World War II and call it *Crusade in Europe*, but if you are straining to assure Muslims the world over that this war is *not* a war of Christians and Jews against Muslims, then do not call your war a crusade! In the Middle East, it is always 1099.

AS 990

That's going to be their pitch. That's going to be their sales pitch, that is. A sidewalk peddler with a pushcart used to be called a "pitchman."

Tinky Holloway, who's a stooge of Orren Boyle. Holloway, a sort of "generic Washington big-shot" in the story, his exact job or title never given, is a stooge of Orren Boyle, head of Associated Steel (read US Steel in real life).

Contrary to what your professors tell you, not all big business tycoons in Atlas are among the heroes. Frank Norris, in *The Octopus*, sets up certain government figures as stooges of "Big Business." Some villains in AS are figures in Big Business, but they do not represent *all* of "Big Business" as a group all sharing the same motivation. Some tycoons are good and some are bad.

what would I do with my neck if that's how I had to keep it? This is why AR's subtitle to *The Virtue of Selfishness* is "A New Concept of Egoism." This is not Nietzsche's or Stirner's egoism. Long-range self-interest is more important than short-range. People allow themselves to be corrupted because they think they can get away with it. Tony is wise enough to realize that he is such a small fry that the same big-time players who reward him today will throw him under the bus tomorrow.

Even if Tony managed to stay alive and prosperous in a corrupt world, he would not be happy with himself. He would not be the person he wants to be, and he would not be living the life he wanted. He had once wanted to be a metallurgist. He had thought that his life would be one of creative, productive work. He is the sort of person who takes that distinction seriously. He wants to *live*, not just survive as the punk of corrupt bosses. He insists on living on his own terms. He dies without reaching full sunlight, like Kira and Johnny Dawes. But he dies on a ledge touched by the sun's rays (see AS 1068).

AS 991

the phone wires were cut. Phone wires got cut a lot, in movies and novels written before cell phones.

they shot me from behind. The bullet hole in Tony's chest is small. An exit wound would be bigger.

like a father's recognition granted to a son's battle. Here, and in Hugh Akston's fatherly attitude toward Dagny, Galt, Ragnar and Francisco, we may be hearing an echo of Zinovy Rosenbaum. BB describes Ayn's relationship with her father as a warm, intellectual friendship.

it wouldn't make any difference to chemicals. This is what Douglas Rasmussen means in saying, in *The Philosophic Thought of Ayn Rand*, that AR can be considered a "real" philosopher because she made this important original contribution to ethics: without the concept of life, no such concept as value can exist. See Galt's Speech, AS 1012.

but it does to me. Living instead of dying? Not just *getting away with living?* Tony learned that distinction. NB wished that AR's fiction had shown more examples of characters reforming themselves after being evil and going on to a life of well-deserved rewards. No sooner does AR reform Tony than she kills him off. But as NB said she said, "the book is too long already anyway."

it makes a difference to an animal, too. AR never produced a theory of animal rights, but she said that she wished she could. Animals suffer, and it does make a difference to them.

AS 992

We finally learn that the Wet Nurse's name is Tony. A small thing like that grows to mountain size when it has been put off so long and shows Hank's new-found respect for Tony. It's almost like hearing *Anthem's* Equality 7-2521 say the word "I" for the first time. This is where the great length of AS pays off. Long build-ups give great emotional impact.

AS 993

I guess I am. Hank and Tony share a light moment, and then Hank kisses Tony's forehead. Frank O'Connor once did a dramatic reading of this passage for AR's circle. There wasn't a dry eye in the house.

Here, and with Ken Danagger calling Hank the only man he ever loved (AS 448), we see these rough, tough American businessmen show a surprisingly tender side. Ayn said that American men tend to be emotionally repressed. Presumably, she meant compared with Russian men. Americans often describe the Russians as an emotional people.

AS 994

a collection of chemicals. A sticker, because this phrase signals that Tony has died. See Tony's remark about "conditioned chemicals" on AS 991 and Dr. Pritchett's remark on AS 131. The next 49 lines angrily indict modern education, which AR expanded upon in *The New Left: The Anti-industrial Revolution.* You have heard, just as this reader has heard, the professors solemnly proclaiming, finger in air, "We can know nothing!"—after which they proceed to tell you what political line you had better parrot if you don't want to be snickered at.

the soft, safe assassins of college classrooms. Sticker. Some professors can be excellent, but others seek to initiate freshmen into the game of intellectual intimidation.

Listen to your profs, but beware of their tricks, like defining and re-defining terms as many times as they need to, to make their current theory work. And confirmation bias.

measured his baby formulas with a jeweler's caution. That's Ayn. BB, at least, describes Ayn as overly cautious in following a recipe. That is why it is hard to credit Roy Childs's claim that Ayn was popping those Dexamyls like popcorn. Given her cautious nature, she would have followed her doctor's advice to the letter.

tortured neurotic. "Neurotic" and "neurosis" were pop psych terms in the 1950s and 60s, but not so much in the 2020s.

cats who teach their kittens to hunt. That is why a mama cat will bring you a half-dead mouse: she is treating you as her kitten. She is training you to hunt by bringing you a mouse to chase who is near death and cannot run away quickly enough. Ayn was a cat person, and she describes this process as a cat "laying a hunting trophy at your feet." She did not explain *why* your cat does that.

AS 995

bureaucrat. One Dixiecrat of FDR's time said, "The Republicans are always complainin' about bureaucrats. You know what a bureaucrat is? A bureaucrat is nothin' but a Democrat with a job some Republican wants!"

perished on his first attempt to soar on his mangled wings. Sticker.

Tony had to die for the same reason that Kira had to die at the end of WTL: the book's theme necessitates it. If Kira had escaped the Soviet Union, that would violate the book's theme: that Communism destroys the best.

swinging a length of pipe at a wall of glass panes. See *Kristallnacht* in the discussion of AS 989.

A wall of glass panes sounds like a typical mid-20th century factory design, more window than wall. Industrial Deco.

a well-planned defense . . . a man who held a gun in each hand. Guess who!

AS 996

a hero of western legend. "Legend" is a favorite Rand word, as in her original title for her play *Night of Jan. 16th: Penthouse Legend*. Western characters, when Ayn arrived in Hollywood in 1926, were not exactly legendary characters. They were either wholly fictional, like the Lone Ranger and the Cisco Kid, or they were real historical figures who would become legends. This was not because little or no surviving written information about them existed, like King Arthur or Robin Hood, but because no one had yet researched the written evidence that did exist on characters like Jesse James, Billy the Kid, Wild Bill Hickok, Calamity Jane, the Clantons, the Earps and Doc Holiday, Bat Masterson, Jim Bowie, Butch Cassidy and the Sundance Kid, and Joaquin Murieta, who may have been the prototype for Zorro, Ayn's prototype for Francisco and Ragnar.

then the club crashed down on his skull. Hank is wounded here, and again on AS 1153. As a swing character, one of Hank's jobs in the story is to suffer—suffer guilt and anxiety for his mistakes, which he eventually triumphs over—and to suffer injuries from the villains, in reinforcement of his theme of suffering. The other heroes suffer only from each other, not from the villains. The exception is Galt getting tortured. He had to be the one to be tortured at the climax, because the climactic action must always be the hero's, in AR's view. He himself says this on AS 1155. Also, see AS 898 for Lillian's remark about Hank getting hit in the head with a club. That is foreshadowing.

allow yourself to rest. He will—because he is now fully on strike.

AS 997

the superintendent. AR gives Rearden's Plant Superintendent no name, no description. He appeared twice before, on AS 211, where he is just a title at the other end of a telephone line, and on AS 982. Now at least he is in the room and we hear his voice, but AR tells us all we need to know about him by the fact that he does whatever Hank asks him to do. He is competent. He is "the man who can carry a message to Garcia." (See the famous 1899 essay "A Message to Garcia," by Elbert Hubbard.)

police or state troopers. Kristallnacht! See AS 989.

Frank Adams. Francisco's face is too well known for him not to be recognized, especially after blowing up his company, so this is an unresolved loose end. Also, this name has the initials F.A., like "Francisco d'Anconia" if you don't count the "d." Francisco follows AR's own practice of keeping his initials. She used to say "Writers—and criminals—keep their initials when they change their names."

not the face itself, but the professors. Ideas matter.

AS 998

let them . . . come in! Let them come in!

The door opened and he lay still. You can see this very scene at the climax of a 1942 movie called *Pittsburgh*. Randolph Scott looks up and is surprised to see John Wayne in the door. Wayne has gone to work for Scott under an assumed name, as Francisco has here. AR must have seen that movie and put that scene down in her notepad, but as always, this is just a guess.

looking like he had a cape waving behind him in the wind. See AS 117.

moved his hand over Rearden's forehead. See AS 993. More tenderness. Dr. Akston makes the same gesture with Galt on AS 736.

You slapped me because. They have not seen each other since the slap. Hank slapped Francisco on AS 640 because Francisco had failed to prevent Ragnar sinking a ship that carried copper for Rearden Steel. Hank naturally saw that as a betrayal of their friendship, and now to find out that Francisco had been Dagny's first lover was too much for him and he slapped Francisco. But later Hank figured out that by the logic of the strike, to prevent the sinking and *help* Rearden Steel would have been a betrayal.

I had no right to look for you. Why not?

You offered me the job yourself. on AS 460.

as my bodyguard. Just as Galt is in the Terminal tunnels, as Dagny's.

AS 999

repeat a word you once offered me. This happened on AS 495. On that page, Francisco, knowing that Ragnar will sink Hank's copper ship, and knowing how hurt and betrayed and murderously angry at him Hank will be, starts to say "Hank" and then changes it to "Mr.

Rearden." That's why Francisco had to reject being on a first-name basis with Hank.

that night I came here for the first time. on AS 447.

The glare of steel being poured. The 1952 movie *Deadline USA* ends with Humphrey Bogart in the pressroom of his newspaper on the phone with a gangster. The presses start and the gangster says, "What's that noise?" Bogart says, "That's the press, baby!" There are other movie scenes like that too, where the button on the end of the story is the resumption of normal operations after a crisis. It was Rand who impressed that lesson on this young reader: the goal of the resolving of a crisis or the solving of a problem is a return to normality, a return to humans doing all the normal things they do to survive. Normality is a moral ideal.

7. "This is John Galt Speaking"

Chapter Overview

Jim tells Dagny that Hank has quit and disappeared. Dagny is relieved that Hank is out of their reach now. The government announces, with great fanfare, that Mr. Thompson will give an address on radio and TV on November 22. Jim takes Dagny to the TV studio to be seen on TV with the leadership.

The TV in the studio goes dead. The voice of John Galt broadcasts on the radio, and he announces that he will speak instead of Thompson. He gives a 3-hour speech in which he explains the strike. He says that what he told his strikers to get them to quit was roughly what he is saying to the world now.

Scene 1: Dagny hears Galt's speech with Mr. Thompson and the nation's leadership.

AS 1000

clock on a distant spire. From 66 Park Avenue or from 139 East 35th Street, or near there, where Ayn and Frank had lived before moving to Los Angeles in 1943, Dagny might be able to see the clock on the Metropolitan Life Insurance Building at Madison Square (where Jim Taggart meets Cherryl). AR may have imagined Dagny living in her own old neighborhood, Murray Hill, because Dagny could walk to work at the New York Central Railroad Building behind Grand Central.

she burst out laughing. Dagny has one of Hank's "heart attacks," but it does not matter anymore. See the entry in the Recurring Themes Index for "Hank's heart attacks".

whatever he had in the safe in his apartment. That would be Ragnar's gold bar.

AR had to make sure that she had mentioned Hank putting the bar in a safe in his bedroom. This is one of the thousands of little loose ends that the author of such a huge novel has to tie up, or count on her typist, editor, copy editor, or proofreader to catch. Think of the eye strain and the aching of the neck and shoulders all five of them must have suffered! Thank you, June Kurisu, Daryn Kent, Mary Ann Rukavina Sures, and anyone else who helped with the typing!

it went through the mills like one of those furnace break-outs. This line is one of the major reasons why this reader wanted to write this commentary. This line has been a sticker all these years, but in a bad way. Jim is not a writer. He would not think to sprinkle his usual panicky outbursts with similes, so AR contradicts her characterization of Jim. But AR also told us that Jim began his career in Taggart's Public Relations Department (AS 51), so maybe he really is a wordsmith at heart.

It is a great simile. We know what happens in a furnace break-out because we saw one on AS 456. Jim might not even know, offhand, what a furnace break-out is. Jim, being a railroad man, might say "It went through the mills like a runaway train," if he were to use a simile at all. That would be a mixed simile, unless the runaway train were on Rearden's industrial siding. But mixing similes would be something a panicky person like Jim might do. Thank you for letting me get this old bugaboo off my chest—if that's not a mixed metaphor.

the superintendent, the chief metallurgist . . . Rearden's secretary. Naturally. The tiny bit we know about the superintendent suggests that he would be the type to go. And Gwen Ives! Once they all get to Galt's Gulch, maybe Hank will eventually marry her. At Inland Steel, in Chicago in 1947, AR interviewed the CEO, the superintendent, and the chief metallurgist.

Deserting, the bastards! Jim and the Washington crowd are of course selling people a military view of society. Directive 10-289 has chained them to their jobs, making any change of job or any change of residence a revolutionary act, and in the government's view, it means going AWOL. No matter how opposed to the Vietnam draft your professors were in the 1970s, do not count on them to be against the draft in principle. They were not. They would have been happy to draft you to fight on the Communist side, that's all.

AS 1001

we've got to have him! This can't be right. The fashionable view is that the individual industrialist is not vital to the *collective* economy.

She looked as if she were seeing him naked and would not endure the sight much longer. Great line!

She wondered dimly. This is Dagny's inner judge, or inner critic, at work.

There's still a chance to win, but let me be the only victim. This is key to Dagny's motivation. She just can't believe she can crash, no matter how close to the boulder field she flies.

The newspapers, like puppets on tangled strings. Someone once compiled the reports in French newspapers of Napoleon's escape from Elba, his landing, and his march on Paris. The closer he got to Paris, the nicer the papers were to him. Control of the contents of the papers and radio and television by propaganda minister Chick Morrison shows the descent of the US, in this novel, into recognizable fascism.

AS 1002

But some news could be witnessed. AR picks up the pace, showing how the loss of Rearden and his key staffers has caused Rearden Steel to largely cease to function, leading in turn to the US economy disintergating.

Public awareness that a pattern of disappearing industrialists exists has started to cause universal panic. Who will disappear next? It is not just the top industrialists. Less famous people have also gone missing. It is like refugees escaping from dictatorships anywhere and anytime. A joke in the USSR went: What's the definition of a quartet? A Soviet symphony orchestra after it has toured abroad.

then noticed that her shoulders were trembling. Dagny does not feel an emotion without taking the time to figure out why she is feeling it.

AS 1003

granted her the exception. Galt would not grant Dagny and Francisco the exception of notifying Hank that Dagny was still alive (AS 761). Galt allowing this exception raises some interesting possibilities. Maybe Galt decided that with Hank on strike, and with the general acceleration of the world's collapse, he does not need to be as strict as before. And maybe he is learning and changing personally, and not being so strict. But mainly the reason for his change in policy is that he hated Hank for being Dagny's lover when *he* could not be. And now he *is* Dagny's lover. Since Galt does not hate Dagny, he will not punish her as he did Hank. He now makes the exception for that reason, and also to let Dagny know that Hank has told him (just guessing here) that he has broken up with Dagny and that Galt is now free to pursue her.

her blankness was a struggle. See AS 775: "When nothing seems worth the effort, it's a screen to hide a wish that's worth too much."

So easily within her reach. See AS 962: All Dagny has to do is chalk a dollar sign on the pedestal of Nat Taggart's statue in the Terminal concourse.

she had no right to take a step to reach it. Again AR has a hero say, "I have no right." But why? Because she is still working for the enemy.

The newspapers did not mention. Now we see the breakdown of civil order, under the impact of Directive 10-289, mainly, and the fact that people are learning, mainly by rumor, about the desertions.

went on to seize all property. This is one difference between Rand and Marx: Marx believed that the process of revolution itself, and the economics of the factory system, would lead to socialism and communism. But Rand saw that socialism, communism, and all the other isms, were ideas, and that people going through a revolution would do the same things their former masters did, over and over again, until someone put forth a better idea. As "The Who" say in their song *Won't Get Fooled Again*, "Meet the new boss, same as the old boss." That song became a libertarian anthem in the 1970s.

AS 1004

soldiers sent out from Washington. For real-life examples of this, see the Russian Revolution, as seen from AR's window in Petrograd, and in an American context, Shays' Rebellion of 1786 and the Whiskey Rebellion of 1794. Resolved without much violence were Coxey's Army, 1894 and the Bonus Army March of 1932, not to mention the Civil War.

the odor of ether in a hospital. Ayn was hit by a taxi before about 1943 (AH 137), and she had an abortion in the early 1930s (AH 128). Those may have been when she smelled ether in a hospital, or wherever she had the abortion, since they were illegal then.

It was as if a volcano were cracking open. AR's idea of a volcano erupting could have come only from newsreels or movies. Before television, people got their visual news from newsreels in movie theaters before the main feature. In 1947, as AR was writing AS, Tyrone Power was starring in *Captain from Castile,* which was filmed in Mexico while the new volcano Parìcutin was erupting and growing. The director, Henry King, decided to film some scenes with the erupting volcano in the background. Cool idea! Mount Popocatepetel had erupted during the conquest of Mexico by Cortéz. This movie probably also gave AR the idea for Sebastian d'Anconia escaping from Spain to the New World due to crossing the lord of the Inquisition (AS 91).

Scene 2: Galt's Speech

AR's 1961 book *For the New Intellectual* has a title essay on Western history, and the rest of the book consists of excerpts from her four novels. (This was before New American Library marketed *Ideal* as "Ayn Rand's fifth novel.") The last and longest of these excerpts is Galt's Speech. Under the title "This Is John Galt Speaking" AR writes "This is the philosophy of Objectivism."

It is not. Even combined with all her nonfiction articles and essays, the speech does not constitute a full treatment of her philosophical system. She never wrote the treatise she had said she would. What she left was the *outline* of a philosophy.

Even with Leonard Peikoff's treatise, *Objectivism: The Philosophy of Ayn Rand*, there is much for other Objectivist philosophers to do.

Galt's Speech is more like the Declaration of Independence. That Declaration was not meant as a treatise on the philosophy of the Enlightenment, either. It was a statement of policy of a revolutionary *junta* and the reasons behind that policy. Same here. Galt is setting out the terms for the return of the strikers.

Mr. Thompson will put an end to those sinister forces. Since Mr. Thompson never gets to deliver this address, we are left to wonder what he was planning to say. Since world leaders do not generally know any response to any problem except more taxes, more stringent controls over everything, and of course war, we can expect that Thompson was planning all three. "a stern way, as befits the gravity of this hour": I'll bet. But after he is knocked off the air by Galt's Speech, why doesn't Mr. Thompson reschedule his speech and give it another night? Apparently because he takes advantage of Galt's intervention to make Galt the focus of his PR. He tells the public that he wants to talk to John Galt.

Compare the idea of a radio or other speech forming the climax of a story to the movies *The Farmer's Daughter*, *Red Planet Mars*, and *The Next Voice You Hear* (not the climax in this case) and to the 1948 Theodore Sturgeon science fiction short story "Unite and Conquer," in the anthology *A Way Home*. And of course, Klaatu's climactic speech in *The Day the Earth Stood Still* with Patricia Neal, who also co-starred in *The Fountainhead*. In *The Great Dictator*, Charlie Chaplin gives a radio speech at the end. Like Galt, he directly addresses his girlfriend in the speech. Since Chaplin puts a Marxist message into the speech, no one complains about the fact that he steps out of character to give it.

Sturgeon uses the familiar trope of uniting mankind by setting up a common enemy. This was also used in an *Outer Limits* TV episode (with Robert Culp) and a different story in an *Outer Limits* comic. Rand would say that this would not work. The nations were largely united against the Axis, but did that produce lasting peace? No. Only ideas can do that.

AS 1005

Public loud-speakers were built in the squares. See William L. Shirer's book, and the movie based on it, *The Nightmare Years*, about his time as a CBS correspondent in Nazi Germany just before the war. There is a scene where Shirer and his wife are having a heated conversation at an outdoor café.

A radio is playing, with a loudspeaker, and a trumpet fanfare is followed by an announcement that *Der Führer* is about to make a speech. The other customers at the café stop talking and prepare to listen intently to the speech. Shirer and his wife ignore this and keep arguing. A middle-aged man sitting at the next table turns and sternly yells at them. "Quiet! Listen to the speech!" he cries repeatedly. That is what it was like in the radio age, when AR was planning AS. Because you could not just rewind and listen later on the internet, everyone had to drop what they were doing and listen to the words of the Great Leader at his convenience, not at theirs. And as the government seizes more power and rules through fear, you had better at least *look* as though you are listening to the speech if you are in a public place.

Why does Galt choose to make the speech? Perhaps because the tremendous publicity for Thompson's speech gave him a target too tempting to pass up. Everyone in the world is listening. And, as Akston said in the valley (AS 748), the world is now collapsing much faster than they had expected. A speech revealing the strike and laying out the issues might be just the one last push that will ignite open rebellion, not just in the US but worldwide. And now the listeners will have the blueprint for a new social order, since there must be people here and there expecting to record and transcribe Thompson's speech. They will now instead record, transcribe, analyze and debate Galt's Speech. Millions of written transcripts will be sold from every news stand in the world.

blank page of a calendar that bore no date. That is the last we will hear of the public calendar. Its work in the novel is done. It announced September 2 of Year 1 of the story on AS 4, September 2 of Year 2 on AS 382, the day of Jim and Cherryl's wedding, and

September 2 of Year 3 on AS 925, when Francisco uses it to deliver his farewell message. September 2, 1946, is when AR dated her first page of the manuscript, and she used that date as a device to help the reader keep track of the passage of time over the three years, and a few months, of the story.

At the broadcasting studio. This is awkward, since no one would say "the broadcasting studio." They would say ABC, NBC or CBS in 1957. But AR's policy in AS, more than in TF, was to avoid names of real people, places or things. She said that she regretted mentioning the Plaza Hotel and Coty perfume in TF. Other writers have made up fictional broadcast networks, such as UBS in the movie *Network*.

Or maybe, by now, the government has already taken over the networks and there is nothing on your dial but PBS! But if that were the case, AR would have said so before this. So, perhaps, she is laying it between the lines.

They wouldn't let you near a microphone! See AS 850.

resigned, yet wondering and curious. That's Eddie! Childlike.

AS 1006

microphones dangling like bait. Ain't it the truth!

The best leadership of the country. President Jerry Ford held just such a televised "conference" in 1974. He had just announced that America would Whip Inflation Now by wearing buttons that read WIN. AR's friend Alan Greenspan, Ford's economic advisor, sat at a big round table with the President, New Deal economist John Kenneth Galbraith (who made a crack about Rand), AFL-CIO chief George Meany (Fred Kinnan in AS), and other VIPs. It was embarrassing.

military marches. Looks like a clue to what Mr. Thompson was about to announce, we might guess.

AS 1007

the kind of look he would have worn if one of the flower vases had suddenly refused to perform its part. Funny.

AS 1008

child's toy. This is what makes Galt's Speech the *coup de grace* of the revolution. If Galt had not had the ability to take the airwaves away from the Head of the State at 7:51, a speech at 8:00 would be just one man's opinion. In an instant, the people have seen that John Galt has the power to turn all broadcasting on and off at will. He has made monkeys out of the government. Therefore, everyone must sit up and listen to what he has to say.

We see straight narrative for the whole page, except for Dr. Stadler's reaction: "There's no such thing! There's nobody on earth to make it!" This reminds the reader that in Dr. Stadler's mind it is still all about exceptional people like himself, and a certain old student of his . . ..

AS 1009

Isn't there a brain left in this country? This is the line that sets up Galt's speech. It repeats the theme of the whole novel, in a nutshell.

Now begins Galt's speech.

Notice that AR gives us the first paragraph of the speech followed by a paragraph of reactions of the people in the room. She next gives us another paragraph of the speech, then a paragraph of narrative, and only then does she go back into the speech and stay there till the end of the chapter. At the beginning of the next chapter, she takes us back into the room for several pages of reaction. She eases us into the speech, and after the end, she re-integrates us back into the story and integrates the speech into the story. The reactions of the government, and of the people, to the speech, the accelerating breakdown of government power due to the speech, and the growing danger to Galt from Dagny become the next thread of the story. This is much more integration of speech to story than Melville gives in *Moby Dick*, before and after the discourse on whales, or Hugo in *Ninety-Three*, before and after the discourse on the Convention. AR was imitating Hugo in WTL when she interpolated a rhapsodic description of Saint Petersburg. The essay is four pages long. It is hard to say where exactly the essay ends and Kira's story resumes, because AR integrates the two pretty well.

the kind of voice that had not been heard on the airwaves for years. That may have been true at the time of Father Coughlin's fascistic radio rants on the radio in the 1930s, but it certainly was not true of the newscasters, like H. V. Kaltenborn, Robert Trout, and Edward R.

Murrow, who all spoke in a calm, businesslike manner. Even Hitler would be hard put to match the radio and TV antics of Howard Stern, the "info-tainment" show hosts, and of course the recent clown-in-chief.

AR spent two years or more writing out philosophical treatises and then translating them into the language and tone of a moral crusader on the radio. When you read the speech, imagine, not a professor lecturing to a class, but a Billy Graham type declaiming dramatic sentences to an enthralled crowd in which each individual feels as though he were on trial.

Galt will later tell Dagny that he had broadcast from the valley (AS 1092). Perhaps he has quit his job at the terminal—his voice and name would be known to his co-workers. But did he give the speech live, or did he record it and play a tape over the radio?

Did he have an audience? It would have been practical to record the speech in ten or twenty-minute chunks in advance and play the tapes on the air.

What if he started to lose his voice after three hours? What if he were interrupted, or just had to go to the bathroom? (The speech is four hours long, not three. I have recorded it, twice.) It might have helped him set the crusading tone if he had had a few people in the room watching him speak, like Dr. Akston, for starters.

I have taken it over. Galt is a radio pirate. A broadcast version of Ragnar. He has seized control of a public property.

It was President Herbert Hoover who claimed that the airwaves are the property of the federal government. Not FDR, but Mr. "Rugged Individualism" Hoover. See AR's 1964 article "The Property Status of Airwaves" in *Capitalism: The Unknown Ideal.* But under the political conditions in this story, you have to ask yourself, not whether Galt has a right to seize Hoover's or FDR's airwaves, but does he not have the right to seize the airwaves from the equivalent of Hitler or Mussolini?

I am the man who loves his life. Notice that this point is what Galt leads off with. This AR's Life-is-not-their-purpose theme. Galt is preaching Aristotelean self-actualization.

only his voice filled the airways of the country. Shouldn't this be "airwaves"? This is not TWA we are talking about. This is one of AR's odd words choices that make us wonder whether Hiram Haydn, at some point, simply gave up trying to edit AS, both because AR refused to be edited (he says), and because he felt guilty helping to publish this "evil" book.

You have heard it said. Galt's speech is uninterrupted from here to the end of the chapter on AS 1069—60 pages. AR explained that in a novel of this length, a 60-page speech is not out of proportion. Just unprecedented. And unfollowed. But since this speech is essentially what Galt told to his strikers to get them to go on strike, it is central to the action of the plot.

We are finally hearing the words that Dagny would have heard from Ken Danagger's office if she had put her ear to the keyhole. This is what Francisco would have said to Hank in his office as Hank lay recovering from being hit in the head with a club. See AS 1015 below.

you who dread knowledge. Galt is a Jeremiah, telling the world what they are doing wrong and what will happen if *they* don't mend *their* wicked ways. Roark, in his courtroom speech, says "We praise an act of charity. We shrug at an act of achievement" (TF 726). He includes himself among the guilty. In the movie *Mass Appeal*, Jack Lemmon plays an older, experienced priest coaching a young priest in the art of preaching a sermon. When the young priest says, "you sin," the old priest tells him "No, never say '*you* sin.' Say '*we* sin.' Otherwise, the congregation will hate you for accusing them of sins that you don't admit to yourself" (or words to that effect). No such niceties for Galt. The gloves are off.

AS 1010

too innocently generous. Generosity is a virtue in AR's moral system.

pursuit of one's happiness. See Jefferson and Locke.

We are useless, according to your economics. A socialist might retort: No, the man of ability is not useless, the heir who inherits millions and does no work is useless. Under socialism, the man of ability will be paid maybe five times as much as unskilled labor, as a People's Manager, but not millions of times as much, for doing nothing, as does a worthless heir under capitalism.

AS 1011

according to your philosophy. Notice that AR goes, in this paragraph, from morality to economics to politics to philosophy. By "philosophy" here, she means epistemology and metaphysics. But since Galt is speaking to the whole world and not to a university audience, AR uses the more familiar term "philosophy."

We do not need you. Sticker! Galt's Gulch is self-sufficient, peaceful and productive. We don't need to ever come back if we don't want to. And this is not, as you have been told, the rich talking to the poor. It is the mind talking to the absence of mind. The honest to the dishonest.

your code was noble, but human nature was not good enough to practice it. Sticker! Yes, that is one of their dodges, all right.

AS 1012

And no one came to say that your life belongs to you and that the good is to live it. Sticker! Compare this line to one in "Toohey's Speech," on TF 67: "But if ever you hear a man telling you that you must be happy, that it's your natural right, that your first duty is to yourself . . . ." Galt's line works just as well. Maybe better. But Toohey's mention of "natural rights" is important. That is the concept that grounds AR's political principles on Locke and the Enlightenment and on Aristotle.

the province of faith and force. AR would use this in the title of a 1960 article called "Faith and Force: The Destroyers of the Modern World" anthologized in her book *Philosophy: Who Needs It?* There are a number of phrases like that, that AR first used in Galt's Speech and later in an article title or elsewhere.

cyclotron. Greek for "wheel-instrument." This was invented by Leo Szilard in Germany in 1929 and patented in the US in 1932 by Ernest O. Lawrence. It was the first particle accelerator, and Dr. Stadler would have used one. Any reminder of physics that brought back memories of Stadler would be painful to Galt, and vice versa.

In any hour and issue of your life, you are free to think or to evade that effort. This is AR's solution to the ancient problem of free will.

Your actions might be called "determined" by the results of your thinking or your evasion of thinking, but you are free to focus on a problem and solve it, or to evade that responsibility.

to be or not to be. This is the most famous line from Shakespeare's play *Hamlet*. AR was not fond of Shakespeare, because of his famous "tragic flaw" formula.

Value is that which one acts to gain and keep. Major sticker! This is the line that inspired this reader with the realization that simple, clear definitions make all things understandable. Philosophy does not have to be incomprehensible.

Virtue is the act by which one gains and keeps it. See *First Principles*, by Thomas E. Ricks, for the importance of the word "virtue" to the American revolutionaries. In Latin, since "vir" means man, virtue simply means being a man and accepting the responsibilities of a man. For General Washington, it meant taking responsibilities in a political community. For Ricks, it means doing so with little or no pay. For the Victorians, it meant little more than female chastity. For Rand, the meaning is much more inclusive. "Virtue" means anything you do to pursue any kind of value.

Washington did not see virtue as a self-sacrifice, but as a means to gain honor in the community, and he valued honor.

It is only to a living organism. This is Rand's "Ethics for Weeds" principle. All plants and animals need to act in order to survive, so yes, we can find a basis in fact and science for a system of good and evil.

AS 1013

It is only the concept of life that make the concept of value possible. Douglas Rasmussen and Doug Den Uyl, in *The Philosophic Thought of Ayn Rand*, explain that this original and important insight gives Rand a claim to be a real philosopher, even though she lacked an academic degree.

Life is a process of self-sustaining and self-generated action. This is why Rand did not find abortion to be murder, and did support its legalization.

Your fear of death is not a love for life. See "Life is not their Purpose," in Recurring Themes Index.

A plant that struggled to mangle its roots. See "Weeds" in Recurring Themes. Notice that AR uses here the neutral word "plant" and not the pejorative word "weed."

Man has been called a rational being. Aristotle defined man as "the animal that thinks."

AS 1014

A doctrine that gives you, as an ideal, the role of a sacrificial animal seeking slaughter on the altars of others, is giving you death as your standard. Osama bin Laden said, "Our youth value death as yours do life." John Galt could not have put it any better.

but to enjoy yourself and live. This does not mean hedonism. Pleasure is not the end of life, happiness is. See the beginning of this paragraph. Sticker!

AS 1015

I told them, in essence, the statement I am making tonight. See AS 1009.

AS 1016

the man who was—no matter what his errors. AR means Aristotle. Rand disagreed with Aristotle in his acceptance of slavery, for starters. Carl Sagan, in his *Cosmos* TV series, explained that Aristotle taught that matter is made up of the Four Elements and the Four Qualities. Democritus of Abdera taught that matter is made up of atoms. Democritus was right on this point and Aristotle was wrong. Sagan's moral for this story is that just the fact that you are a genius does not guarantee that on any particular point, you can't be dead wrong.

the greatest of your philosophers. Galt is here speaking as if from outside of mankind. Aristotle is one of *his* philosophers, too! Galt sounds not only like a Jeremiah, but like a visitor from another planet, like Klaatu! But he is also making his speech more personal. It is about *you*—the individual hearing this speech and having to come to a decision as to what you are going to do about it. Aristotle is one of *your* philosophers.

Existence is Identity. Consciousness is Identification. This is the most important of all stickers. This is all human knowledge, in a nutshell.

A thing is itself. In his 1978 movie *The Deer Hunter*, director and writer Michael Cimino has Robert De Niro hold up a bullet and say

"This is what it is. It ain't something else." Cimino wanted to film TF and Atlas, but never did.

Or if you wish it stated in simpler language. This a case where AR annoys the really smart reader by saying the same thing two or three times, in highbrow, middlebrow, and lowbrow language, just to make sure everyone gets it.

Reason is the faculty that perceives. AR later admitted a mistake here. Perception is not included under the definition of reason.

AS 1017

The most depraved sentence. This is an example of AR's intimidating style. The reader who sees this, and decides to climb onboard, then imitates this style and becomes a notorious arrogant pain in the ass. Word gets around, and people shun him. Then he wonders why he can't get any girls. This line is appropriate to a speech by a moral crusader, and to a declaration of independence that lays out a bill of grievances against an unjust world, but day to day conversation calls for diplomacy, not accusation.

reality is the court of final appeal. Sticker! "You have to do it because Mom says" is not good enough. You have to do it because there will be bad consequences in reality if you don't. Your opinion is not good enough. As Dr. Akston said (AS 735), we do not tell. We show. We do not claim. We prove. A high standard to live up to!

Does the nature of atmospheric electricity. Galt is describing his motor. Why does he use that example? Is this reference intended for some particular listener? Dagny? Stadler?

a man who assumes the responsibility of thinking. If this reader fully noticed this line on first reading, at thirteen, he would have been scared to death, since, as a fourth and last child, he was totally unused to taking any responsibility, or being given any.

soul or spirit is your consciousness. AR explained that this was Aristotle's use of the Greek word (*psyche*) usually translated as "soul."

Thinking is man's only basic virtue. This whole paragraph should be a pull-out quote for the whole book.

the source of all his evils. This, not money, is the root of all evil.

blanking out. Galt will use this expression many times in the pages to come, as AR and NB later used it in articles intended mainly for readers who had already read Atlas.

AS 1018

Who am I to judge? This line gave this reader a life-long aversion to the "humble act": Who am I to judge? Who am I to say? Who am I to do anything?

desert island. Sticker! Morality is connected with practical reality? Who knew?

Galt uses words like "premise" and "axiom," which most teenaged listeners would not know. Some might look them up the next day.

A moral commandment is a contradiction in terms. Sticker! This was another eye-opener to this young reader.

My morality, the morality of reason. Here AR begins her listing and description of her Three Values and her Seven Virtues. She uses the magic numbers 3 and 7. This is another of AR's parodies of religion, here the Trinity and the Seven Deadly Sins.

AS 1019

pinch-hitter. A baseball term. Will baseball be as important and its terms as familiar to Americans in 2057 as in 1957?

subordination of your mind to the mind of another. Do you think she's exaggerating? Consider this Nazi slogan: "Leader command! We follow!" On point, yes?

Honesty. This is a hard one for most people to believe. Coarsened as we all are by centuries of dishonesty, and of man's inhumanity to man, we all find it hard to believe that we can't get away with some dishonesty, *and that we don't need to.* After all, we assume our victim must be just as dishonest as we are, and deserves to get fooled and victimized in turn.

to withhold your contempt from men's vices. AR and NB took this one a bit too far in the NBI days.

AS 1020

Black Mass. This is a Satanic parody of the Catholic Mass.

all work is creative work if done by a thinking mind. All work that solves problems, whether done by a janitor or a genius, is creative.

It is all the use of one's mind. That is what makes us human.

a routine he has learned from others. NB used to say, "My definition of a hack is someone who is doing exactly the same thing next year that he did last year—no matter how good what he did last year was."

the man who makes another man his goal. See AR's play *Think Twice*. This whole paragraph is a delightful string of metaphors on the theme of motors and cars. And there is more on the next page.

as man is a being of self-made wealth, so he is a being of self-made soul. Often quoted by AR and NB.

AS 1021

Virtue is not its own reward. Cicero, a Stoic, said "The only reward of virtue is virtue."

Just as your body. This is the relation of emotion to reason.

a loophole in the law of causality. If the world ever really does achieve the much-touted "paper-free office," readers will have to go to the Museum of Paper to learn what a loophole is.

AS 1022

it has brought you where you wanted to go. AR told Johnny Carson that her philosophy "has brought me where I am today."

not the joy of a drunkard. Here, young readers will learn to mature from the idea of sobriety-as-duty, hearing others joke about wishing to be drunk, to asking why anyone would ever *want* to be drunk, or drugged.

One friend of Rand's said that the most fun she had at a party was to be the only one sober, so she could watch all the others make fools of themselves. This is also where a reader learns to distinguish between momentary pleasure and real joy and happiness, and so between hedonism and Aristotelean self-fulfilment.

no contradictions in my values. This is what Chris Sciabarra means when he says that AR's approach to ethics is dialectical: you look for contradictions and heal them.

there are no victims and no conflicts of interest among rational men. This is crucial. This is AR's reply to the Marxists, who believe that their theory of historical determinism and class struggle entails, of *necessity,* conflicts of interest.

In Rand's view, though, the only necessary struggle is the struggle against mistaken thinking of the past. You don't do that by dying on a barricade. You do it by learning and thinking. Many people are so hardened by centuries of war and statism that they refuse to believe Rand on this point, so she wrote an article expanding on this idea, "The 'Conflicts' of Men's Interests," in *The Virtue of Selfishness*, 1962.

the trader. This is AR's Trader Principle. She did not write articles specifically about her "Trader Principle" but searching through Google will produce some entries on the subject.

what moral obligation I owe. This could be the springboard for whole books.

AS 1023

if I am right, he will learn; if he is right, I will learn. The honest reader will learn here that the purpose of all conversation is either teaching or learning. This distinguishes the honest person from the con man, for whom words are only weapons.

no man may initiate force. Crucial! This is the Non-Initiation of Force Principle, or Non-Aggression Principle, that serves as the defining principle of the Libertarian Party, which likes to call itself "the party of principle." Its 1976 presidential candidate, Roger MacBride, called his private plane "No Force One."

morality ends where a gun begins. Perhaps AR was inspired in this line by the Natural Rights slogan "My right to swing my fist ends where your nose begins."

If there are degrees of evil. It is unusual for AR to admit uncertainty about anything. Does she or doesn't she believe in degrees of evil? Altghough she did not sort that point out before finishing the Speech, for the purposes of this paragraph, she did not have to. This came up before, on AS 303 and AS 745.

AS 1024

No, I do not share his evil. This is the difference between AR's non-aggression and a pacifist's non-force. It is okay to use force to stop force.

a holdup man seeks to gain wealth by killing me. This is why AR saw the US as having an advantage over the USSR in a nuclear war: If the Soviets are trying to seize real wealth, as they seized factories in

Manchuria toward the end of World War II, then they have to be careful in a war not to destroy too much of the goods they want to loot. But in defending herself, the US may destroy what little there was to destroy in the USSR. With his strategy of *Blitzkrieg*, Hitler was seizing neighboring nations intact, in order to loot them to pay the workers he had set to work building arms. You readers growing up in the 21st century are hard put to imagine what it was like for us of the 1950s and 60s, who half expected to be vaporized at any moment by Soviet ICBMs. That fear was hanging over us as Atlas went to press in 1957. For most Americans, Atlas was the name of a missile, not a book.

it will be on our moral terms. See *Ayn Rand and Song of Russia*, by Robert Mayhew, page 97, to see what happened when AR told Parnell Thomas, the Chairman of HUAC, that if she ever came to testify again it would be on her terms. She must have remembered that comical moment when she wrote these words.

Intelligence is not the absence of stupidity. A friend of AR's used this line once, but she did not mean it in Galt's sense. She meant that even highly intelligent people can sometimes be stupid. See Carl Sagan on Aristotle on AS 1016 above.

Building is not done by abstaining from demolition. For a moment, AR has slipped from Galt's speech back into Roark's. She still did that in 1979, telling Tom Snyder on his *Tomorrow* show, that writing a novel is "much more complicated than designing a building. You have to hold in your mind an enormous context. It's killingly difficult. But wonderful when you succeed."

AR was still thinking about architecture.

AS 1025

Original Sin. Ayn said "Frank is more of an atheist than I am." I know what she means. I was brought up in the Presbyterian Church, which does not have Saturday confession and does not preach Original Sin. Ayn was brought up in a secular Jewish family. Both of us, then, got off pretty light. But Frank was brought up Catholic. He got the full treatment. And he bore a lifelong resentment of it. Thomas Jefferson suffered under a strict Anglican tutor as a boy, with the same result.

Original Sin was the doctrine that Frank found particularly enraging. A newborn baby is born already damned to hell? Other Catholics say their pet peeve is having to confess their "sins" to some guy in a booth. "There the guy who's got religion'll / Tell you if your sin's original . . . " (Tom Lehrer)

Notice that Galt is here speaking as if Original Sin were a tenet of all of mankind's belief systems. It is not. Ayn had learned about Catholicism from Frank and whatever books she read on the subject. Perhaps from Frank's brother Nick, too. Russian Orthodoxy (which AR had to learn about in school under the Czar) has a slightly different spin: only Adam and Eve are *guilty* of the Original Sin, but all their descendants bear the *punishment* of death for it. So we remain condemned to death even though God does not hold us guilty of the sin. How Russian. Kafka-esque.

AS 1026

What are the evils man acquired? This paragraph is a *tour de force.* You have heard the story of Adam and Eve all your life. Have you ever thought about its meaning? What it implies about what religion thinks would be paradise for you?

the rack with two wheels . . . digging his way to that glorious jailbreak. Ayn draws upon the Spanish Inquisition. She might have learned stories about torture and jailbreaks when she had her first job: tour guide at Petrograd's Peter and Paul Fortress.

AR's picture of digging your way out of jail probably came from a novel everyone read in Ayn's day: *The Count of Monte Cristo,* by Alexandre Dumas.

a corpse and a ghost. AR might have gotten this from Nietzsche's *Also Sprach Zarathustra.* "Do I bid you become a plant or a ghost?"

AS 1027

the mystics of spirit and the mystics of muscle. That is: Immanuel Kant, AR's pet peeve, and the Marxists, who called themselves "materialists." They accepted the existence of matter only and not spirit, while the Kantians accepted the existence of a "higher reality." But in their materialism, the Marxists believed in "historical necessity," a kind of determinism, which works on recruits much as religious prophecy

"This is John Galt Speaking"

does, hence AR's term "Muscle-Mystics." "Muscle-Mystics" became a favorite image of AR and her circle.

AS 1028

This whole page and the next are about the nature of sacrifice. Isabel Paterson asked Rand about saving a child at the expense of her own life. Perhaps she was thinking of the climax of Victor Hugo's *Ninety-Three*. Would it be different if it were her own child?

worthless stranger. Does AR mean that any fellow human being is worthless to you until you bond with him as a friend? See bottom of AS 1033, and the top of AS 1060.

a vegetable seeking to be eaten. AR's favorite example of this is the schmoo: an animal in the *Li'l Abner* comic strip. It seeks to be eaten.

as it slashes your desires away from your reach. Think of the look of anguish on James Stewart's face, in *It's A Wonderful Life*, as he realizes that he cannot move away from his small town and pursue his dream of being a big-time engineer because he has to clean up the messes others have made.

AR was very much aware of that movie while starting to write AS. Her complaint was that "Mr. Potter," the evil banker, was such a stock character in fiction. Who wouldn't become a socialist if all we ever see in fiction are stock "evil businessman" characters?

AS 1029

I am concerned with no other. Neither are you. Galt gives no quarter. He permits no Caesars. Sticker!

feeds him only from a sense of duty. That would be Ayn's mother. She had the nerve, Ayn recalls, to not only have children only out of duty, but to *tell* her children that.

cause to be just ... donates his money. Notice that Galt is speaking approvingly of donating money to non-profit organizations.

devotes his effort to the production of trash. AR must be thinking of the first meeting of Roark and Steven Mallory on TF 343.

AS 1030

another life in heaven or a full stomach on this earth. This, once again, depicts the conflict between the religious crowd and the Marxists. AR may have been blissfully ignorant of the Dorothy

Day crowd: the Catholic Communists, or "Liberation Theology" crowd.

The greatest good for the greatest number. This was the slogan of Utilitarianism. John Stuart Mill (1806-1873) was the movement's star philosopher. He published *Utilitarianism* in 1861.

a fumigator of any action, even the slaughter of a continent. AR refers to the Holocaust, among other enormities.

anything goes. An expression of AR's time. Cole Porter wrote a Broadway show called *Anything Goes* in 1934.

AS 1031

booby-trap. The Booby is a sea bird. Sailors used to set traps for them on the decks and masts of their ships.

AS 1032

each to the extent of his distance from that ideal. Nota bene! From AR's perspective, the real world does not consist only of absolute heroes and absolute villains. That sort of division happens only in fiction. In the real word, you find that everybody is to some extent good and to some extent bad, as defined by various moral systrems, such as altruism or egoism.

Notice that each of these paragraphs lists four or five examples. The clever reader, who gets the point from the first example, will often skip the others in his impatience, but in the process may miss something interesting by doing so.

AS 1033

every man is both victim and parasite. Compare "each to the extent" on AS 1032

To love is to value. Sticker!

worthless. See AS 1028 above.

AS 1034

Love . . . the greatest reward you can earn. This is Ayn's last line in the 1999 TV movie *The Passion of Ayn Rand* with Helen Mirren, who brought to the role her own native Russian accent. Contrast this paragraph with the Greek word *agape*.

stockyards. As with Rearden's "steel mills," AR pluralized the word. It should be just "stockyard." But that is the way people usually say it.

a means of knowledge higher than the mind. Saint Augustine famously said, "I believe it *because* it is absurd."

AS 1035

In the hardcover edition, you will notice a bad print job on this page. One character was cut off on the left end of each of the top 16 lines.

They offer you, as proof of their superior knowledge, the fact that they assert the opposite of everything you know. Professors do this with every book they write and tout on TV.

The mystics of muscle call it "the future." AR is again talking about the Communist Party of the Soviet Union. See her 1958 Foreword to WTL, on the Soviet promises and Five-Year Plans. She mentions Sputnik in that Foreword. See Sputnik, two paragraphs below.

rivers run with milk and coffee. The biblical line is "a land of milk and honey." AR must have liked coffee better than honey, or just wanted to update the phrase.

they travel from planet to planet at the cost of a wish. Sputnik, the first artificial satellite, was launched on October 4, 1957. Atlas was published October 10.

Space travel was much talked about in magazines at the time. When Atlas was published, manned spacecraft were still on the drawing boards. But what AR talks about here is the mystic trying to get us to believe his magical claims. See the "Heaven's Gate Comet Cult" for some real wack jobs.

If an honest person. One of the few times AR writes "person" and not "man." NB, in the 1980s, said that in the fifties it would never occur to anyone not to say, "All men are created equal."

esoteric philosophies. Around 2018 or so, suddenly replacing the word "philsophy" with "philosophies" became fashionable.

dialectics. A word of Aristotle's, but associated in everyone's mind but Chris Sciabarra's with Karl Marx.

AS 1036

lift it to the roof of a skyscraper. The image of the skyscraper is never far from Rand's consciousness. To this day, Saint Petersburg has only three skyscrapers, and those are recent and far from the city center. The onset of skyscrapers from the 1880s to the 1920s was seen by

Rand and others as something new and interesting, not yet taken for granted as they are in 2024.

Things as they are. Kant's phrase.

a child's nightmare where identities switch and swim. You have had such dreams, haven't you? Your point of view switches from first person to third and back.

It looks like AR had much the same kind of dream. But she calls this "a child's nightmare." Didn't she have nightmares in adulthood?

AS 1037

an emotion you cannot explain or control. AR claimed that she could explain the cause of her every emotion. She may not have succeeded in every case, but how many people have ever even tried?

let me have my one irrational whim. This line was a major sticker and a challenge. Galt permits no exceptions, no Caesars.

How many people have told you that they accept the absoluteness of reason 99% of the time, but reserve their right to fall back on faith as their epistemological Plan B.

For such people, NB said, "Either reason is an absolute for you or it is not, and if it is not, you will tend to flee from reason and rely on faith during a crisis—which is exactly when you need your reason the most."

a fixed jury who take orders from a secret underworld. How many gangster films of the 1930s and 40s did AR see? One such was *Tight Spot,* starring AR's friend Ginger Rogers. It was released in 1955, as AR was working on Galt's Speech.

All actions are caused by entities. See Aristotle's Four Causes, in Mortimer J. Adler's *Aristotle for Everybody*. This solves the problem of how to explain causality if the only cause of an event is a previous event. The causes of an event should include the nature of the *entities* that caused it.

have your cake and eat it too. AR is thinking of her friend Henry Hazlitt's book *Economics in One Lesson*. The lesson is: You cannot consume what you have not produced. The old saying is "You can't have your cake and eat it too."

AS 1038

unearned love . . . unearned wealth. Notice how she integrates love and economics.

Who pays for the orgy? In these two paragraphs, it is important to remember that AR is not talking about captains of industry. She is talking about any human being who ever did productive work or took any kind of responsibility, great or small. That same person will usually also exhibit all the flaws she is decrying. People have mixed premises.

Most people are Galt part of the time and Jim Taggart part of the time, and in between most of the time.

You—who leap like a savage out of the jungle of your feelings into the Fifth Avenue of our New York. Galt has just explained, over the past few pages, that he is not saying that feelings are evil, but that many people have made evasions in their thinking which have caused feelings they don't enjoy and don't understand.

By "savage" AR means anyone who tries to replace reason with "magical thinkinIf I forget my umbrella, that fact will somehow make it rain. See AS 1039 below. But when she puts together in one sentence the words "savage" and "jungle," many will interpret it as racism. Fifth Avenue, in AR's day, was the luxury shopping district of New York and almost of the world. It represented the luxuries paid for and made possible by productive work. Before AR's day, Fifth Avenue was where the mansions of the super-rich were, and so was again a symbol of luxury.

created by miracle out of non-matter. This is why the looters called Rearden Metal "Miracle Metal."

AS 1039

bootleggers. In the 1880s, a "bootlegger" was someone who concealed a flask of liquor in his boot top. Later, during Prohibition, 1919 to 1933, a bootlegger was anyone who made, sold or transported illegal liquor. When AR arrived from Russia in 1926, the US was right in the middle of the "noble experiment."

blank-out. This is another term from Galt's Speech that AR would use again in her essays.

running railroads . . . running steel mills. If the FBI analyzed Galt's speech, as they must have done, they might have twigged to the fact that Galt was gunning for Dagny as he had just nabbed Rearden.

a savage, who believes that the magic words he utters have the power to alter reality. This is what AR means by "savage." She does not mean a literal primitive person. She is giving the word a new and deeper meaning. You do not have to live in a hunter-gatherer society to fall into the "umbrella" kind of faulty thinking mentioned on AS 1038 above.

so they feed on stolen concepts in mind. NB wrote a whole article on "The Stolen Concept" in the January 1963 *Objectivist Newsletter*.

turn the cranks of the machines. There was a union hymn from the 1940s that said, "They have taken untold millions that they never toiled to earn (Marxist economics) /But without our brain and muscle not a single wheel would turn."

Ah, so there *is* a role for the mind in production, according to whoever wrote this song. The union members would not sink as far as the professors, who had students believing that "we can be certain of nothing"—see below.

nothing exists but change. You have heard that cliché many times. This reader has heard professors say that change is the only constant condition.

AS 1040

he doesn't choose to accept the axiom that he exists. On the Ed Sullivan Show, in the 1960s, Joan Rivers, in her comedy routine, bemoaned the fact that she had gotten married after getting a degree in philosophy in college. "Now I have to spend my time shopping for hamburger I can prove doesn't exist."

She got a laugh, and she knew she would get a laugh, from a general audience, not just a college audience. This shows how widely philosophy had become a laughing stock. The general public saw philosophy as nothing more than a parlor game disconnected from reality. AS, and AR's career, interested people in philosophy again, as they had been in previous centuries.

An axiom is a statement. Here Galt defines "axiom."

caveman... anthropoid... witch doctor... headhunter... pygmy... cannibal. Most people would not use these words today, even as metaphors. "Pygmy" is a Greek word that is defined as an ethnic group with an adult male average height of 4 feet 11 inches or less.

People of this description have been studied in Africa, southeast Asia and the Pacific. They are mainly hunter-gatherers. Their short stature may be adaptive and recent.

The African Pygmies have a rich inheritance of choral singing. They have spoken languages related to those of surrounding peoples, but they have no written languages. Despite language similarities with the surrounding peoples, their genes vary from those of their neighbors.

Rand is not the first writer to use the metaphor of "moral pygmies." Again, as in defining "savage" on AS 1039, AR does not mean these words literally. She is giving them all a new and deeper meaning. These images are about ideas, not average adult male stature.

a skyscraper needs no foundation. Another skyscraper metaphor.

your history. Again, Galt sounds as though he is speaking from outside the earth and the human race.

the era of pre-language. Newspeople on TV almost never bother to define the fashionable word of the month, words like "empathy".

AS 1041

it is a city's reflection. AR had never seen a mirage, unless it was in driving from Los Angeles through Arizona and New Mexico. When you see a mirage, you don't see a city. That happens only in the movies. You see a pond.

offering them sacrifices in token of his gratitude. AR may have gotten this from Fustel (see Bibliography). But to the Greeks and Romans and other ancients, burning an animal was not a sacrifice in Rand's sense. It was a straight business transaction. I will burn sacrificial lambs if you grant me rain and a bumper crop, O Jupiter!

part man, part animal, part spider. A spider is an animal. But in Rand's day, people often spoke of "animals" as the four-legged kind and did not include arachnids, insects and fish.

the world of non-A. This should not be confused with *The World of Null-A*, a 1945 science fiction serial and 1948 novel by A. E. Van

Vogt. The Null-A stands for non-Aristotelean logic. Might AR have read or heard of this novel?

AS 1042

Man can be certain of nothing! These exact words were spoken by one big shot visiting professor at Cortland State in the 1970s. And he smirked. AR is not making this up.

electric light . . . generator. This is another allusion to Galt's role as an inventor, and a set up for the torture scene in the chapter titled "The Generator."

New York City does not exist. This was not literally true even in 1957. It is certainly not true today. But if we say that the belief systems of the world deny the possibility of a city of freedom, achievement and happiness, and opportunity for the immigrant, and upward mobility, of people of different religious and ethnic groups living together in peace, then yes, the world would be skeptical that such a place could exist.

If you added that New York City also has some municipal corruption—*that* they'd believe. Sticker.

and call it a revolt against believing. This is the Marxist arguing against religion. Tweedledee and Tweedledum.

they proclaim that there is no mind. AR is thinking of the Behaviorists, who taught that everything you do is a "conditioned reflex." Everybody controls you but you. See her article on B. F. Skinner's *Beyond Freedom and Dignity* in ARL.

AS 1043

rubber meanings. Listen to the newsmen on TV, and to the big shots they interview. They all misuse the same words, because those misuses are currently fashionable.

They don't seem to understand that words have meanings. They think that words have only fashions. We are all supposed to say "empathy" everywhere we used to say "sympathy." No one bothers to look up the meanings of these words. So, it is easy for Comrade Professor to get away with switches in definitions—rubber meanings—like "Oh, the Soviet Union was never socialist. It was State Capitalist. So, it wasn't socialism that failed in Russia. It was a form

"This is John Galt Speaking"

of Capitalism." A professor said those very words to me in the 1970s—with a straight face. Again, AR is not making this up.

reactions, drives, condition. Q. E. D. These were the fashionable words of the. 1950s.

a scientist working on an invention. AR is again reinforcing Galt's role, the torture scene climax, and more: the centrality of the inventor in man's rise.

a psychologist helping a neurotic. AR refers to NB helping several members of Rand's circle, although not always successfully.

The problem of production has been solved. The only problem left is distribution. This reader was taught this in college by a professor who called himself a "liberal." It did not even take one of the socialist professors to say it. A statist nostrum. AR is not making this up.

every man born is entitled to exist without labor. The current version of this comes from Robert Reich, who is now pushing an automatic, unconditional income. Does this mean that we won't have to work anymore? Of course not.

Since the money will come from government taxes, and half of it will just be taken back again by government taxes, we will be forced to work for government under the direction of government economic experts like Robert Reich.

Frantic cowards. Was AR thinking of Wendell Willkie, the Republican presidential candidate of 1940? She worked for his campaign, until disillusioned with him. Would she later put William F. Buckley in this category? Friedrich Hayek, the economist?

an adjustment between the unlimited. An actual quote from some conservative economist?

Any stray mediocrity. The 1930s—the Great Depression—were particularly rich in "plans." Will Rogers, noting the Huey Long Plan and the Townsend Plan, proposed his own "Rogers Plan." But at least Rogers *knew* he was a comedian.

Random females with causeless income. Eleanor Roosevelt, surely. This reader saw her on TV frequently, just before she died in 1962, doing a Public Service Announcement about "the poor people of the world." Who *made* them poor?

AS 1044

If you permit it to be done, you deserve it. Was it Ben Franklin who said, "Those who trade freedom for security deserve neither"? And they will get neither. But AR and BF were both wrong on this point. Every human being deserves freedom, because of his nature, even if he does not "deserve" it because of his ideas.

AS 1045

Faith in the supernatural begins as faith in the superiority of others. A thesis to be debated and expanded on.

His feelings become his only guide. This is one of many lines in AR's writings that make it look to the first-time reader as though AR is somehow opposed to feelings or emotions. But wherever you see those two words in AR, just substitute the word "fear." Then look at the end of this paragraph: "the nature of his feelings is terror." Q.E.D.

Feelings are not the enemy. Evasion of reality leads to fear, and fear paralyzes needed efforts, as FDR said, to convert retreat into advance. See NB's book *The Disowned Self*: You can't disown your unpleasant feelings without destroying your capacity to feel anything at all.

like a blind man who depends on the sight of a dog, he feels he must leash them in order to live. Touchè! Compare Wynand: "You were a ruler of men. You held a leash. A leash is only a rope with a noose at both ends (TF 705).

Every dictator is a mystic. This is a thesis. It probably becomes more true as the dictator becomes more and more surrounded by yes-men and cut off from reality.

faith and force. See AS 1012 above.

Compare this paragraph about dictators to this wartime quote from Winston Churchill: "You've seen these dictators on their pedestals, surrounded by the bayonets of their troops and the truncheons of their police. But in their hearts lies an unspoken, unspeakable fear. They're afraid of words! Of thoughts! Of words spoken abroad. Of thoughts stirring at home, all the more powerful because forbidden. A mouse—a tiny mouse of thought appears in the room, and even the mightiest potentate trembles."

parasite in spirit, who plunders the ideas created by others. As with Aristotle, "spirit" means "mind."

AS 1046

gargoyle. This means a monstrous carving on a European church. But any such carving is called a "grotesque." A gargoyle is specifically a rainspout, with the run-off coming out of the monster's mouth.

The word "gargoyle" is related to the words "gargle" and "gurgle." Victor Hugo, AR's model and mentor in novel writing, was probably inspired by the gargoyles of Notre Dame to create the character Quasimodo the hunchback for his novel *Notre Dame de Paris*.

not deterred by piles of human corpses. AR imagined Hitler and Stalin.

the excuse that the end justifies the means. Gary Weiss, in *Ayn Rand Nation*, misquotes Frederick Cookinham, in *The Age of Rand*, as saying that one of the things that AR has in common with M.K. Gandhi is that "they both believed that the ends justify the means" (Weiss, page 26–7). Mr. Cookinham mentioned "the ends justify the means" on page 229 of *The Age of Rand*, in order to say that both AR and MKG *rejected* the idea that the ends justify the means.

to believe that you could adjust yourself to a mystic's dictatorship. See AS 606: One of the victims of the tunnel disaster believes he can get along under any system.

swinish indulgence . . . not enjoyment, but escape. How did John Belushi die? (Belushi died on March 5, 1982, and AR died March 6.) Life was not his purpose.

AS 1047

scum . . . torrent . . . dam . . . sewer . . . reservoir. This is a complex metaphor. It works except that you don't find dams in sewers.

not to live, but to get away with living. This is yet another example of the Life-is-not-their-purpose Principle. It is what Dr. Akston asked Dagny as she was about to leave the valley (AS 807). Do they really want to live, or do they just want to get away with self-destructive behavior by getting more virtuous people to clean up the messes they make?

businessman . . . chaining the ability of competitors. You should always be sure to notice when AR's heroes criticize businessmen, lest you fall for the claim by the Rand Bashers that Rand is simply "pro-business."

demolishing greatness. That is what Ellsworth Toohey does, in TF.

last in human history . . . first to vanish. Since 1957, you might add astronaut and web designer, but the point is the same: high tech came last and will be the first to go. Sticker! Look into the lives of inventors and especially inventor-entrepreneurs, like Madame C. J. Walker.

legends about a thundering god. Sticker! How inspiring that a man should tame a source of energy that his ancestors had feared and personified as Thor, the thunder god, and his equivalent gods around the world! It was said that Franklin "ripped lightning from the heavens and the scepter from tyrants." Hero of Alexandria built a steam engine, but in a world where slaves were available to do work, no one started an industrial revolution with it. It was merely a toy. See the life of James Watt, the first builder of steam engines. Edwin L. Drake read about people near the Caspian Sea collecting oil from seeps and burning it for light, and he had the idea of drilling for it. Inventors!

AS 1048

three parasites. Jeff Allen's story of the Twentieth Century Motor Company, on AS 654. Imagine Jeff Allen listening to Galt's speech! And the six thousand others who had heard Galt say, "I will stop the motor of the world." Allen's is one of the reactions you might film in an AS movie that shows the whole Speech, or more than just fifteen minutes of it.

by reason of their incompetence. Galt does not mean incompetence makes you evil. The exploitation of people through guilt makes you evil. This might have been clearer if he had said, "by reason of their *relative* incompetence."

the willingness of the good to serve it. The triumph of evil is possible only if the good people serve it. But Tolstoy, in *War and Peace*, said that the only thing required for the triumph of evil is that good men do nothing. That's the opposite, isn't it? Or is it?

The word was 'No.' Communist screenwriter Dalton Trumbo, in his script for the movie *Spartacus*, had Tony Curtis ask Kirk Douglas, "Could we have won, Spartacus?"

Spartacus replies, "Whenever even one man says No, the empire begins to crumble. And we were tens of thousands who said No."

AS 1049

electronic tube. AR means the vacuum tube. John Ambrose Fleming invented the oscillation valve in 1904, and Lee de Forest invented the audion in 1906. The transistor was invented at Bell Labs in New Jersey in 1947. The most common type of transistor, invented by Bell Labs in 1959, appeared two years after AS was published.

Let your women take a look at a jungle female. Here you can see that Galt is addressing his words mainly to a typical man with a wife. Today he would address the wife equally.

ideas are created by men's means of production. This is a Marxist idea.

the skyscrapers and smokestacks around you. In AR's *Capitalism: The Unknown Ideal*, she mentioned smokestacks in a way that has been ridiculed. She pointed out that the only time in history when population suddenly shot up was the industrial revolution, the era of smokestacks and coal and steam-powered factories and railroads. An agricultural society, she said, was more vulnerable to famine and other limiters of population growth.

AS 1050

It's only human. AR got this from Nietzsche's 1878 book *Menschliche, Allzu Menschliche—Human, All Too Human.*

The public, to you, is whoever has failed. See Rearden asking, "Why is Orren Boyle more "the public" than I am?" (AS 981).

Did you want to know who is John Galt? It is extraordinary to hear a character talk about himself and his role in history while he is still alive, but this is the tone of the whole speech. Galt, like Patrick Henry, bids defiance to the world. Why do you think AR created a fictional "Patrick Henry University"?

I have done by plan and intention. Galt is every slave who ever ran away. Every indentured servant who ever signed onto a ship bound for the colonies. Every immigrant landing at Ellis Island.

AS 1051

who went on strike, in protest and despair. Ayn considered Frank to have "gone on strike" from acting. Which of the men she describes in this paragraph would be Frank? This is what Eddie meant, on AS 649, when he said that Dan Conway had not been taken out on strike by the destroyer. He had just given up.

the Dark Ages. The image of Roman civilization falling was an important one to AR, and not only in AS. " . . . it feels like I'm living in the last days of the Roman Empire . . . " (BB 302). AS ends on a hopeful note, but AR did not feel very hopeful for years after finishing it. This was partly due to her "post-partum depression."

The game of the mystics is up. Leonard Peikoff says that thanks to Rand, the "Guilt Game is up."

humanity's brief summer. That is, since the American and Industrial Revolutions.

power . . . glory. This comes from The Lord's Prayer. See Matthew and Luke. Google Andrea Bocelli singing it. Gay Talese likes to use biblical quotes for his book titles, such as *The Kingdom and the Power*, his history of the *New York Times*. ("For Thine is the kingdom, and the power, and the glory forever, amen.") Talese's wife Nan Talese was the Doubleday editor of Anne C. Heller's *Ayn Rand and the World She Made.*

AS 1052

you honor a fortune-teller above a fortune-maker. Touchè!

the man who sleeps on a bed of nails. AR is referring to Nikolay Chernyshevsky (1828-1889), Russian literary critic and novelist, and a leader of the Russian socialist movement in the 1860s and 70s. He was a follower of Hegel and an inspiration to Lenin. His literature students went on to be revolutionaries. He wrote his famous novel *What Is to Be Done?* while imprisoned at Saints Peter and Paul Fortress in Saint Petersburg, a sort of Russian Bastille. His hero was totally devoted to revolution. He sleeps on a bed of nails and eats only raw steak, to build up his strength for the revolution. Lenin later used "What Is to Be Done?" as the title for a famous article. Like her fictional Kira in WTL, AR's first job was tour guide at that fortress. She would have told visitors about Chernyshevsky.

the Atlantic skyline of New York. Why "Atlantic" skyline? In 1957, especially for AR, there was still a cachet to the North Atlantic

Ocean. Even people who lived in other parts of the world looked to London, Paris, New York and Washington for leadership, political, cultural, you name it. Madrid, Lisbon and other Atlantic capitals too. And of course, here, in *Atlas Shrugged*, we can guess that Rand is hinting at Atlantis, and at the Atlantes (the plural of Atlas) who hold civilization on their shoulders. But today, some people make the mistake of being chauvinists of "Western Civilization."

With millions jetting around the world routinely, it is time to forget about Western or Eastern Civilization. From now on, we are living in one world civilization.

I have foreshortened the usual course of history. It must be terrifying for people to hear Galt say this. He is not just another guy with an opinion. He has taken away the broadcast of the Head of the State. He has just seized static electricity from the heavens and the airwaves from tyrants. (See AS 1047 above.)

the will to love one's life. Not Nietzsche's "will to power."

AS 1053

vicious circle. This is an old expression. The more an addict gets, the more he craves, for example. Dorothy Parker, Robert Benchley and their friends, who had lunch at the Algonquin Hotel in the 1920s, called themselves "The Vicious Circle." Gandhi spoke of breaking the vicious circle of violence and revenge. "The practice of an eye for an eye accomplishes nothing but to make the whole world blind."

an amoral jungle where anything goes. Calling an immoral person "amoral," suggests that the individual does not know the difference.

You believe they are the masters of existence. See the title essay in AR's *For the New Intellectual*, for AR's psychological archetypes of the "Attila" and the "Witch Doctor."

some animal's race. Sounds like AR thinks it is stupid to bet on a horse race. See AS 932. Betting more than you can afford to lose is stupid, but horse racing is intensely interesting to those in the horsy set. And until the "horseless carriage" was invented, *everyone* was in the horsy set. Wine, women and betting, and we can throw in drugs and gun ownership for reasons of machismo—these are the things your clergy will condemn as selfish, thus insuring the continuance of both the vice trade and the Saturday confession trade. The Guilt Game.

a liquor-soggy brain. Long before reading AR, some of us were contemptuous of alcohol, drugs and cigarettes. With AR, except for her cigarette smoking, we found a kindred spirit. Contempt for grownup failings is one big reason for AR's enormous appeal to youth.

AS 1054

private profit or public good. This is an important point for all the talking heads on TV who are constantly setting up this very alternative—this very false alternative. The freedom of eight billion human beings to make their private profits *is* a public good.

straddling for two hours. Two hours is AR's estimate of the time it takes to declaim the speech up to this point. This line makes us picture people in their homes or in bars listening for two hours, and Galt still has an hour to go. How are those millions reacting in the radio audience? In a movie, we should see lots of reaction shots. Perhaps the actors will show something of the awed and dazed expressions of the people in the movie *Close Encounters of the Third Kind* as they watch the alien spacecraft land.

cast the first stone. A biblical reference. In John 8, a mob was about to stone a woman caught in the act of adultery. Jesus picked up a stone and held it out to the crowd, saying, "Let him who is without sin cast the first stone." Jesus is mistaken if he thinks that no one is entitled to make moral judgments unless he himself has never committed an immoral act. But to the woman, Jesus very sensibly says "Go and sin no more." That is what the conscious, reasoning self must say to other sinners—and to himself too. And then Jesus tells the crowd, "I am the light of the world." Not literally, though. He had not invented a light bulb, like *Anthem's* Equality 7-2521, or ripped static electricity from the heavens and turned it into current.

Whether you live or die is an absolute. Perhaps Hank has told Galt about the death of Tony the Wet Nurse.

willing to sit out the course of any battle. In the 2020 movie *The Trial of the Chicago 7*, William Kunstler, defending the 7, says to Dave Dellinger, a pacifist, "You refused to fight against Hitler!

You sat out World War II! Even *I* want to slug you!" AR is not alone in her contempt for the uninvolved.

In any compromise between good and evil, it is only evil that can profit. AR quoted herself more than once on this point, expanding on it in her article "Doesn't Life Require Compromise?" in *The Virtue of Selfishness*, and "The Anatomy of Compromise" in *Capitalism: The Unknown Ideal*.

AS 1055

When some barefoot bum in some pesthole of Asia yells at you: How dare you be rich. Asia has had plenty of socialists and Communists, but they have been well-educated lawyers and professors. They can afford shoes. She may have been referring to Gandhi, in her ignorance of what he was all about. Sadly, the head games AR describes in this paragraph are as much a fact of 2024 life as of 1957 life, except that many more American kids go to college now, and learn all the bullshit intellectual games from the professors.

champions of reason and science. This is for Ronald Reagan and subsequent Republicans who have more and more become wholly the Religious Right. Barry Goldwater, once part of the "Cold War Conservative" trend that came between the so-called "Isolationist Right" of the 1930s and the "Religious Right" of the 1980, when CBS *60 Minutes* interviewed him, said, "the Religious Right scares the hell out of me!" AR, though, had already scored this debating point, in this page of Galt's speech. The religious folks had, long before 1957, conceded science and modernity to the Marxists.

concentration camps. This is as close as *Atlas* comes to mentioning Hitler and Stalin by name. The first use of "concentration" in this context came from the Spanish army in the 1890s. They forced villagers into fortified camps, and called those villagers "*re-concentrados*."

AS 1056

People's States will surpass this country in material production. See the "Kitchen Debate" between Vice President Richard Nixon and Premier Khrushchev in Moscow in 1959.

half-crazed delinquents. "Juvenile Delinquent" was the word of the day in 1957. There were also the "Beatniks" in the 1950s, but

AR had yet to see the "hippies" of 1967, who did really have to be seen to be believed.

the looters' conquests keep creeping closer to your doors. AR must be referring to the Soviet takeover of eastern Europe after World War II, as she was writing this book, and its conquest of China and North Vietnam and Laos. In 1959 came Cuba.

their bloodiest horrors are unleashed to punish the crime of thinking. Do you think she's exaggerating? When Pol Pot's Communist army captured Cambodia's capital in 1975, all educated people were shot.

AS 1057

This page expands on Galt's briefer description of self-esteem on AS 1018.

A lot of this page reflects what we have seen in Hank Rearden's lifelong struggle against guilt. Galt would have made this point to Rearden personally on Hank's arrival in the valley, or Francisco would have done so in Hank's office or on a plane flying Hank and company to the valley.

To fear to face an issue is to believe that the worst is true. That's the truth!

shyster. Wikipedia reports some interesting theories as to the origin of this word.

self-made night . . . nameless fire. You will find almost these exact words in NB's recorded lecture "Discovering the Unknown Self" and his book *The Disowned Self*. Did he even realize when he wrote those words that he had gotten them from Galt's Speech?

It is fascinating to see how AR's circle picked up on her words and made habits of them.

Observe the persistence. Here begins a fascinating speculation on Atlantis, as Galt already analyzed Adam and Eve on AS 1026.

AS 1058

That is the paradise which you have lost. AR is referring to John Milton's *Paradise Lost*. Milton (1608-1674) published this in 1667. It is an epic poem running to ten thousand lines of blank verse. Milton was blind, and in the gallery room of the New York Public Library you can see a painting of Milton dictating the poem to his wife and daughters.

On AS 1011, Galt says "You wanted to know John Galt's identity." On AS 1021 he asks, "Are you beginning to see who is John Galt?" On AS 1050 it's "Did you want to know who is John Galt?" Here, it's "Some of you will never know who is John Galt."

This repetition is one of the touches that makes the whole 60-page speech hang together better.

you have known the state of being a man. This is the Enlightenment use of the word "man." This is virtue—the Roman quality of *virtu*: to be a man. A few lines below on this page, Galt says "Accept, as your moral ideal, the task of becoming a man."

you who are alone with my words at this moment. Picture millions of radio listeners aware of how challenged they are by these words.

I am, therefore I'll think. Rene Descartes (1596-1650) wrote *Discourse on The Method* in 1637. In it, he wrote "Cogito, ergo sum": I think, therefore I am.

He had been doubting everything, including his own existence, but he concluded that there is obviously someone doing this doubting, so he exists. If I doubt, I think. If I think, I exist.

Some philosophers in our time believe that the most Descartes could reliably say is that doubting is going on. Galt would ask how doubting can go on if there is no entity doing the doubting. Rand relies on Aristotle.

Descartes was mainly responsible for an increased interest in epistemology in his time and is considered the father, or one of the fathers, of modern philosophy.

Live and act within the limit of your knowledge. Compare this to Francisco saying to Hank "Within the limit of your knowledge, you are right" (AS 641).

his nature, his morality, his glory. On the Phil Donahue Show, Rand was asked whether she considered herself a perfect being. She said yes. A more complete answer might be: Morality is more forgiving than practicality. No one can fault you morally as long as you did the best you could with the knowledge and other means you had. You are morally perfect as long as you did your best. As a practical matter, though. your best may not be good enough.

Nevertheless, morally, at least, you are on safe ground as long as you can say, with Harry Truman, "On my tombstone I want written, 'He done his damndest'."

AS 1059

The top half of this page explains the foregoing better.

errors of knowledge and breaches of morality. See AS 641 again.

an action you know to be evil. Spencer Tracy, playing an American judge in the 1961 movie *Judgment at Nuremberg*, hears a German judge say, "I did not know it would come to that."

Tracy replies, "You knew it would come to that the first time you condemned a man you knew to be innocent."

just feel it. AR may have heard people say this a lot in her day, but have you ever heard anyone try to get away with this dodge? Perhaps the saying has just gone out of style—and perhaps partly through AR's influence.

the achievement of your happiness. See Jefferson's Declaration of Independence. In *Who Is Ayn Rand?*, BB (page 237) quotes AR on "... a moral revolution to sanction and complete the political achievement of the American Revolution," and in *The Passion of Ayn Rand* (page 230), BB writes, "She was to repay her adopted country for the gifts it offered her. She was to repay it by giving America its voice."

discipline you did not value yourself enough to assume. This is what self-esteem means. You are worth the effort it takes to survive and thrive!

you will learn to live like a man. See AS 1058 above.

Do you ask if it's ever proper to help another man? This is crucial, if you want to meet the anger and fury of the Rand Bashers.

AS 1060

treason you committed . . . to your country. Here, and again at the bottom of this page, AR makes the common mistake of saying "country" when she means "nation."

A country is land, real estate, dirt. A nation means the people and their institutions they maintain *on* that piece of land. She focuses on the United States when she should focus on the world. In many places in this book, AR sets her ideas in the context of man and his world,

"This is John Galt Speaking"   219

so, when she shifts to a patriotic theme, it surprises, and not in a good way. That is the difference between 1957 and, perhaps, 2057.

a pile of dead scrap. We saw Dagny and Hank find Galt's motor in the ruins of the Twentieth Century Motor Company in Starnesville, Wisconsin back on AS 279.

and you failed to know me when I passed you in the street. Interesting! Galt faults the world for not making him as famous and honored as Edison.

His motor is a good reason for his faulting the world. They *should* know and honor him. Something has gone terribly wrong in a world where people don't use his motor and he lacks fame. On top of that, there is this irony:

When you cried in despair for the unattainable spirit which you felt had deserted your world, you gave it my name. Dr. Stadler told Dagny, on AS 360, that his student must be dead, because if he were alive, a man of his ability, the whole world would be speaking of him now. And Dagny replies: the whole world *is* speaking of him!

the disguise of a playboy . . . the role of a pirate. This is what people miss if they skip the speech.

Lines like this relate to characters: there are more below.

my fellow fighters. AR autographed her books to her friends with these words (BB 143 (quoting *Anthem* page 118), and 294).

what I am now completing. Galt sees this speech as the *coup de grace* to the looters. Millions will replace them with new leaders, political and intellectual, under the impact and influence of this speech.

this greatest of countries. See twenty lines above. Here he identifies this nation as based on "man's right to exist" and that is the important point: not the land, but the principle of natural rights.

AS 1061

unequaled in history. Two big reasons for America's fantastic growth after the revolution were immigration and European investment. Millions of entrepreneurs came hither looking for opportunity, and European bankers put their investment capital into America because it was politically stable and safe, and because there was unlimited opportunity here for growth.

rocket-explosion of its youth. Remember Eddie, on AS 9, being reminded, by Ellis Wyatt, of stories he had read in school books and never quite believed, of the nation's youth? Perhaps we can hope for that kind of growth for the whole world in the 21st century.

until the road is clear. See AS 1168, below.

inalienable right. Jefferson's words in the Declaration of Independence.

gift of God . . . gift of society. President Kennedy, in his inaugural speech, spoke of the American Revolutionary "belief that man's rights come, not from the generosity of the state, but from the hand of God." (Just substitute "nature" for "God" in that line.)

A sophisticated Harvard man like JFK would have to reach his own sensible accommodation between his Catholic upbringing and his Harvard professors, who had to find their own compromise between religion and Marx. But at least in this case, JFK, or Ted Sorensen, his speech writer, was using AR's and Aristotle's, and Locke's and Jefferson's, principle of natural rights.

Do you hear me now, Hank Rearden? Why does Galt add the word "now" in Rearden's case?

Rights are conditions of existence. Here Galt defines natural rights.

which means . . . which means. Jerome Tuccille, in *It Usually Begins with Ayn Rand*, tells of members of Rand's circle finishing each other's sentences with "which means . . . ." See Recurring Themes.

AS 1062

so a nation can't, or a country. Why the distinction?

The only proper purpose of a government. These words are in the Preamble of the Libertarian Party Platform. That Preamble was written by AR's former friend Dr. John Hospers, who taught philosophy at Brooklyn College when he met Rand, and at USC when he was the LP's first presidential candidate in 1972.

AS 1063

But a government that initiates the employment of force. This terrific quote by George Washington on the nature of government appeared in a Libertarian Party pamphlet. "Government is not reason, it is not eloquence, it is force! And like fire, it is a dangerous servant and a fearful master."

ninety-nine year contracts. Sticker! This consideration will not have occurred to most thirteen-year-old readers. This is what Milton Friedman and the "Chicago Boys" told General Augusto Pinochet of Chile, who had overthrown Marxist President Salvador Allende.

Pinochet wanted Friedman to magically produce a plan whereby Chile would have the benefits of capitalism without having to offer protection of civil liberties to its citizens. Pinochet thought he could attract foreign investment in spite of his reign of terror. Friedman tried to tell him that it just does not work that way. You can't have economic liberty without civil liberty. That conversation would have been the same in principle as the scenes, below, where Mr. Thompson and his henchmen try to cajole, entice, and threaten Galt into "fixing" the US economy. The story of Friedman and Pinochet was told, in 1973, to the Syracuse University Young Americans for Freedom chapter, by Milton's son David Friedman, also an economist, and author of the anarcho-capitalist book *The Machinery of Freedom*.

Nor will he give ten years. Galt refers to Rearden Metal.

AS 1064

When you work in a modern factory. This page and the next explain AR's "Pyramid of Ability" theory. It impressed her publisher, Bennett Cerf of Random House.

This page is AR's answer to Marx's Labor Theory of Value. Galt does not have to concentrate much on Nazi theories here, since Hitler had just finished doing a really great job of discrediting them. If AR had written AS before the war, she might have had Galt denounce the pseudo-science of genetics and Aryan superiority alongside Marxist economics. A Jeremiah has to attack whatever ideas are fashionable at the moment.

the philosopher who taught men how to think. Aristotle.

AS 1065

Such was the price we asked. Roark, in his courtroom speech, says "That was the price I set for my work. I was not paid" (TF 730). AR thinks here along the same lines.

should own our palaces and yachts. This was a sticker, and not altogether welcome. This is Rand's view of the world and the human future on a very practical level. Most of us have a modern apartment, a car, a radio, movies, a refrigerator, but the industrialists have palaces and yachts. The thirteen-year-old reader might wonder whether John Galt would be interested in owning a yacht. Would Rand fancy yachting if she had made tens of millions with her writing? Galt would be more the type to be so engrossed in his laboratory that he would not be interested in a yacht.

Rand's point is that in a free society, more and more people would have more and more choices. No matter the lifestyle of each individual tycoon, the real wealth he makes possible will become the capital that will make possible more jobs that will lift more people out of poverty.

you saw no difference between economic and political power. Your socialist professors said, "Free enterprise is not free." And they all repeat the cliché that "a hungry man is not free." The socialists always claim to want to *free* us from capitalism, though.

AS 1066

there can be no such thing as a disinterested action. This is part of the reason there cannot be real, full altruism. William Lyon Phelps (1865-1943), the Yale literature professor and wit, said, "This is the final test of a gentleman: his respect for those who can be of no possible service to him." Galt would not admit the possibility of a human being who is of no possible service to him. Phelps probably meant *literal* service, such as a train porter. But any human being doing productive work anywhere in the world is of service to me, directly or indirectly. And I am, to him. Every human being owes a certain basic respect to every other human being.

Do you hear me, Dr. Robert Stadler? But it is not to him that I wish to speak. This is where Galt turns from flailing his audience with moral damnation to speaking words of comfort and encouragement to those who might still be salvageable. This would typically be the young.

one owes a rational statement. Jefferson: "A decent respect to the opinions of mankind requires that they should declare the causes . . .." See AS 1004: Galt's Speech is akin to the Declaration of Independence.

"This is John Galt Speaking" 223

stop supporting your own destroyers. This is AR's Sanction of the Victim principle, or Gandhi's "Non-co-operation with evil" principle. It is very sensible advice: do not play the looters' game, thinking that you will win. You won't. First of all, they are more practiced than you are, and more ruthless, and secondly, you would be playing on a sinking ship.

AS 1067

white blackmail. This is a chapter title on AS 423.

Since you're captive, act as a captive. Galt will do this after they capture him.

raise a standard to which the honest will repair. General Washington makes a third appearance in the novel: see AS 534 and 549.

or with a few of your chosen friends. See *Anthem*, page 122.

the founder of a modest community on the frontier of mankind's rebirth. Sticker! At the end of this angry tirade to a collapsing word, at last a note of optimism. Like *Anthem*.

then and on that day we will return. Sticker! She must have thought of General MacArthur's famous line "I shall return!"

We will open the gates of our city. The Book of Revelations 21: 1 and 2: "And I saw a new heaven and a new Earth . . . And I, John, saw the holy city, New Jerusalem, coming down from God out of Heaven . . . ." Ayn, with her Jewish background, might have been a little spotty on the New Testament, but she may have looked over the whole bible for points from which to draw parallels in AS. Frank might have made suggestions. In any case, some readers might be reminded of this line of John of Patmos by that line of John of Galt.

a city of smokestacks, pipelines, orchards, markets and inviolate homes. Sticker! Of course, again, we have to point out that smokestacks are going the way of the horse and buggy. They were only a temporary means to the end of energy, and cleaner sources of energy have been invented. The city AR describes is a city of and for the kind of person the socialists hate: the "middle class." The "Bourgeoisie." This impression of the post-strike world is not like southern England, where millions work as domestic servants in places like Downton Abbey. It is not a world of golf resorts for Trump's billionaire friends. Picture a world where North Korea, Haiti, Somalia, Syria, Iraq and Afghanistan are dotted with the booming and bustling middle-sized and middle-class US manufacturing cities of the 1950s, but with solar power.

We will act as the rallying center. Here is a rare clue as to what Galt plans to do after the novel ends. Colorado will get its Second Renaissance. Galt doesn't tell the world the location of Galt's Gulch yet, but after the looters' government falls, we can guess that he will. Or the information will leak out.

free trade and free minds. In 1968, Lanny Friedlander founded *Reason Magazine: Free Trade and Free Minds.* Since then, it has become the leading and most successful libertarian magazine.

hordes of savages have never been an obstacle to men who carried the banner of the mind. This is ominous. It is a historical reference, though, not a vision of the future. And the history it recalls is one of white armies with Gatling guns shooting down non-white warriors with spears. Not a good note for Galt to hit.

AR had been thinking of white settlers defending themselves from Indians, as in the movie *Drums Along the Mohawk*. But note that in the Mohawk Valley, during the War for Independence, the Oneida and Tuscarora nations sided with the Americans while the other nations of the Iroquois Confederacy sided with the British. It was not about skin color. It was about ideas. AR would be the first to criticize governments for violating rights and treaties, including government treachery toward the Indians.

AS 1068

The political system we will build. This sounds ominous. Is Galt hinting at throwing out the Constitution? No: see AS 1167. Perhaps this was the line Robert Kirsch, of the *Los Angeles Times*, meant when he wrote in his review of AS that Galt is arguing for a dictatorship.

In that world, you'll be able to rise in the morning with the spirit you had known in your childhood. Sticker! And this whole paragraph! "*Eagerness, adventure . . . as consistent and reliable as facts*" This image might help to keep the young reader going over the years. This is the most inspiring paragraph in the book.

touched by its rays. Walter Donway, of the Atlas Society, used this line as the title of a 2008 book of poetry. This sentence is too long and convoluted for a spoken speech.

the endurance that carries their burdens. Go to the Chanin Building, across E. 42nd Street from the Grand Hyatt next to Grand Central Terminal. It has three entrances. In each entrance there are four *repoussé* panels together called "New York: City of Opportunity." In the east entrance, on Lexington Avenue, is one called "Endurance." It shows Atlas on one knee, straining to hold up the sky. It looks just like the Nicholas Gaetano cover of AS.

AS 1069

the generosity that responds to their cries of despair. See? AR has placed generosity among the virtues, not the vices. But it can be abused.

which makes you believe that they are men and that they love it, too. Life is not their purpose—a Recurring Theme.

Do you hear me . . . my love? This whole paragraph is addressed to Dagny. Go back over the whole paragraph and hear what Galt is saying to Dagny to get her to join the strike at last. But this creates a problem. AR never says so, but Mr. Thompson must have people not only recording Galt's speech—after all, they must have been ready to record his speech for the ages—and they must have combed the speech for any clue as to Galt's whereabouts and anything else they could learn about him that would help them use or destroy him, like the fact that there is some woman out there whom he calls "my love." And on AS 1105 below, Thompson asks Galt whether he has a sweetheart.

In the name of the best within you. Since this was a line Eddie remembered a minister saying in his childhood (AS 6), maybe Galt got it from Eddie in one of their cafeteria chats (but it is not in any of the five chats AR lets us in on). In this paragraph, and in the whole speech, Galt is speaking to Dagny. The whole world too, of course, but mainly to Dagny. And she knows it. This is where AS is revealed as a love story, just as Albert Ruddy said to Ayn when he approached her in 1972 about making a movie from the book, and Ayn's reply was: "That's all it ever was." Now go back and read the whole speech again, as a love letter.

The world you desired can be won, it exists, it is real, it is possible, it's yours. Galt used this line to Dagny on AS 813. Notice that AR writes "it is" twice, but then contracts it to "it's." The line sounds better with the contraction. It quickens the pace when spoken. It looks like she meant this line, and perhaps all of her writing, to be read aloud. But especially this speech, of course, since it is a speech.

Might some composer make a cantata out of these last four paragraphs of the speech?

It took AR over two years to write the speech. BB reports that once AR finished the speech, the rest of the novel was relatively easy. It was just a matter of writing regular narrative, description and dialog and tying up loose ends. AR could to some extent relax and have fun writing "like a happy child."

8. The Egoist

Chapter Overview

Mr. Thompson orders a tail be put on Dagny, and a search made for Galt. Eddie realizes that Galt is the track worker, and that he has told a lot of personal information about Dagny to him, as well as information about Taggart Transcontinental and the state of the economy, information the government is trying to cover up. Starvation and inflation are worsening.

Against Galt's wishes, Dagny looks up his address in her employee records, goes there, and finds him home. Police have followed her and they arrest Galt.

Thompson visits Galt at the Wayne-Falkland Hotel, where he has been imprisoned. He tries to persuade Galt to somehow fix the national economy. Other leaders have no success trying to get Galt to take over and "run" the national economy. Dagny persuades Thompson that she has turned against Galt and hates him. Otherwise, they will torture her before Galt's eyes. Francisco slips Dagny a note with a phone number to reach him at. Galt asks to see Stadler. Stadler comes and frantically tries to justify himself to Galt.

Galt is ordered to put on formal clothes and appear on TV at a banquet, to trick people into believing that he is now co-operating with the government. Dagny is at the banquet, observing the leaders and shedding her last doubts about going on strike. She sees the proof of Galt's and Akston's words: These people do not want to live, or to see reality. When called upon to speak, Galt turns so the TV audience can see the gun in his ribs. He makes a curt comment that shows that he is not co-operating. The TV audience can see that this banquet is phony.

Thompson and the other leaders confer, and we can see that they know the jig is up. Fighting has broken out between armed gangs around the country. Industry is at a standstill. They are making plans to escape.

Ferris takes Galt on a plane to his torture chamber. Dagny hears this and reports to Francisco.

Scene 1: Dagny with the leadership in the studio after the speech.

AS 1070

Tinky Holloway and Chick Morrison. On AS 990, Tony told Hank that Peters, of the Unification Board, was a stooge of Tinky Holloway, who was a stooge of Orren Boyle. So maybe Holloway is the head of the Unification Board or a lobbyist for the steel industry. On AS 587 we learn that Wesley Mouch favors Holloway.

We see Holloway calling Hank on AS 965 and 966. He meets with Hank on AS 977, where we see his description. Other than these slim clues, we never learn his actual title or function, so AR apparently wants to restrict Holloway to the identity of a generic Washington big shot.

Chick Morrison, though, is given the title "Morale Conditioner," in other words, propaganda minister.

Imagine any recent US President in this situation. He has been bumped, humiliatingly, off the air by someone who seems to have the upper hand, who can stop your broadcast at will, and can mesmerize the whole world with a three-hour speech. In other words, that President is toast.

We don't have to believe it, do we? NB uses this line in his recorded talk "The Moral Revolution in Atlas Shrugged," and that talk is also a chapter in *Who Is Ayn Rand?* "

"No, they don't have to believe it. They are free to think or not to think." Contrast that with Dagny's line on AS 702, "We never had to take any of it seriously, did we?"

AS 1071

goose-stepping. This reference to the Nazis hints that Mr. Thompson will order the muzzling of the TV and radio commentators, and so he does, making real the suggestion that Mr. Thompson has the Hitler-like power to force uniformity of opinion on the media.

The goose step, invented by a sergeant in the Prussian army of Frederick the Great, is well known to American audiences from the newsreels of the 1930s and 40s as a Nazi practice, but the Soviet Union and other nations also used it.

Its purpose was to make men look like mindless automata, thus frightening the enemy. This was psychological warfare. Ironically, it is therefore a sort of Gandhian technique: why fight your enemy when you can frighten him into running away, thus allowing you a bloodless victory?

"Would you rather have the public think that we didn't?": Great touch!

Which is worse for the government—letting the public think they authorized Galt's speech, or letting people think they did not?

amateur at a master. Up to now, Mouch overshadowed Thompson in the story, gradually Bormannizing Thompson's Hitler. But now we see that Mouch is the bureaucrat and Thompson is the politician. This adds some wily depth to Thompson's character.

Chick Morrison uses the expressio, "mystical insight" but then pauses, as if afraid someone will slap him. That is the lingering effect of Galt's speech on all of them, even in this crowd. In AS 1074 below, Thompson refers to "the people" with Dagny, but he quickly changes that to "everybody" as he realizes that Galt's speech made slogans like "the people" obsolete.

AS 1072

The workingmen won't go for it. AR lists all the groups that, as a group, won't be swayed by Galt's speech. There is much satire, and much truth, to these expected group reactions to the speech.

except maybe of big business. AR knew exactly what the book reviewers and intellectuals would say about AS. And this has changed not a bit since 1957, or 1857.

they don't want to starve. Notice that it is always Fred Kinnan, the labor leader, who offers the most honest and practical comments, as when we first met him when planning Directive 10-289 on AS 538.

knowing that the man who answered would, thereafter, be the man in power. Good point, psychologically and dramatically—because the one who does answer is Dagny.

AS 1073

Let those who can, take over. That's a line the Rand Bashers could use if they wanted to thoroughly comb AS for dirt. They could easily spin that to mean Dagny proposes a dictatorship for Galt! See AS 1068 above. But it won't wash, because "take over" would mean that Thompson and his gang withdrew Directive 10-289 and the Railroad Unification Plan, and the Fair Share Law. It would also require that the Railroad Association rescind the Anti-Dog-Eat Dog Rule.

Furthermore, government control of information would have to be lifted. All of those changes would have to come from public demand, not because of any dictation from Galt. Because of his speech, Galt and the strikers have influence, but not power.

In 1968, Lyndon Johnson was committed to the war in Vietnam. Nixon could run against him for President on a platform of admitting that Johnson's war had been a mistake. When a leader's policy has fallen out of favor with the public, he usually leaves office rather than admit that his policy had been wrong. Some candidate, after the end of the strike, would run against Thompson for Head of the State on a Galt's Speech platform, unless political instability has increased to the point of Thompson fleeing the country. In that case, his VP or someone farther down the line of succession would complete his term, two or more candidates would run in the next election on various platforms, and Thompson just would not run. He and Jim Taggart, and Mouch, Ferris, and their cronies would be in Switzerland, counting the loot in their numbered bank accounts.

On this page, Dagny launches into her own angry speech at the nation's rulers, both out of long pent-up frustration and because of just having heard Galt on the radio. His tirade has revved up Dagny for her own. Later, she will realize that she needs to play it cool with these characters and pretend to hate Galt.

began as a shock of astonishment and ended as an obituary. Dagny is already mourning Dr. Stadler. Soon, he will literally die.

AS 1074

ivory-tower intellectuals who stick to some pet theory and haven't any sense of practical reality. One student of history was confused when he learned that Frederick the Great and Bismarck had as much to do with the birth of socialism as Marx did.

"But Bismarck hated the socialists!" he objected.

"Sure, because they were his competitors for the same loot."

But more, it was that they were professors and he was a savvy political dealmaker.

If you mentioned the socialists, Bismarck might retort: Those professors with their theories and books! They would not know how to get a law passed! For that they would need a practical politician like me!

This was a case of the *Attila* versus the *witch doctor*. (See *For the New Intellectual*.)

for the people—that is, I mean, for everybody. See AS 1071 above.

and could not move to any further thought. AR sometimes oversells the idea of Eddie's helplessness. If he were as helpless as that, what use would he be to Dagny as her assistant?

AS 1075

Watch that Taggart woman. But her brother James is standing right there with Thompson and Stadler!

On AS 1005, Jim arrives at the broadcast studio with Dagny and Eddie.

On AS 1006 Jim introduces Dagny to Mr. Thompson. He is there on AS 1070, too. But when Thompson tells his goons to put a tail on Dagny, Jim is nowhere to be heard. Wouldn't he curry favor with Thompson by volunteering to report on Dagny's movements and put his own spies on her? Or else object to Thompson tailing her because she is his sister?

Isn't it sheer chance she hasn't deserted you long ago? If Dagny is "his kind," then why is she still sticking around? Unless Stadler means that Dagny is a spy. And shouldn't he say "is" and not "isn't"?

He'll tell us what to do. So it is Thompson who just nominated Galt for dictator and Messiah.

Scene 2: Dagny and Eddie after the speech.

AS 1076

in the street outside the radio station. Picture the walk from the RCA Building of Rockefeller Center (later the GE Building and now Comcast), past the sculpture of Prometheus, down Fifth Avenue, east on 46th Street and into the New York Central Building (now the Helmsley Building), straddling Park Avenue between 45th and 46th.

a few lone figures stood in whispering clusters. Imagine people on the street asking each other "Did you hear the speech?!"

broadcasting a domestic comedy. Amos and Andy and *Fibber McGee and Molly* were still on the radio past 1957. *Our Miss Brooks*" with Eve Arden, ended its radio run that year. Radio was giving way to television just as AS went to press.

above the twenty-fifth-floor limit. See AS 500. The city had closed all buildings above the 25th floor. Jim had the pull to get an exception for the Taggart Building. Here again, AR does show the favoritism government gives to big business—but only to those big businesses in favor at the moment.

He used to ask questions. This is where those five conversations between Eddie and the track worker come home to roost.

Eddie is mortified that he may have blabbed information to Galt that helped Galt destroy Taggart Transcontinental, as Eddie would see it.

AS 1077

what I look like, when I'm asleep. AS 439.

a sudden connection crashed into place in his mind. Eddie had asked Galt why he should want to know what Dagny looked like asleep. Galt had asked Eddie why he wanted to *talk about* what Dagny looked like asleep. Now, knowing that Dagny had met Galt in the valley, Eddie twigs to the fact that Galt has fallen in love with Dagny as he himself has.

In fact, Galt fell in love with Dagny *through* his conversations with Eddie. And now Eddie knows about Dagny and Hank. And Eddie is revealing to Dagny that he has a kind of "bromance" love for Galt.

Since when? she asked sharply: Dagny wants to know when Galt left New York for the valley.

the full understanding of its meaning struck him together. That's when Eddie had blurted out to Galt that Dagny had been sleeping with Hank, on AS 653.

AS 1078

There will be no looters' government within ten days. Notice that Eddie had just said that there would be no trains running in a week if Dagny quit. He uses the conditional "would," but Dagny uses the declarative "will." Does she mean there will be no looters' government in ten days if she quits, or does she mean there will be no looters' government ten days from now because of Galt's speech? In either case, what would happen?

It sounds, from what Eddie just said at the top of the page and from the general breakdown reported on every page, that people are everywhere defying Directive 10-289 and going on strike or going rogue, with or without the speech. But now, the world has heard from Galt himself that the disappearances, and Francisco blowing up d'Anconia Copper, and the activities of Ragnar, are all part of a coordinated rebellion against Directive 10-289, led by a man who can make a monkey out of the Head of the State and the whole broadcasting field. AR avoids, probably wisely, mentioning any political activity. Where is the party politics here? When is the next presidential election?

Then men like Cuffy Meigs will devour. That is as close as Dagny and AR come to a prediction. Mass desertion will mean the breakdown of the nation into the fiefdoms of local warlords, like China between the empire and Mao.

Should I lose the battle by failing to wait one more moment? Dagny is still justifying her hope for a turn around, but . . . .

They're finished. Who is finished? Thompson and friends, but they will be followed by Meigs and Meigs types, unless some opposition party promises to follow Galt's ideas. Do you see Galt running for office? Some politician declaring for Galt's ideas, then. That is Dagny's only hope, and even she no longer quite believes it.

Scene 3: Thompson hears public reaction to the speech, asks Dagny for advice.

AS 1079

The flames that went up. Is AR describing things she saw or heard about in Russia as the Reds drove back the Whites and took over? On this page and those to come, we see the public reaction to Galt's speech superimposed on the descriptions of general breakdown.

AS 1080

beaten up . . . fractured jaw. Here's more ammunition for the Bashers: Ayn Rand advocates beating up people who teach their kids to share their toys. But here, the injured woman has told her five-year-old to *give away* his best toy, not just share it. AR must have thought of the toy story that Harry Binswanger recounted in his "Ayn Rand's Life: Highlights and Sidelights" talk, which is available. Ayn's mother told little Alisa and her sisters to give her half of their toys, so she could put them away for a year. Natasha and Nora gave their mother the half they liked least, but Alisa gave her mother the half she liked best, so she would have something to look forward to. A year later, Alisa asked her mother when they would be getting their toys back. Her mother said she had given them all away. Alisa was shocked that her mother would lie to them.

whistle-stop tour. Fresh in AR's mind would be Harry Truman's whistle-stop tour during the 1948 presidential election. A whistle stop is a stop that a train makes only on the request of someone on the train. A flag stop is a stop a train makes to pick up a passenger who flags the train down.

the better men. AR would have seen this happen in Russia. She apparently never knew that her old philosophy professor had escaped and was living out his life on the Upper West Side, a mile from her. (Sciabarra, page 44)

regal glory . . . hemophilia. AR must have been thinking of the Tsarevich Alexis, son of Tsar Nicholas II, who had hemophilia, which the boy's mother believed her friend Rasputin could cure.

There was no answer. Galt must have said to himself "Now let it work. Mischief, thou art afoot! Take what course thou wilt."

He is not appearing anywhere as a candidate for anything.

no longer to be mined . . . never to be filled. This is a nice metaphor.

AS 1081

Give us men! AR quotes this paragraph on page 162 of *Capitalism: The Unknown Ideal*, in the essay "Is Atlas Shrugging?"

The Order of Public Benefactors. In the Soviet Union, it was the "Hero of Socialist Labor" medal.

John Galt will solve our problems! They are doing to Galt what they did to Rearden Metal. You either destroy something, or you take credit for it ("Miracle Metal"). You make every human action either mandatory or forbidden.

AS 1082

There's an unskilled railroad laborer. Galt had skipped town for the valley, but they would find that he had until recently worked in the Terminal, right under Dagny's nose. They might put two and two together.

The wads of worthless paper money. This is the novel's only mention of gathering hyperinflation. Look up the German hyperinflation of 1923. Inflation in the US would not become a much-talked about problem until the 1970s, under Nixon. As Chairman of the Federal Reserve, AR's friend Alan Greenspan, in 1987, stomped on the brakes of the money supply and caused a brief collapse in the stock market. He hated and feared inflation above all else, and often cited the example of Germany in 1923.

squadrons joined the people they had been sent to punish. This is what AR had seen happen in Petrograd in 1917. The Cossacks were sent to break up riots at the bread lines, but joined them instead.

the 'Indians'—the attacks of any looting savages. Sorry, Ayn, but this line will have to go. Here, AR is using the word "savage" to mean "violent." Real Indians—Native Americans—First Peoples—could have given AR many examples of the wrongdoing, and the violence, of the "Washington crowd." And ironically, insofar as they live in somewhat self-sufficient farm communities, today's Native Americans could ride out a societal collapse better than many city folks. The people in this paragraph fleeing into the wilderness might have to *join* an Indian community to survive and fend off the Washington crowd.

Each individual Indian will choose his own mixture of preservation of an ancient way of life with adoption of modern technology. Russell Means, of the American Indian Movement, liked to say that "It is possible to be an Indian and yet function in the modern world." Means sought the Libertarian Party nomination for President in 1988, losing to Congressman Ron Paul.

But no soldiers could be persuaded. That depends on whether the individual soldier wants to just follow orders and stay out of Leavenworth, or whether even the army has started to break down, as it did in Vietnam, where, by the early 70s, orders were considered merely a starting point for negotiation between the enlisted men and the officers.

We will meet any terms you set. Notice that in the course of this page, they have gone from "We wish to negotiate" to "We might meet your terms" to "We will meet any terms you set."

AS 1083

the night of January 22. A sequel to *Night of Jan. 16th*? AR must have smiled—or grimaced, since her play of that title would have brought back painful memories. It was the triumph of Atlas that brought new life to that play, to WTL, and to her other early writings.

smoke, soot, fumes, noise. This theme will be followed later by AR's scornful comments on the "environmentalists"—later called "Greens."

We have the luxury today of pining for wilderness, now that we have industry. Our ancestors had no choice but to live in pre-industrial wilderness. Nano technology will someday give us steel and materials even better than steel, and will do it without the smoke, soot, fumes and noise.

policemen nor state troopers. The ones who attacked Rearden's mill?

AS 1084

Guatemala. It is ironic that in 1954, the Washington crowd installed a dictator in Guatemala. He was assassinated in 1957. Today, Francisco Marroquin University in Guatemala City has a bust of Ayn Rand on its campus.

In 2020, Guatemala produced 20,000 tons of steel.

to let him take over. As we will see when they meet, Thompson's idea of Galt "taking over" is to offer Galt Wesley Mouch's job: economic dictator. Just as Milton Friedman could not convince Pinochet that dictatorship does not work, neither can Galt convince Thompson. See AS 1063 above.

AS 1085

I can't hold my own boys in line any longer. Mr. Thompson is playing Good Cop—Bad Cop with Dagny. Bobby Kennedy did the same thing to Soviet Foreign Minister Gromyko in the 1962 Cuban Missile Crisis. He said the Joint Chiefs under Chairman Air Force General Curtis LeMay were pressuring the President to invade Cuba or just let them sink the island with hydrogen bombs. Bobby told Gromyko that he did not know how long the Joint Chiefs could be held in check.

AS 1086

Wesley won't go for strong-arm methods. AR is giving us another peek at the full face of fascism, not just the corrupt economics.

Scene 4: Dagny goes to Galt's apartment.

the glassy rustle that was the East River somewhere close by. In 1957, before gentrification, the East River south of the UN was a landscape of power plants, slums, and boats bringing bananas from places like Guatemala. Nikola Tesla, Ho Chi Minh, Sun Yat-sen, and Leon Trotsky had lived on the Lower East Side at one time or another.

her mind seemed inaccessibly relaxed. This is one of AR's unusual images.

if a naked bullet could feel in mid-flight. And this is another.

AS 1087

an 'if' with which she could not exist any longer. This explains why she is doing something so reckless as going to Galt's address. Thompson has scared the bejeezuz out of her. She can't stand not knowing whether Galt is alive or dead.

We must not underestimate Thompson. He figured out that Dagny might have some connection with Galt (actually he got the idea from Stadler, but he saw the possibility and acted on it), and he scared her into showing her hole card. Dagny is not perfectly successful all the time, despite the belief of many, both fans and bashers, who have not read the book carefully, or at all.

as she looked at a vault. This is the vault containing the motor. This whole page shows why AR told Albert Ruddy that Atlas was a love story. A love poem.

She had not seen him. Galt could hardly go on working every day at the Terminal. Someone would have recognized his voice, as Eddie had. He must be staying home. How then will he see Dagny's dollar sign on the Nat Taggart sculpture? He must have spies among the Taggart workers, spies whose name, face and voice no one would know. Maybe Pop Harper! See AS 11. Maybe the young brakeman.

coat collar . . . brim of her hat. Picture Ingrid Bergman at the end of *Casablanca.*

AS 1088

an abandoned city. AR is seeing *The Little Street*, (JAR) and Petrograd and Odessa and other cities and villages in war-torn Russia, and Depression-era towns on the road from Los Angeles to New York, and Stephen Vincent Benét's "The Place of the Gods."

he who possessed such extravagant power to lighten the job of human existence. See Preface.

But this is New York City! New York no longer looms so large for us in the twenty-first century, because we are seeing so many other cities springing up out of nothing. The years since 1957 have brought us Dubai, not Starnesville. Perhaps man has "passed through the midnight, toward the dawn, without knowing it" (Edward R. Murrow).

The moment when she saw the number. This is another example of what Wynand and Roark discussed on TF 578 about "stops, points reached, and then the typing rolled on again."

5th floor, rear. As AR was finishing Atlas, she and Frank lived on the 5th floor of 36 East 36th Street. Her study faced the Empire State Building, so it must have been in the rear of the building.

AS 1089

it was not disaster she expected. Just as Kay Ludlow does not expect to hear of Ragnar's death at sea, so Dagny is confident of finding Galt,

The Egoist

alive and here, not in the valley. AR did not quite make a convincing case for that, but she pulled so many other rabbits out of hats that we should not too quickly dismiss her sense of life as unrealistic. AR said this is how she felt about finding Frank after meeting him once. She did not know his name or address, but she felt as if it were inevitable that she would see him again.

This whole paragraph is one long, complex sentence, but it is worth going back over slowly, to see how AR integrates Dagny's thoughts, feelings and actions, and the meaning of the scene.

crack of a board . . . the sliding wail of a tugboat. AR is putting these bits of movie business into the scene after Dagny pushes the doorbell, because they raise our hopes and then dash them.

Does she hear Galt coming to the door? No, it's a floorboard on another floor. Is that some sound from within his apartment? No, it's just a tugboat siren. AR is keeping us in suspense. Just as she delayed Galt's appearance in the novel for 701 pages, so she is building up his appearance again.

AS 1090

long, bare garret. Picture Van Gogh's painting *Chambre des artiste*, updated to the 20th century with a gas stove, and to the 21st with Galt's lab. In 1957, you may have still been able to see the New York Central Building from the lower East Side, from certain angles.

Your presence in this district. No one uses the word "district" in New York. He would say "neighborhood." Maybe that was different before 1957.

every policeman in the district. Another aspect of the breakdown of civil liberties would be the breakdown of the separation of federal, state and local government, including law enforcement. This is where you see the difference between the US and even good ol' Canada. The latter has the Mounties—the Royal Canadian Mounted Police—a national police force; the US has no federal police, only state and local police. There is a well-honored tradition of local law enforcement here. But the FBI, the ICE, the ATF, and other armed government agencies will never stop trying to see what they can get away with. They all want to become a national police force.

If you did not quite understand what I said on the radio. Galt anticipates that even someone as smart as Dagny might need to read a transcript of the speech and study it to get every point. And she has been awfully busy.

the man in the middle. Galt discussed this on AS 1054. There used to be a libertarian button that read "1776—1984. There is no middle ground."

AS 1091

I will kill myself. This is one of the most interesting lines in the book. Imagine John Galt, of all people, contemplating suicide! But not for Hamlet's reasons. Read his reasons yourself, through Dagny's eyes, on this page, and see whether you agree that death would be preferable to seeing Dagny tortured to death. This is where Galt becomes Johnnie Dawes! (in Rand's play and novelette *Ideal*). When the bad guys have reduced the quality of your life to that extreme, you might choose quality over quantity. A long, miserable life or a short, principled, defiant life? Which would you choose? Of course, if Galt killed himself, they might kill Dagny anyway, because she knows too much.

See ARL 372, for more on why a John Galt might, in extreme circumstances, consider suicide. The looters torturing Dagny would not be the end. They would go on finding other ways of making life impossible for Galt, and everyone else.

we owe no morality to those who hold us under a gun. Rand might have put this a bit more accurately: Morality *requires* us to lie to the bad guys in order to defeat them.

Afterwards, you'll claim—and accept—the five-hundred-thousand-dollar reward. You can see that Galt has expected Dagny to come, and has had time to plan for this contingency. This is like the scene in TF where Dominique comes to Roark's apartment and he says, "I expected you to come." He could have gotten away to the valley—in fact he is about to tell Dagny that he had broadcast from the valley, so he was already there. He came *back* just to be ready to grab Dagny when she decided to go on strike. The days since Galt and Dagny met in the tunnels have given him a chance to do all the planning you see on this page, so AR does not have to strain believability by having him figure all this out in one half hour.

The Egoist

It will happen. This is Galt the ruthlessly realistic, un-self-deluding marble lover of truth, as Rand has characterized him all along. AR calls this chapter "The Egoist," meaning, not "egotist," which means a braggart, but "egoist," meaning a man who practices Aristotelean self-fulfillment. Even to the extent of killing himself? Yes—under extreme conditions that only a dramatist could think of.

AS 1092

You didn't want to wait any longer. This is why she came, and why he stayed here waiting and expecting her to come, even though it might mean their deaths.

Dagny, Dagny! Galt gets emotional. Don't blink or you'll miss it!

longer than is necessary to fight them. This is what Kay Ludlow should have said to Dagny in the valley when she found it incredible that Kay could live eleven months of the year not only without her husband, Ragnar, but knowing that at any moment he might get killed.

Don't struggle not to be happy. You are. Don't borrow trouble.

At the risk of destroying you? Galt is saying that Dagny should not fault herself for coming and putting his life in danger. He is turned on by the thought that she is so irresistibly attracted to him that she would recklessly come to his apartment. After all, he could have stayed in the valley after the speech. He came back to New York just to be close to Dagny and pull her out the moment she agreed to go on strike. What he is not mentioning is that he has some tricks up his sleeve, namely the rescue operation the strikers are about to mount. On AS 1157 below, it sounds as though Galt knew nothing about the rescue plan. But he must have made some contingency plans, and he must have discussed them with Francisco and Ragnar. That is a loose end AR should have tied up.

AS 1093

'Come in,' he said, grinning. You see? John Galt grins sometimes.

Either-or. The title of Part II, and one of Aristotle's laws of logic. It recalls, and Dagny's thought here recalls, Lincoln's insight on the slave states and the free states: "A house divided against itself cannot stand. I do not believe this government can endure half slave and half free. I do not expect the union to dissolve. I do not expect the house to fall. But I do expect that it will cease to be divided. It will become all one thing or all the other."

On the royalties Midas Mulligan pays me. Remember that Galt's Gulch is Mulligan's land. The banker pays Galt to build and maintain the powerhouse, the ray screen and the radio.

radio cabinet. This is the kind of radio Ayn and Frank owned in the 1930s, the size of a small TV of the 1960s. Look up the name "Suffens, Ev" in the index of LAR for the fan letters Ayn wrote in the Age of Radio to a favorite disc jockey. How would you like to power your home with a device the size of a breadbox? No fuel, no pollution. Maybe someday.

coils of wire. Those would be what gather static from the air for the machine to turn into current.

like a sacred relic. And so it is. We of the secular age would not exactly *worship* the motor's prototype, but we would look at it with awe, like Edison's prototype light bulb. We would not expect it to produce miracles, like a relic of the True Cross. But we would recognize it as a miracle of human problem solving. When the first moon rock was brought back to earth and displayed at the 1970 Osaka World's Fair, visitors lined up for an hour just to see it. It was the sensation of the fair. Look up Lewis Latimer, a Black associate of Edison's. He improved Edison's light bulb.

in a glass coffin in a vault. Could AR have been thinking of the Grail, in Wagner's operas *Lohengrin* and *Parsifal*? But AR was not a Wagner fan. Did she see relics in Russian churches? Did she ever have occasion to visit an Orthodox church? There was a chapel in the Peter and Paul Fortress in Leningrad when she was a tour guide there. She must have attended a Catholic funeral at a church in Lorain, Ohio when Frank's father died. She certainly went to weddings, too.

a picture of her. Here is another "humanizing" touch for John Galt. The picture is of Dagny at the opening of the John Galt Line, AS 238.

AS 1094

The doorbell rang. The person closest to the leader has betrayed him to soldiers who have come to arrest him. This chapter should be

The Egoist

called "Gethsemane." But Dagny's motivation is not that of Judas selling out Jesus. AR has, as always, given the Judas story a new and deeper meaning.

a neat mustache. This was a Hollywood Golden Age convention: the mustachioed villain. And this is a villain with blue eyes. Don't let anyone tell you that AR's heroes all have blond hair and blue eyes. Some do, some don't. And some of her villains have blond hair or blue eyes too.

AS 1095

keep your stool pigeon away from me. There is a similar moment in the 1953 movie *Thunder Bay*. James Stewart, after meeting alone with Joanne Dru, tells someone to "keep her away from me." Also, when his crew, building an oil platform, complain that he is driving them too hard, Stewart tells them to leave. He will finish the job himself. That sounds like the story Dagny tells about Nat Taggart on AS 513. *Thunder Bay*, along with *Pittsburgh* and *Tycoon,* belong to the genre of business-adventure movies. A small genre, but it shows that not every businessman in the movies is Mr. Potter, in *It's a Wonderful Life.*

AS 1096

no louder than the sigh of a weary mind. Sticker! Nice metaphor.
the machinery would collapse into rubble. That was on AS 732.
as if abandoned by a receding tide. Another good metaphor.

Scene 5: Thompson's first visit with Galt.

AS 1097

This scene, between Mr. Thompson and Galt, has always been a favorite for this reader, because of Galt's snappy comebacks.

sixty-first floor. Actually, the Waldorf-Astoria is a hotel only up to the 18th floor. The "Waldorf Towers" above that have always been residential. Cole Porter, General Douglas MacArthur, Marilyn Monroe and President Herbert Hoover lived there. You can see Porter's piano in the lobby.

Notice that they do not just arrest Galt for the crime of jamming the airwaves—"our" airwaves. That shows how fast the nation is disintegrating. They know that Galt has something they want. They just overlook his act of radio piracy.

bulges in places where the garments of businessmen have no cause to bulge. Sticker.

Tommy gun. Officially called the "Thompson submachine gun" after the inventor, an American general named John Thompson, it arrived as World War I neared its end. Prohibition era gangsters loved it.

looking at the ceiling. What could Galt be thinking about? Physics? He would want paper and pencils for that, but he does not want the looters to seize his ideas. Planning for a possible rescue by Francisco and the strikers, perhaps.

John Galt is in New York! The Head of the State is in New York, and Galt is kept in New York. Mr. Thompson must have flown up from Washington to meet him. Perhaps they don't want to give rescuers a chance to rescue Galt in the course of getting him to Washington, but that seems unlikely. They had only to get him, that very night, from the Lower East Side to LaGuardia or Idlewild (later JFK) and fly him to Washington. Perhaps Ayn was just indulging a fantasy that New York, her favorite city, was, or should be, the capital. Or perhaps she is applying Aristotle's dramatic principle of "unity of place."

So you're the young fellow who's started all the trouble. This is what Lincoln said on meeting Harriet Beecher Stowe, author of *Uncle Tom's Cabin*, which AR cited as a novel that had a great influence on history. No doubt AR had similar hopes for this novel. "So you're the little woman who wrote the book that started this great war." Stowe had published the novel in 1852, and the war started in 1861, but that is just *post hoc ergo propter hoc*. It was outrageous of Lincoln to blame the war on her book.

I'm Mr. Thompson, you know. This where AR giving Thompson no first name seems weird. A politician would stick out his hand and say "Hi, I'm Dick Nixon!" And he brought no entourage with him into the room. No photographers.

How do you do. This is how people used to greet each other in Ayn's time and before. It's how Ayn greeted this reader when we met in 1978.

AS 1098

I'm always open to a deal. Sticker! It is a convention, a cliché, in fiction for the villain to offer the hero a deal and for the hero to scornfully say "I don't make deals with criminals!" Or with tyrants. Captain Kirk, for example, in the *Star Trek* episode "Mudd's Women." Rand turns this cliché on its head. Galt is all for deals—with someone who has a value to offer him.

fool intellectual theorizers. See Bismarck on AS 1074.

AS 1099

I don't recognize your right to speak in the name of the country. This is revolution.

You see? I told you we had nothing to discuss. Wouldn't you love to hear this dialog done as a comedy routine? The movie version of this scene is not as good.

We've got to preserve the system. On March 8, 2021, Oprah Winfrey's interview with Harry and Meghan, the Duke and Duchess of Sussex, was broadcast. According to them, any amount of lying and cruelty to members of one's own family is permitted, in order to preserve "the firm": the Royal Family and the institution of the monarchy. That interview may be one more step toward the end, perhaps in this century, of not only the British monarchy, but the state as we know it.

AS 1100

"How?" "Somehow." This dialog is almost like Abbott and Costello's "Baseball" routine, isn't it? A few pages of comic relief for the novel.

AS 1101

What is it you're after? What was General Washington after, putting his neck in a noose to lead an army that he had to build up from scratch? He could have sailed to England, made money, and lived a comfortable life in a castle like Downton Abbey.

Want a billion dollars? If AS 1094 was Gethsemane, this page is the Devil tempting Jesus, which story is told in all four Gospels.

AS 1102

What will it buy me? This point is also made in, of all places, Richard Wagner's opera *Das Rheingold*. Alberich boasts that he is forcing the

Nibelungen to mine treasure for him in Nibelheim. Wotan asks what good this will do Alberich, since Nibelheim is "joyless" (*freudlos*). There is nothing there for his treasure to buy. So, this argument against crime and dishonesty is not new. Reality is objective. The same facts and principles are out there for anyone to independently discover. AR, Wagner, you, me. No one thinker has a monopoly on truth. A is A.

It's not yours to offer.

The removal of a threat is not a payment.

Not if he was the one who broke it.

Stickers all!

AS 1103

He doesn't waste his time wishing things to be different or trying to change them. He takes things as they are. Who hasn't heard that speech from his parents? This is why AR's appeal is to youth.

This is another page of debating points—zingers—for Galt at the expense of Thompson. Don't you wish real life were like that? Hiram Haydn, AR's editor at Random House, recalls how clever AR was at this kind of repartee. He is in the Bibliography.

How will your guns make me do that? Contra Mao tse-tung, power does not grow out of the barrel of a gun. Before you can loot, your victims have to have something worth looting.

AS 1104

I'll bash your teeth in. This is not among this reader's favorite lines. It is "verging on being overly broad," as Leonard Peikoff describes the tone of the short story "Good Copy" in *The Early Ayn Rand*, page 35.

For the same reason that makes you offer it. Galt is not saying this off the cuff. He has had time to plan what to do if captured. This line expands on Tony's line about "what would I do with my neck if that's how I had to keep it?" on AS 990. Those who ride on the back of the tiger end up inside.

Passionately. This is one of the best examples in the book of AR's Life-is-not-their-purpose Principle: the principle that you cannot assume that you have common ground with the evil people. Do not assume that they want to live. They don't. But how could that be?

How could any human being not want to live? AR's insight is that an animal running in panic from the danger of the moment is different from a human being wanting to live. Wanting passionately to live means jumping into life, with all of its challenges, with both feet, and taking the bad with the good. The bad things in life are problems you are eager to face and solve, and the good things in life are the rewards.

That is what Galt is talking about. Thompson is talking about just getting through another day of evading problems. In the same volume of *Playboy* interviews with Rand's, you will find one of Frank Sinatra. Asked about his religious views, Sinatra said "I'm for anything that will get you through the night, whether it's prayer or a fifth of Jack Daniels." Isn't that sad? Not a very exalted view of life. That is the Thompson view of life, not the Galt view.

AS 1105

I want to be your friend! Thompson is a politician. He lives by winning elections by promising everyone everybody else's money. He wants to call everyone "My friends." Remember who used to open his every radio talk—his "Fireside Chats"—with those words during the Great Depression? President Franklin Roosevelt.

have you got any family? Now we know why AR could not let Galt have any family living. Thompson could arrest them too.

Scene 6: Thompson confers with Dagny. Francisco sends Dagny a note. Thompson, Ferris, and Stadler visit Galt. Eddie leaves for California.

a pile of unsold newspapers on the stand of a ragged, shivering vendor. One of the most minor of all the minor characters in the novel, but AR gives him two adjectives and paints a picture that helps set the scene. Chick Morrison, whose business is public opinion, notices that people are not even glancing at the guards with their machine guns.

AS 1106

a ragged old woman. Eddie gave a dime to a beggar on AS 1. Morrison does not do so on AS 1106.

They don't believe anything any more. Does this line come from AR's impressions of St. Petersburg in 1917? Los Angeles in 1933?

Notice that AR and Haydn and Krantz spell "anymore" as two words. Your computer thinks it always has to be one word. Young writers today do not know anything but what their computers tell them.

he's a man who talks straight. Fred Kinnan, the labor leader, once again shows that he is the best of a bad lot. He has no self-delusions. Notice that both Kinnan and Mouch, on this page, look up at the ceiling when they think about Galt. Why?

AS 1107

You can't make me lose my faith in humanity. Lawson is the "Banker with a heart" from Dagny's search for the motor's builder, AS 309.

a ruthless egoist. This is just the way Toohey, in TF, describes Roark when addressing a crowd before Roark's trial.

a man who wants to live. If Kinnan understands that much, he must be close to switching sides and going on strike.

Jim screams, as he does when someone mentions living, as on AS 885. This continues to build up to Jim's big climax on AS 1145. Jim, much more than Thompson and the rest, *really* does not want to live.

He is the opposite of Rearden, "the man who belongs on earth." Jim panics at the thought of immutable facts. He has, from early in life, a profound and crippling lack of self-confidence in dealing with reality itself.

AS 1108

that I'm not a . . . . Thompson is not a monster, not an evil man. But he is a man of limited imagination, and he is at the end of his rope.

If he goes, we perish. Thompson has come to understand that much, at least.

an apartment house whose front wall had collapsed. Soviet housing was notorious for problems like this—especially if built with convict labor.

marching on the state capital. Angry citizens are marching, but in response to real problems, not fantasies, as on January 6, 2021.

every home worth more than ten thousand dollars. The Rand Bashers would expect critics of government help to burn homes worth *less* than ten thousand dollars. Ayn Rand hated the poor, they say. In the Russian Revolution, peasants set fire to manor houses and crops, as young Alisa Rosenbaum knew well.

People's Party . . . former oil-field owners. That's just like California. So little has changed in this regard since 1957. The health food crowd versus the Religious Right.

Ayn and Frank, during the war, would have known the conservative religious types as profiteers on the imprisonment of the Nisei, like Frank's ranch hands, the Kato family. See page 80 of Jeff Britting's book for a photo of Ayn and Frank at the wedding, in 1950, of June Kato to George Kurisu. June was Ayn's first typist for AS. She and her parents worked on the O'Connor ranch after release from the camps.

his hotel room. Thompson is again, or still, in New York! He spends as much time away from the White House as Woodrow Wilson!

a man who has no desire to command. Naturally, Thompson, as a world leader, cannot understand a man who does not want to be a world leader.

Benjamin West, a famous portrait artist, was painting King George III in London. The King asked West what General Washington planned to do now that the War for Independence was over. When West said that Washington planned to resign as Commander in Chief and become a private citizen again, the astonished King said that in doing that, Washington would be "the greatest character of the age."

If AR had wanted to write historical fiction, she might have made a very Galt-like figure out of GW.

Late in life, West wrote his memoirs with the help of a Scots novelist named John Galt. Mr. Galt sold Canadian real estate on the side, so you will find a John Galt Park in downtown Guelph, Ontario. And there is a city of Galt, Ontario.

AS 1109

language as a tool of honor, always to be used as if one were under oath. This is not just a sticker, but a moral *charge*, a commandment, to a thirteen-year-old.

adding machine. See the nurse in my comment on AS 711. Dagny is a woman of action, an Energizer Bunny, and she likes the feeling of being brought back to working order by Dr. Hendricks. What the nurse thought was more like the "adding machine" metaphor in this paragraph. Dagny is reduced to the unfeeling routine of mechanically spitting out calculated lies for the fooling of fools. What she feels strongly about is the need to lie, to save Galt's life, and maybe her own.

the kind of ticking he understood. See Mayhew's *Ayn Rand and Song of Russia*, page 97, for a funny exchange between AR and HUAC Chairman J. Parnell Thomas, ending with the words "Oh, I thought you meant money."

AR must surely have been thinking of that incident when she wrote this line about Mr. Thompson. Like "Truman," "Thomas" begins with a T. Perhaps AR was picturing Chairman Thomas more than President Truman in the Mr. Thompson role.

the state in which they lived. It has taken years for this reader to believe that many, perhaps most, people lie constantly as a way of life. It seems close to the mind of a Ted Bundy, a psychopath, for whom every other human being is an enemy.

Constantly trying to get away with lies, to be concerned only with the fooling of everyone around you all the time, was inconceivable to this thirteen-year-old, and another reason why he felt the precious discovery of a kindred soul in AR.

This is another paragraph that makes you wonder what the effect is, of such a paragraph, on a thirteen-year-old reader—and what effect the *lack* of such paragraphs have on other thirteen-year-old readers.

AS 1110

till they destroyed the world. On page 152 of BB's and NB's *Who Is Ayn Rand?* (and also in BB and AH) you will read of a story Alisa wrote at the age of eight. A woman's husband is captured in a war and faces execution within hours. The woman makes a rescue plan, but as she leaves to carry it out, their child falls deathly ill and needs her. The woman has to choose, and she chooses her husband: her "top value," as Ayn would say. Unusual choice for an eight-year-old author. (The woman succeeds in rescuing her husband and the child recovers.) Dagny faces a similar choice here, but it is hard to believe that Dagny is worried that the looters will destroy the world just by holding on to Galt a little longer.

As repeatedly pointed out in these pages, nothing, not even Galt's help, would save their system now.

preventing catastrophes. AR is setting us up for one more disaster—the Taggart Bridge.

AS 1111

Did they want him to live? [. . .] *Did they want to live?* Dagny approaches her moment of going on strike. Her decision hinges on the question asked by Dr. Akston in the valley, back on AS 807. Do they want to live? She asks herself this question at the bottom of AS 1109 and again here.

It was not a token of value. This recalls Bennett Cerf's story about the cheap bracelet he bought Ayn (AS 156 above). But the Bashers say that Ayn was in favor of "greed." Galt told Dagny not only to claim the reward, but to accept it. He should have told her to also use it for something, just to complete the deception.

OR6-5693. Before "The Break" between AR and NB, the text of AS was followed by an "About the Author" page. On that page, AR wrote, "if you are interested in further information, please inquire: Nathaniel Branden Institute, 165 East 35th Street, New York 16, New York, MUrray Hill 6-5693. (That's how mailing addresses used to look, before the ZIP Code in the 1960s, and how phone numbers looked when local telephone exchanges had names instead of all numbers, and before Area Codes.)

The address belonged to Nathaniel's and Barbara's one-room apartment, where they typed *The Objectivist Newsletter* on their kitchen table.

When NB spoke at a seminar of The Objectivist Center (now the Atlas Society, and originally the Institute for Objectivist Studies) in 2004, this reader showed him that page with Francisco's phone number. I asked him, "Do you remember this? Did you know that Ayn gave Francisco your old phone number?" NB looked back and forth from one phone number to the other, shook his head, and said, "Amazing."

AS 1112

Next to Jim Taggart, Thompson looks like a Rand hero.

You would—. AR has finally had enough of bombarding us with Jim's incessant hysteria, leaving the rest of his rant to our imagination. It's not like Jim is likely to say anything original and interesting.

watching Galt's movements with such hatred. Just like Toohey watching Roark at the party (TF 271).

AS 1113

present from an anonymous admirer. This is totally unbelievable. Anyone attempting to give a present for a prisoner to a guard would immediately join Galt in the clink.

The fact that someone (Francisco or Ragnar probably) did this suggests that Galt did not have any rescue plan already worked out with the strikers, which seems unlikely. Or else they did have such a plan and the cigarettes were a signal to Galt that the plan was about to go into effect.

But it does not seem to have gone into effect before the TV appearance. A loose end, but a minor one.

They might have had only a very general contingency plan. They could not have known exactly where Thompson would keep Galt. He could have sent Galt to Guantanamo.

AS 1114

This page shows the kind of moral ruthlessness that AR admired and some readers have tried to emulate, not always successfully. NB recalls Ayn telling him, "What I admire about you is the ruthlessness of your moral judgments." (NB, page 264.)

If others agree with you, they will admire you for standing up for what is right. If they disagree, they will call you "judgmental" and a "moralist."

But I, who do, should obey them? This is how AR appeals to the rebellious teen. He will thrill to Galt's debating ability, to his devastating ripostes, his brilliant zingers.

every third ... put to death. See "The Courtship of Eddie's Father" story on AS 976 above.

Tell the bastard to look at me. This is what AR did to a woman in the audience of the Phil Donahue show. The woman had begun her question by saying, "I used to believe in your philosophy, but then I became educated." AR found this so insulting that she would not speak to the woman, but would accept the same question if Donahue asked it.

AS 1115

I've changed my mind. What made Galt think of Dr. Stadler just now? Look seven lines up. Slapping a face? Probably selling a soul, and Galt has just met Ferris, whom he knows to be Stadler's Number Two.

No grapefruit juice. See AS 837. The Smather brothers and other members of the "aristocracy of pull" show that the US is sliding into fascism, not socialism.

the Taggart Bridge on the Mississippi. This helps to set us up for the coming disaster.

no other railroad bridges across the Mississippi. See AS 499-500. Of course, in real life there is more than just one railroad bridge across the Mississippi. The first one south of the Missouri River, where the Mississippi becomes wider, was the Eads Bridge at St. Louis, opening in 1874. It was named after its designer and builder, James B. Eads. It is today the oldest surviving Mississippi bridge. It occasioned the first large-scale use of steel rather than wrought iron. The largest and deepest caissons ever built were used in its construction. The center arch was the longest rigid span ever built, at 520 feet. Nat Taggart's bridge is apparently farther north, between Iowa and Illinois, as we will see when it is destroyed.

Cornelius Vanderbilt had quite a struggle to get his railroad built up the Hudson. The politically-connected Livingston family owned the boats on the river and had friends in the state governments of both New York and New Jersey. See Stiles in the Bibliography.

AS 1116

'Dagny,' said Eddie Willers, that evening. Here is an abrupt change of scene, unheralded even by a scene break. A fast dissolve in the movie. Always picture the story as AR pictured it: through the eyes of a screen writer. And AR starts quickening the pace here as we approach the climax.

That's why it's I who'll go there. This is a neat solution to one of AR's endless plotting problems all over this huge, complex novel. Eddie knows that Dagny must go to San Francisco, and he knows that she can't, and he knows why: because Galt needs to be rescued. So, AR found it convenient to separate Eddie from Dagny at this point, in order to give her main characters, Dagny and Galt, a happy ending while Eddie's arc ends unresolved. Does he survive or not? AR had a reason for leaving Eddie's fate unresolved, which we will discuss on AS 1167.

Here we see Eddie initiating a plan, not just taking orders. He is growing in his job, thanks in part to the mounting disasters, and in part by Dagny placing him in charge on three occasions while she builds the John Galt Line, when she goes to her cabin, and when she goes after Quentin Daniels.

Did you know how I felt about you? We might wonder whether Joseph Mankiewicz had read AS before writing the screenplay for *Cleopatra* (1963). Cleopatra gives her final instructions to her devoted slave Apollodorus before going off to kill herself.

He says he will carry them out.

She asks, "Is there anything else?"

"I've always loved you."

"And I've always known."

AS 1117

He gripped the edge of a table. This is the Royal Suite, but is that Francisco's old suite, where Francisco gripped the table edge to keep from throttling Hank? And where Mouch and company tried to talk Hank into a pooling arrangement with Associated Steel? AR does not say so.

They're mindless animals. This is AR's familiar image of Steven Mallory's "mindless beast" on TF 346.

their greedy, grasping, blind, unaccountable feelings. Dr. Stadler has long since gone over to the Dark Side: AR's heroes would not use the word "greedy." But "unaccountable feelings" shows that AR still gives her Judas some of her heroes' fear and hatred of "feelings"— but only "unaccountable" ones.

AS 1118

It would have worked. This page condenses quite a lot of the novel's theme. Stadler's speech is like one of Eddie's one-sided dialogues

The Egoist

with Galt. It is almost "stream of consciousness" writing. He knows exactly what arguments Galt will make and he argues back, before Galt has said a word.

It would have worked, he says, maybe for his lifetime. Maybe, if Galt had not called the men of ability out on strike, the world would have kept going at least long enough for Stadler to get that next telescope or cyclotron at the taxpayers' expense.

AS 1119

No! . . . No! . . . No! Stadler is cracking up much the same way Jim will, as Galt, without even saying anything, shows the objective nature of reality that Stadler and Jim cannot evade. Facts are stubborn things.

Scene 7: Galt forced to ballroom for broadcast.

His skull was shaved except for a patch of faded blond curls on top. This guard may be a thug, but he is sixty years ahead of his time in hair styles. And blond! A blond villain—for those who think Rand's heroes, and only her heroes, are all blond.

"Don't make any false moves." "I never do." This line is a sticker. Cute. Hollywood-type line. A Spock line. Dissolve.

AS 1120

through the long, dim corridors. The corridors were deserted. Awkward to end one sentence and begin the next with the same words. Well, it's not too bad.

But if AR was as particular as Hiram Haydn claimed, never putting two rhyming words in the same paragraph, then you would think she would want to re-word this paragraph. Or perhaps AR is suggesting the repetitious motion of walking down a corridor with a repetition of words. She is creating rhythm in words.

right arm was linked to Galt's left. Four paragraphs above, the strong-arm man had his right hand on his gun in his pocket, then he was holding Galt's arm and pressing the gun against his ribs. It is hard to picture this. He must have changed position twice as they walked.

gold-copper hair. When we first met Galt back on AS 701, his hair was "chestnut brown," which means brown with just a hint of red. Now it is blond and red. Is this a mistake or is AR doing this on purpose? And again, where is Hiram Haydn's blue pencil?

He says in his memoir that he eventually gave up trying to edit AS, because AR simply refused to be edited. This reinforces that conclusion.

jewels on the naked shoulders. Perhaps AR uses the word "naked" so much precisely because it *was* old fashioned by 1957. Naked shoulders had become invisible and unnoticeable to the typical reader. Perhaps she anticipated that clothing styles would become even more casual in fifty years than they were in 1957. Maybe they were more daring at the French and Russian courts of the 18th century. So, to make this a meaningful part of the scene, AR reminds us of what we have now become too blasé to even notice. This is another difference between 1957 and 2024.

with the eager, anxious look. For once, AR omits her usual "as if."

news cameras, microphones, television cameras. The looters do not know what to do about the economy, but they know how to stage a public spectacle. They are like the Romans, and AR was always thinking, during and after the writing of Atlas, of the fall of the Roman Empire.

as those of you who can find a television set. Grim humor—too grim for a TV announcer who knows that the government's "Morale Conditioner" is breathing down his neck.

He should be reminding his viewers that only the brilliant economic planning of the Great Leader, or the Brain Trust, allows them to own a TV set. Dagny and Galt appreciate the bizarre quality of the scene.

Comedian George Carlin pointed out in the 1970s that in the 1930s people spoke of "radio sets," and in the 1950s, "television sets." "The word 'set' appears only briefly every twenty years, then it disappears again."

AS 1121

receiving an industrial award. This is a sticker. This is central to the theme. This is what Galt's life should have been, in a normal world.

Remember what Dr. Akston said on AS 786 about superhuman creatures. It's not about being superhuman, but about remaining normal in an abnormal world. And remember what Galt told Dagny

The Egoist 257

on AS 959 about "what my years would have brought me," if he had lived in a normal world.

This is what Galt gave up for the strike, but it is also why the strike is necessary. The world after the strike is the "pearl of great price" that is worth whatever it costs.

in the days of a distant past. Under the entry "Normalcy" in the Recurring Themes Index, you can see how many times AR refers to the normal world being the world of the past, but that is a trap. Don't get lost in nostalgia for a golden past. Galt and his strikers never lose sight of the world *after* the strike, as we saw in the previous paragraph. AR says, "Those who fight for the future live in it today."

Celebrations should be only for those who have something to celebrate. Dagny said this on AS 150, at Hank and Lillian's anniversary party.

The faces were drawn and twisted by the most obvious and least dignified form of tension: by forced smiles. Good line.

not by means of their reason, but by means of their panic. This is what NB, on the first of his "Seminar" records, says about Toohey: He understands, about Roark, not the concept of what Roark means, but only what his fear of Roark tells him. See Toohey spotting Roark at Enright's party, on TF 271.

neither their God nor their guns. AR does not put in too many of these direct slaps at religion. That would be strained, like a forced smile.

a slush of ice cream in a crystal bowl. Have you ever before seen ice cream presented in a negative way? But we understand that Dagny is too tense to enjoy her food. The word "slush" is not an adjective, but an unattractive noun.

AS 1122

and of any other that's able to listen. More grim humor, as on AS 1120 above.

a television screen to project for the guests. They did not have large TV screens in 1957. Today, every occasion like this would have giant screens behind the dais.

General of the Army Whittington S. Thorpe. This is an example of AR's talent for making up character names that sound exactly right for such a character.

"Whittington" as a given name suggests old money, and in 1957, old money and high-ranking military careerists still went together, more than they do in 2024. "Thorpe" might have come from AR's Fountainhead research: Ely Jacques Kahn, AR's architect boss, designed a department store in midtown called Jay-Thorpe.

Majority Leader of the National Legislature, Mr. Lucian Phelps. We noted before AR replacing "Congress" with "Legislature." It must be unicameral, since in real life there is a Majority Leader of each house, not one for the whole Congress. If AR was getting character names from prominent men of her time she read about in the papers, the "Lucian" might come from General Lucian Truscott, of World War II, or from Lucius Beebe, theater critic of the New York *Herald Tribune.* AR might have met him, and if so, it would have been through Isabel Paterson, who wrote a book review column for that paper. The "Phelps" might have come from William Lyon Phelps, a famous Yale literature professor of AR's time, a critic, popular speaker and wit. He's the guy who said, "If at first you don't succeed, find out if the loser gets anything." See the AS 1066 comments for another Phelps quote.

invulnerable by virtue of self-esteem. In the 1959 Disney animated movie *Sleeping Beauty,* Prince Phillip is armed, by the fairy godmothers, with the Sword of Truth and the Shield of Virtue. AR would like the image of Truth as a sword, because Truth cuts through all the BS.

"Virtue" for Disney and his writers may have been interpreted closer to the Victorian meaning, but if you are virtuous and innocent, no one can blackmail you by threatening to reveal your guilt, because you have none, so virtue is your shield against blackmail, and that is one of the themes of AS. Hence the "White Blackmail" theme. If you have self-esteem, you are less manipulable through guilt, or through the promise of a title, a uniform, and a gun. The cults look for kids with low self-esteem. The group identity they give the kid is a stand-in for his leaky self-esteem.

implacable by virtue of serenity. The serene cannot be frightened, panicked, and stampeded, or stopped dead in their pursuit of values.

Did they want him to be real? This is a corollary to "Do they really want to live?" If they really want to live, they will be looking for a

John Galt, the man who makes life possible, and not running from him in terror and denying his existence.

AS 1123

the man of the 'know-how' Have you ever seen "the" in front of "know-how"? Another one of AR's peculiar word uses. The political pros deal with Galt the only way they know how. He made a speech, people are talking about it, and he seems to be gaining support, so they try to co-opt him, just as they tried to co-opt Rearden and his Metal.

In 1978, California voters approved a ballot initiative called Proposition 13. It was a governor's race year. Libertarian candidate Ed Clark supported Prop 13. The Republican candidate remained non-committal and Democrat Jerry Brown stood against it until it started to look like it would pass. Brown suddenly became Prop 13's leading cheerleader.

One political analyst said, "In two weeks he will have everyone thinking that 13 was his idea!" AR is not making this stuff up. It's what they do.

Once they have seen him. This page shows Galt through Dagny's eyes. This is a woman in love, combined with a woman in crisis: her railroad, her whole world, are at stake. Thus, AR integrates the love story with the politics and economics of the story.

the Mouches as the human. This is Nietzsche's "Human—All Too Human" theme.

The camera was roving over the ballroom. This sounds like the TV show broadcast in the 1950s from The Stork Club (see the Cub Club on AS 69) and hosted by the restaurant's owner, Sherman Billingsley. The TV camera would follow Billingsley as he roved between the tables. He would introduce famous visitors, like the Duke and Duchess of Windsor, and tout his store brand of cigarettes ("Fatima") as he handed a pack to each guest.

Billingsley's sister-in-law, Barbara Billingsley, played June Cleaver on *Leave It to Beaver*, which premiered on TV on October 4, 1957—the same day that the USSR launched Sputnik and the Space Age, and six days before AS was published.

the sincerity of the dishonest. Another of AR's paradoxes that make perfect sense once you grasp her insight and the deeper meaning she has found. Compare the first page of TF: "The water looked immobile, the stone, flowing." And "I am not brave enough to be a coward. I see the consequences too clearly." (*Who Is Ayn Rand?*, by NB and BB, page 239) In Asia, the words that translate as "sincerity" really mean a sincere effort to be insincere. Politeness is valued there and bluff frankness is not, so they value the person who tries hardest to be politely phony. In America and other frontier countries, traditionally, diplomacy bows to honesty.

AS 1124

Did they care to live? Again, Dagny is inching toward the big reveal; the key to whether to go on strike or not. Dr. Akston's question: Do they want to live?

so they'll recognize your voice. Galt will take Thompson's advice on the next page, if he had not already thought of it himself.

Mouch's paragraph parodies Galt's speech, at least the economics of it. Dagny sees how the speakers are translating Galt's speech into the assumptions they know.

they feared the precision of his face. Here, AR is giving Dagny her own belief in one's ability to read all about a person by a look at his face. AR should have been a poker player.

On this page, AR switches back and forth between the scene in the ballroom and Dagny's mind, as she interprets the action around her and reaches conclusions and finds meaning in what is happening. This stretches out the time of the scene. It gives us a look into Dagny's thoughts and feelings. (AR does not show us the full wording of Thompson's and Mouch's speeches. A summary is enough.) This gives AR time to build suspense: we can see that the chapter will end on the next page, and we are wondering what Galt will do when called upon to speak to the nation. The switching back and forth is like the silent movie scene that switches back and forth between Nell on the tracks and the onrushing train. We see Nell seeing the train approach, and the terror on her face infects us. So, Dagny's thoughts and feelings do not slow down a scene that should be fast, they build

The Egoist

up suspense. Also, Dagny has been working so hard, cooped up in her office, and so pre-occupied with Galt's safety, that this banquet may be the only chance she has had lately to observe the leaders (except for a couple of meetings with Thompson) and other big shots, and have leisure to look at them and ask: do they want to live? What is their plan, if any? So it is at this dinner that she is able to take some steps toward her final decision to join the strike.

AS 1125

eady, willing and able. This was an old expression, even in AR's time. Since 1990, New York City has had a non-profit group called Ready, Willing and Able—The Doe Fund, a service that gives jobs to men with a history of incarceration and poverty. AR's use of the phrase was probably inspired by a 1941 Frank Capra-Gary Cooper movie, *Meet John Doe,* which she must have seen since it starred her favorite actor, Gary Cooper, and which may have been in the back of her mind as she wrote this scene, and perhaps throughout the book. BB points out that Cooper and Frank could have been brothers, they looked so much alike. In picturing John Galt, then, we can feel free to put Coop's face or Frank's on the hero.

some sort of a motor. Ah! So Thompson's people *have* listened to, transcribed, read and analyzed the Speech! They know about the motor. They just don't know that it is in a vault in the tunnels under the Terminal, unless Stadler has told them, since Dagny showed it to him on AS 358. There is no indication that he has. Would he want to? Maybe he would like to do a Quentin Daniels on the motor and get it working himself. But AR does not so indicate.

No man is an island unto himself. This famous line comes from John Donne's 1624 poem, "Devotions Upon Emergent Occasions." Donne was recovering from a deathly illness when he wrote this, and death was on his mind. His "island" line was addressed to the King and his advisors, and Donne hoped they would notice his meaning and the censor would not. Even a King's private actions can have public consequences. In the other famous line from this poem, he writes, "Therefore never send to ask for whom the bell tolls. It tolls for thee." This is where John Steinbeck got his novel title, *For Whom*

The Bell Tolls. This novel, set during the Spanish Civil War, became a movie starring Gary Cooper.

Get the hell out of my way! This reader has never been satisfied with this line. Even at thirteen, I was expecting something from Galt a bit more profound. AR has given the line a long build up, and the reader might feel let down. The thirteen-year-old reader might expect Galt to vanish into thin air, having invented the *Star Trek* Transporter. Beam me up, Scotty! There is no intelligent life on this planet! But the line perfectly sums up Galt's feelings at that moment. And it signals the TV audience that he is not cooperating with the government, and therefore that everything Thompson and the others have just said has been lies. And he had just had his three hours to say all that needed saying. If Galt has nothing more relevant or lofty to say, that too sends a message. The looters are irrelevant. All that is relevant now is the need for the world to get out of Galt's way. The more thoughtful will read: We need to get out of *each other's* way. And I have to get out of my own way. And if the audience notices the gun in Galt's ribs, that fact will, as AR said on the previous page, "add a silent paragraph."

9. The Generator

Chapter Overview

Stadler drives to Iowa and Project X. He finds that Cuffy Meigs and an army detachment have seized it. Stadler tries to explain that Meigs should let him take command of the sound ray machine. Meigs is drunk, and in a defiant gesture against Stadler, starts pulling levers. The machine blows up, killing Meigs and Stadler and taking out a circle with a 100-mile radius, including the Taggart Bridge across the Mississippi, which is the only such bridge left. Dagny is in her office when she hears of the destruction of the bridge. She starts to grab a phone, but then pulls back. She has finally reached her point of decision and gone on strike. She runs to meet Francisco, and gives him the Strikers' Oath.

Ferris, Mouch, and Jim torture Galt. Their generator fails. Jim breaks down when Galt tells them how to fix the generator. The technician runs away. Ferris and Mouch get Jim into their car, leaving Galt alone.

Scene 1: Stadler to Project X. Meigs blows it up.

AS 1126

part gasp, part scream, part laughter. Perhaps three different reactions from different members of the live audience when they saw the gun and heard Galt's line.

All stations were off the air. You can see how total the government's control of information has become.

like a jockey. AR had no use for betting "on some animal's race" (AS 932), but maybe she saw a horse race somewhere, sometime. With Frank and Nick, perhaps?

or at those in the city. Here is Ayn the New York City snob. Stadler is in Iowa. He has just come from New York, and he feels as though he is being pursued by Galt, but he himself lives in New Hampshire. For Ayn, there were only two places in the world: New York City and not New York City.

like a net of lines traced in acid. Was Ayn familiar with copper etching? Perhaps it came up in her research on the copper and steel industries. You can google "copper etching" and see how etchers, like Francisco Goya, etched pictures on a copper plate with acid.

You can also see this in the movie *Goya's Ghosts*. She did go to art galleries, so perhaps she learned about etching that way.

AS 1127

you're the only one he asked for. Thompson questioning on this point, and threatening Stadler, is more credible than his guards not questioning whoever brought the dollar sign cigarettes to the hotel. Was Galt thinking of this possibility when he asked for Stadler?

mushroom-domed structure. Another reminder of the Mushroom Cloud of an atomic bomb.

private feudal domain. AR draws on her history of the fall of the Roman Empire, when Roman landowners hoped that Ostrogoth kings would let them keep their land. They, or their successors as owners of vast manors, became semi-independent in time if they turned their villas into castles and their serfs into pikemen.

AR paints the fall of the American empire in the same colors. This would have been unbelievable to the American reading public of 1957, when America dominated the post-war world. They can believe it better now, in 2024.

Today's problem is that China believes the United States to be a spent power, and sees this as an opportunity to press further in its desire for world domination.

cunning for obtaining illegal purchases of gas. This would be familiar to anyone, in 1957, old enough to remember gas rationing during World War II. You would have to be only twelve or thirteen.

I'm Robert Stadler. Think of *Citizen Kane*. Kane tries to overawe people, bellowing "I'm Charles Foster Kane!"

the vibrating steel of the Taggart Bridge. This is how we know that the bridge is between Illinois and Iowa, not at St. Louis: Stadler is heading for Project X, in Iowa. Apparently, the Taggart Bridge, like the Eads, has an upper level for cars and a lower level for trains. The steel deck of the Brooklyn Bridge used to vibrate loudly, before they asphalted it over.

AR surely had ridden over the Brooklyn Bridge. Out came her notepad.

AS 1128

Are you one of the new or one of the old? Cuffy Meigs has beaten Stadler to his re-enactment of the fall of Rome.

Perhaps these are the troops sent to guard the bridge (AS 1115) and Meigs was in command. In any case, Meigs has seized Project X with troops he got from somewhere. AR must have been remembering Petrograd, 1917.

I'm Joe Blow. A 20th century expression.

AS 1129

No notes for this page.

AS 1130

semi-military tunic. AR never makes it exactly clear whether Meigs is in the military or not.

When we first met him back on AS 364, he "wore civilian clothes and the leather leggings of a traffic cop."

It would be characteristic of AR to not make a military man a bad guy since she still considered the US military as the organizational descendant of General Washington's forces. Its sacred tradition of respecting civilian authority has remained unbroken since March 15, 1783, when His Excellency warned his officers, gathered in the "Temple of Virtue" at the New Windsor Cantonment, that any breach of that trust would "plunge (the army) into a gulf of civil horror from which there might be no receding."

outer spaces. Not "outer space." Peculiar.

AS 1131

This page consists of a dialogue between Stadler and Meigs. This is straightforward storytelling.

AS 1132

that mysterious, occult breed, the intellectual. This is the theme of "Attila versus the Witch Doctor" that AR later developed in *For the New Intellectual.*

enclosing parts of four states. Those would be Iowa, Minnesota, Wisconsin and Illinois. Edward Teller had hoped that the largest version of his hydrogen bomb, detonated at a great altitude, could devastate one hundred thousand square miles of Soviet territory. A radius of one hundred miles has about 30,000 square miles.

AR wants us to think of the atomic and hydrogen bombs when she concocts her Xylophone. To get an idea of what we all worried about in those Cold War years, see movies like *Dr. Strangelove, On the Beach,* and *Fail-safe.* After 1980, even more horrifying nuclear war movies included *The Day After* and *Testament.*

Scene 2: Ferris, Jim, and Mouch get Galt to the torture chamber. Dagny hears of the collapse of the Taggart bridge, meets Francisco, and gives the oath.

AS 1133

she looked at the sky, as her feeling was more solemn than joyous. Take some time to study this sentence. When you feel solemn, you look up at the sky. When you have a sublime thought, you feel sublime yourself, and feel entitled to look up with pride, not down in humility.

the crash of microphones being shattered. Why are microphones being knocked over? Are the people at the head table fleeing?

The ballroom was like a ship without captain. Not "a" captain? Peculiar. Could this be a typo?

oddly expectant intensity. Why? Jim now expects violence, mainly directed against Galt. Or, being subject to panic himself all the time, he is relieved when others are as panicky as he is. He is thinking: Ha! You are no more calm and cool than I am!

AS 1134

He has a hide-out all stocked for himself in Tennessee. This is ironic. The Establishment big-shots have become the survivalists, like

The Generator 267

Himmler donning a private's uniform, shaving his mustache, and trying to escape by sneaking through British lines.

In a societal breakdown like this, though, there is always an enemy—usually an invader. However, AR has stipulated that all the other nations are going through the same breakdown and in no position to invade the US. Then there must be some *internal* enemy.

We have seen Cuffy Meigs in Iowa and more than one armed group in California, so that checks. But AR has not mentioned any opposition party or rising charismatic figure running for Head of the State against Thompson. This must be deliberate.

All these villains are sideshows to the main plot: Dagny slowly coming to the point of going on strike. So, AR leaves the villains and the breakdown as an impressionistic background. We can have fun imagining the details on our own.

Compare this scene to the movies *Hitler: The Last Ten Days, The Bunker,* and *Downfall,* and the episode of the TV series *The Great Adventure* about the flight of Confederate President Jefferson Davis and his cabinet.

These are the appointive government figures and their Big Business friend Jim and their government-science ally Ferris. Thompson is in the room, but he was the last one to speak. He waits for one of his underlings to offer some useful advice. As appointees, Mouch and Tinky serve at the pleasure of the Head of the State, and hope to get Galt on the program and report their success to Thompson, their boss. They are afraid, not only of Meigs and the California armed groups (we would call them "militias" now), but afraid of the millions who have heard Galt's speech, and have by now read transcripts of it and have had time to digest it and organize resistance to Directive 10-289 and its enforcers. The disaster in Iowa is happening at the same time as this scene, or a few hours later.

the end justifies the means. This is the old favorite among moral principles. See Recurring Themes Index.

AS 1135

Mr. Thompson was struggling not to see that they were all looking at him. This is the last we will see of Mr. Thompson.

within three hours. Why did AR make it three hours? Apparently, they hope to resume the broadcast tonight, after some "technical difficulty," but three hours is not enough time to get Galt to an airport, get him to New Hampshire, torture him, get him back to New York, and put him on the air.

She knew. In this paragraph, Dagny takes another big step toward going on strike. The last.

Now she has had lots of time in the company of the villains and has at last convinced herself that Dr. Akston was right (on AS 807) that they do not want to live. They want Galt to die.

This paragraph, and many others like it, shows AR the silent film scenarist. Explanatory paragraphs like this one are like the narrative cards in a silent movie.

Nirvana. This means Buddhist heaven. It is the same as the Hindu Moksha. It is a state they describe as "no-mind." Perfect rest, with none of the cares and woes of existence and desire for any goals or values.

the wrench of a switching perspective. Somewhere in her writings, AR refers to the odd experience of looking at a drawing of a transparent cube. At first you think you are looking at it at an upward angle, then suddenly you are looking at it at a downward angle. If AR found any change of perspective more "wrenching" than you might, then perhaps that explains her angry reaction to the surprise party her friends threw for her when AS was published (BB 295). But BB also writes that AR had no trouble switching, every six months, from writing screenplays for Hal Wallis to writing AS and back.

the subhuman. This line shows what AR really means by "subhuman." A Rand Basher might try to read something else into her use of this term.

AS 1136

past the stage of worrying about her. Don't they still have goons shadowing her? Maybe Thompson called them off after she accepted the reward money.

jewelry and any valuables. Now everyone in the story is a survivalist, and with good reason.

AS 1137

northwest corner, two blocks east of the main entrance of the Taggart Terminal. Dagny has left the Waldorf-Astoria, let's say by the Lexington Avenue exit. She has gone to a bar. There are no bars on Park Avenue near the Waldorf, but there would have been some on Lexington. She calls Francisco from a phone booth in the bar.

She hails a cab. It takes her south on Lex and west on 36th—let's say she lives at or near where Ayn herself lived in 1957: East 36th Street between Park and Madison. The streets and avenues were two-way before about 1980. She packs and changes clothes.

She walks up Park Avenue, through Grand Central Terminal concourse, and into the New York Central Railroad building and her office. She collects a few things, then walks back through the concourse onto East 42nd Street and east two blocks. She meets Francisco on the northwest corner of East 42nd and 3rd Avenue. Oddly enough, the building on that corner, the Kent Building, was where David H. Koch had his office, Koch Engineering, which built pollution control equipment as a subsidiary of Koch Industries. Francisco has given Dagny only forty minutes to do all this. A little tight.

She broke the two frames. Could AR have gotten this idea from the story of Dolley Madison? When the British took Washington in September 1814, President Madison was in the field with his troops. Dolley, back at the White House, ordered the Gilbert Stuart portrait of Washington cut out of its frame, rolled up, and evacuated with her. The British arrived after Dolley and her staff had escaped, and the Redcoats burned the White House, the Capitol, and the Library of Congress. AR might have seen this historical incident recreated in the 1946 movie *Magnificent Doll*, with her friend Ginger Rogers as Dolley Madison. Out comes Ayn's notepad again. That movie had a good integration of action with political theme. David Niven played a power-mad Aaron Burr.

everything in that circle has been wiped out. Project X must have been somewhere around Waterloo, Iowa. The bridge would be around Davenport or Dubuque, and the city of Des Moines would have been destroyed. That's why the Manhattan Project, under

General Leslie R. Groves and Dr. J. Robert Oppenheimer, put the Trinity test site in a desert section of New Mexico called the *Jornada del Muerto*—the Journey of Death.

At first, the scientists were not sure whether the atomic bomb might produce a heat so great that it would make the nitrogen in the atmosphere react with the oxygen, thus setting fire to the whole atmosphere of the earth.

Stadler and Meigs meet their Waterloo.

The science fiction aspect of the novel fascinated many teenaged boys. They loved spectacles of destruction.

AS 1138

She leaped to her desk. This is it! The moment that Dagny goes on strike. This is the climax of the novel.

a promise she had made. On AS 962, Dagny promised Galt that she would chalk a dollar sign on the pedestal of Nat Taggart's statue in the Terminal concourse.

she took the lipstick from her bag. Elizabeth Taylor does the same thing in *Butterfield 8*. She leaves a parting message in lipstick on a mirror.

"BUtterfield 8" was a local telephone exchange, like "MUrray Hill 6," from the days before numbers replaced the names of telephone exchanges. Maybe personal names too, someday, like Equality 7-2521 in *Anthem*. In *Butterfield 8*, Liz plays a high-priced call girl on the Upper East Side. But that movie came out after AS. What AR would have had in mind is the scene in *A Tale of Two Cities*, where we see only the hand of some revolutionary chalking a message on a wall under a public clock: "It is later than you think."

See AR's article "It Is Earlier Than You Think" in the December 1964 *Objectivist Newsletter*.

gates of his own domain. Here again, AR is drawing a similarity, and a dissimilarity, between the unearned wealth and distinction of royalty and the earned wealth and distinction of industrial fortunes.

AS 1139

I swear—by my life . . . . Francisco wins again! He had wanted to beat Galt to the bagging of the big elephant: Rearden, and he did, and now

The Generator 271

he has bagged the only bigger elephant, Dagny. But he knows that he did not *cause* these conversions, as Galt had caused Ken Danagger's, he merely happened to be the witness when they happened.

Scene 3: The torture scene.

Only the small gray patch of the unit's roof could be seen from the Institute's windows. Perhaps AR got this picture from her visit to Frank Lloyd Wright's estate, "Taliesin," in Spring Green, Wisconsin, in 1947. The roof could have been that of the garage as seen from the main house. In a space under that garage was the emergency generator for the estate. Did that suggest Galt's motor in its vault? Also, Ayn and Frank must have stayed in a guest room or a whole guest house at Taliesin. Hank and Dagny at Ellis Wyatt's? That is why AR advised young writers to keep a notepad handy at all times. Anything you see might become a scene in your future writing, or a Maguffin.

Ferris, Mouch and Taggart. Thompson is not present. The big boss is always insulated from the dirty work done by his appointees. He might be on a plane back to Washington, dealing with other weighty matters of state besides what to do with Galt. He is preparing two speeches: one to take credit if Galt comes across, and the other to shift the blame to someone else if Galt does not.

But what is Jim Taggart doing here? He is neither an employee of the State Science Institute nor the Thompson administration. Maybe they figure that what the nation needs most right now is a working national railroad system.

Jim, as president of the nation's biggest railroad, is the closest thing the government has to a national railroad Czar, and Jim wants to be just that. So, he wants to wring national rail transportation strategy out of Galt, just as he has always done with Dagny. Also, since California and some other states are on the verge of secession and local war, Thompson needs a national railroad to help hold the nation together. That is why Lincoln subsidized the Central Pacific and Union Pacific Railroads. He wanted a transcontinental railroad as soon as possible, to help hold the new states of California and Oregon to the Union, as the southern states were seceding. Like

Thompson, Lincoln was watching the United States falling to pieces. For a history of the subsequent corruption and ruin of the subsidized railroads, see *The Myth of the Robber Barons,* by Folsom, listed in the Bibliography.

Does Mouch know Thompson offered Galt Mouch's job, back on AS 1100? Perhaps not, since Mouch seems, on AS 1140, and again on AS 1142 and AS 1143, to be genuinely concerned about Galt dying.

dials, screens, knobs, buttons, levers. Picture the laboratories of the science fiction movies of the 1950s.

AS 1140

pale blue eyes. Blues eyes on a villain, not a hero? But you have been told that all AR's heroes all have blue eyes and blond hair. See AS 1119.

stethoscope. On TF 685, AR writes that a doctor had once let Wynand listen to his own heartbeat. Perhaps some doctor had done the same for Ayn.

We want ideas—or else. This is the meaning of the scene, and of the novel, in a nutshell.

The mechanic pressed a button under one of the dials. Google the Milgram Experiment. Stanley Milgram, a Yale psychologist, performed his famous experiment in 1961, so AR could not have gotten the idea from him. Oddly enough, Stanley was the uncle of Shoshana Milgram, author of the forthcoming biography of AR. Another odd connection: Stanley designed his experiment to see how obedient people are to figures of authority, being intrigued about this question by the news coverage of the arrest and trial of Adolf Eichmann. Anne C. Heller followed her biography *Ayn Rand and the World She Made* with one on Hannah Arendt, the German-Jewish philosopher who got in some trouble, when covering the Eichmann trial for the *New Yorker* Magazine in 1961, by seeming to let Eichmann off too easy. There was an excellent movie about that called *Hannah Arendt.*

This is one of two torture scenes in AR's *oeuvre.* Equality 7-2521 is beaten on page 70 of *Anthem.*

AS 1141

his hands gripped the edge of the mattress. So, Galt's arms are not pinioned flung out to the side. That would be too obvious: If his arms were all the way out, at right angles to his torso, and if his body were held up vertically instead of supine on a mattress, what would this scene look like? AR herself refers you to Salvador Dali's painting *Corpus Hypercubus*—a painting of Christ on the cross: "One of the reasons it was her favorite painting was that it reminded her of Galt's bearing while he was on the torture rack" (McConnell, *100 Voices*, page 330). See also Britting, page 93.

Had enough? A favorite Rand expression. In her articles, she would describe some outrage, and, framed in a separate paragraph, say "Had enough?"

by a controlled effort at relaxation. This is a line this reader had never noticed before. Galt is fighting possible heart failure the only way he can: by forcing his breathing to slow down. You might even say Galt is meditating.

His naked body. This whole paragraph is about sculpture. To see how an Objectivist sculpture professional develops these ideas, see Diane Durante in the Bibliography.

the meaning of a statue of ancient Greece—the statue of man as a god. Q.E.D. "Man as god" is one of the major themes of the whole novel.

AS 1142

not attempting to negate it, but to bear it. Compare this line to the scene in *Lawrence of Arabia*, where Lawrence fascinates his fellow army officers with his ability to hold a flaming match between his fingers. Another man tries it and yells, "Ow! That hurts! What's the trick?"

"The trick is not *minding* that it hurts."

Do not deny an unpleasant fact. Just deal with it.

The terror of hearing one's own heart struggling. Today, this is called "bio-feedback."

I want him to believe! Now this sounds like the 1962 movie *The Manchurian Candidate* or George Orwell's *1984*. Richard Condon wrote the 1959 novel *The Manchurian Candidate*, from which George Axelrod adapted the screenplay and produced the movie. Axelrod is mentioned in Bennett Cerf's memoir *At Random*. After a long evening at Ayn's, Cerf left the party with Axelrod, who said "She knows me better after five hours than my analyst does after five years!"

He hasn't even screamed yet! Maybe Stanley Milgram got the idea for his experiment from Atlas! How many people have gotten how many ideas from AR, but won't admit it, because one simply does not read Ayn Rand?

AS 1143

The generator gives out just as Galt is near death. The religious folks would call this a "Pit Experience": a moment when you are helpless and can survive only through divine or other intervention. AR would retort that the real cause of Galt's salvation is the incompetence of men chosen for political reliability rather than for competence at their jobs.

AS 1144

He ran out of the room. AR just having the technician run out of the room is not very credible. He should have said, "I'll get Joe" before running out of the room. Then AR should have him run out of the building, never to be seen again. And she should have shown the man getting, previous to this scene, some inkling of how close to fleeing to hideouts in Tennessee his bosses are.

It's the vibrator that's out of order. At the bottom of AS 1141, Ferris reminded us that Galt was "some sort of electrical expert." That was to help set up this moment. And back on AS 961, Galt asked Dagny whether she would like him to fix the terminal signal system. AR must have called some electrician and asked him what might stop a generator, and how to fix it. But why does Project F need a generator anyway? Can't the torture machine run off the building's regular current? See AS 866 for some of AR's set-up for Jim's final mental breakdown.

AS 1145

The protective walls of emotion. AR should have said "anxiety" instead of "emotion." All emotions are not at fault; it is just Jim's evasions, creating anxiety, that are at fault. You can see, all over this page and so many others, how AR makes it look as though emotions as such are the bad guy, which was not her position at all.

On this page, Jim must be understood as a fictional character who embodies a certain principle. In Romantic fiction, it is okay to skate pretty close to the edge of unbelievability. It is unbelievable that Jim, after a lifetime of evasion and hatred for unavoidable truth, should suddenly have a moment of clarity. But notice that AR says, "It was not by means of words that this knowledge confronted his consciousness."

What Jim sees are tunnels with all exits blocked, and he sees that only in terms of terror, not conceptual clarity. In the same way, NB explained, on his first *Seminar* record, that "Toohey could not have given Roark's speech if he had wanted to. He does not have that kind of conceptual understanding of Roark. He knows only that Roark is the man whom he can't intimidate or manipulate, but he knows that only in terms of the *fear* that a man like Roark evokes in him."

that realm of which Galt was so radiant a son. A pun! And a pagan pun. Helios the sun god. Apollo. Mithras. Who but AR would make the thirteen-year-old first-time reader see the modern inventor in ancient Greek terms as the Prometheus who brings the fire of the gods to man? Religion has been robbed of its monopoly on reverence. Did AR's friend Cecil B. DeMille read AS? He died on January 21, 1959, so he could have. If DeMille had lived longer, Charlton Heston might have played Galt.

He was no longer able to summon the fog. On AS 868, AR writes "a foghorn, not to warn, but to summon the fog."

AS 1146

On this page, we see the last of Jim Taggart, Mouch, and Ferris.

the stamp and proof of objectivity. Sticker! It means Jim sees that Galt knows what he is thinking. His words and actions over the past few minutes have provided Galt with the objective facts and clues he needs to understand Jim's scream and breakdown. Others in the room see it too, but they are busy trying to escape the inevitable conclusion.

We'll be back. Great touch! Sticker!

This is the perfect button to put on the end of the scene, the chapter, and in a way, the whole story. The evil represented by these men will never go away completely. This could be the set-up for a sequel to AS. But this novel is so unique that it is hard to imagine a sequel, as it is hard to put AS in a category with any other novel. It is in a class by itself. It will never be repeated.

Arthur C. Clarke says that the last line in his novel *Rendezvous with Rama* was an afterthought. Leaving the deserted alien vessel Rama, the hero remembers that "the Ramans do everything in threes." That sets us up for a sequel, *Rama II*, because perhaps the same species that built Rama will send two more.

But what do Ferris and Mouch plan to do now? How can they just leave Galt there after all their talk about needing him? AR does not make this clear. Perhaps, they can't do anything just now anyway since the torture machine is on the blink, and those hideouts in Tennessee beckon. It would be funny if one of these bigshots had a hideout in southwestern Colorado. Ironically, the bad guys are now themselves "going Galt." If things are getting that bleak for them, we might guess that they would be leaving the country, perhaps to follow their numbered bank accounts to Switzerland, as other deposed leaders have done. AR does not tie up all these loose ends, because she is more concerned with the next moves of her heroes. Suffice it to say that Thompson, Mouch and company are out of power, like their generator, and out of our story.

10. In the Name of the Best Within Us

Chapter Overview

Dagny, Francisco, Ragnar and Hank fly to the State Science Institute and Ferris's torture chamber. They overcome the guards and get Galt into their plane. As they are flying over New York City, its lights go out.

Eddie is on the Taggart Comet in Arizona. The train breaks down. All the passengers, and all the crew but Eddie, hitch a ride with a passing wagon train. Eddie is left trying to start the train.

The people of the Gulch are all busy preparing for the resumption of their lives and careers in a post-strike world. Galt tells Dagny that the road is cleared, and it is time for the strike to end.

Scene 1: Assault on Project F.

AS 1147

Remember that Aristotle—*Aristoteles*—means "best end or purpose, or far in the distance." *Tele*vision means to see at a distance. *Aristos* means best. You will find the phrase "the best within themselves" on TF 312.

Here begins the scene where Dagny shoots the guard. We will discuss that on that next page. The theme of this scene, as always, is the necessity for every human being to think and choose.

AS 1148

Get out of my way. AR is echoing Galt's *very short* radio speech.

But how do I know you really have an order? This is totally unrealistic. A guard looks only for written permission to enter handed him by a visitor and confirmed by a list he has in his guard house. The only plausible reason for this setup is that the man is not a trained guard, and he was put here in haste without clear instructions because of the spreading panic. He has no guard house and no "Admit" list. Otherwise, this can be taken only as a morality play. A fairy tale. The lesson, though, is clear. Think or die.

You could also say that AR's writing style is simply impressionistic. She did not see a need to tie up all the loose ends, especially here at the climax, when she has to quicken the pace.

she pulled the trigger and fired. This line is a problem. Rand's friend Joan Kennedy Taylor (see Riggenbach in the Bibliography) was not satisfied, she told this reader, that it was necessary for Dagny to kill this guard. After all, Francisco, Hank and Ragnar are just around the corner of the building. They could plead division of labor, though: they were busy with the four guards posted among the trees while Dagny was dealing with the guard at the door. There are sixteen guards altogether. Five down, eleven to go.

This reader asked Leonard Peikoff about this problem in 1978, after getting Rand's autograph at a lecture of Peikoff's at the Hotel Pennsylvania. He instantly and confidently told me why Dagny's action was perfectly reasonable and moral, but in very few and unsatisfying, words (which I don't remember). As Peikoff strode quickly away, I thought that he sounded very practiced in answering this question. Others have also asked this question. This is probably another one of the mistakes AR made in that part of the book following Galt's speech (the *very long* one). At the end of a long, exhausting project is when you tend to make mistakes, because you are looking impatiently forward to finishing. Also, AR had convinced herself that she need pay little attention to her editor, Hiram Haydn, thinking that she knows better than he does how to write her book. That was Haydn's, and Cerf's, impression.

Peikoff's defense was something like: Dagny needs to shoot him because he is blocking her way and refuses to think and take responsibility and make a decision. That was no more than what I could read for myself on this page. I had noticed in Peikoff's answers to other questions after the lecture that I already knew his answers word for word, having read them in AR's books and articles.

AR's very first published work, back in Russia, was an article about Polish-American film star Pola Negri. It was published in a Russian film fan magazine. She mentioned that Negri, in leaving Poland, was stopped by a Polish border guard who refused to let her pass until she had handed over her jewelry. Negri, writes young Alisa Rosenbaum, "was ready to crush the man who dared to stand in her way." Perhaps this line crossed AR's mind as she wrote the Dagny-guard scene.

Here's another interesting point. AR says that Dagny would "hesitate to fire at an animal." Here is AR's reverence and respect for all life, even weeds (see Recurring Themes Index). And it is true that Dagny tells the guard "You may try to shoot me first," though she has her gun levelled at his heart as she says this.

When AR wrote this scene, she was probably thinking of a scene in the 1943 movie *Watch on The Rhine*, which was based on a 1941 play written by Lillian Hellman, with a screenplay written by her lover Dashiell Hammett.

(There is a funny Hellman-Rand connection. BB tells that story on page 207 and AH on pages 89, 164 and 205. It is probably no accident that AR named Hank Rearden's wife "Lillian.")

Paul Lukas plays the hero, a German in the US who calls himself a "professional anti-Fascist." He shoots in cold blood a Nazi collaborator. The Production Code Administration and the Hays Office objected: no murder in a movie may go unpunished. As Lukas is preparing to shoot the collaborator, who has demanded money or he will rat on Lukas to the Nazis (Lukas is about to go back into Germany to rescue other resistance workers), he says "You are not even a coward. By tomorrow morning you will have forgotten your fear" and will expose Lukas. So, Lukas has no choice but to silence the collaborator by shooting him. Lukas figures that his victim is quite capable of taking the hush money and squealing anyway. But the Hays office insisted that even if the victim is a Nazi, you may not murder him and get away with it, so the writers wrote an ending where Lukas has not returned from his mission and is presumed dead. Lukas's wife stoically dealing with him going back into Germany may have also inspired AR's bit about Kay Ludlow facing eleven months out of the year with Ragnar facing death on the high seas, but again, that is only speculation.

AS 1149

These next five pages are pure gravy, pure action, and for Francisco, this page is pure Zorro. The 1920 silent movie *The Mark of Zorro* was AR's inspiration for Francisco. That was Douglas Fairbanks Senior. Douglas Fairbanks Junior starred in the 1947 adventure movie *Sinbad the Sailor*. Junior laughs his way through danger and action, just like his father used to, and it is that light-hearted adventurer character that makes Francisco everyone's favorite in this book.

"*The name's too long to tell you.*" "*I'm asking the questions!*" "*I'm not answering them.*" Don't you wish real life were like that? That is the point of Romantic literature: not realism, but *hyper*-realism.

Francisco's hand was too fast. This would not be so credible if AR had not established, back on AS 997, that Francisco is a deadly marksman. But was Francisco's gun already in his hand? Without the guard noticing?

AS 1150

a gang of highwaymen. AR could have said "robbers," but "highwaymen" has a romantic, 18th century sound. See the 1906 Alfred Noyes poem *The Highwayman*.

AS 1151

his face was too well known. Who, in the business world, would be this familiar to the public today? Suppose Bill Gates or Elon Musk suddenly walked into your poker game.

AS 1152

The animals in the cages make a nice, unexpected touch. They reinforce AR's picture of the guards trapped between their bosses and these sudden invaders.

Oh, thank God! This line shows that the general public grasps that the key men in the economy have gone on strike and they need those men to come back before everyone starves or gangs take over and kill everyone. They got that much from Galt's speech and from what they could read between the lines of the government's statements, and what they can see going on around them.

Throughout the book, AR has shown us, many times, all sorts of ordinary people suffering from the deepening depression, such as the Minnesota wheat farmers.

AS 1153

we don't want to tangle with those people, they're—. They are what? Capable of seizing the airwaves and getting feted by the Head of the State? This attack by Francisco and friends is all about bluff. AR must have been thinking of the German stereotype: blind obedience to constituted authority, but what does the helpless bureaucrat do when he is not sure who constitutes authority?

We should make that *Ragnar* and friends. He is more accustomed to rough stuff than these business tycoons. They had not approved of his mode of fighting the looters, but now we can bet they are glad of his experience.

AS 1154

fired at the deserter. And Francisco does not fire fast enough to stop him? And does not shoot the chief after he kills his own man?

as from a catapult. Ragnar jumps from a tree limb through the window. Funny, I thought I remembered him swinging on a rope. Do not trust your memory! Memory plays tricks. AR may have had Ragnar swing on a rope, but maybe she changed her mind because that would be too obviously Hollywood, even for her. My false memory of a rope probably comes from seeing Errol Flynn swinging into the frame in the 1938 movie *The Adventures of Robin Hood*. Not to mention Tarzan! This is the problem so many readers have with AS: They vaguely remember, forty years after reading the book, what they *think* AR wrote, and they believe what academia and media *say* AR wrote.

AS 1155

beyond the tangle of electric wires. AR does not put the "octopus" image in this line. AR has refrained from throwing in more adjectives, now that they are no longer needed. And when she described the wires as octopus-like before, it was to scare us. Now the wires and the torture machine are powerless—literally and literarily. AR does not need to scare us anymore.

We never had to . . . ." Dagny said this to Galt back on AS 701.

radiant certainty. That is why they call it The Enlightenment! But if you appear certain of anything, all the intellectuals in the room will get scared and become angry, demanding to know who you are to claim to know anything, and accusing you of being an incipient dictator, forcing your dogma on helpless victims.

a flask of brandy. This is a Francisco thing to do. A swashbuckler, an Errol Flynn, a Zorro thing to do.

Give me a cigarette. Smokers used to claim that cigarettes calmed their nerves.

there's nothing left of them to kill. Think of the fleeing Nazi leaders as the war ended. Without the apparatus of the state to command, they scattered individually to Franco's Spain or Peron's Argentina, changed their identities, and lay low, trying to avoid detection.

AS 1156

the only things that were to matter from now on. Here we see the faintest little suggestion of the married life that awaits John and Dagny. Judge Narragansett will have some hitchin' to do.

the rest of his clothing. One unglamorous detail of torture is that the victim's bladder and bowels might empty themselves in the process. AR would not be so literal as to mention this. Today's writers, alas, would.

demolish the torture machine. This recalls Galt leaving the remnant of his motor at the Twentieth Century Motor Company. But maybe AR did not intend this echo. Sometimes a writer just gets lucky.

State Science Institute. Most of the guards there had been rushed down to Project F, so maybe there is no one around this late at night but a janitor or two. It may be a while before the guards left tied up are able to summon help, and by that time Galt and friends will be long gone. But some farmer may be calling the cops if he does not like people landing planes on his fields.

beyond the next hill. Can Galt walk that far, and the wounded Rearden?

stretch out in a reclining chair. Planes do not have chairs. They have seats. As when Dagny was half out of her seat in her plane chasing Galt's plane (AS 697), AR shows that she has no idea how small and cramped a light plane cabin is. Francisco helps Galt lie down, then he dresses Rearden's wound. This is after they are in the air. Ragnar is at the wheel. He glances over his shoulder to look at Hank. Where is Francisco sitting?

There are five people in this plane. How big a plane is it? Maybe AR was counting on the guess that not so many people had flown in light planes in 1957. Perhaps more people today would wonder about the size of the plane than would have in 1957. Maybe AR had been watching *Sky King* on TV. Sky had at least two planes, one a two-seater and the *Songbird*, which was bigger: a four- or eight-seater, but not big enough for any "reclining chairs." How big is the field? This is January or February, weeks after the speech on November 22, so the ground should be hard enough, but New Hampshire is pretty hilly. Is this field long enough for a take-off? AR describes this as a meadow with ruts, not an actual airfield. Not even a grass airstrip.

he was leaving the outer world. This line would be a little too expository for this action sequence, except that it comes at the end of the action, as a summing-up. AR should have dialogued it or made it a thought of Francisco's perhaps, since AR does show him, first in Project F and now in the plane, respecting Dagny's right to be closest to Galt. That is significant in view of the attention AR has paid throughout the novel to the rivalry for Dagny's hand among Francisco, Hank and Galt. Francisco, with his ducal chivalry and gallantry, is gracefully accepting his status as merely an old flame, now, to Dagny. That is why, back on AS 769, Galt says to Francisco "You're the one who's taken the hardest beating." He means Francisco had to give up Dagny. Ragnar is the only man in this plane who has not had sex with Dagny.

AS 1157

That is why I thank you. Sticker! How many young readers learned the true nature of gratitude from that line?

the message he had sent her from the valley. That was on AS 1002. "I have met him. I don't blame you."

in conversation with empty space. Around the year 2000, we all had to get used to seeing people walking down the street talking to people who weren't there, because they were having telephone conversations on tiny microphones and earpieces. But in 1957, it would have been momentarily surprising to Dagny.

Hank Rearden got a flesh wound. This is an old Hollywood line: "It's only a flesh wound, Ma'am."

To about half the male population. Here, AR is putting a bunch of exposition into an explanation Francisco is giving to Galt about the Gulchers' plan to rescue him.

Couldn't AR have left out the word "male"?

he won't have much longer. What does AR have in mind for the top men in the looter government? Their comeuppance would depend on some newly-elected Head of the State who would prosecute Ferris for torturing a prisoner and other crimes. AR wisely steers clear of any speculation on what political developments will follow this story. It is not necessary, for purposes of this novel, to know what happens after AS 1168, especially to the villains. Who would like to offer a sequel to Atlas about the flight and capture of Floyd Ferris? What about Wesley Mouch? He is the economic czar of the nation. AR would point to Harry Hopkins and other top FDR appointees. In World War I, in the Wilson administration, it was Bernard Baruch. Robert Reich and Paul Krugman would never torture Elon Musk or any other industrial visionary or inventor for advice on how to run the nation's economy, since that would mean having to admit that they don't know how to run it themselves. Instead, they torture *us* with their latest schemes of universal income and such.

Google the flight of President Jefferson Davis and his Confederate cabinet after the Civil War.

AR wrote the novel so as to, as much as possible, eliminate other nations as a factor. But we can imagine a second General Santa Anna taking power in Mexico with a promise to take advantage of the American breakdown to regain the territory lost in the war of 1846.

Maybe he could conclude a non-aggression pact with Canada and divide the US between them, like Hitler and Stalin did with Poland. But keeping just within the US context, Thompson will, like any national leader, care more about armed bands taking over parts of the country than a few deserting engineers. He might replace the disabled Jim Taggart with Lancelot Clokey or some other flunky and nationalize the railroads, for starters.

Correction: That should be Clifton Locey. Lancelot Clokey is in TF. Similar villain names. Maybe AR just rearranged the sounds to make a similar-sounding name. But she was probably thinking of Clifton Fadiman, who had been one of her models for Toohey. Fadiman (1904-1999) was a writer, editor, anthologist, and a radio and TV host, of the "witty intellectual" type favored in the 1950s. Since TV sets were expensive, the networks thought the viewers would be well-educated and would like to watch witty intellectuals. That soon changed. Fadiman's nickname was "Kip," like AS's Kip Chalmers. AR met him and liked him. Perhaps he mentioned that his father had been a druggist and had fled Imperial Russia. AR must have thought: If only my own druggist father had done the same!

Millions of people studying Galt's speech carefully will start all kinds of movements, ranging from peaceful and constructive to violent. And all those *not* influenced by Galt will be doing the same. When Galt and company announce their return, Galt will hold, we can suppose, a press conference, announcing on what terms his strikers will return. That may get Thompson to rescind Directive 10-289 and the other regulations Galt demands the repeal of. Some elected officials will declare that they are siding with the Galt faction, and the laws will be changed. Those elected officials' hand will be strengthened when the public learns of Galt's capture and torture.

mind and force. In other words, human beings banding together in self-defense against bandits.

AS 1158

started to build their homes in the valley. Here is another clue to the post-strike world. The strikers do not plan to leave the valley any time soon. A great deal of education will have to radiate out from

Mulligan's Valley first. A few more radio speeches, perhaps, and not just by Galt. A few "walking delegates" of the strike, visiting the settlements Galt suggested people start.

AR, in 1957, was thinking almost exclusively of the US as a patient to be resuscitated in the foreseeable future, although Francisco did once speak of reform reaching from the US to Argentina, on AS 771. Today, we can see a post-strike world as a *world*. North Korea has to be salvaged, and Syria, just for starters. Ragnar looks forward to selling his ship for use as a trans-Atlantic passenger liner. AR must have been thinking of the *De Grasse*, the French liner that brought her from Le Havre to New York.

But why trans-Atlantic and not trans-Pacific or Caribbean cruise service? Here is AR's Atlantic bias again.

Ragnar and Francisco, it seems, will be the ones to take charge of the international spread of American principles. Maybe Ragnar will teach philosophy at a university back in his native Norway.

our teacher's first teacher. Dr. Akston and Aristotle, that is.

thriftless. This is an old-fashioned term for careless and wasteful. In the days of candles, you had just one candle in a candle holder, and you carried it from room to room if you were still up at all after dark.

rations, quotas, controls. AR is thinking of World War II sugar and gasoline rationing, and even greater stringencies she remembered from World War I and the Russian Civil War.

still extending its lights to the sky. AR always comes back to the theme of light and those who bring it.

the continent's severed artery. This is the main thing on the minds of the people down there on the ground, great and small. Suppose there *were* only one rail and truck bridge over the Mississippi, and it had been suddenly destroyed, along with the city of Des Moines and a few others, and a quarter of Iowa. This happened on the same night that the Head of the State and other bigwigs had put John Galt on TV, only to hear him say "Get the hell out of my way," while the gun in his ribs had been exposed, along with the lies of the leaders. The TV audience couldn't be more shocked if Mr. Thompson had told them to drink Clorox.

panic had reached the power stations. The looter government would not be so concerned about panic—the power station workers would stay at their posts until the coal and oil failed to be delivered—as about putsches.

In the widening gyre of economic breakdown, the government would be more worried about extremist groups of all kinds doing what Cuffy Meigs did with Project X—*seizing* the power stations.

Don't look down! Why would Galt say that, and say it as a "sharp order?" Perhaps, in the minds of these characters in the plane, seeing the lights of New York go out must be like the person who does not want to look at his father or mother in a casket, because you "can't un-see" that, as they say. He prefers to remember the loved and lost as he was, alive and thriving.

AS 1159

the story Francisco had told her. On AS 766, Francisco told Dagny about Galt saying to him and Ragnar that when they saw the lights of New York go out, they would know that their job was done.

as she had seen him look at an untouched countryside. Remember Hank's reaction to wilderness, as he and Dagny drove through Wisconsin back on AS 282?

Anne Heller finds that there was a 1922 movie AR may have seen in Russia called *The Lights of New York.*

rise like a phoenix. Dagny saw Galt's plane rise from the airfield on AS 692.

knowing that one has a continent to build. Sticker!

the words of a businessman's language: "Price no object." Sticker! This young reader saw, in this line, the soul of a human being who is *efficacious* (a favorite Rand adjective)—a person who can make things actually happen. Not one of "those who can *only* dream."

It's the end. It's the beginning. Similar lines have been much used, for example in the title of the 1947 MGM movie *The Beginning or the End*, about the building of the atomic bomb. Hal Wallis assigned AR to write a movie script about the Manhattan Project—that's how she met and interviewed J. Robert Oppenheimer—but then he sold AR's script to MGM, who did not use it.

You have to notice inconspicuous lines like that to realize that AR's focus is not on the decline and fall of America and the world, but on Churchill's "broad, sunlit uplands" that await man, once he gets through the horrors of the twentieth century.

Then they lay still. Read this paragraph slowly, then get married. Johann Wolfgang von Goethe said "The sum which two married people owe to one another defies calculation. It is an infinite debt which can be discharged only through all eternity."

AS 1160

I had to be. A is A. Why did he have to be all right? In this line, Galt sounds much more young and vulnerable than elsewhere.

Scene 2: Eddie is stranded on the Comet.

Mr. Willers. For one brief moment, on this page and the next, we see Eddie out of Dagny's shadow. It's *Mr.* Willers to you!

any attempt to explain made any unadmitted terror easier to bear. Good line.

the range of the moment. This was a favorite line of AR's. After the "Saturday Night Massacre" in 1973, AR, at the Ford Hall Forum, said "One can speak today *only* on the range of the moment," meaning that unexpected developments in the Watergate scandal were coming too thick and fast to analyze at the leisure of news analysts.

AS 1161

He had never had to work so hard. This is Eddie's version of building the John Galt Line. He is no longer just Dagny's assistant. He is in charge. Perhaps he *could* have been a Dagny, if he had started early enough. Perhaps AR is redeeming Eddie now, as she redeemed Peter Keating by making him a frustrated painter (TF 620-1).

borrowed track of the Atlantic Southern that ran through Arizona. Ah! That would explain why the Comet is going out of its way from San Francisco.

AR has brought the "Atlantic Southern" Railroad into the story before (AS 500), so she uses it again rather than have Eddie use the tracks of some railroad to the north, like the real-life Northern Pacific or Jim Hill's Great Northern. There is only one Mississippi bridge, and only one way around the destroyed tunnel in Colorado, and that way leads south all the way from San Francisco to Arizona. And Eddie does not know it yet, but he cannot hope to get closer to New York than Iowa because the bridge is gone. This scene must be happening on the same night as the Project X disaster, Galt's appearance on TV, gun in his ribs and all, and his later rescue from Project F. AR is not, in this case, foreshortening time, but expanding time: it seems like days must have passed since Ferris hauled Galt down to the ballroom, and got him to New Hampshire, and Galt got rescued, but it has all happened in one evening and night.

he wondered why he felt it with such urgency. Dagny, back on AS 15, said that the Comet has never been late. This is Eddie's role as the "feudal serf of Taggart Transcontinental" as Jim called him on AS 11. Eddie accepted the title. Years later, Leonard Peikoff would reportedly proudly call himself "the feudal serf of Objectivism."

AS 1162

From Ocean to Ocean, Forever. We saw this on AS 6.

Don't let it go! It was Dagny who first said this line, back on AS 655, in a kind of industrial prayer. This will be the theme of the rest of this scene, and the title of an article in ARL.

Go down the length of the train. It is such a relief to hear Eddie turning into Mr. Willers, having the ideas and giving the orders that Dagny would have given.

the occupied ones, that is. AR never misses a chance to throw in a line that reinforces multiple themes: in this case, the line reinforces the "decay" theme of the whole novel, *and* reinforces what she said on the previous page about how few passengers there are on the Comet, *and* reinforces Eddie's newfound confidence as the boss of this part of Taggart Transcontinental.

The engineer had exhausted his meager store of knowledge. Why is this engineer running the Comet when he has such meager knowledge? Because the best engineers, like Pat Logan, have long since gone on strike against Directive 10-289 and other outrages.

but without the child's conviction that knowledge is possible. AR's references to children are many, and they show love and respect for children, despite what the Bashers say about AR hating children because she puts none in her novels.

AS 1163

motor units. We know about motor units from Dagny walking into one on AS 245, during the first run on the John Galt Line.

a man who seemed to be the leader. AR based this character on Bennett Cerf, of Random House Publishing, the man who published this novel.

Cerf was a regular panelist on a game show on CBS called *What's My Line?* in the 1950s and 60s. Just google "*What's My Line?*" and you can see Cerf in action and hear his voice. Google "*What's My Line?*, September 22, 1957" and you can see Dorothy Kilgallen introduce Cerf as the publisher of the "due soon" *Atlas Shrugged.*

it was a train of covered wagons. The TV show *Wagon Train* premiered September 18, 1957, just a bit late to give AR this idea, but in 1951 there was a movie called *Westward the Women*, with Robert Taylor as wagon master Buck Wyatt (as in Ellis).

AS 1164

for a price. This shows that people are reading transcripts of Galt's speech, or listening to recordings, and Galt's ideas are spreading. Perhaps his influence will extend to the Legislature, and maybe Mr. Thompson himself, who might fire Wesley Mouch and scrap Directive 10-289.

Remember, that was a Directive, not a law, so the Legislature cannot repeal it, but they and others might get Thompson to rescind it, along with the Railroad Unification Plan and other unpopular directives. Then you will see Tom Colby return to Rearden Steel, Pat Logan to Taggart Transcontinental, and millions of others.

Then you haven't heard? Now Eddie learns of the bridge being destroyed.

You would think that Taggart Division offices, stations, and the Comet would have been among the first to hear of it, but two hundred miles of the Taggart system have suddenly disappeared in Project X's one-hundred-mile radius of destruction. Apparently, the trains do not have radios, since they have to get to track phones to communicate, which seems unlikely, for 1957. Is this a case of dramatic license?

Step right up, folks! This might be Bennett Cerf hosting the surprise party for Ayn at the Plaza Hotel after the publication of AS. He had the famous dollar sign cigarettes made for the occasion (BB 295, AH 282).

AS 1165

grease-monkey. Are mechanics called grease-monkeys anymore?

The 'People's Party' crowd grabbed the crops. This is the last and the worst of all the thousands of signs of decay, economic and political, in the novel. Seizure of power by local warlords, like Vasily Chapayev and Nestor Makhno in the Russian revolution (AR mentions Makhno in WTL, on page 13), for example, and the warlords all over China who stepped into the power vacuum as the empire crumbled. By the time Mao took over in 1949, as General MacArthur said, "The masses are desperate, and eager to follow any leader who promises to relieve local stringencies." It was easier for a refugee like AR, than a born American, to imagine a societal breakdown, since she had lived through one. Yes, it *can* happen here.

Some critics faulted AR for the unrelieved gloom of the novel. See the movie *Blade Runner*. It is always dark and rainy throughout the whole movie. Then, the hero and heroine escape Los Angeles in a plane. Suddenly we see the mountains, valleys and lakes of northern California from the plane, and all is bright sunlight and color. The contrast is stunning. AR will do something of that on the last two pages of this book, just as the sudden appearance of the word "I" at the end of *Anthem* is stunning and gives a dramatic sense of relief. Or see the sudden appearance of color in The Wizard of Oz when Dorothy arrives in Oz.

Got to travel by night, on account of the Washington crowd. Today, this type might call themselves Survivalists, and wear camouflage. This line, like Galt's Gulch, is no longer possible. Satellites and infrared detectors make it impossible to avoid detection by "the Washington crowd" merely by traveling by night.

secret, free settlement. Eddie has been thinking about the immediate future, with people everywhere taking Galt's advice and starting imitation Galt's Gulches. The Republic of San Marino began that way. Escaped slaves fled to Monte Titano—Mountain of the Titan—as the Roman Empire crumbled. Today it is the world's oldest surviving republic.

Escaped slaves in the southern states formed a settlement in Spanish Florida called Saint Marks. Escaped slaves and free Blacks formed communities in Staten Island (Sandy Ground), Brooklyn (Weeksville), and Seneca Village, inside what would become Central Park, between West 82nd and West 89th Streets. Black Loyalists fleeing with the Redcoats founded Shelburne and Birchtown, Nova Scotia. Escaped Hessians, Redcoats, outlaws, Indians, and hillbillies became the Jackson Whites of the Ramapo Mountains along the New York–New Jersey state line. There were many others. History and the whole world are strewn with Galt's Gulches.

AS 1166

he was stepping on the dead man's pedal, which was dead. AR made a funny, but do you think she meant to? This is supposed to be a sad scene, and AR succeeds at pathos here better than she does with the death of the Wet Nurse. "Pulling levers at random" may have made her chuckle involuntarily, too. It would be Bennett Cerf pulling the levers at Random. "Dead man's pedal" can be found on Wikipedia under "Dead man's switch." On trains, though, the fireman is always near the engineer and can stop the train if the engineer is incapacitated.

In the name of the best within us. This was on AS 5 and 6. Business and earning a living, not just the unlikely events of winning battles, climbing mountains, or saving people from fires, is the real meaning of life. Sticker! Perhaps the most important sticker of all. You don't have to wait for someone to need saving from a fire to find meaning and a justification for your existence. Some of us, when young, are genuinely surprised to learn this. If you spend your childhood watching TV, you do tend to think that life's only meaning is solving an unusual crisis, as Captain Kirk does every week.

he lunged in the direction of the rabbit. For the same reason, Dagny lunged at a weed on AS 519. Eddie and Dagny are both rebelling against signs of decay.

AS 1167

Then he collapsed. NB explained why Eddie's fate had to be left undetermined, in his essay "The Literary Method of Ayn Rand" on page 122 of *Who Is Ayn Rand?* Just as Kira had to die at the end of WTL, since the theme of the novel was that dictatorship destroys the best, so Eddie had to be left suspended between life and death, like Schrödinger's Cat, to reinforce the theme that we all depend on man's mind, and we depend the most on those whose minds have given us the most. Surely Dagny and friends, once safely landed in the valley, will try to find Eddie and a few others. It will not be necessary any more to keep the valley a secret from Eddie and other sympathizers.

Scene 3: Dagny and Galt in the Gulch. Strikers plan for the future.

It was a symphony of triumph. At last we see the repetition of the paragraph on AS 13 where Dagny first heard Halley's Fifth Concerto.

the snow still covering the ground. Galt's speech was on November 22. It took some weeks for Galt to be captured, so Galt's TV appearance, his torture and rescue, the Project X explosion, and Eddie's marooning must have been in January or February, and now spring is coming, so it might be March or April.

the rectangle of light. The camera glides around from house to house. AR might be thinking of *It's a Wonderful Life*. It begins that way. In each house there is someone praying for George Bailey.

New York . . . New York . . . New York. New York City gets one last homage from the reverent city girl.

for these truths hold good. In the 1956 movie *Alexander the Great*, with Richard Burton, we hear Aristotle ranting maniacally about the superiority of Greeks over the barbarians. Many first-edition readers of AS probably had seen that movie just a year before, and might have wondered whether AR's reverent view of Aristotle was more accurate than the ranting view. In any case, at the end of the movie, we hear either Aristotle or some voice-over representing Sophocles saying his famous quote from *Antigone*: "There are many wonderful things in nature, but the most wonderful of all is man." This is also translated as: "Wonders are many, but the greatest wonder is man himself."

Here, AR is giving us Aristotle's own explanation of why his Law of Identity (which she words succinctly as "A is A") is an axiom and not just a hypothesis. You cannot make any statement about any subject without being confidant that the subject is what it is.

AS 1168

Congress shall make no law. Judge Narragansett is adding a free enterprise clause to the Constitution. There has been a movement for many years now to do just that. It has never picked up much steam. It was advertised in *Reason* magazine years ago. Google "abridging the freedom of production and trade" and you will see lots of discussion of this idea.

Here we see the clearest glimpse of the plan for a post-strike world. Judge Narragansett and others in the legal field will present the legislators with proposed changes in the law, probably beginning with Thompson or his successor rescinding Directive 10-289. They would also want to rescind the authority by which the Head of the State was *allowed* to issue Directives like 10-289. Robert Kirsch, reviewing AS for the *Los Angeles Times*, writes that Galt is arguing for a dictatorship. Dictators have no need to tinker with a constitution. They can just throw it out. See Article 48 of the Weimar Constitution, which allowed Chancellor Hitler to suspend that Constitution and rule by decree.

Contained in the sentence he had heard. This sentence is the payoff. It is the *Bladerunner* ending. It is the light at the end of the tunnel.

the eyes of youth looking at the future with no uncertainty or fear. Youth was Rand's target audience. NB explained that Big Business was never among AR's fans or intended audience. Her appeal was to youth.

She will probably try to take the shirt off my back. Sticker! This is a counterpart to Hank's negotiation with Dagny about rails of Rearden Metal on AS 82. To many young readers of 1957, this was new: grown-ups who respect each other can speak frankly and not try to snow each other. They can drive a hard bargain but still be friends.

He stood looking. Google *Roaring Guns.* Robert Shayne (remember Inspector Henderson in *Superman* on TV?) stars in this 1944 Warner Bros. 19-minute short set in the west in the 1880s. (Jay "Tonto" Silverheels is in it too.) At the end, you see the hero and heroine on a mountaintop saying a few solemn words relative to the movie's theme. Did AR get this last scene of AS from this obscure short?

the defiantly stubborn flame of Wyatt's Torch. It is always fun to see a, not a running gag in this case, but a running reference. Wyatt's Torch here makes its seventh and last appearance. The torch of liberty is a useful literary and visual symbol of defiance and freedom. Know any statues with torches? Besides the one on Bedloe's Island, there was another one, briefly, in Tiananmen Square, Beijing, the "Goddess of Democracy."

He raised his hand and over the desolate earth he traced in space the sign of the dollar. Perhaps AR was thinking of her old hero Zorro, with his sword, tracing in people's shirtfronts the sign of the Z. Are you satisfied with this as the last line of the novel, like the last note of a symphony or opera? When have you ever seen any adult trace anything in the air with his finger?

What might AR have had Galt do instead? Perhaps he could take a remote control out of his pocket and turn off the ray screen. Today, he could summon a flock of drones to form a dollar sign a thousand feet tall. Instead of hiding the valley, Galt could start advertising its location, to attract fellow rebels.

What is the meaning of Galt's words "We are going back to the world"? AR is playing one last trick on Jesus: Going back to the world is also called resurrection.

Appendix A
Rand Qua Writer

(*Page numbers refer to the printed version of Atlas Shrugged.*)
While many readers appreciate the political values and polemics expressed in Ayn Rand's *Atlas Shrugged*, it is important to recognize the literary excellence of the novel. As discussed in the Commentary, *Atlas Shrugged* should not be viewed as a political manifesto, but rather as a novel that exhibits excellent literary merits. Ayn Rand, after all, is first and foremost a novelist. To showcase her skills and talents as a writer, I have curated a collection of passages from the novel in several categories that highlight the literary value of the work.

The Journey of Dagny Taggart

Atlas Shrugged, as a novel, traces the story of Dagny Taggart's journey from an enemy of the strike to a passionate supporter. Here is a partial list of passages tracing that emotional journey.

- The thought of leaving Taggart Transcontinental did not belong among the things she could hold as conceivable. 55
- What would I say if you asked me to consider the idea of committing suicide? 113
- "Hank, what if anything happens to Ted Nielsen?" . . . "Why should anything happen to him?" " . . . well, there was Dwight Sanders. He vanished . . . ." 282

- There were times when she wondered why she wanted to rebuild the motor. What for?–some voice seemed to ask her. Because I'm still alive, she answered. 352
- ... if they sentence you to jail tomorrow, I'll quit–without waiting for any destroyer to prompt me. 474
- She had found it, everything she had ever wanted, it was here in this room, ... but the price was that net of rail behind her, the rail that would vanish, the bridges that would crumble, the signal lights that would go out. 749
- But so long as I choose to go on living, I can't desert a battle which I think is mine to fight. 807
- "I don't want to see *you* working as their serf!" "And yourself?" "I think that they're crumbling and that I'll win. I can stand it just a little longer." 961
- ... the heavy indifference she now felt for her railroad was hatred ... Did they want him to live, those who had heard him? 1110
- She leaped to her desk and seized the telephone receiver. Her hand stopped in mid-air. 1138

The Atlas Theme

The *Atlas* theme—the punishing of the productive by the parasitic—connects the novel's story to the book's title.

- "If there's any trouble, are you taking responsibility for it, Miss Taggart?" "I am." 17
- At every step of her rise, she did the work long before she was granted the title ... 51
- Don't you see that that's what you're being punished for—because it was good? 78
- It's we who move the world and it's we who'll pull it through . 88
- When a problem came up at the mills, his first concern was to discover what error he had made; he did not search for anyone's fault but his own; it was of himself that he demanded perfection. 128

- Because they're a bunch of miserable children who struggle to remain alive, desperately and very badly, while I–I don't even notice the burden. 147
- He thought that Gwen Ives and Mr. Ward could look to him for hope, for relief, for renewal of courage. To whom could *he* look for it? 215
  . . . what's going to support a seven-thousand-ton train on a three-thousand ton bridge?" "My judgment." 238
- "Oh, you'll do something!" cried James Taggart . . . he felt a deafening crash within him. 986
- You have nothing to offer us. *We do not need you.* 1011

Some Lovely Passages

I particularly enjoy many of Rand's beautifully written sentences. I found these examples especially delightful.

- But from the sunset far at the end of the street, yellow glints caught his eyes, and the eyes looked straight at Eddie Willers, mocking and still–as if the question had been addressed to the causeless uneasiness within him. 3
- An incoming freight train hid the view, filling the windows with a rushing smear of noise. In a sudden break above the flat cars, the passengers saw distant structures under a faint, reddish glow in the sky; the glow moved in irregular spasms, as if the structures were breathing. 27
- It was Halley's Concerto swung into a popular tune. It was Halley's melody torn apart, its holes stuffed with hiccoughs. The great statement of joy had become the giggling of a barroom. Yet it was still the remnant of Halley's melody that gave it form; it was the melody that supported it like a spinal cord. 155
- The earth was snow-covered now, and what remained was like the skeleton of the countryside she remembered – a thin design of bare branches rising from the snow to the sky. It was gray and white, like a photograph, a dead photograph which

- one keeps hopefully for remembrance, but which has no power to bring back anything. 196
- The green-blue rails ran to meet them, like two jets shot out of a single point beyond the curve of the earth. 239
- Uncoiling from among the curves of Wisconsin's hills, the highway was the only evidence of human labor, a precarious bridge stretched across a sea of brush, weeds and trees. The sea rolled softly, in sprays of yellow and orange, with a few red jets shooting up on the hillsides, with pools of remnant green in the hollows, under a pure blue sky. 279
- She stood there silently, watching, without interest or purpose, like a chemical compound on a photographic plate, absorbing physical shapes because they were there to be absorbed, but unable to ever form any estimate of the objects of her vision. 286
- He saw her look of sudden attentiveness, the look of thought rushing into a breach torn open upon a new direction. 408
- Clouds had wrapped the sky. 633
- . . . he had a look of satisfaction, but satisfaction could not soften his features, it merely struck them like flint and sent sparks of humor to glitter faintly in the corners of his eyes, a humor that was shrewder, more demanding, yet warmer than a smile. 734

Rand's Sense of Humor

Rand can be quite funny. These gave me a few chuckles.

- . . . who had crossed into age from adolescence, without the intermediate stage of youth. 7
- I don't think the signal's going to change." "Then what are you doing?" "Waiting for it to change." 15
- He had started out with a hundred thousand dollars of his own and a two-hundred-million-dollar loan from the government . . . This proved, he liked to say, that individual ability still had a chance to succeed in the world. 45

- . . . in a momentous drama giving the answer to the great problem: Should a woman tell? 66
- "It is disgraceful that artists are treated like peddlers and that art works have to be sold like soap." "You mean, your complaint is that they *don't* sell like soap?" 141
- In the bluish light of the snow, his skin had the tinge of butter. 166
- In any group of three, his person became indistinguishable, and when seen alone it seemed to evoke a group of its own, composed of the countless persons he resembled. 532
- "Is that what you learned from Dr. Akston?" "That, among other things." 712
- The way she now looked at him was worse than her smile—she looked as if she were seeing him naked and would not endure the sight much longer. 1001
- "You won't?" he asked blankly, with the kind of look he would have worn if one of the flower vases had suddenly refused to perform its part. 1007

Parodies of Christianity

In the novel, Rand takes a few well-placed shots at Christianity.

- The vaulting held the solemn peace of a cathedral, spread in protection high above the rushing activity of men. 59
- In her childhood, his statue had been Dagny's first concept of the exalted. When she was sent to church or to school, and heard people using that word, she thought that she knew what they meant: she thought of the statue. 60
- The motors were a moral code cast in steel . . . . They *are* alive, she thought, but their soul operates them by remote control . . . . She was making her way back toward the cab, feeling that she wanted to laugh, to kneel or to lift her arms, wishing she were able to release the thing she felt, knowing that it had no form of expression. 246

- ... at the foot of a structure that looked like an ancient temple – and she knew what rite was the proper form of worship to be offered on an altar of that kind. 731
- ... let the world rack him or ruin him, he will not bear false witness to the evidence of his mind! 783
- Every man builds his world in his own image. 791
- "Take it," he said. "You've earned it – and it wasn't chance." 810
- If I were to speak your kind of language, I would say that man's only moral commandment is: Thou shalt think. 1018
- They had known that theirs was the power. I taught them that theirs was the glory. 1051
- And as the meaning of a statue of ancient Greece–the statue of man as a god – clashed with the spirit of this century's halls, so his body clashed with a cellar devoted to prehistorical activities. 1141

Rand's Words Refute Critical Attacks

Rand bashers frequently criticize Rand for a variety of literary failures that have no basis in fact. In most instances, they probably haven't read *Atlas Shrugged*. Here are a few examples that refute some of the erroneous charges.

Critique: Ayn Rand hates the poor

- A worker saw him and grinned in understanding, like a fellow accomplice in a great celebration, who knew why that tall, blond figure had had to be present here tonight. 29
- And kitchenware that will be bought at the dime store and passed on from generation to generation 87
- Better find another supplier at once, if you don't want to have a famine on your hands. 165
- ... she shuddered, realizing what things she now called luxury ... things once available to the poorest: dry cleaning – electrical appliances – gas station. 519
- Let him be my guest. 656

Critique: Ayn Rand favors big business

- "Your brother – he wouldn't have taken a coach." She laughed. "No, he wouldn't have." 17
- Because I'm going to beat the Phoenix-Durango if necessary– only it won't be necessary, because there will be room for two or three railroads to make fortunes in Colorado. 21
- Rearden disliked the subject. . . . He could not quite convince himself that it was necessary. (lobbying). 40
- He seemed unusually skillful at obtaining favors from the Legislature. 52
- He never sought any loans, bonds, subsidies, land grants or legislative favors from the government. 59

Critique: Ayn Rand lacks compassion

- It's so hard for him, thought Rearden, and so easy for me. 39
- "I'm sorry," he said, his voice low. It sounded, not as an apology, but as a statement of compassion. *Akston to Dagny.* 329
- His voice tense with the anger of compassion. 488
- "Cherryl, I don't want you to go home tonight." 892

Critique: Atlas Shrugged has inadequate characterization

- She waved to him on her way out. 59
- "Well, what do you want me to call it?" she snapped, worn down to anger. 196
- "Mr. Willers, I'm looking for a job as a station operator." 218
- She saw the shot of pain in his eyes and wished desperately that she had not said it. 372
- . . . he looked like a truck driver, so she asked . . . "No, ma'am," he answered. "I was a truck driver." He added, "But that's not what I wanted to remain." 721
- And suddenly, broken by the whole of this day and of that month, she was sobbing in his arms, slumped against him,

sobbing as she had never done in her life, as a woman, in surrender to pain and in a last futile protest against it. 855

Critique: **Ayn Rand Hated The Poor**

- A worker saw him and grinned in understanding, like a fellow accomplice in a great celebration, who knew why that tall, blond figure had had to be present here tonight. 29
- And kitchenware that will be bought at the dime store and passed on from generation to generation. 87
- Better find another supplier at once, if you don't want to have a famine on your hands. 165
- . . . she shuddered, realizing what things she now called luxury . . . things once available to the poorest: dry cleaning– electrical appliances – gas station. 519
- Let him be my guest. 656

Appendix B
A List of the Strikers

(The list is organized in descending order of narrative importance. Page numbers indicate the page in *Atlas Shrugged* where the individual is identified as a striker.)

Strikers	Professions	Page
John Galt	physicist, Twentieth Century Motor Company, Wisconsin	671
Dagny Taggart	Operating Vice President, Taggart Transcontinental Railroad	1138
Francisco d'Anconia	d'Anconia Copper	112
Hank Rearden	Rearden Steel, inventor of Rearden Metal	1000
Ragnar Danneskjöld	pirate	573
Midas Mulligan	Mulligan. Bank, Chicago	315
Ellis Wyatt	Wyatt Oil, Colorado	336
Ken Danagger	Danagger Coal, Pittsburgh	443
Dr. Hugh Akston	Head of the Philosophy Department of Patrick Henry University, Cleveland	330 —332
Judge Narragansett	Illinois State Superior Court	318
Dick McNamara	Cleveland railroad construction contractor	63
Dwight Sanders	Sanders Aircraft	219
Andrew Stockton	Stockton Foundry, Colorado	344
Lawrence Hammond	Hammond Motors, Colorado	348

Roger Marsh	Marsh Electric, Colorado	380
Ted Nielsen	Nielsen Motors, Colorado	518
Calvin Atwood	Atwood Light and Power Company, New York	723
Richard Halley	composer	24
Kay Ludlow	movie star	727
Dr. Thomas Hendricks	surgeon	711
n.a.	a professor of economics	719
n.a.	a professor of history.	719
n.a.	a professor of psychology	719
n.a.	Francisco's superintendent	770
n.a.	Francisco's former metallurgist	770
n.a.	The old Taggart Terminal Manager, before Owen Kellogg	779
n.a.	Rearden's superintendent	1000
n.a.	Rearden's chief metallurgist	1000
n.a.	Rearden's chief engineer	1000
Owen Kellogg	Taggart Terminal Manager	25
William Hastings	Chief Engineer, Twentieth Century Motor Company, Wisconsin	324
n.a.	A writer with large eyes	719
n.a.	a sculptor	724
n.a.	a chemist	724
Gwen Ives	Rearden's secretary	1000
n.a.	The young brakeman on Taggart Transcontinental. Works for Wyatt in the valley while taking piano lessons from Richard Halley	13
n.a.	A truck driver	721

Appendix C
My Fifteen Favorite Stickers

Page numbers refer to the printed version of Atlas Shrugged.

- This was like the stories — 9
- He asked who had started him — 31
- I could ask twice that — 83
- My judgment — 238
- A feeling that forbade him — 375
- To lie for the first time in his life — 650
- As if I had moved my grave two hours further away — 722
- That's the only sort of men I like to hire — 725
- Well done — 736
- The wealth of selection, not accumulation — 736
- Not the fact that you felt, but that you felt what I wished you to feel — 782
- No, through our own choice — 888
- Not because you suffer, but because you haven't deserved to suffer — 888
- It went through the mills — 1000
- In that world, you'll be able to rise in the morning — 1068

Appendix D
My Dreamcast for
Atlas Shrugged

Dreamcasting *Atlas* has been a popular game among many fans of *Atlas Shrugged*. Here is my list. While many of the performers are no longer with us, this is, after all, a fantasy exercise. Imagine them as they might have looked in years past. Whom would you cast?

Character	Casting
Dagny Taggart	Elizabeth Montgomery
	Greta Garbo
	Katherine Hepburn
	Gretchen Corbett
Henry Rearden	Robert Lansing
	Charlton Heston
Lillian Rearden	Jane Wyatt
James Taggart	Martin Landau
	Bruce Dern
Francisco d'Anconia	Douglas Fairbanks Jr.
	Tyrone Power
John Galt	Eric Braeden
	Charlton Heston
	Yul Brynner
	Henry Fonda
Dr. Hugh Akston	Spencer Tracy
	Sidney Poitier
	Henry Fonda
Jeff Allen	Morgan Freeman

Mr. Thompson	Ed Flanders
	Howard da Silva
	Ed Begley
Eddie Willers	Bill Bixby (Tim in *My Favorite Martian*)
Ellis Wyatt	Yul Brynner
	Clint Eastwood
Midas Mulligan	John Doucette (Gen. Lucian Truscott in *Patton*)
Dr. Floyd Ferris	Vincent Price
Dr. Robert Stadler	Cillian Murphy (Oppenheimer in *Oppenheimer*)
	Raymond Massey
Cherryl Taggart	Sandy Dennis
The Wet Nurse	Michael J. Fox
Judge Narragansett	Chief Justice Warren Burger
	Dean Jagger
	Henry Fonda
Wesley Mouch	William Talman (Hamilton Burger in (*Perry Mason*)
	James Gregory
Cuffy Meigs	Larry Storch
	Anthony Denison (Cuffy Meigs in *Atlas Shrugged Part III*)
Fred Kinnan	John Doucette
	John Wayne
	Lee J. Cobb
Orren Boyle	John Randolph (the Mayor in *Earthquake*)
	Ed Begley
Dan Conway	Edward Binns (*12 Angry Men*)

Bibliography

Adams, Henry "The Virgin and the Dynamo," in *The Education of Henry Adams*, New York: Modern Library, 1918.
Adler, Mortimer J., *Aristotle For Everybody: Difficult Thought Made Easy*, New York: Macmillan Publishing Co., 1978.
Anderson, Poul, "The Light," *Galaxy Science Fiction*, March 1957.
Ayer, A. J., *Language, Truth and Logic*, London: Penguin Books, 1990. Originally published 1936.
Bastiat, *The Law*, Irvington-on-Hudson: Foundation for Economic Education. Originally published 1850.
Blanshard, Brand, *Reason and Analysis*, London: George Allen and Unwin Ltd., 1962.
Bradbury, Ray, *The Illustrated Man*, New York: Doubleday & Company, Inc., 1951.
Branden, Barbara, *The Passion of Ayn Rand*, Garden City: Doubleday & Company, Inc., 1986.
Branden, Barbara, *Who Is Ayn Rand?*, New York: Random House, 1962.
Branden, Nathaniel, *Judgment Day: My Years With Ayn Rand*, Boston: Houghton Mifflin, 1989.
Branden, Nathaniel, *The Disowned Self*, New York: Bantam Books, 1972.
Branden, Nathaniel, *The Psychology of Romantic Love: Romantic Love in an Anti-Romantic Age*, New York: Jeremy P. Tarcher/Penguin, 1980.
Branden, Nathaniel, *The Psychology of Self-Esteem: A Revolutionary Approach to Self-Understanding that Launched a New Era in Modern Psychology*, San Francisco: Jossey Bass, 2001. Originally published 1969.
Britting, Jeff, *Ayn Rand*, New York: Overlook Duckworth, 2004.
Burdick, Eugene and Harvey Wheeler, *Fail-Safe*, New York: McGraw-Hill, 1962.
Burdick, Eugene and William Lederer, *The Ugly American*, New York: W. W. Norton, 1958.
Burton, Richard, *Meeting Mrs. Jenkins*, New York: William Morrow and Company, 1966.
Cerf, Bennett, *At Random: The Reminiscences of Bennett Cerf*, New York: Random House, 1977.
Cheney, Margaret, Robert Uth, and Jim Glenn, *Tesla: Master of Lightning*, New York: Barnes & Noble Books, 1999.
Chernow, Ron, *Alexander Hamilton*, New York: Penguin Books, 2004.

Christie, Agatha, *They Came to Baghdad*, London: The Collins Crime Club, 1951.
Clarke, Arthur C., *The Fountains of Paradise*, London: Millenium, 2000. Originally published 1979.
Clarke, Arthur C., "The Nine Billion Names of God," first published in *Star Science Fiction Stories* No. 1, in February 1953. James Randi's favorite Clarke story.
Condon, Richard, *The Manchurian Candidate*, New York: McGraw-Hill, 1959.
Cookinham, Frederick, *The Age of Rand: Imagining an Objectivist Future World*, Lincoln, NE: iUniverse, 2005.
Cookinham, Frederick, *Man in the Place of the Gods: What Cities Mean*, Lincoln, NE: iUniverse, 2016.
Cooper, James Fenimore, *The Last of the Mohicans*, Philadelphia: Carey & Lea, 1826.
Cornuelle, Richard, *Healing America: What Can Be Done About the Continuing Economic Crisis*, New York: G. P. Putnam's Sons, 1983.
Cornwell, Patricia, *Portrait of a Killer: Jack the Ripper – Case Closed*, New York: G. P. Putnam's Sons, 2002.
Cross, Milton, *Milton Cross' Complete Stories of the Great Operas*, New York: Doubleday, 1948.
Cullen, Countee, "The Shroud of Color," poem, published in the November 1924 issue of *The American Mercury*. That was H. L. Mencken's magazine.
Cunningham, Mary with Fran Schumer, *Powerplay: What Really Happened at Bendix*, New York: Simon & Schuster, 1985.
De Kruif, Paul, *Microbe Hunters*, New York: Harcourt, 1926.
Dershowitz, Alan, *America Declares Independence*, Hoboken: John Wiley & Sons, Inc., 2001.
Dickens, Charles, *A Tale of Two Cities*, London: Chapman & Hall, 1859.
Dickens, Charles, *A Christmas Carol*, London: Chapman & Hall, 1843.
Donway, Walter, *Touched By Its Rays*, Washington: The Atlas Society, 2008.
Dumas, Alexandre, *The Count of Monte Cristo*, New York: Everyman's Library/ Random House, 2009. Originally published 1845.
Durante, Dianne L., *Outdoor Monuments of Manhattan: A Historical Guide*, New York: New York University Press, 2007.
Durante, Dianne L., *Forgotten Delights: The Producers: A Selection of Manhattan's Outdoor Sculpture*, New York: Dianne L. Durante, 2003.
Edwards, Frank, *Stranger Than Science*, New York: Lyle Stuart (now Kensington Books), 1983. Originally published 1959.
Eisenhower, Dwight D., *Crusade In Europe*, New York: Doubleday & Company, Inc., 1948.
Ellison, Harlan, "I Have No Mouth and I Must Scream," in *IF: Worlds of Science Fiction*, March, 1967.
Empak Publishing Company, *A Salute to Black Scientists and Inventors*, Chicago: Empak Enterprises, Inc., 1985.
Engel, Lehman, *This Bright Day: An Autobiography*, New York: MacMillan, 1973.

Farago, Ladislas, *Patton: Ordeal and Triumph*, Yardley, PA: Westholme Publishing 2005. Originally published 1964.
Fitzgerald, F. Scott, *The Great Gatsby*, New York: Charles Scribner's Sons, 1925.
Flaubert, *Madame Bovary: Provincial Manners*, serialized in *Revue de Paris*, 1856, published by Michel Lévy Frères, 1857.
Folsom, Burton W., *The Myth of the Robber Barons: A New Look at the Rise of Big Business in America*, Reston, VA: Young America's Foundation, 1991.
Friedan, Betty, *The Feminine Mystique*, New York: W. W. Norton, 1963.
Friedman, David, *The Machinery of Freedom: Guide to a Radical Capitalism*, Chicago: Open Court Publishing Company, 1973.
Fuller, R. Buckminster, *I Seem To Be A Verb: Environment and Man's Future*, New York: Bantam Books, 1970.
Fustel de Coulanges, Numa Denis, *The Ancient City: A Study on the Religion, Laws and Institutions of Greece and Rome*, Garden City, NY: Doubleday & Company, Inc., 1864.
Gaitskill, Mary, *Two Girls, Fat and Thin*, New York: Scribner's, 1991.
Gelb, Arthur, *City Room*, New York: Berkley Books, 2003.
Gimpel, Jean, *The Medieval Machine: The Industrial Revolution of the Middle Ages*. New York: Penguin Books, 1976.
Gladstein, Mimi Reisel, *Feminist Interpretations of Ayn Rand*, University Park, PA: Pennsylvania State University Press, 1999.
Greenspan, Alan and Adrian Wooldridge, *Capitalism in America: A History*, New York: Penguin Publishing Group, 2018.
Greer, Germaine, *The Female Eunuch*, London: Flamingo, 1970.
Hailey, Arthur, *Airport*, New York: Doubleday, 1968.
Hamlin, David, *The Nazi-Skokie Conflict: A Civil Liberties Battle*, Boston: Beacon Press, 1980.
Harlow, Alvin F., *The Road of the Century: The Story of the New York Central Railroad*, New York: Creative Age Press, 1947.
Haydn, Hiram, *Words and Faces*, New York: Harcourt Brace Jovanovich, 1974.
Hayek, Friedrich, *The Road to Serfdom*, Milton Park, Oxfordshire, UK: Routledge, 1944.
Hazlitt, Henry, *Economics in One Lesson*, New York: Harper & Brothers, 1946.
Heinlein, Robert, *The Moon is a Harsh Mistress*, New York: Tom Doherty Associates, 1966.
Heinlein, Robert, *Stranger In A Strange Land*, New York: G. P. Putnam's Sons, 1961.
Heller, Anne C., *Ayn Rand and the World She Made*, New York: Nan A. Talese/ Doubleday, 2009.
Heller, Anne C., *Hannah Arendt: A Life in Hard Times*, Seattle: Amazon/New Harvest, 2015
Hemingway, Ernest, *The Sun Also Rises*, New York: Scribner's, 1926.
Herrnstein, Richard J. and Charles Murray, *The Bell Curve*, New York: Free Press,1994.

Hessen, Robert, *Steel Titan: The Life of Charles M. Schwab*, Pittsburgh: University of Pittsburgh Press, 1975.
Hill, Ruth Beebe, *Hanta Yo: An American Saga,* Garden City: Doubleday, 1979. In the Introduction, Ruth's Dakota collaborator, Chunksa Yuha, uses the line "They have to check their premises."
Hubbard, Elbert, *A Message To Garcia*, East Aurora, NY: The Roycrofters, 1914. A very influential pamphlet. Inaccurate story of Rowan and Garcia.
Hugo, Victor, *Les Miserables*, Brussels: A. Lacroix, Verboekhoven & Cie., 1862.
Hugo, Victor, *Ninety-Three*, Oklahoma City: OK Publishing, 2021. Originally published 1874.
Hugo, Victor, *Notre Dame de Paris*, Paris: Gosselin, 1831.
Hugo, Victor, *The Man Who Laughs*, Brussels: A. Lacroix, Verboeckhoven & Cie., 1869.
Hugo, Victor, *Toilers of the Sea*, New York: Modern Library, 2002. Originally published 1866.
Ibsen, Henrik, "A Doll's House," First performed at the Royal Theatre, Copenhagen, 1879.
Isaacson, Walter, *The Innovators: How a Group of Hackers, Geniuses, and Geeks Created the Digital Revolution*, New York: Simon & Schuster, 2014.
Johnson, M. Zachary, *Emotion in Life and Music: A New Science*, New York: MZJ Music, 2016.
Josephson, Matthew, *The Robber Barons*, New York: Harcourt, 1934.
Kipphardt, Heinar, *In the Matter of J. Robert Oppenheimer*, New York: Macmillan, 1969.
Kerouac, Jack, *On The Road*, New York: Viking, 1957.
Lamont, Lansing, *Day of Trinity*, New York: Scribner's, 1965.
Lamprecht, Barbara and Julius Shulman, *Neutra: Complete Works*, Cologne: Taschen, 2010.
Lawrence, Colonel Thomas Edward, *The Seven Pillars of Wisdom*, Garden City: Doubleday, 1935.
Lepanto, Paul, *Return To Reason*, Pompano Beach, FL: Exposition-Phoenix Press, 1971.
Levy, Shawn, *The Last Playboy: The High Life of Porfirio Rubirosa*, New York: Fourth Estate/HarperCollins, 2005.
Lewis, Sinclair, *Ann Vickers*, New York: Doubleday, 1933.
Lewis, Sinclair, *Elmer Gantry*, San Diego: Harcourt, 1927.
Lipstadt, Deborah, *Denying The Holocaust: The Growing Assault on Truth and Memory*, London: Penguin Books, Limited (UK), 2016. Originally published 1993.
McConnell, Scott, *100 Voices: An Oral History of Ayn Rand*, New York: New American Library, 2010.
Mann, Thomas, *The Magic Mountain*, Berlin: S. Fischer Verlag, 1924.
Martin, Albro, *James J. Hill and the Opening of the Northwest*, Oxford: Oxford University Press, 1976.
Maugham, W. Somerset, *The Razor's Edge*, New York: Doubleday, 1944.

Bibliography

Mayhew, Robert, *Ayn Rand and Song of Russia*, Lanham, MD: The Scarecrow Press, Inc., 2005.
Melville, Herman, *Moby-Dick; or, The Whale*, London: Richard Bentley, 1851.
Merwin, Samuel and Henry Kitchell Webster, *Calumet "K"*, New York: Macmillan, 1901.
Metalious, Grace, *Peyton Place*, New York: Julian Messner, Inc., 1956.
Milton, John, *Paradise Lost*, London: Samuel Simmons, 1667.
Mitchell, Margaret, *Gone With The Wind*, New York: Macmillan, 1936.
Morris, Jan, *Manhattan '45*, New York: Oxford University Press, 1987.
Murray, Charles and Richard Herrnstein, *The Bell Curve*, New York: The Free Press, 1994.
Nasar, Sylvia, *A Beautiful Mind*, New York: Simon & Schuster, 1998.
Nietzsche, Friedrich, *Also Sprach Zarathustra: Ein Buch für Alle und Keinen*, Chemnitz: Ernst Schmeitzner, 1883.
Nietzsche, Friedrich, *Human, All Too Human*, Chemnitz: Ernst Schmeitzner, 1878.
Nietzsche, Friedrich, *The Will to Power: An Attempted Transvaluation of All Values*, Edited by Elisabeth Förster-Nietzsche. Leipzig: C. G. Naumann, 1901. [4]
Nock, Albert J., *Memoirs of a Superfluous Man*, New York: Harper, 1943.
Nordhoff, Charles and James Norman Hall, *The Bounty Trilogy*, New York: Little, Brown and Company, 1936.
Norris, Frank, *The Octopus: A Story of California*, New York: Doubleday, 1901.[5]
Noyes, Alfred, "The Highwayman," First published in Blackwood's Magazine, August 1906, Edinburgh.
Orczy, Baroness, *The Scarlet Pimpernel*.[6]
Orwell, George, *Nineteen Eighty-Four: A Novel*, London: Secker & Warburg, 1949.
Orwell, George, *Animal Farm: A Fairy Story*, London: Secker & Warburg, 1945.
Paterson, Isabel, *Never Ask The End*, New York: William Morrow & Co., 1933.
Paterson, Isabel, *The God of the Machine*, New York: G. P. Putnam's Sons, 1943.
Peikoff, Leonard, *The Ominous Parallels: The End of Freedom in America*, New York: Stein and Day, 1982.
Peter, Laurence J. and Raymond Hull, *The Peter Principle*, New York: HarperCollins, 1969.
Puzo, Mario, *The Godfather*, New York: G. P. Putnam, 1969.
Rand, Ayn, *The Ayn Rand Column*, New Milford, CT: Second Renaissance Books, 1998.

---

[4] You should read the Wikipedia entry on this book before you blame it on Nietzsche. It was a case of "creative editing" by his sister Elisabeth.
[5] Famous novel about the oppression of the farmers by the corrupt railroads. The "Robber Baron" story we are all taught in school. They never teach about Jim Hill.
[6] Produced on stage, 1903, re-worked as a novel, 1905 (London: Greening). Became a movie in 1934 and again in 1982.

Rand, Ayn, *Capitalism: The Unknown Ideal*, New York: New American Library, Inc., 1966.
Rand, Ayn, *For The New Intellectual: The Philosophy of Ayn Rand*, New York: Random House, 1961.
Rand, Ayn, *The Fountainhead*, Indianapolis: The Bobbs-Merrill Company, Inc., 1943.
Rand, Ayn, *Ideal,* New York: New American Library, 2015.
Rand, Ayn, *The Journals of Ayn Rand*, New York: E. P. Dutton, Inc., 1997.
Rand, Ayn, *The Objectivist*, New Milford, CT: Second Renaissance Books, 1966–1971.
Rand, Ayn, *Philosophy: Who Needs It?*, Indianapolis: The Bobbs-Merrill Company, Inc., 1982.
Rand, Ayn, *The Ayn Rand Column Written for the Los Angeles Times*, New Milford, CT: Second Renaissance Books, 1998.
Rand, Ayn, *The Early Ayn Rand*, New York: New American Library, 1984.
Rand, Ayn, *The New Left: The Anti-Industrial Revolution*, New York: New American Library, 1971.
Rand, Ayn, *The Romantic Manifesto*, New York: New American Library, 1971.
Rand, Ayn, *The Voice of Reason: Essays in Objectivist Thought*, ed. Leonard Peikoff, New York: New American Library, 1989.
Rasmussen, Douglas B., and Douglas Den Uyl, *The Philosophic Thought of Ayn Rand*, Champaign: University of Illinois Press, 1984.
Ricks, Thomas E., *First Principles: What America's Founders Learned From The Greeks and Romans and How That Shaped Our Country*, New York: HarperCollins, 2020.
Riggenbach, Jeff, *Persuaded By Reason: Joan Kennedy Taylor and the Rebirth of American Individualism*, New York: Cook & Taylor Publishing, 2014.
Robbins, Harold, *The Carpetbaggers*, New York: Simon and Schuster, 1961.
Rosen, Barbara and Barry Rosen, with George Feifer, *The Destined Hour: The Hostage Crisis and One Family's Ordeal*, New York: Doubleday, 1982.
Rostand, Edmond, *Cyrano de Bergerac*, premiered December 28, 1897 in Paris.
Rothbard, Murray, *Man, Economy, and State: A Treatise on Economic Principles*, New York: Van Nostrand Publishing, 1962.
Russell, Bertrand, *The ABC of Relativity*, London: George Allen & Unwin, 1925.
Sanders, James, *Celluloid Skyline: New York and the Movies*, New York: Alfred A. Knopf, 2003.
Sciabarra, Chris, *Ayn Rand The Russian Radical*, University Park, PA: The Pennsylvania State University Press, 1995.
Schrecker, Ellen W., *No Ivory Tower: McCarthyism and the Universities*, New York: Oxford University Press, USA, 1988.
Scoggins, C. E., *Tycoon*, New York: Thomas Y. Crowell, 1934.
Sellers, Charles Coleman, *Mr. Peale's Museum: Charles Willson Peale and the First Popular Museum of Natural Science and Art*, New York: W. W. Norton & Company, Inc., 1980.

Bibliography 317

Shirer, William L., *The Nightmare Years*, New York: Little, Brown, 1984.
Shirer, William L., *The Rise and Fall of the Third Reich*, New York: Simon & Schuster, 1960.
Sienkiewicz, Henryk, *Quo Vadis, A Tale of the Time of Nero*, Philadelphia: Henry Altemus, 1897.
Skinner, B. F., *Beyond Freedom and Dignity*, New York: Alfred A. Knopf, 1971.
Speer, Albert, *Infiltration*, New York: Macmillan, 1981.
Speer, Albert, *Inside the Third Reich*, New York: Macmillan Publishers Ltd., 1970.
Steinbeck, John, *The Grapes of Wrath*, New York: The Viking Press, 1939.
Stiles, T. J., *The First Tycoon: The Epic Life of Cornelius Vanderbilt*, New York: Vintage Books, 2009.
Sturgeon, Theodore, *A Way Home*, New York: Pyramid Books, 1955.
Swanson, Gloria, *Swanson on Swanson*, New York: Random House, 1980.
Talese, Gay, *The Kingdom and the Power: Behind the Scenes at the New York Times: The Institution that Influences the World*, Cleveland: World Publishing, 1969.
Tolkien, J. R. R., *Lord of the Rings*, London (now Sydney): Allen & Unwin, 1954.
Tolstoy, Leo, *War and Peace*, first appeared as a serial in *The Russian Messenger*, Moscow, 1867.
Torres, Louis and Michelle Marder Kamhi, *What Art Is: The Esthetic Theory of Ayn Rand*, Chicago: Open Court, 2000.
Tuccille, Jerome, *It Usually Begins With Ayn Rand*, New York: Stein and Day, 1971.
Tuchman, Barbara W., *A Distant Mirror: The Calamitous 14th Century*, New York: Random House, 1987.
Turner, Frederick Jackson, *The Frontier in American History*, New York: Holt, 1920.[7]
Twain, Mark, *The Adventures of Huckleberry Finn*, London: Chatto & Windus, 1884.
Twain, Mark, *The Adventures of Tom Sawyer*, Hartford: American Publishing Company, 1876.
Twain, Mark, *The Prince and the Pauper*, Boston: James R. Osgood & Co., 1881.
Verne, Jules, *Twenty Thousand Leagues Under the Sea*, Paris: Pierre-Jules Hetzel, 1870.
Walker, Jeff, *The Ayn Rand Cult*, Chicago: Open Court, 1999.
Weiss, Gary, *Ayn Rand Nation: The Hidden Struggle for America's Soul*, New York: St. Martin's Press, 2012.
Whitbeck, R. H. and V. C. Finch, *Economic Geography*, New York: McGraw-Hill, 1935.
Willkie, Wendell, *One World*, New York: Simon and Schuster, 1943.

---

[7] Includes his famous paper "The Significance of the Frontier in American History", which he delivered to the American Historical Association at the Columbian Exposition in Chicago in 1893, which exposition is mentioned in *The Fountainhead* in connection with Henry Cameron, who is based very closely on Louis Sullivan.

Wolfe, Tom, *Radical Chic and Mau-Mauing the Flack Catchers*, New York: Farrar, Straus & Giroux, 1970.

Yergin, Daniel, *The Prize: The Epic Quest for Oil, Money, and Power*, New York: Free Press, 1991.

Zamyatin, Yevgeny, *We*, New York: E. P. Dutton, Inc., 1924.[8]

---

[8] My copy, published by Penguin in 1993 with an Introduction by Clarence Brown, was given to me by Anne C. Heller. In his Introduction, Brown writes: "And for George Orwell, author of *1984*, and for certain others bent on creating their own dystopias, it appears to have been *the* crucial literary experience." *Anthem* comes to mind, but not *Atlas Shrugged*, although recently it too has been called "dystopian."

About the Author

Frederick H. Cookinham, 70, was born in Syracuse, New York in 1954. He earned a BA in American History from Cortland State College in 1976 and a Masters from Brooklyn College in 1987. He is the author of *The Age of Rand: Imagining an Objectivist Future World*. He currently edits *Broadside*, the newsletter of the American Revolution Round Table of New York. He has retired from a career in legal proofreading and now leads walking tours in Manhattan. Five of his tours concentrate on Ayn Rand, whose life and work he has been studying since the age of thirteen. Six more show sites from the American Revolution in New York City. He lives in Queens with his wife Belen.

Advance Echoes

As the readers work their way through the novel, they may catch a phrase or idea that suggests something they read earlier and would like to check back on. I call these instances "Advance Echoes." However, locating the earlier passages in such a long novel might be nearly impossible, and the reader might ignore the insight.

In the following listing, I have collected several instances that I think of as "Advance Echoes." In some cases, AR may have deliberately intended to reference an earlier passage that had expressed a parallel thought. In other instances, the influence of the earlier passage may have occurred subconsciously.

These pairings showcase some of the tedium involved in writing a book this big and complex. Imagine the difficulty AR might have had drafting later portions of the novel and having to look through more than a thousand handwritten pages, without a modern word processor, to find just the right two or three earlier words that she wanted to parallel in the later passage.

Some of these "Advance Echoes" are almost subliminal (AS 749: bridges and signal lights: we will see both fail later). Others may be the repetition of a particular word, like "flea-bait," of no great significance, but it repeats Ayn's use of a popular expression of her time, which has now fallen out of use.

The list follows the chronological order of appearance of the first part of each pairing. You might enjoy checking word targets by scanning through the list and going back to see how they appear in context.

The Journey of Dagny Taggart

(All page references are to the printed version of Atlas Shrugged.*)*

your days are numbered, 4, 12, 379
deliverance, 13, 531, 1167
Dagny the take-charge woman, 16, 779
Owen Kellogg, 24, 269, 674, 761
Woman cutting fruit, Lillian cutting plum pudding on 30, 465
cigarette collector, 61, 382
fire tamed at his fingertips, 61, 672, 684
Wyatt bursts in, but Dagny does not, 81, 442; see 552, Dagny bursts into Jim's office.
motor in a glass case, 84, 300, 358
Flashback bookended, 90, 117
I can do it, 93, 94
lights and flowers, 103, 363
Taggart Transcontinental wall calendar, 106, 197
cape, 117, 998
Francisco and Galt crucified, 122, 1140
Axiom, 127, 1015
collection of chemicals, 131, 994
first of their return, 142, 330
take it seriously, 143, 702
AR establishes Dagny's femininity, 154, 155 (when she demands the bracelet)
sex speech, 160, 484
torch, 162, 351
knowing he would understand and follow, 183, 955

Stadler, 184, 185
motto cut in stone, 185, 731
portrait of Nat Taggart's grandson and bridge, 193, 513, 1137
map, 197, 1138
check your premises, 199, 331
Minnesota harvest, 209, 936
Gwen's tears and Hank's slump, 213, 214
Hank slumps, 214, Dagny slumps, 220
Dagny flies, 218, 289
string of lights, 220, 221
Dagny wants Hank, 220, 236
Look here, Rearden! 224, 448
Pat Logan, 233, 238, 248, 675
glass-enclosed formality – glass case for Galt's motor, 253, 300
Look up, 255, 260
flea bait, 259, 435
ten years added to life, 290, 722
soul for a nickel, 321, 412
Hank tied to a rack, 334, 1139
patch of green and sunlight, 340, 349
Wyatt's torch, 343, 351
ruby pendant, 367, 558
Hank as seen by Galt, 372, 959
Hank starts to see things Francisco will explain to him in the Sex Speech (on 489), 374, 376, 378
Hank has insights too! 377, 860
torture rack, 378, 1139
destroyer, 379, 380

Advanced Echoes

Danagger to coal as Hank to wheat, 383, 939
suntan, 394, 404
ticker tape, 406, 408
account overdrawn, 413, 496
your first man, 426, 638
trail, 434, 435
cigarettes, 442, 447
Hank and Ragnar, 448, 571
sanction, 454 top, 454 bottom
if *this* is the enemy, 459, 463
furnace foreman, 460, 998
Winston, Colorado, 497, 501, 550, 587
Atlantic Southern bridge, 499, 500, 1161
modern judges, 530, 571, 932
radio speech, 535, 1004
Jim's crackup, 540, 839, 912, 1145
"We'll discuss it, you and I", 542, 548
Lillian's trip to Florida, 556, 559
Statue of Liberty, 558, 727
law, ethics, politics, epistemology, 596-598, 600-602
Taggart terminal, 612, 703
Francisco knew Dagny was at her cabin, 615, 637, 795
Hank and Dagny to meet in Colorado in a week, 648, 799
Hank flies, 648, 800
where no one would see the body: Jeff's or Tony's 656, 989
generator stopped, 669, 1143
Taggart bridge destroyed, 728, 1137
Akston as Dagny's prospective father-in-law, 736, 786, 791

"the bridges that would crumble": an almost subliminal advance echo of the Taggart bridge disaster, 749, 1137
signal lights, Subliminal! 749, 943
Kay Ludlow, 755, 759, 784, 1167
Galt sees Dagny for the first time, 800, 956
underground vault, 800, 955
they had left no value behind them. The one value he had wanted to win, 801, 1156
Spilled water bookends Jim-Cheryl flashback, 873, 883
swaying on an edge, 885, 908
impotent, 899, 900
Meigs, Canadian trolleys, conquest, 914, 948
harvest, 917, 936
speech, 954, 1009
Don't come to my home, 961, 1086
Repair signals, repair generator, 961, 1038, 1144
Hank's safe, 964, 1000

Recurring Themes Index

(All page references are to the printed version of Atlas Shrugged. This version of the Recurring Themes Index has some additional entries misssing from Volume 1.)

AR's poetry 256, 286, 291, 327, 388, 608; A dead photograph, 196; Devouring, 335; Taut like a string, 450; The first rays of the sun, 549; Weightlessly, stretching, 554; Twisted bolts of satin, 557; Tail of a nervous animal, 584; Stars tinkling against each other, 586; The twilight, 654; Take-off, 690; No journey to recapture it, 691; The sun had trickled down, 716; Pages riffled, 726; Abyss, 743; Photo on a cloud, 749; Glittering drops of water which were the stars, 750; Slithering slowly, 774; Dragon-fly, 799; Shadows cast by a distant sea, 808; If she were not so far away, 814; Single smile, 888; To be shaped by them as they please, they who have no shape of their own, 905; Paragraphs 4 and 5, 906; Dawn, 967; A flower reaching for the sun, 1059; Sunrise, 1073; Glassy rustle of the East River, 1086; Weary mind, receding tide, 1095; A vision both distant and close, 1166.

Astronomical References earth's crust, 29; earth, 146, 208, 241, 246, 768, 831, 914, 985, 1033, 1037, 1052, 1058, 1066, 1069; universe, 161, 265, 322, 565, 624, 701, 867, 892, 1036, 1054, 1058; cosmic rays, 170-1, 185; star, 191, 685; live on earth, 191; comet, 242; heart of the universe, 339; cosmic rays, 340; give up the world, 382, 494; like an uncooled planet, 520; "run the world," not just the nation, 539; our world, 544; world scale, 561; world, 577, 578, 671, 672, 692, 701, 708, 746, 750, 765, 788, 846, 850, 859, 863, 904, 946, 955, 959, 960, 988, 997, 1048, 1054, 1066, 1069; world reborn, 580; looters' world, 629, 645; world scale, 669; moon, 673; moonlight, 676; planet, 678; stars whose light remains after they are gone, 682; globe of moonlight, 684; globe, 690, 865, 985, 1055, 1062,; stars, 691, 692; earth's crust cooling, 695; lunar soil, 749; moonlight,

782; earth rolling, starlight, sun, 788; a world falling apart, 805; a star in the process of extinction, 815; cosmic space, 830; dead surface of the moon, 849; control this earth, 858; world ending, 890; encircle the earth, 906; on earth, 925, 933; cosmic disturbance, 1008; destroyed your world, 1009; solar system, 1016; remaking the earth, 1020; bureaucrat of the universe, 1034; planet to planet, 1035; sun and moon, 1041; birth of the globe, 1047; world problems, 1079; surface of the moon, stars, 1084; everyone on earth, 1125; as in the cabin of a ship about to take off for a different planet, 1136; dead glow of the moon, 1156.

Atlantis 153, 438, 633, 637, 701, 749, 783, 801, 812, 813, 921, 956, 960, 1002, 1003, 1052, 1096; Vanishing land, 789; Persistence in myth, 1057.

Atlas and other classical references 53, 61, 112, 147, 259n, 300, 307, 411, 425, 427, 561, 681n, 692, 738, 813, 915, 917, 929, 933, 943, 971, 972, 1052; The power of Atlas: Jim knows he needs Dagny, 195; The only one who kept a job, 261; He can find a way, 333; Devouring the unborn children of greatness: Was AR thinking of the Goya painting "Saturn Devouring his Son"? 335; Chained to his desk: Was AR thinking of Odysseus, chained to the mast of his ship, hearing the sirens sing?; Caligula, 390; Olympian: 400; Pyramids, 414; Keeps the whole world going . . . a tower to the sky . . . wings made of wax, 431; To shrug, 455; Unbound, 531, 557n; Grecian goddess, 778; Minerva, 786; Would-be decent... moves the world, 788; Caesar's wife, 898; Was AR thinking of the Medusa when she wrote "smites the observer"? 913; Burden, 958; Responsibility you dropped, 1047; The endurance that carries their burdens, 1068-9; Bearing too much, 1160.

Benevolent and malevolent universe 32, 133, 374, 457, 483, 491, 499, 635, 653, 759, 766, 788, 790, 797, 798; Gulch kids, 785; pain is the core of existence, 906; by the grace, 1014.

Best within us 6, 412, 451, 483, 560, 561, 564, 619, 1021, 1069, 1147, 1166; Anything left within you, 200.

Betters 414, 577, 581, 668, 743, 1050, 1062, 1068, 1104, 1157; Inferior, 1118.

Calendar, September 2 4, 12, 50, 174, 227, 274, 379, 382, 428, 550, 802, 864, 866, 886, 905, 909, 910, 921, 925, 939, 1005, 1111.

Cannibal 31, 335, 478, 722, 740, 744, 914, 916, 1011, 1021, 1022, 1030, 1040, 1059, 1062, 1079.

Check your premises 199, 331, 378, 382, 489, 618, 710, 732, 737, 790, 807.

Compassion, sympathy and pity 52, 146, 147, 148, 183, 302, 309, 316, 370, 375, 389, 404, 465, 468, 470, 472, 488, 490, 529, 565, 577, 603, 608, 637, 641, 658, 726, 729, 767, 769, 794, 801, 855, 856, 862,

Recurring Themes Index

863, 864, 888, 962; Hand plow, 323; Self pity, 515; Pity v. justice, 788; Akston's face and "unpitying", 802; Pity, 879, 880, 901, 917, 974, 1050, 1053, 1068, 1113, 1118; Gnawing drabness of pity, 882; Sympathy, 889; Lechers of pity, 915; Pity, compassion, 968; See also TF pages 621 and 711.

Competence and incompetence 4, 14, 15, 52, 100, 105, 170, 206, 226, 300, 327, 328, 349, 357, 358, 411, 420, 453, 560, 562, 619, 620, 662, 665, 679, 711, 739, 765, 791, 996, 1012, 1032, 1047-9, 1062; Tunnel, 558; Clifton Locey, 567-9; Tunnel disaster sequence, 584-607; Do things badly, 635; Mediocracy, 743; Shiftless, 744; Loafing failures, 766; Ineptitude, 789, 1065.

Dagny's attraction to Francisco, Hank and Galt 94, 108, 116, 126, 137, 149, 220, 240, 268, 276, 279, 300, 368-78, 643, 701, 730, 767, 777, 796, 852, 854, 921, 954, 957.

Dagny's inner judge, and others' 104, 323, 330, 440, 775, 776, 781, 886, 949, 1001, 1124; Jim's inner judge, 257; Stadler's courtroom, 340; Hank's courtroom, 398; Hank's verdict, 533; Nat Taggart, 554; The verdict of Hank's emotion, 563; Eddie, 653; She was thinking of herself, 803; The day when I would stand before you, 812; Jim, 867, 869; You knew it, she had told herself severely, 886; Cherryl, 881, 887; Jim sees Dagny as judge, 912.

Ecstasy 67, 87, 96, 108; A picture of her, 1093-4; *Anthem*, 95; NB makes a theme of ecstasy in *Judgment Day* on pages 10, 128, 434 and 436.

Eddie's dialogs with Galt 62, 217, 438, 567, 651.

Emotions or feelings 10, 17, 24, 26, 29, 31, 38, 51, 52, 100, 102, 111, 116, 121, 136, 147, 165, 167, 192, 193; Jade vase, 85; Revulsion, 194; Hank slumps, 214; Dagny's loneliness, 219; Larkin's fear and guilt, 220, 222-3; Hank's hatred, 224; Jim's panic, 229; Jim's feelings, 245, 253, 254, 260; Hank's hatred for his family, 271, 283, 304; Lillian's feelings, 306; Shocked at his own brutality, 308; Personal feeling, 309, 316; Never feels the human side, 318; Sensitive feelings, 321; Hank's integration of principles and emotion, 329, 339, 340, 347, 353, 372, 374, 380, 396, 398; Sentiment, 417, 421, 429, 436; Unfeeling rigidity, 438, 443; No time to feel, 444, 450, 457; Philip's lifeless eyes, 470; Suppressed emotion, 481, 488, 491, 493; Loss and hatred, 495; Feeling, left unsealed by his mind: Hank wants to understand, 528, 530; Jim's fear, 363, 574, 578, 600, 605, 611, 613, 623; To indulge any personal loneliness, 629, 639, 649; That love of existence he was alone to feel, 656, 682, 694, 703, 730, 732, 733, 739; Dark emotions, 739; Feeling nothing, 743; Emotions be damned, 753, 761, 773, 780, 782; Halley, 783; No regard for cost or feeling, 789, 794,

796, 802; The unemotional Miss Ives, 812, 818, 819, 831, 833; Pain worth feeling, 835; Feeling in Lilian's lifeless eyes, 849; Impervious to feeling, 865; Fear, 874; Feelings, 880, 881; Permit herself no emotion, 882, 887; What I felt when I was a child, 889, 891; no emotion save respect, 897, 914; Philip's feelings, 918, 920, 927, 931; Unemotional tone, 932, 934; Limit of her capacity to feel, 943, 948, 951, 957; Feel without thinking, 968, 970, 972; Non-logical feelings, 973; Jungle of your feelings, 1036, 1037, 1038; To feel, 1046, 1047, 1050; Feeling, terror, guilt, 1056, 1057; Terror, 1058; Just feel it, 1059; Feel he believed it, 1084, 1097; Feeling, 1108; Savage emotion, 1127; The panic of their nameless emotions, 1135; A diffused hatred and an unfocused terror, 1141; It was death his emotions had chosen . . . as all his knowledge had consisted of emotions, 1145; No visible emotion, 1156.

Ends do not justify means 135, 208, 584, 605, 1025, 1046, 1118, 1134.

Envy 19, 55, 93, 100, 166, 264, 352, 358, 389, 391, 453, 492, 537, 559, 766; Jealousy, 397; Evading thoughts they know to be good, 417.

Errors of knowledge 149, 177, 392, 451, 641, 807, 960, 972, 1059; They don't know, 79; Fair share law, 500.

Fred Kinnan and unions 299, 555, 604, 609, 1072, 1106, 1121; Directive 10-289, 532-549.

Generosity 75, 619, 656n, 739, 887; Kindliness, 657.

Greed 42, 54, 58, 66, 99, 133, 175, 190, 191, 213, 228, 252, 285, 310, 315, 322, 352, 356, 383, 434, 454, 467, 475, 476, 484, 520, 540, 543, 569, 670, 741, 766, 819, 825, 849, 867, 878, 884, 957, 1004, 1042, 1046, 1061, 1080.

Gwen Ives 42, 127, 206, 212-3, 360, 437, 524-5, 557, 571, 833, 1000.

How much a man can bear 321, 418, 423, 431, 450, 581, 630, 659, 489.

I want to understand 38, 76, 100, 103, 119, 139, 146, 182, 186, 189, 191, 240, 309, 331, 392, 444, 531, 559, 618, 657, 872, 873, 882, 904, 968, 982, 994; I like to learn things for myself, 109; Mrs. Rearden does *not* want to understand, 467; Philip doesn't, 470; Lillian doesn't, 528; Hank wants to understand, 530; Clarity, 857; The Cherryl-Dagny scene, 887-892; Never been able to understand, 932; Struggling to understand, 959; Neither ignoring it nor responding, 1120.

Laws, directives, policies and corruption Anti-Dog-Eat-Dog Rule, 73-76; Equalization of Opportunity Bill, 130, 395; Mouch directives, 132, 133, 134, 135, 333; Laws to kill Colorado, 299-300; Unfreeze bonds, 352; Fair Share Law, 361; Directive 10-289, 532-549; Railroad Unification Plan,

Recurring Themes Index

606, 836, 911; California tax, 926; Steel Unification Plan, 964-5, 977-987.
Life is not their purpose 61, 218, 266, 295, 1078, 1081, 1102, 1104, 1107, 1109, 1111, 1123, 1124, 1135; Self-interest was not Jim's motive, 300; Being alive, 317; Ivy Starnes, 322; The anti-living, 543n, 636, 667-8, 679, 740, 781n, 807, 842, 864, 867, 932; We want to live, 973; I can get away with it, 975, 983; Fear of death, 1009, 1013; Quality of being alive, 1021, 1024, 1046-7, 1069, 1073; Did they want him to be real? 1122.
Look up and not down 255, 260, 268, 354, 358, 377, 566, 730; Light and unimportant, 150; Head bowed, 368.
Mind-body dichotomy 123, 158-60, 177, 240, 252, 322, 490, 528, 564, 611, 631, 636, 692, 757, 781, 858, 862, 954, 1019, 1020, 1026, 1027, 1029, 1054, 1061, 1062.
Naked 18, 32, 38, 87, 103, 108, 117, 136, 137, 150, 154, 156, 157, 163, 176, 191, 221, 252, 253, 255, 279, 281, 303, 305, 367, 396, 397, 400, 475, 490, 519, 531, 559, 583, 626, 640, 642, 661, 705, 732, 739, 752, 757, 778, 780, 813, 851, 948, 949, 954, 1001, 1025, 1058, 1090, 1106, 1120, 1121, 1140, 1149, 1156, 1167; See too much, 104; See through her clothes, 106; Naked bones, 162; Her face naked in bewilderment, 308; Naked trees, 313; A naked plea, 357; Indecent in its exposure, 422; Naked shoulders, 779; Naked ribs of the roof, 821; Too much of her were seen, 850; Some invention of his own, 886; Naked bullet, 1086; Naked rock, 244, 792, 1139; Naked savage, 163, 662, 739.
Normalcy 145, 198, 199n, 203n, 210, 230, 277, 303, 475, 477, 598, 603, 612n, 630n, 659, 668, 735, 736, 737, 786, 799n, 1094; Not the world I expected, 220; Nat Taggart, 243; Hank's Purchasing Manager, and ARL, page 122: "A Nation's Unity," 302; "You did *what?*" 317; Clear-cut standards, 321; Mrs. Hastings, 324; Wherever such may be left, 347; Whoever is left, 445; Not some revelation, but what you normally live by, 447; Modern judges, 530; There had once been a society, 597; Go down with the last wheel, 632; The old days, 657, 658; Subhuman age, 758; Their century, 771; Vanishing age, 789; Lose the battle, 1078; The better men, 1080; Respect for human beings, 1108; Days of a distant past, 1121.
Objective 198, 374n, 436, 596, 737, 917, 933, 1030, 1040, 1042, 1045, 1056, 1063, 1065, 1146; TF page 126.
Old money 135, 136, 143, 158, 390, 430, 505n; Betty Pope, 71; The whole party scene, 127; From a good family, 195; Lee Hunsacker, 313; Cuffy Meigs, 364; Horsewoman, 399; Heirloom, 420; Tennis player, 977.
Our own guilt 10, 52, 459, 483, 565, 619, 858, 933, 1034, 1044; Not to some superior power, 611; My sanction was its only power,

1048; Power to enslave them, 1049; Nothing but the sanction you give it, 1066.
Paradox 28, 102, 109, 213, 352, 362, 773, 775, 784, 789, 830; Jolted into calm, 215; Furniture, 219; Dagny too dignified and Hank too casual, 233; Notorious success, 238; Cold eyes, narrowed and grim . . . profound sympathy, 302; Hunsacker's face, 313; Perversely intentional contrast, 369; Static and kinetic, 380; Enormity of the smallness, 483; Rich and poor, 576; Long-distance short cut, 585; Smile/ not smiling, 616; More astonishing than supermen, 786; Studiously sedate pirate, 787; Pitiless gentleness of certainty, 791; Her distance from people seemed longer, 832; Hard face made of soft muscles, 836; Unprovoked tips, 866; Yet knew that it was true, 877; Overbearing timidity, 959; Her face frightened them – because it was devoid of fear, 1073; Stationary motion of the stars, 1084; Who was prisoner, 1121; The sincerity of the dishonest, 1123; Chuckled/ terror, 1163.
Purpose 87, 94, 120, 205, 214, 241, 245, 280, 282, 286, 308, 354, 371, 374, 376, 411, 421, 424, 430, 445, 448, 451, 454, 526, 527, 575, 580, 582, 608, 609, 612, 615, 616, 634, 658, 679, 690, 739, 742, 775, 784, 808, 846, 912, 913, 921, 954, 959, 988, 1012, 1014, 1020, 1050, 1061, 1067, 1068, 1093, 1111, 1118, 1154, 1156, 1167; The most depraved man is the man without a purpose, 99; The only depraved man is the man without a purpose, 148; Moral purpose, 560; A goal and a motive, 703; Purpose defined, 1018; No goals to reach, 1161.
Sanction of the victim 377-8, 416, 454, 470, 477, 740, 845, 1066-7.
Savage 26, 246, 284, 291, 346, 362, 365, 404, 446, 501, 641, 650, 654, 696, 746, 773, 801, 818, 825, 913, 917, 933, 945, 1038, 1039, 1040, 1041, 1049, 1062, 1063, 1067, 1073, 1082, 1127, 1166; Jungle barter, 556; Voodoo, 669; Primeval violence, 924; Sale of Manhattan, 952; Primitive terror, civilized control, 1007; JAR page 232, to be guarded savagely.
Self-esteem or self-respect 159, 208, 255, 305, 353, 375, 412, 413, 431, 490, 491, 492, 743, 1010, 1028, 1031, 1032, 1033, 1034, 1046, 1053, 1056, 1057, 1059, 1060, 1122, 1145; Defined, 1018.
Sense of life 40, 116, 781.
Smiles of morning, summer, or childhood 14, 28, 31, 69, 107, 117, 247, 404, 424, 443, 458, 530, 550, 566, 576, 583, 612, 613, 705, 706, 752, 767, 788, 797, 798, 799, 967, 998, 1057, 1138, 1155, 1160, 1168; Morning, 608; Young, triumphant smile, 708; First morning, 727; Not since childhood, 784; Sound of youth in Hank's voice, 834; Youth, 976; In that world 1068.
Spirituality, or AR giving religious formulas a new and deeper meaning 40, 59, 98, 123, 125, 136, 177, 191, 199,

Recurring Themes Index 331

209, 220, 240, 240n, 241, 246, 252, 298n, 323, 325, 389, 412, 453, 510n, 512n, 537, 545, 546, 564, 572, 609, 617, 620, 634, 634n, 684, 723, 730, 739, 812, 813, 859, 1021, 1022, 1026, 1028, 1029, 1032, 1034, 1035, 1044, 1045, 1046, 1052; Altar, 742; A rest granted to her, 553; Battle hymn, 210; Bear false witness, 783; Childish enjoyment – of a steel mill, 472; Contentment on earth, 933; Dagny in the motor compartment, 245; Die by the sword, 757; Eden, 1058; Faith, 955, 967; Funeral, 518; Galt's image, 792; Ghosts in heaven, 1012; Hank's feelings about a slag heap, 371; Heaven, 707; He permits no Caesars, heaven and earth, 636; Hope, 243; Idol, 327; immortality,789; It must not stop me, 213; Join him, not in death, 554; Like words addressed to the. dead, 448; Looter in spirit, 743; Materialistic place, 929; Mortal sin, 789 ; Mystic, 913; Original sin, 1025; Prayer, 514, 788, 890, 904, 920, 955, 1001, 1161; Ransoms in spirit, 619; Realm of no return, 447; Religious novice, 874; Reverence, 768; Sacred, 898, 914, 1117; Sacred idol, 577; Sacrilege, 117; Soul, 560, 778, 904, 906, 907, 931, 948, 960, 987, 997, 1033, 1056, 1057, 1059, 1060, 1066, 1069, 1093, 1123, 1124, 1145; Soul and essence, 997; Spirit, 740, 784, 865, 893, 914, 948, 967, 1060, 1095; Spiritual son, 1132; Standing at attention, 238; Steel-embodied thought, 928;

Supernatural apparition, 1163; Supernatural terror, superstitious awe, 820; Superstitious, 846; Temple of Nat Taggart, 835; Unattainable,772; Unlimited promise, 612; Unspiritual, 461; Vision, 856, 886; Voodoo, secret rites, 818; Withdrawing man's spirit, 757; Woman of great spirit, 530; Worship, 955; Wyatt in hell, 721; TF page 449, soul defined.

Subconscious 4, 5, 121, 144, 215, 318, 330, 331, 348, 377, 398, 442, 471, 688; flash, 697; music, 705; she thought of Jeff Allen, 721, 803; by some will of their own, 886; causeless certainty, 892.

Subhuman or retarded retarded, 476; moron, 519; apes, 560; inferior animals, 564; morons, 581, 662, 689; sub-animal, 715; subhuman, 758; vermin, 766; not human, 948; less than animal, 1015; nothing less is human, 1020; anthropoid, 1040; birth as a *human* being, 1041; sub-human, 1047; the title of human, 1062; mirth of a halfwit, 1071; subhuman, 1135.

Temple 59, 962, 731 (More pagan references!).

Violent: a favorite AR term. But metaphorical except where noted. Notice that literal violence increases toward the end of the novel as the US falls apart. 13, 28, 81, 100, 111, 117, 120, 125, 158, 197, 250, 251, 253, 368, 403, 481, 482, 527, 528, 552; literal violence, 554; 562, 563, 576; literal, 578; violate, 582, 614, 622, 637, 639, 640, 641, 642, 644, 650; literal,

673, 685, 691, 694, 697, 717, 718, 720, 734, 751, 757, 758, 760, 774, 777, 780, 784, 791, 797, 804, 806, 828; 852, 856, 865, 924, 936, 943, 953; literal, 964; violate his mind, 970; literal, 974, 979, 990; violent pain, 996; literal, 1062, 1063, 1073, 1083, 1092, 1105, 1108, 1130, 1136, 1140, 1153; violent anger, violent grip, 1155; 1156; literal, 1158.

Weeds, jungles and animals 15, 31, 37; neglected machine, 64; 137, 176, 279, 280, 282, 283, 321, 323, 335, 446; Roger Marsh factory, 519; 560, 572, 609, 659; jungle, 715; positive image of a weed struggling to survive, 722; 723, 737, 814, 815, 821, 822; plant, cat and jackal metaphors, 842; Cherryl a plant with a broken stem, 892; 990, 993, 1013, 1045; a bird or flower reaching for the sun, 1059; firing at an animal, 1148; 1156; Eddie scares off a rabbit, 1166.

Which means... which means.... See also "Do you mean..." above.783. See also Tuccille making fun of AR's circle using this expression to show that they can finish each other's sentences. Galt uses this formula in his speech, on these pages: 1018, 1047, 1059, 1061 and 1062. Also, see page 134: "Just as... just as," and 249 and 487: "Do you mean... I mean."

Wyatt's Torch 343, 351, 498, 520, 605, 607, 692, 1168.

Youth 238, 834, 921, 976, 1068, 1089.

Index to Volume 2

(*All page references are to the printed version of* Atlas Shrugged.)

Akston, Dr. Hugh on telling and showing, 735; why he went on strike, 741; world crashing faster than expected, 748; on supermen, 786; tells Dagny of Galt's college days, 786; Do they want to live?, 807

Boyle, Orren has transportation pull, 913; inefficient, 981; Holloway is his stooge, 990; 1070

Chalmers, Ma 937; at Thompson's speech, 1006

d'Anconia, Francisco arrives in gulch, 764; explains his strange behavior to Dagny, 765; serves Eucharist to Galt and Dagny, 810; farewell message to the world, 925; saves Hanks mills, gives Hank the speech and removes him from his mills, 997; slips note under Dagny's door with Nathaniel Branden's phone number, 1111; appears in rescue scene, 1148; the regime won't have open airports much longer, 1157

Danagger, Ken tells Dagny "Well done", 736; 1009

Danneskjöld, Ragnar arrives in Gulch, 753; on Galt's future fame, 755; moral right to choose piracy, 757; reminds Dagny that she has benefited from corporate welfare, 758; married to Kay Ludlow, 759; appears in rescue scene, 1148

Ferris, Dr. Floyd at opening of Project X, 816; plays the hip intellectual game, 823; and McCarran Act, 825; threatens a dissident reporter with Directive 10-289, 831; at conference with Rearden, 977; at Thompson's radio speech, 1005; meets Galt, 1114; at banquet for Galt, 1121; proposes Galt's torture, 1134

Galt's Gulch chapters 701-815

Galt, John speaks to Dagny for the first time, 701; mercilessly perceptive eyes, 710; no wish for fame, 710; makes Dagny breakfast, 712; explains to Dagny about gold, 717; shows Dagny the powerhouse, 730; explains the strike, 738; plans for after the strike, 748; everyone has to enter through my house, 751; does not allow messages sent out of the Gulch, 763, 769; tells of his first sight of Dagny, 778; nobody stays here by faking reality, 795; refuses to let Dagny stay with Francisco, 795;

decides to return to New York, 809; his most dramatic scene with Dagny, 812; first sex with Dagny, reveals much personal information, 954; shows pain, 958; envies Rearden, 959; allows Hank to send a note to Dagny, 1003; what he told people to get them on strike, 1015; tells Dagny he will kill himself if they torture her, 1091; tells Thompson he is open to a deal, 1098; meets Mouch, Kinnan, Lawson, Morrison and Ferris, 1106; meets Jim Taggart, 1112; gives a very short radio speech, 1125; tortured by Ferris, Mouch and Jim Taggart, 1139; tells them how to fix the generator, 1144; "Don't look down!", 1158; declares strike over, 1168

Galt's speech begins on page 1009; ends on page 1069; initiation of force, 1023; references to Rearden and Dagny, 1039; the ends do not justify the means, 1046; inventors, 1047; the Starnes heirs, 1048; legend of Atlantis, 1057; four repetitions of "Who is John Galt?", 1058; refers to a playboy and a pirate, 1060; "until the road is clear," 1061; addresses Rearden, 1061; proper purpose of government, 1062; pyramid of ability versus labor theory of value, 1064; addresses Stadler, 1066; founding modest communities, 1067; the gates of our city, 1067; the political system we will build, 1068; addresses Dagny, 1069; the world you desired, 1069

Halley, Richard 705; on his Fifth Concerto, 737; why he went on strike, 743; on art, 782

Hendricks, Dr. Thomas 712
Holloway, Tinky invites Rearden to a conference, 965; Steel Unification Plan, 980; stooge of Orren Boyle, 990; at Thompson's radio speech, 1005; no title given, 1070; at banquet for Galt, 1121
Ives, Gwen usually unemotional, 833; goes on strike with Hank, 1000
Kinnan, Fred at Thompson's radio speech, 1005; reaction to the speech, 1072; meets Galt, 1106; at banquet for Galt, 1121
Lawson, Eugene gives radio speech, 911; at conference with Rearden, 977; at Thompson's radio speech, 1005; meets Galt, 1106; at banquet for Galt, 1121
Ludlow, Kay 727
Meigs, Cuffy running Taggart Transcontinental, 836; insulting view of women, 843; superstitious, 939; on conquering Mexico and Canada, 948; meets Stadler at Project X, 1130; blows up Iowa, 1132
Morrison, Chick control of media, 1001; at Thompson's radio speech, 1005; in charge of event, 1007; propaganda minister, 1070; mystical insight, 1071; at banquet for Galt, 1121
Mouch, Wesley at opening of Project X, 821; encroaching on Thompson's power, 826; at conference with Rearden, 977; at Thompson's radio speech, 1005; admires Mr. Thompson as a master of public opinion, 1071; at banquet for Galt, 1121; agrees to torture Galt, 1134

Mulligan, Midas 706; hosts his friends one month per year, 714; minting coins, 727; wealth of selection, 736; why he went on strike, 742; on the dangers of a collapsing world, 805
Narragansett, Judge marble face, 735; on non-objective law, 737; why he went on strike, 742; to act as arbiter, 748; revises Constitution, 1168
Pritchett, Dr. Simon at Thompson's radio speech, 1005; at banquet for Galt, 1121
Railroad Association and Anti-Dog-Eat-Dog Rule, 1073
Railroad Unification Plan 836; and profit pooling, 911; and Fair Share Law, 1073; 1164
Rand's cameo 719
Rearden, Henry flies over the Gulch, 799; gets phone call from Dagny and learns that she is alive, 834; reconciles with his loss of Dagny to a new lover, 854; becomes the strong one for Dagny, 855; confesses his love for Dagny, 857; blames himself too much, 898; realizes that Francisco kept his oath of friendship, 921; discusses saving the Minnesota wheat harvest with Dagny, 923; learns to deal with the underground economy, 926; refuses his brother a job, 927; warned by his divorce lawyer that something may be about to happen to his mills, 934; open minded to the Wet Nurse, 934; final rejection of his family, 976; hears Mouch's proposal of a Steel Unification Plan, 977; Hank's last straw, making him go on strike, 986; finds the Wet Nurse dying, 98; hit and knocked out by rioter, 996; Francisco gives Hank the strike speech, 997; appears in rescue scene, 1148
Rearden, Lillian tells Dagny she is blackmailing her, 847; visits Jim to ask him to stop Hank divorcing her, 893; has noticed the infiltration of thugs in Washington, 894; begs Hank for money, knowing the Mouch crowd is about to stage a *pogrom* on his mills, 968
Rearden, Philip begs Hank for a job, 927; lets slip that something may happen to Hank's mills, 930; a psychology like Jim Taggart's, 932; rats on Hank, 966
Stadler, Dr. Robert Galt does not intend to reclaim him, 778; at opening of Project X, 816; pleasure at watching a baby goat, 822; suffers Galt guilt, 831; gives in and endorses Project X, 831; says the mind is a myth, 938; at Thompson's radio speech, 1005; confronts Galt, 1117; drives to Project X in Iowa, 1126; meets Cuffy Meigs, 1128
Taggart, Cherryl now sees through Jim, 868; flashback showing Cherryl's year of marriage to Jim and disillusionment, 873 to 883; trying hard to learn, 873; Finds the key to Jim, 884; visits Dagny to apologize, 887; Dagny accepts her as a sister, 888; why Cherryl must commit suicide, 890; comes home to find Jim in bed with Lillian, 900; too close to the unnamed, 904; meets a social worker, 907; kills herself, 908

Taggart, Dagny arrives in Gulch, 701; meets Kay Ludlow, 727; meets Richard Halley, 737; becomes Galt's housekeeper, 760; falls in love with Galt, 775; hears Halley's views on art, 782; hears Kay Ludlow's views on acting, 784; meets two children, 785; sees Hank's plane, 799; on abdication of choice, 803; decides to return to New York, 806; her most dramatic scene with Galt, 812; returns to New York, 831; speaks on radio, 850; lets Hank be the strong one, 855; and two kinds of guilt, 856; advises Cherryl, 887; shows Cherryl the relevance of philosophy to her life, 890; still seeing Hank, but no longer lovers, 921; thinks of Galt's powerhouse as the "temple of Atlantis," 921; combats Minnesota wheat disaster, 936; listens to Jim, Mouch, Ferris and Meigs scheming, 944; femininity, 945; regrets a mistake, 945; rushes to the Terminal when the traffic signals fail, 948; inner judge, 949; hires a man from a competitor, 950; shows anger, 952; spots Galt, they have their first sex, 954; why she is still holding out, 961; at Thompson's radio speech, 1005; hears the leaders' reactions to the speech, 1071; "the man in power," 1072; defends her decision to stay, for the last time, 1078; pretends to help Thompson, 108; goes to Galt's apartment, 1086; why she would risk going there, 1087; chooses Galt over the world, 1110; brought still closer to striking by seeing Galt onstage with Thompson, 1122; goes on strike, 1138; shoots guard, 1148; on plane with Galt, Hank, Ragnar and Francisco, 1156; sees the lights of New York go out, 1158; first to hear Galt end the strike, 1168

Taggart, James starting to crack up, Dagny notices, 838; celebrates deal with Chile to nationalize d'Anconia Copper, 864; uses a line AR got from Isabel Paterson, 876; Almost reveals his innermost self, 878; brags to Lillian of his double-crossing Francisco, 897; sadism, 899; has sex with Lillian, 900; envies Rearden, 902; hits Cherryl, 904; expects cheap copper, once Chile has taken over d'Anconia copper, 910; running to Dagny instead of avoiding her, 912; invokes his privileges as Dagny's brother, 917; at conference with Rearden, 977; tells Dagny of Rearden's disappearance, 1000; at Thompson's radio speech, 1005; in the room with Thompson, 1075; meets Galt, 1112; at banquet for Galt, 1121; looks forward to torturing Galt, 1134; has a nervous breakdown, 1145

Thompson, Mr. at opening of Project X, 820; announces his coming speech, 1004; ready to give radio speech, 1005; master of manipulating public opinion, 1071; puts a tail on Dagny, 1075; meets Galt, 1097; tempts Galt, 1101; hoping for a hostage, 1105; understands that if Galt dies, they die, 1108; at banquet for Galt, 1121; greenlights Galt's torture, 1135

Torture Scene starts on page 1139; ends on page 1146
Unification Board 963; 990; 1070
Utopia 752
Wet Nurse asks Rearden for a job, 934; warns of some move against Rearden, 936; Hank finds him on slag heap, 989; real name is Tony, 992; why his death is necessary for the story, like Kira, 995
Willers, Eddie explains to Dagny about Meigs, 836; a warm moment with Dagny, 846; Tells Cherryl the truth about Jim and Dagny, 880; realizes he had blabbed everything to Galt, 1077; leaves for California after confessing his love to Dagny, 1116; in charge of abandoned train, 1160; fate left undetermined, 1167
Writer with large eyes 719
Wyatt, Ellis 720; manufacturing time, 722; in charge of rescue, 1157

PERESET PRESS

A message from Pereset Press

Pereset Press is proud to have published this landmark study of Ayn Rand's *Atlas Shrugged*, and we hope you will help spread the word about this remarkable book. If you enjoyed it, please go to Amazon or your preferred bookseller and place a review on its book page.

On the following pages, you will find information about other titles from Pereset Press that you might enjoy.

The Werewolf of Wall Street
By Gary Greenberg and Jerome Tuccille

I was up most of the night reading The Werewolf of Wall Street. Gary Greenberg and Jerome Tuccille are marvelous story tellers. I had to know how the book would end, and, somehow, I utterly suspended disbelief. - **Barbara Branden, author of *The Passion of Ayn Rand***

A political satire expressed in the form of a horror story . . . Some of their ideas really are clever. Their secretive master villain's ultimate secret really is ingeniously chosen. - ***Prometheus*, Newsletter of the Libertarian Futurist Society**

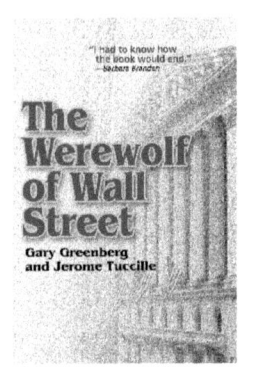

Rival revolutionaries, a deadly monster, a friendly vampire, and tough choices

Ever since that odd night at The Pentagram Pub six years ago, left-wing revolutionary Alex Mallum has had strange dreams and unexplained blackouts. Shortly thereafter, the mysterious Luke Fenris appeared, and in just a few short years, he became the idol of Wall Street and was talked about as an American savior. Each has secret revolutionary plans to change the face of American politics, and their radical paths are on a collision course. But unbeknownst to each, the two share a mysterious link to a deadly monster. Only Ludwig von Dracula, self-proclaimed descendant of the infamous count and head of the Vampire Liberation Front, knows the secret of the homicidal beast that binds these two rivals together. Still, he's not sure he should intervene. Not his problem. But if Alex Mallum doesn't die before the completion of the upcoming eclipse of the Harvest moon, the world may never be the same. Unless . . .

Gary Greenberg has written several books about myth and history, including his popular *101 Myths of the Bible*. In 1978, he was the Libertarian Party candidate for Governor of New York.

Jerome Tuccille has written numerous popular books, including the libertarian classic *It Usually Begins With Ayn Rand*. In 1974, he was the Libertarian Party candidate for Governor of New York.

ISBN-13: 978-0981496627

PEREJET PREJJ

King David Versus Israel: How a Hebrew Tyrant Hated by the Israelites Became a Biblical Hero

By Gary Greenberg

In this controversial biography of one of the Bible's most revered figures, biblical historian Gary Greenberg challenges the conventional image of King David as a much-beloved hero of the ancient Israelites. Originally published as *The Sins of King David: A New History*, the author has re-edited the manuscript, refined some arguments, and added many additional biblical citations.

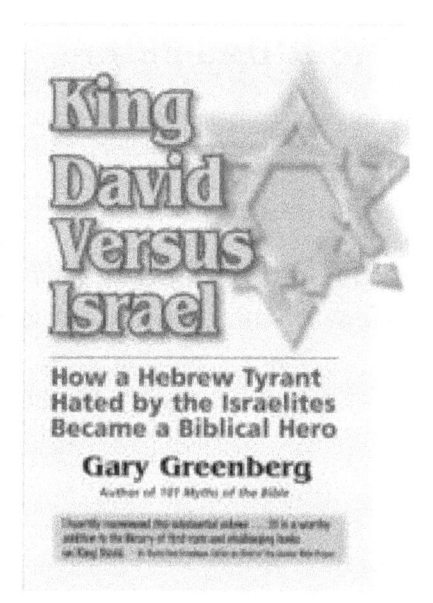

I heartily recommend this substantial volume . . . [It] is a worthy addition to the library of first-rate and challenging books on [King] David. – *Dr. David Noel Freedman, editor of the Anchor Bible Dictionary and the Anchor Bible Project*

Placing these texts into their historical, political, and geographic setting, Greenberg is able to separate much historical fact from biblical fiction . . . Greenberg shows David to be an ambitious mercenary, ruthless politician, unjust tyrant, and military imperialist. – *Library Journal*

Gary Greenberg will make you think. He might even make you angry. In his latest book he paints a portrait of a ruthless, deceitful, corrupt leader who was a traitor to Israel. – *Green Bay Press-Gazette*

[Greenberg] offers compelling new evidence that changes our perceptions—turns David, in essence, from a mythological figure into a living, breathing human being. - *Bookloons.com*

ISBN-13 : 978-0981496610

PEREJET PRESS

THE JUDAS BRIEF

A Critical Investigation into the Arrest and Trials of Jesus and the Role of the Jews

By Gary Greenberg

Judas did not betray Jesus. He tried to save his teacher's life.

The Judas Brief offers history's first full-scale, historically-based rebuttal to Gospel accusations that Judas betrayed Jesus and that the Jewish priesthood demanded that Pilate crucify him. This book compares the Gospel accounts of Judas, Pilate, and Herod Antipas with the historical evidence and demonstrates how false and unreliable the Gospels are.

Some astonishing revelations from The Judas Brief

- Pre-Gospel Christians did not believe that Judas betrayed Jesus.
- Pontius Pilate's contemporaries described him as a cruel, corrupt murderer who tolerated no disagreement from Jewish leaders and brutally suppressed any protest against his rulings.
- The chief Jewish priests had no political leverage over Pilate and little political support from the Jewish population.
- The only prominent Jewish leader who felt threatened by Jesus was Herod Antipas, Rome's puppet king of Galilee, who beheaded John the Baptist for speaking out against Herod's wickedness.
- The Gospel of John radically differs from and contradicts the other three Gospels regarding the events leading up to the arrest of Jesus.

"Presses important historical questions and rightly insists on a fresh consideration of the evidence."—**Catholic Biblical Quarterly.**
"This well-documented work . . . presents some interesting history."—**Library Journal.**

ISBN 978-0-9814966-4-1

PEREJET PRESS

The Moses Mystery
The Egyptian Origins of the Jewish People

By Gary Greenberg

What do history and archaeology really say about the origins of ancient Israel?

Although the bible says that Israel's formative history took place in ancient Egypt, biblical scholars and Egyptologists have steadfastly refused to explore the role of Egyptian history and literature on the origins of Jewish religion. *The Moses Mystery* attempts to set the record straight.

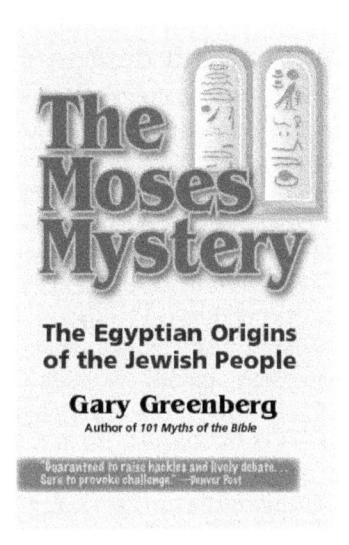

Based on extensive research into biblical and Egyptian history, archaeology, literature and mythology Greenberg argues that the first Israelites were Egyptians, followers of the monotheistic teachings of Pharaoh Akhenaten.

Some of the many intriguing revelations in The Moses Mystery include:

- Ancient Egyptian records specifically identify Moses as Akhenaten's chief priest and describe the Exodus as the result of a civil war for control over the Egyptian throne
- Abraham, Isaac, and Jacob were characters from Egyptian mythology
- The Twelve Tribes of Israel never existed

Mr. Greenberg seems to delight in a game of scholarly "gotcha."—*NY Times*

An ingenious comparison of Biblical and Egyptian history.– *St. Louis Post-Dispatch*

Sure to provoke challenge and debate—Denver-Post

A must read for those interested in biblical scholarship. – *Tennessee Tribune*

ISBN 978-0-9814966-9-6

PEREJET PREJJ

MATTHEW, MARK, LUKE, AND JOHN DID NOT WRITE THE GOSPELS

—at least, not according to modern New Testament scholarship. The evidence shows that all four Gospels were written anonymously, and for almost two centuries after they were completed, early Christians had no idea who had written them. Eventually, guesses became traditions, and traditions became dogma. The evidence also shows that during these first few centuries, orthodox Christian scribes deliberately altered or added to the Gospel texts, and many of these changes remain in our modern Gospels. Yet, few members of the lay public know very much about this history. Gary Greenberg takes you inside the complex and poorly understood world of modern Gospel text and source criticism and provides a simple, easy-to-follow guide that shows how New Testament scholars arrive at these challenging conclusions.

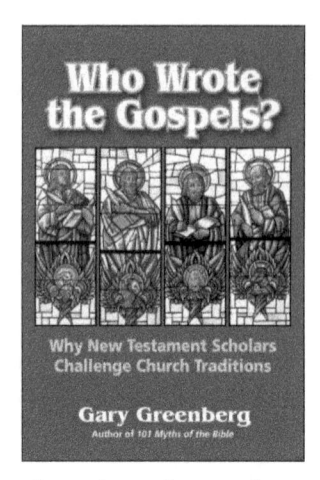

SOME OF THE FASCINATING TOPICS COVERED IN *WHO WROTE THE GOSPELS?*

- What is the Synoptic Problem, and how do scholars resolve it?
- What is the mysterious Q source that influenced Matthew and Luke?
- Is there a literary relationship between the Gospels of Mark and John?
- Did the original Gospel of Mark depict the resurrection of Jesus?
- Did Evangelists agree with each other about crucial story details?
- Why did orthodox Christian scribes alter the Gospel texts?
- When scholars encounter contradictory ancient Gospel manuscripts, how do they decide which text comes closest to the original?
- What manuscripts stand behind our modern Gospel texts, and how accurate are they?

Gary Greenberg is the author of several popular and controversial books, including *101 Myths of the Bible*, *The Moses Mystery*, and *The Judas Brief: Who Really Killed Jesus?* His works have been translated into several languages. He has presented papers at numerous academic conferences and has been published in several scholarly journals.

ISBN: 978-0-9814966-3-4

PERESET PRESS

www.ingramcontent.com/pod-product-compliance
Ingram Content Group UK Ltd.
Pitfield, Milton Keynes, MK11 3LW, UK
UKHW050429050625
6233UKWH00044B/20